CAMBRIDGE GREEK AND LATIN CLASSICS

A HELLENISTIC ANTHOLOGY

SELECTED AND EDITED BY

NEIL HOPKINSON

Fellow of Trinity College, Cambridge

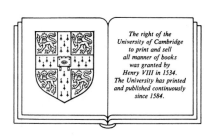

The right of the
University of Cambridge
to print and sell
all manner of books
was granted by
Henry VIII in 1534.
The University has printed
and published continuously
since 1584.

CAMBRIDGE UNIVERSITY PRESS

CAMBRIDGE

NEW YORK   NEW ROCHELLE

MELBOURNE   SYDNEY

Published by the Press Syndicate of the University of Cambridge
The Pitt Building, Trumpington Street, Cambridge CB2 1RP
32 East 57th Street, New York, NY 10022, USA
10 Stamford Road, Oakleigh, Melbourne 3166, Australia

First published 1988

Printed in Great Britain at the
University Press, Cambridge

566 0295010

British Library cataloguing in publication data

Hellenistic anthology. – (Cambridge Greek
and Latin classics).
1. Greek poetry
I. Hopkinson, N.   II. Cambridge Greek and
Latin classics
881'.01'08   PA3431

Library of Congress cataloguing in publication data

A Hellenistic anthology.
(Cambridge Greek and Latin classics)
Includes indexes.
1. Greek literature, Hellenistic.   I. Hopkinson, N.
II. Series.
PA3423.Z5H45   1987   880'.01'09   87–6359

ISBN 0 521 30696 5 hard covers
ISBN 0 521 31425 9 paperback

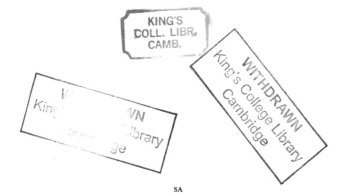

SA

CONTENTS

CONTENTS

PREFACE

Undergraduates who wish to read and appreciate Hellenistic poetry are faced with a forbidding range of scholarly commentaries, many of them written in Latin, German, French and Italian. The aim of this book is to make accessible to English-speaking students a small but varied sample of Hellenistic poetic texts. Wherever possible I have tried to aid literary appreciation by including whole poems rather than extracts. In making my final selection I have been influenced by the advice and opinions of colleagues engaged in teaching Hellenistic poetry in several British universities. Theocritus may be thought under-represented; but he is at least available to undergraduate readers in the useful edition of K. J. Dover. Dr G. O. Hutchinson's forthcoming *Hellenistic Poetry* will discuss in greater detail topics touched on in my own necessarily brief introduction.

I am most grateful to Professor W. S. Allen, Mr P. J. Callaghan, Dr G. C. Horrocks and Professor C. M. Robertson for their advice on matters philological and artistic; to Professor R. G. G. Coleman, Mr I. C. Cunningham, Mr N. C. Denyer, Mr H. B. Freeman, Dr S. D. Goldhill, Professor E. W. Handley, Dr R. L. Hunter, Professor D. A. Kidd, Professor H. Lloyd-Jones, Dr K. J. McKay, Dr M. Schofield and Professor F. H. Sandbach, who read various sections of the commentary; to my colleague Dr R. D. Dawe, who scrutinized the entire typescript and made many chastening criticisms and improving suggestions; to the General Editors, Mrs P. E. Easterling and Professor E. J. Kenney, for their detailed comments and helpful guidance; to Mr A. R. Munday and Professor E.W. Handley, for reading the proofs; and to the staff of Cambridge University Press, for the care which they have expended on the production of this book.

Cambridge   N.H.
December 1986

vii

ABBREVIATIONS

CA	*Collectanea Alexandrina*, ed. J. U. Powell (Oxford, 1925).
CAF	*Comicorum Atticorum fragmenta*, ed. T. Kock (Leipzig, 1880–8).
CHCL I	*The Cambridge history of Classical literature.* I *Greek literature*, eds. P. E. Easterling & B. M. W. Knox (Cambridge, 1985).
Denniston, *GP*	J. D. Denniston, *The Greek particles* (2nd edn, Oxford, 1954).
Fraser	P. M. Fraser, *Ptolemaic Alexandria* (Oxford, 1972).
FGE	*Further Greek epigrams: epigrams before* A.D. *50 from the Greek Anthology and other sources . . .*, ed. D. L. Page (Cambridge, 1981).
FGH	*Die Fragmente der griechischen Historiker*, ed. F. Jacoby (Berlin, 1923–).
Goodwin, *GMT*	W. W. Goodwin, *Syntax of the moods and tenses of the Greek verb* (London, 1889).
GP	*The Garland of Philip and some contemporary epigrams*, eds. A. S. F. Gow & D. L. Page (Cambridge, 1968).
HE	*The Greek Anthology: Hellenistic epigrams*, eds. A. S. F. Gow & D. L. Page (Cambridge, 1965).
K.–B.	R. Kühner & F. Blass, *Ausführliche Grammatik der griechischen Sprache. Erster Teil: Elementar- und Formenlehre* (Hanover, 1890–2).
K.–G.	R. Kühner & B. Gerth, *Ausführliche Grammatik der griechischen Sprache. Zweiter Teil: Satzlehre* (Hanover/Leipzig, 1898–1904).
LSJ	*A Greek–English lexicon*, eds. H. G. Liddell, R. Scott, H. Stuart Jones, R. McKenzie (9th edn with Supplement, Oxford, 1968).
Newman	J. K. Newman, *Augustus and the new poetry* = Collection Latomus 88 (Brussels, 1967).

Pfeiffer, *HCS*   R. Pfeiffer, *History of Classical scholarship from the beginnings to the end of the Hellenistic age* (Oxford, 1968).

PMG   *Poetae melici Graeci*, ed. D. L. Page (Oxford, 1962).

SH   *Supplementum Hellenisticum*, eds. H. Lloyd-Jones & P. Parsons (Berlin/New York, 1983).

SLG   *Supplementum lyricis Graecis*, ed. D. L. Page (Oxford, 1974).

SVF   *Stoicorum ueterum fragmenta*, ed. J. von Arnim (Stuttgart, 1905–24).

TGF   *Tragicorum Graecorum fragmenta*, eds. B. Snell, R. Kannicht, S. Radt (Göttingen, 1971–   ).

West, *GM*   M. L. West, *Greek metre* (Oxford, 1982).

Periodicals are abbreviated as in *L'Année philologique*.

> = 'the source of' or 'leading to'
< = 'derived from'
~ = 'corresponding to' or 'contrasting with'

Italic numbers (*1–1739*) refer to the continuous line numeration printed to the right of the text.

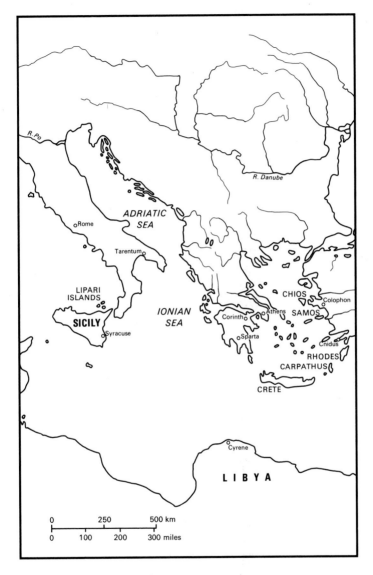

Map 1. The central Mediterranean

Map 2. Greece and Asia Minor

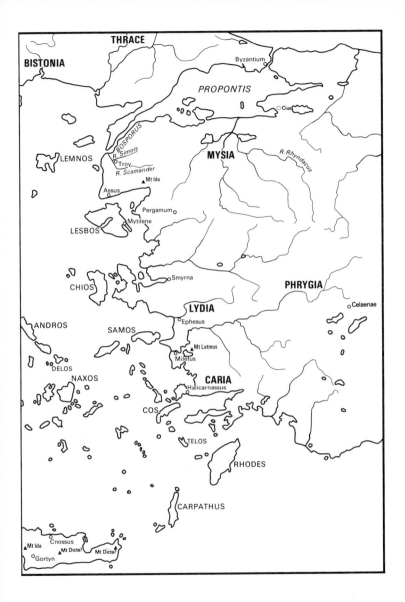

Map 3. The eastern Mediterranean and the Black Sea

INTRODUCTION

᾿Α μάκαρ, ὅστις ἔην κεῖνον χρόνον ἴδρις ἀοιδῆς,
Μουσάων θεράπων, ὅτ᾿ ἀκήρατος ἦν ἔτι λειμών·
νῦν δ᾿ ὅτε πάντα δέδασται, ἔχουσι δὲ πείρατα τέχναι,
ὕστατοι ὥστε δρόμου καταλειπόμεθ᾿, οὐδέ πηι ἔστι
πάντηι παπταίνοντα νεοζυγὲς ἅρμα πελάσσαι.

(*SH* 317)

Blessed indeed the man who was skilled in song in those days, a
'servant of the Muses' when the meadow was still undefiled! Now,
when everything has been portioned out and the arts have
reached their limits, we are left behind in the race, and one looks
everywhere in vain for a place to drive one's newly yoked chariot.

These are the gloomy words of Choerilus of Samos, an epic poet writing
in the late fifth century B.C. Earlier writers have explored every avenue,
have excelled in every type of poetry. What way is still untravelled by
the chariot of song? Choerilus' response to this problem was an epic
poem which dealt, unusually, with a recent historical subject – the
Persian Wars.

More than a century later Callimachus, most influential of all the
Hellenistic poets, employs similar imagery in a famous polemical
defence of his own approach to poetry. He rejects warlike themes and
says that Apollo advised him not to use the well worn high-road, but to
drive his chariot along untrodden by-ways (*1–40*).

The texts collected in this book illustrate some of the highly diverse
'by-ways' followed by Hellenistic poets as they selected and combined
elements from earlier writers to create a new, sophisticated type of
poetry far different in tone and technique from anything that had gone
before.

1. THE BACKGROUND[1]

By the middle of the fourth century B.C. many of the old Greek city-states had become weakened by decades of almost continuous warfare, and the centre of power shifted to wealthy Macedonia. Philip II of Macedon allied Greece with his own kingdom; his son Alexander conquered Egypt, Syria, Persia and Asia as far east as the Indus. At Alexander's death in 323 the empire was divided amongst his generals, and bitter wars ensued. By about 275 four main dynastic kingdoms had emerged:

(1) Macedon and Greece (capital Pella), ruled by the Antigonids, descendants of Antigonus 'Monophthalmus', a son of Philip II.

(2) Asia (capital Antioch), ruled by the Seleucids, descendants of Alexander's general Seleucus.

(3) Asia Minor (capital Pergamum), which between 283 and 240 gradually expanded within Seleucid territory; ruled by the Attalids, descendants of Philaenetus (son of Attalus), who had administered Pergamum for Seleucus.

(4) Egypt (capital Alexandria), ruled by the Ptolemies, descendants of Ptolemy (son of Lagus), a Macedonian general of Alexander.

In Greece and Asia Minor the old city-states maintained their democratic machinery and had some local autonomy; but ultimate power resided with the kings, who lived in splendour at their courts in Pella, Pergamum, Antioch and Alexandria, surrounded by official 'friends' and advisers and by large administrative staffs.

Rivalling the Athenian example of state patronage for the arts the Hellenistic monarchs established their capital cities as centres of culture equipped with libraries, facilities for scientific inquiry and schools of art and philosophy, the latter modelled on the Athenian Peripatos and Academy. The prospect of royal patronage attracted artists and men of learning from all over the Greek world. These international centres promoted the exchange of ideas between scholars and artists living in close proximity, and resulted in an intellectual culture more unified than that which had existed in the πόλις-orientated Greece of earlier times. The Greek language, too, became more uniform: a common

[1] See further *The Cambridge Ancient History* VII[2] 1, eds. F. W. Walbank & A. E. Astin (Cambridge, 1984), W. W. Tarn & G. T. Griffith, *Hellenistic civilisation* (3rd edn, London, 1952).

speech, the κοινή, gradually replaced the ancient dialects. (The stylized and artificial *literary* dialects, which had long since lost their geographical and ethnic associations and had become linked with particular types of poetry, continued to be used by Hellenistic poets.)

During the second and first centuries B.C. the monarchies gradually came under Roman domination. Egypt retained a token independence until the death of Cleopatra in 31 B.C. The deaths of Alexander and Cleopatra are taken conventionally to mark the limits of the Hellenistic period (323–31 B.C.). Pergamum, Antioch and Alexandria continued as cultural centres until well into the Christian era.

2. ALEXANDRIA[2]

i. The social and religious background

Alexandria, situated on the western edge of the Nile delta, was founded by Alexander in about 331, shortly after his conquest of Egypt; his main aim was probably to provide easy sea communication with Europe. In 323 Ptolemy set up residence in the town and made it the seat of government; in 305 he declared himself king.

Alexandria had been founded from nothing, and all its Greek-speaking inhabitants were of immigrant stock. In addition there was a large population of Jews, Syrians, slaves and native Egyptians: it has been estimated that in the province as a whole the Egyptians numbered about seven million, the Greeks only about one hundred thousand. For those Greeks who were citizens the trappings of democracy were established, but Ptolemy kept control of affairs through his own officials.

The first four Ptolemies were:

(1) Ptolemy I 'Soter' (a cult title often given to great benefactors), d. 283, who married his step-sister Berenice (I).

(2) Ptolemy II 'Philadelphus' (so called because he married his sister Arsinoe), son of Soter and Berenice, 283–246.

(3) Ptolemy III 'Euergetes' (= 'benefactor'), son of Philadelphus and Arsinoe, 246–221; he married Berenice (II) daughter of Magas, king of Cyrene.

(4) Ptolemy IV 'Philopator', 221–204, son of Euergetes and Berenice.

[2] See further Fraser *passim*, Pfeiffer, *HCS* 87–279, L. D. Reynolds & N. G. Wilson, *Scribes and scholars* (2nd edn, Oxford, 1974) 1–18, *CHCL* 1 16–36.

It was not unusual in Greece for divine honours to be paid to a great benefactor after his death. Hellenistic monarchs went a step further and instituted dynastic cults and ruler-cults as a focus for the loyalty and patriotism of their Greek citizens. Soter set up a cult of Alexander, whose body was buried in the city. A full dynastic cult was introduced by Philadelphus; it was administered by a hierarchy of provincial priests who were official 'friends' of the king. Philadelphus and his sister-wife Arsinoe, whose incestuous marriage had at first scandalized the Greeks in Egypt (notwithstanding the alleged precedent of Zeus and Hera), were worshipped during their lifetimes as Θεοὶ ᾿Αδελφοί;[3] Arsinoe was in addition identified with Aphrodite[4] and with Isis, and after her death in 270 she was given a separate cult with its own priesthood. These cults, together with those of the traditional Olympian gods (especially of Dionysus, from whom the Ptolemies claimed descent), provided opportunity for public show as well as for ruler-worship. In 279 Philadelphus founded the Πτολεμαιεῖα, a festival with competitions in gymnastics, music, etc., modelled on the Olympic Games. A long fragment of the historian Callixinus of Rhodes (*FGH* 627 F 1–2) describes a spectacular πομπή or procession, an amazing pageant of the colourful and the exotic, which took place through the streets of Alexandria in honour of Dionysus.[5] In the second *Idyll* of Theocritus (*574–738*) Simaetha describes how she fell in love whilst on her way to watch a procession of this sort.

Other deities, such as the Egyptian Isis and Osiris, and the newly introduced Sarapis, played a large part in religious life but left very little trace in Alexandrian poetry, which concerned itself with treating, often in novel ways, the gods familiar from earlier Greek literature.

Native Egyptians worshipped the Ptolemies as Pharaohs. It was in imitation of Pharaonic tradition that Philadelphus married his sister.

ii. Alexandria as cultural centre

The Ptolemies were themselves learned and cultured men. Soter composed a history of Alexander's campaigns; Philadelphus was interested in science; Euergetes published a narrative of his own entry

[3] Cf. *1400* & n.
[4] See on *1646–57*.
[5] See E. E. Rice, *The Grand Procession of Ptolemy Philadelphos* (Oxford, 1983).

into Antioch; Philopator wrote a tragedy called *Adonis* and founded a temple to Homer. Throughout the third century conditions were favourable to literature and learning. Patronage was nothing new: the Greek tyrants of the sixth and fifth centuries had earned praise from poets for their beneficence. But the Hellenistic approach was quite different. Under the early Ptolemies permanent conditions were established in Alexandria for academic study totally at the royal expense. Facilities included an observatory, a school of anatomy and a zoo; but the most famous Alexandrian institution was the Μουσεῖον, literally 'shrine of the Muses', founded by Soter probably with advice from Demetrius of Phalerum, an exiled governor of Athens, pupil of Aristotle and author of philosophical works. The Museum was built close to the royal palace area. For those fortunate enough to secure royal patronage it provided free meals and accommodation and the opportunity to pursue research in most branches of learning. Given the Peripatetic (Aristotelian) influence on its foundation, it is hardly surprising that scientific as well as artistic and literary inquiries were carried on there. In overall charge was a ἱερεύς of the Muses or ἐπιστάτης, who administered rites for the patron goddesses: the Museum was literally dedicated to the arts and to learning. Its concentration of scholars and artists in one place meant that there was much opportunity for interaction between disciplines – and for disagreements. Timon of Phlius, a writer of satirical lampoons, drew an amusing analogy between Ptolemy's zoo and his well fed scholars:

πολλοὶ μὲν βόσκονται ἐν Αἰγύπτωι πολυφύλωι
βιβλιακοὶ χαρακῖται ἀπείριτα δηριόωντες
Μουσέων ἐν ταλάρωι.

(*SH* 786)

Lots of pedantic cloisterlings are kept in multiracial Egypt, squabbling incessantly in the Muses' birdcage.

The scholars who flocked to enjoy Ptolemaic patronage needed texts from which to work. To facilitate their studies a Library was set up at the same time as the Museum. (Again Aristotle's influence is likely: he is said to have been the first serious manuscript collector.[6]) The list of

[6] Strabo 13.1.54.

Chief Librarians during the third and second centuries, many of whom were tutors to successive crown princes, includes some of the most famous names in Hellenistic scholarship: Zenodotus, Apollonius of Rhodes, Eratosthenes (mathematician and poet), Aristophanes of Byzantium, Apollonius Εἰδογράφος ('Classifier'), Aristarchus (p. 10). Under their direction the Library staff attempted to collect and classify the whole of Greek literature; Callimachus, who probably never became Chief Librarian, compiled the Πίνακες, a 120-volume catalogue (p. 83). A small army of scribes must have been employed in copying papyrus rolls of works commonly consulted; and other members of staff were sent out to mainland Greece in search of rare works. Euergetes went to even greater lengths. He ordered that all books found on board ships which docked at Alexandria should be seized and copied; and he borrowed from Athens for a deposit of 15 talents the official performance texts of the three tragedians; then he kept the originals, sent back copies, and forfeited his deposit.[7] Philadelphus is said to have commissioned the κοινή translation of the Hebrew bible from 72 Palestinian Jews, who completed it in 72 days (hence the title Septuagint). The total holdings amounted to perhaps half a million papyrus rolls. A large proportion of the books were burnt in 48 B.C., when Julius Caesar was besieged at Alexandria. In that fire many obscure works of earlier Greek literature were lost for ever.

The city long continued as a centre of learning, and the techniques of painstaking study and exegesis pioneered there were disseminated throughout the civilized world. Modern Classical scholarship in these fields is part of an unbroken tradition which had its origins in the work of Alexandrian scholars.

3. HELLENISTIC POETRY[8]

i. Problems

Insuperable difficulties face the would-be historian of Hellenistic poetry. In the first place, except for the plays of Menander almost nothing survives from the century preceding the generation of Lycophron, Aratus and Callimachus: we have very little idea how non-dramatic poetry developed during those years, and it follows that we

[7] These two stories are told by Galen: see Fraser II 480–1 n. 147.

[8] For a full treatment see G. O. Hutchinson, *Hellenistic poetry* (Oxford, 1987).

cannot adequately assess the originality of the third-century works which do survive. In the second place, both absolute and relative chronologies even for the works of major poets are extremely uncertain. Callimachus, Apollonius and Theocritus in particular frequently allude to each other's work; but who alludes to whom in any given case it is usually impossible to decide. This problem is compounded by the fact that long poems such as the *Aetia* and *Argonautica* were probably recited as 'work in progress' over many years before their final publication; this makes it quite likely that poets reacted to each other's works actually during the process of composition. Thus even when it can be proved that one passage antedates another (and such 'proofs' are rarely convincing), the fact is of very limited use in establishing an absolute chronology. Moreover, several of the Hellenistic poets cannot be dated even to within 50 years. In the third place, only a small fraction of the poetry written during this period survives. Most of what does survive is broadly in line with the aesthetic principles often called 'Callimachean' – so called not because Callimachus originated them, but because he was their most outspoken advocate (see *1–40* nn.). But the existence today of so many poems written according to 'Callimachean' artistic criteria may well not be a true reflection of the popularity of those criteria at the time. It seems quite likely that for every 'Callimachean' poem to have survived a hundred more traditional ones are lost: we have scant fragments or mere titles of many such poems, and their number is increasing as new papyri come to light. This is not to say that the new poets were less significant in their own time than they appear to us with historical hindsight; but clearly their criteria did not command anything like universal support.

In other words, a literary history of the Hellenistic period cannot be written. All we can do is to consider the works which survive and describe some of the broad characteristics which most of them appear to share – always bearing in mind that our sample is probably unrepresentative. On the whole such generalizations are of limited value. It seems that the only characteristic shared by every poem in this volume is that each is striving in its own way to be different.

ii. Poetry and learning

Hellenistic poetry is often characterized as learned and allusive – as if the earlier epic, lyric, tragic and comic poets were not constantly indulging in puns and etymological play; as if they too were not preoccupied with roots, causes, origins and aetiologies. Every ode of Pindar, every play of Euripides bears witness to the fact that Hellenistic poets were not the first to display wide knowledge of myth or to exploit the possibilities of word-play. Nevertheless, there is a palpable difference in emphasis between the 'learned' details of earlier poetry and the learned nature of many Hellenistic texts. That difference could be said to lie in the degree of self-consciousness, cleverness, subtlety or 'wit' which Hellenistic poems display in their learning. It is tempting to go further and to suggest that 'self-consciousness' is a prime characteristic of many Hellenistic poems, which by alluding to and echoing earlier writers seek to draw attention to their own place in the poetic tradition, to point their similarities to and differences from past literature. Appreciation of this poetry requires an alert and learned reader: alert enough to spot an allusion, learned enough to remember details of a passage to which allusion is made. Allusion can consist in a single word or in the construction of a whole work. Callimachus wrote his *Hecale* (p. 84) for an audience familiar with the Eumaeus episode in *Odyssey* 15; appreciation of Theocritus' *Cyclops* (*493–573*) depends in part on our remembering the words of *Odyssey* 9 and of a dithyramb by Philoxenus; when Jason and Medea finally meet as lovers (*Argonautica* 3.948 ff.) we must recognize allusions to Homeric encounters in battle; the reader of Moschus' *Europa* (*1045–1210*) must know his Aeschylus, Homeric Hymns, Apollonius and Theocritus (see p. 200–1). These are texts to be read through other texts; learning and allusion are absolutely integral to their meaning.[9]

Even in the poor state of our knowledge about the Hellenistic poets' predecessors we can see that poetry of this learned and allusive nature did not appear fully formed in the early third century. It is clear, for example, that Antimachus of Colophon (born c. 440) anticipated many of the characteristics of Hellenistic poetry. His most controversial work was the *Lyde*, a long elegiac poem which dealt with heroes and heroines disappointed in love; the ostensible reason for its composition was the poet's loss of his own mistress, Lyde. Antimachus was a scholar as well as a poet: he produced an edition of Homer often referred to by textual critics in following centuries. The results of these philological inquiries

---

[9] This aspect, too, is not in itself novel: cf., for example, Euripides' pointed allusions to the *Choephoroe* in his *Electra*.

can be seen in his use of rare Homeric 'glosses', or words of debated meaning, in his poetry; in addition he used rare words and neologisms, and was notorious for his obscurity. These characteristics point to a linguistic self-consciousness akin to that of Hellenistic poets, some of whom (not Callimachus: see p. 93) we know admired the *Lyde*.

Of Antimachus' work only the most meagre fragments survive,[10] and it is not possible to say how he made use of allusion on a wider, non-verbal level. Nor can we be sure of the extent of his influence on fourth-century poetry; certainly no evidence survives of other authors immediately following his lead. The next scholar-poet of whom we know is Philetas of Cos (born c. 320). Philetas was described by Strabo (14.2.19) as ποιητὴς ἅμα καὶ κριτικός; and, like Antimachus, he combined these two aspects in learned poetry.[11] He wrote a prose treatise called Ἄτακτοι γλῶσσαι, 'Miscellaneous Glosses', explaining rare Homeric and dialectal words, which became a standard reference work. It is possible that he was the first poet to concentrate on small-scale verse (e.g. the famous elegiac *Demeter*) as opposed to long epics. Callimachus pays tribute to him,[12] and Theocritus is said to have been his pupil. Propertius and Ovid allude to him as their inspiration for love-poetry, and to his mistress Bittis, whom he celebrated in elegies and epigrams. He is said to have been so slender (λεπτός – cf. p. 90) that he had to wear lead in his boots to prevent himself being blown away in strong winds.

It seems, then, that Philetas was a pioneer of the 'Hellenistic' approach to poetry. Ptolemy Soter had appointed him tutor to his young son (the future Philadelphus), who was born on Cos; and it is likely that Philetas followed his employer to Alexandria. He was succeeded as royal tutor by one of his own pupils, Zenodotus. In 284 Zenodotus was made first head of the newly established Library. Although he too was a writer of poetry, he was known in antiquity chiefly as a scholar. He began a systematic examination of the Homeric epics, a διόρθωσις, obelizing with a marginal mark lines which he thought later interpolations; he seems also to have added explanatory notes. It may have been Zenodotus who divided the *Iliad* and *Odyssey* into the 24 books in which they are still printed today. The exact nature of this 'edition' is uncertain; but Zenodotus' critical study of Homer

---

[10] There is an edition by B. Wyss (Berlin, 1936); later discoveries in *SH* 52–79.
[11] His fragments are collected in *CA* pp. 90–6 and supplemented in *SH* 673–5D.
[12] See *9–12* n.

aroused much interest at the time, especially in respect of the controversial obelized lines. Aided by two collaborators he went on to
produce texts of Pindar, Hesiod and tragedy; and like Philetas before
him he compiled a Homeric glossary, as well as a work entitled Λέξεις
ἐθνικαί on foreign words in literary texts. During the next century and a
half successive librarians, chief among them Aristophanes of Byzantium
and Aristarchus, were to continue this tradition of detailed textual and
literary study.

This was the atmosphere of critical scholarship which received the
third-century men of culture who arrived at Alexandria. The word
'critical' is important here. Works of the past were being read not as
formerly for enjoyment or moral improvement alone; rather they were
being examined scientifically, explained, discussed, catalogued and
classified. The individual word took on a new importance. Little
wonder that poets of the Hellenistic period, most of whom were
themselves scholars, philologers and grammarians, should include in
their work Homeric *hapax legomena* (words occurring only once) and
allusions to topically contentious passages; or that, themselves steeped
in earlier literature, they should write for an elite of readers equally
learned. Of course many aspects of these poets' works can be appreciated and enjoyed without this kind of detailed knowledge; but modern
readers, who do not have even Homer by heart, are liable to miss much
that is important, and can easily gain a false impression of tone, style
and 'literary texture'. One aim of the present commentary is to provide
help towards a fuller reading of these difficult and allusive poets.

iii. The nature of Hellenistic poetry

Self-consciousness, learning and allusion have been discussed at some
length because they are the aspects of Hellenistic poetry which readers
have found most difficult to appreciate. It is not necessary to dwell at
equal length on other characteristics, which will become clear from a
reading of the texts presented in this volume. They include: great
interest in the power of Eros and its workings; choice of unusual subject-
matter, or novel aspects of well-known subject-matter; pseudo-naive
concentration on smallness, poverty and the Simple Life, paralleled by a
concentration on smaller-scale, less 'pretentious' types of poetry; novel
fusions of metre, dialect and genre; variety of tone within individual

poems, and variety of metre, dialect and subject within the oeuvres of individual writers.

Literary historians have suggested several possible reasons for the new direction taken by poetry in the Hellenistic period.[13] One alleged reason is concerned with the function of poetry within society. Poetry (including tragedies and comedies) continued to be performed at festivals and competitions throughout the fourth and third centuries, and panegyrics of cities and their founders kept poetry in the public eye; but the decline of real democracy under the Hellenistic monarchies and the development of prose as a medium for communicating much that had formerly been expressed in verse meant that the public role of poetry was far more limited than it had been in the fifth and earlier centuries. Many poets, it has been argued, began to cater instead for an audience of well-read private individuals. To this rarefied urban audience the simple life of rustics and the lower classes appealed because such people were outside their own experience and, paradoxically, 'exotic'.

These and similar arguments could be greatly elaborated, but we should perhaps be wary of explanations couched in such general terms. By ignoring the fact that a thousand and one different motives characterize individual poets and individual readers, and by seeking to accommodate within a single 'spirit of the age' the varied and diverse talents of many writers, such theories are open to a charge of credulous determinism. In the light of the problems described above (p. 6–7) truly circumstantial answers are most unlikely ever to be found.

[13] See, for example, *CHCL* I 543, Pfeiffer, *HCS* 87–8.

THE APPARATUS CRITICUS

It is not feasible in an anthology of this type to deal separately with the manuscript tradition of each author. It has therefore seemed best to present the most important variants using the following abbreviations:

M	= reading of the whole MS tradition.
m	= reading of part of the MS tradition.
pap.	= reading given by a papyrus.
test.	= testimonium, reading given by a source quoting independently of the MS tradition.
schol. u.l.	= variant reading recorded by an ancient commentator.

For papyrus texts see pp. 91, 234 and 272.

Manuscripts of ancient authors invariably contain errors, which have arisen in the process of copying and re-copying over many generations. Since the Renaissance, textual critics have laboured to restore original readings by conjectural emendation. Except for the most elementary corrections, all such emendations adopted into the present text are attributed to the scholars who made them, and the corrupt MSS readings are given directly afterwards (e.g. 'γε Bentley: τε m: δέ m' means that the MSS have either τε or δέ, but Bentley restored the true reading, γε). Where the choice is between readings given by various MSS, unadopted readings are mentioned in the app. crit. only if they might possibly be right. By the same token, a few modern conjectures are mentioned which, though very attractive, do not seem certain enough to be adopted into the text.

A HELLENISTIC
ANTHOLOGY

I

CALLIMACHUS

REPLY TO THE TELCHINES (fr. 1)

Πολλάκ]ι μοι Τελχῖνες ἐπιτρύζουσιν ἀ⌊οιδῆι
νήιδε⌋ς, οἳ Μούσης οὐκ ἐγένοντο φίλοι,
εἵνεκε⌋ν οὐχ ἓν ἄεισμα διηνεκὲς ἢ βασιλ[ήων
πρήξι]ας ἐν πολλαῖς ἤνυσα χιλιάσιν

5 ἢ προτέρ]ους ἥρωας, ἔπος δ' ἐπὶ τυτθὸν ἐλ[ίσσω   5
    παῖς ἅτ⌋ε, τῶν δ' ἐτέων ἡ δεκὰ⌊ς⌋ οὐκ ὀλίγη.
φημὶ δὲ] καὶ Τε[λ]χῖσιν ἐγὼ τόδε· "φῦλον ἀ[κανθές,
    μοῦνον ἐὸν] τήκ[ειν] ἧπαρ ἐπιστάμενον,
ἢ μὲν δὴ γὰ]ρ ἔην [ὀλ]ιγόστιχος· ἀλλὰ καθέλ⌊κει

10 γρηῦν] ⌊πο⌋λὺ τὴν μακρὴν ὄμπνια Θεσμοφόρο[ς·   10
    τοῖν δὲ] δυοῖν Μίμνερμος ὅτι γλυκύς, α⌊ἱ⌋ κατὰ λεπτὸν
    ῥήσιες,] ἡ μεγάλη δ' οὐκ ἐδίδαξε γυνή.
μακρ]ὸν ἐπὶ Θρήικας ἀπ' Αἰγύπτοιο [πέτοιτο
    αἵματ]ι Πυγμαίων ἡδομένη [γ]έρα[νος,

15 Μασσα⌋γέται ⌊κ⌋αὶ μακ⌊ρὸν ὀιστεύ⌋οιεν ἐπ' ἄνδρα   15
    Μῆδον·] ἀ[ηδονίδες] δ' ὧδε μελιχρ[ό]τεραι.
ἔλλετε Βασκανίη⌋ς ὀλοὸν γένο⌊ς⌋· αὖθι δὲ τέχνηι
    κρίνετε,] ⌊μὴ σχοίν⌋ωι Περσίδι τὴ⌊ν⌋ σοφίην·
μηδ' ἀπ' ἐμεῦ διφᾶ⌋τε μέγα ψοφέουσαν ἀοιδὴν

20 τίκτεσθαι· βροντᾶ⌋ν οὐκ ἐμόν, ⌊ἀλλὰ⌋ Διός."   20
καὶ γὰρ ὅτ⌋ε πρ⌊ώ⌋τιστον ἐμοῖς ἐπὶ δέλτον ἔθηκα
    γούνασι⌋ν, 'Α[πό]λλων εἶπεν ὅ μοι Λύκιος·

I *P.Oxy.* 2079; uu.14–21 mutilos habet *P.Oxy.* 2167   1 suppl. Lobel 2 Μούσης Wilamowitz (pl. sicut u.37; cf. *498*): -ης pap.   3–4 suppl. Lobel, 5 init. Wilamowitz, fin. Hunt, 7 init. Hunt, fin. Pfeiffer, 8 init. Housman, med. Hunt, 9 init. Pfeiffer: Κῶιος δὴ γὰ]ρ Puelma   10 suppl. Maas: δρῦν Housman: θεῦν Matthews   11 suppl. Housman, 12 Rostagni: Κώιαι Puelma   13 suppl. init. Pfeiffer, fin. Lobel, 14 Pfeiffer, 16 init. Pfeiffer, med. Housman, 18 Housman

"μέμνεό μοι, φίλ'] ἀοιδέ, τὸ μὲν θύος ὅττι πάχιστον
θρέψαι, τὴ]ν Μοῦσαν δ' ὠγαθὲ λεπταλέην·
25 πρὸς δέ σε] καὶ τόδ' ἄνωγα, τὰ μὴ πατέουσιν ἅμαξαι   25
τὰ στείβε∫ιν, ἑτέρων δ' ἴχνια μὴ καθ' ὁμὰ
δίφρον ἐλ]ᾶν μηδ' οἷμον ἀνὰ πλατύν, ἀλλὰ κελεύθους
ἀτρίπτο]υς, εἰ καὶ στε∟ι∫νοτέρην ἐλάσεις."
τῶι πιθόμη]ν· ἐνὶ τοῖς γὰρ ἀείδομεν οἳ λιγὺν ἦχον
30 τέττιγος, θ]όρυβον δ' οὐκ ἐφίλησαν ὄνων.   30
θηρὶ μὲν ο∫ὐατόεντι πανείκελον ὀγκήσαιτο
ἄλλος, ἐγ]ὼ δ' εἴην οὑλ[α]χύς, ὁ πτερόεις,
ἆ πάντ∫ως, ἵνα γῆρας ἵνα δρόσον—ἣν μὲν ἀείδω
πρώκιο∫ν ἐκ δίης ἠέρος εἶδαρ ἔδων,
35 αὖθι τ∫ὸ δ' ⌊ἐκ⌋δύοιμ⌊ι⌋, τό μοι βάρος ὅσσον ἔπεστι   35
τριγ∫λώ⌊χι⌋ν ὀλ⌊οῶι⌋ νῆσος ἐπ' Ἐγκελάδωι.
οὐ νέμεσις· Μοῦσαι γ∫ὰρ ὅσους ἴδον ὄθμα⌊τ⌋ι παῖδας
μὴ λοξῶι, πολιοὺς∫ οὐκ ἀπέθεντο φίλους.
Μουσάων δὲ καὶ ὄρνι]ς, ἐ[πεὶ] πτερὸν οὐκέτι κινεῖν
40 οἶδε, πέλει φων]ῆι τ[ῆ]μος ἐνεργότατος.   40

II

ACONTIUS AND CYDIPPE (frr. 67 + 75)

Αὐτὸς Ἔρως ἐδίδαξεν Ἀκόντιον, ὁππότε καλῆι
ἤιθετο Κυδίππηι παῖς ἐπὶ παρθενικῆι,
τέχνην—οὐ γὰρ ὅγ' ἔσκε πολύκροτος—ὄφρα λέγο[ιτο
τοῦτο διὰ ζωῆς οὔνομα κουρίδιον.
5 ἦ γάρ, ἄναξ, ὁ μὲν ἦλθεν Ἰουλίδος ἡ δ' ἀπὸ Νάξου,   45
Κύνθιε, τὴν Δήλωι σὴν ἐπὶ βουφονίην,

23 suppl. Hopkinson exempli gratia, 24 Pfeiffer, 25 Hunt   26 δ' test.: om. pap.
27 suppl. Hunt, 29 Wilamowitz, 30 Lobel, 32 Hunt, 39 init. Rostagni, med.
Hunt, 40 Hunt

II fr. 67 = P.Oxy. 2211   3 et 7 suppl. Lobel

αἷμα τὸ μὲν γενεῆς Εὐξαντίδος, ἡ δὲ Προμηθ[ίς,
καλοὶ νησάων ἀστέρες ἀμφότεροι.
πολλαὶ Κυδίππην ὀλίγην ἔτι μητέρες υἱοῖς
10   ἐδνῆστιν κεραῶν ᾔτεον ἀντὶ βοῶν·   50
κείνης ο[ὐ]χ ἑτέρη γὰρ ἐπὶ λασίοιο γέροντος
    Σιληνοῦ νοτίην ἵκετο πιδυλίδα
ἠοῖ εἰδομένη μάλιον ῥέθος οὐδ' Ἀριήδης
    ἐς χ]ορὸν εὐδούσης ἀβρὸν ἔθηκε πόδα ...

.   .   .

ἤδη καὶ κούρωι παρθένος εὐνάσατο,   55
τέθμιον ὡς ἐκέλευε προνύμφιον ὕπνον ἰαῦσαι
    ἄρσενι τὴν τᾶλιν παιδὶ σὺν ἀμφιθαλεῖ.
Ἥρην γάρ κοτέ φασι—κύον, κύον, ἴσχεο, λαιδρὲ
5   θυμέ, σύ γ' ἀείσηι καὶ τά περ οὐχ ὁσίη·
ὤναο κάρθ', ἕνεκ' οὔ τι θεῆς ἴδες ἱερὰ φρικτῆς,   60
    ἐξ ἂν ἐπεὶ καὶ τῶν ἤρυγες ἱστορίην.
ἦ πολυιδρείη χαλεπὸν κακόν, ὅστις ἀκαρτεῖ
    γλώσσης· ὡς ἐτεὸν παῖς ὅδε μαῦλιν ἔχει.
10 ἠῶιοι μὲν ἔμελλον ἐν ὕδατι θυμὸν ἀμύξειν
    οἱ βόες ὀξεῖαν δερκόμενοι δορίδα,   65
δειελινὴν τὴν δ' εἷλε κακὸς χλόος, ἦλθε δὲ νοῦσος,
    αἶγας ἐς ἀγριάδας τὴν ἀποπεμπόμεθα,
ψευδόμενοι δ' ἱερὴν φημίζομεν· ἢ τότ' ἀνιγρὴ
15   τὴν κούρην Ἀ[ίδ]εω μέχρις ἔτηξε δόμων.
δεύτερον ἐστόρνυντο τὰ κλισμία, δεύτερον ἡ πα[ῖ]ς   70
    ἑπτὰ τεταρταίωι μῆνας ἔκαμνε πυρί.
τὸ τρίτον ἐμνήσαντο γάμου κάτα, τὸ τρίτον αὖτ[ε
    Κυδίππην ὀλοὸς κρυμὸς ἐσωικίσατο.
20 τέτρατον οὐκέτ' ἔμεινε πατὴρ [ἐς Δέλφιον ἄρας
    Φοῖβον· ὁ δ' ἐννύχιον τοῦτ' ἔπος ηὐδάσατο·   75

12 πιδυλίδα Pfeiffer: πηγυλίδα pap.   14 suppl. Lobel   post h.u. reliqua
octo uu. satis mutila
fr. 75 = *P.Oxy.* 1011   7 εξανεπει pap.: diuisit Housman   15 suppl. Crusius
et Housman, 18 Pfeiffer   20 fin. sic dispexit Hunt

"'Ἀρτέμιδος τῆι παιδὶ γάμον βαρὺς ὅρκος ἐνικλᾶι·
Λύγδαμιν οὐ γὰρ ἐμὴ τῆμος ἔκηδε κάσις
οὐδ' ἐν Ἀμυκλαίωι θρύον ἔπλεκεν οὐδ' ἀπὸ θήρης
25   ἔκλυζεν ποταμῶι λύματα Παρθενίωι,
Δήλωι δ' ἦν ἐπίδημος, Ἀκόντιον ὁππότε σὴ παῖς   80
ὤμοσεν, οὐκ ἄλλον, νυμφίον ἐξέμεναι.
ὦ Κήϋξ, ἀλλ' ἤν με θέληις συμφράδμονα θέσθαι,
νῦν γε] τελευτήσεις ὅρκια θυγατέρος·
30   ἀργύρωι οὐ μόλιβον γὰρ Ἀκόντιον, ἀλλὰ φαεινῶι
ἤλεκτρον χρυσῶι φημί σε μειξέμεναι·   85
Κοδρείδης σύ γ' ἄνωθεν ὁ πενθερός, αὐτὰρ ὁ Κεῖος
γαμβρὸς Ἀρισταίου Ζηνὸς ἀφ' ἱερέων
Ἰκμίου οἷσι μέμ[η]λεν ἐπ' οὔρεος ἀμβώνεσσι
35   πρηΰνειν χαλεπὴν Μαῖραν ἀνερχομένην,
αἰτεῖσθαι τὸ δ' ἄημα παραὶ Διὸς ὧι τε θαμεινοὶ   90
πλήσσονται λινέαις ὄρτυγες ἐν νεφέλαις."
ἦ θεός· αὐτὰρ ὁ Νάξον ἔβη πάλιν, εἴρετο δ' αὐτὴν
κούρην, ἡ δ' ἂν' ἐτῶς πᾶν ἐκάλυψεν ἔπος
40   κῆν αὖ σῶς· [ὅ τε] λοιπόν, Ἀκόντιε, σεῖο μετελθεῖν
νύμφην τ]ὴν ἰδίην ἐς Διονυσιάδα.   95
χἠ θεὸς εὐορκεῖτο καὶ ἥλικες αὐτίχ' ἑταίρης
ἦιδον ὑμηναίους οὐκ ἀναβαλλομένους.
οὔ σε δοκέω τημοῦτος, Ἀκόντιε, νυκτὸς ἐκείνης
45   ἀντί κε, τῆι μίτρης ἥψαο παρθενίης,
οὐ σφυρὸν Ἰφίκλειον ἐπιτρέχον ἀσταχύεσσιν   100
οὐδ' ἃ Κελαινίτης ἐκτεάτιστο Μίδης
δέξασθαι, ψήφου δ' ἂν ἐμῆς ἐπιμάρτυρες εἶεν
οἵτινες οὐ χαλεποῦ νήιδές εἰσι θεοῦ.
50   ἐκ δὲ γάμου κείνοιο μέγ' οὔνομα μέλλε νέεσθαι·
δὴ γὰρ ἔθ' ὑμέτερον φῦλον Ἀκοντιάδαι   105
πουλύ τι καὶ περίτιμον Ἰουλίδι ναιετάουσι,
Κεῖε, τεὸν δ' ἡμεῖς ἵμερον ἐκλύομεν

24 θρύον Hunt: θριον pap.   29 suppl. Pfeiffer: ῥίμφα Trypanis   30 ἀργύρωι
Mair: -ον pap.   33 et 40 suppl. Housman, 41 Barigazzi   43 ἦιδον
Wilamowitz: ειδον pap.   45 τῆι Murray: της pap.   50 μέλλεν ἔσεσθαι
Crusius, Brinkmann

τόνδε παρ' ἀρχαίου Ξενομήδεος, ὅς ποτε πᾶσαν
55 νῆσον ἐνὶ μνήμηι κάτθετο μυθολόγωι,
ἄρχμενος ὡς νύμφηισιν ἐναίετο Κωρυκίηισι,   110
τὰς ἀπὸ Παρνησσοῦ λῖς ἐδίωξε μέγας,
Ὑδροῦσσαν τῶ καί μιν ἐφήμισαν, ὥς τε Κιρώ[δης
ἥρως εὐσίτοις] ὤικεεν ἐν Καρύαις·
60 ὥς τέ μιν ἐννάσσαντο τέων 'Αλαλάξιος αἰεὶ
Ζεὺς ἐπὶ σαλπίγγων ἱρὰ βοῆι δέχεται   115
Κᾶρες ὁμοῦ Λελέγεσσι, μετ' οὔνομα δ' ἄλλο βαλέσθ[αι
Φοίβου καὶ Μελίης ἶνις ἔθηκε Κέως·
ἐν δ' ὕβριν θάνατόν τε κεραύνιον, ἐν δὲ γόητας
65 Τελχῖνας μακάρων τ' οὐκ ἀλέγοντα θεῶν
ἠλεὰ Δημώνακτα γέρων ἐνεθήκατο δέλτοις   120
καὶ γρηῦν Μακελώ, μητέρα Δεξιθέης,
ἃς μούνας, ὅτε νῆσον ἀνέτρεπον εἴνεκ' ἀλ[ι]τρῆς
ὕβριος, ἀσκηθεῖς ἔλλιπον ἀθάνατοι·
70 τέσσαρας ὥς τε πόληας ὁ μὲν τείχισσε Μεγακ[λ]ῆς
Κάρθαιαν, Χρυσοῦς δ' Εὔπ[υ]λος ἡμιθέης   125
εὔκρηνον πτολίεθρον 'Ιουλίδος, αὐτὰρ 'Ακαῖ[ος
Ποιῆσσαν Χαρίτων [ἴδρ]υμ' ἐυπλοκάμων,
ἄστυρον Ἄφραστος δὲ Κορή[σ]ιον, εἶπε δέ, Κεῖε,
75 ξυγκραθέντ' ἀνίαις ὀξὺν ἔρωτα σέθεν
πρέσβυς ἐτητυμίηι μεμελημένος, ἔνθεν ὁ πα[ι]δὸς   130
μῦθος ἐς ἡμετέρην ἔδραμε Καλλιόπην.

III

THE BATH OF PALLAS (*Hymn* 5)

Ὅσσαι λωτροχόοι τᾶς Παλλάδος ἔξιτε πᾶσαι,
ἔξιτε· τᾶν ἵππων ἄρτι φρυασσομενᾶν

58 suppl. Murray, 59 Barber   62 βαλέσθαι Lobel: βαλεισθ[pap.: καλεῖσθαι
Hunt   68 suppl. Wilamowitz, 70 et 71 Hunt, 72 Pfeiffer, 73 Wilamowitz
74 Κορήσιον Hunt: καρη[.]ιον pap.   δέ, Κεῖε incerta   75 ἀνίαις Maas: αυταις
pap.

τᾶν ἱερᾶν ἐσάκουσα, καὶ ἁ θεὸς εὔτυκος ἕρπεν·
σῶσθέ νυν, ὦ ξανθαὶ σῶσθε Πελασγιάδες.   135
5 οὔποκ᾿ Ἀθαναία μεγάλως ἀπενίψατο πάχεις
πρὶν κόνιν ἱππειᾶν ἐξελάσαι λαγόνων·
οὐδ᾿ ὅκα δὴ λύθρωι πεπαλαγμένα πάντα φέροισα
τεύχεα τῶν ἀδίκων ἦνθ᾿ ἀπὸ γαγενέων,
ἀλλὰ πολὺ πράτιστον ὑφ᾿ ἅρματος αὐχένας ἵππων   140
10 λυσαμένα παγαῖς ἔκλυσεν Ὠκεανῶ
ἱδρῶ καὶ ῥαθάμιγγας, ἐφοίβασεν δὲ παγέντα
πάντα χαλινοφάγων ἀφρὸν ἀπὸ στομάτων.
ὦ ἴτ᾿ Ἀχαιιάδες, καὶ μὴ μύρα μηδ᾿ ἀλαβάστρως
(συρίγγων ἀίω φθόγγον ὑπαξόνιον),   145
15 μὴ μύρα λωτροχόοι τᾶι Παλλάδι μηδ᾿ ἀλαβάστρως
(οὐ γὰρ Ἀθαναία χρίματα μεικτὰ φιλεῖ)
οἴσετε μηδὲ κάτοπτρον· ἀεὶ καλὸν ὄμμα τὸ τήνας.
οὐδ᾿ ὅκα τὰν Ἴδαι Φρὺξ ἐδίκαζεν ἔριν,
οὔτ᾿ ἐς ὀρείχαλκον μεγάλα θεὸς οὔτε Σιμοῦντος   150
20 ἔβλεψεν δίναν ἐς διαφαινομέναν·
οὐδ᾿ Ἥρα· Κύπρις δὲ διαυγέα χαλκὸν ἑλοῖσα
πολλάκι τὰν αὐτὰν δὶς μετέθηκε κόμαν.
ἁ δὲ δὶς ἑξήκοντα διαθρέξασα διαύλως,
οἷα παρ᾿ Εὐρώται τοὶ Λακεδαιμόνιοι   155
25 ἀστέρες, ἐμπεράμως ἐνετρίψατο λιτὰ λαβοῖσα
χρίματα, τᾶς ἰδίας ἔκγονα φυταλιᾶς,
ὦ κῶραι, τὸ δ᾿ ἔρευθος ἀνέδραμε, πρώιον οἵαν
ἢ ῥόδον ἢ σίβδας κόκκος ἔχει χροϊάν.
τῶς καὶ νῦν ἄρσεν τι κομίσσατε μῶνον ἔλαιον,   160
30 ὧι Κάστωρ, ὧι καὶ χρίεται Ἡρακλέης·
οἴσετε καὶ κτένα οἱ παγχρύσεον, ὡς ἀπὸ χαίταν
πέξηται, λιπαρὸν σμασαμένα πλόκαμον.

III 3 ἕρπεν Schneider: ἕρπει M   14 ὑπαξονίων m: ὑπ᾿ ἀξονίων
Schneider   18 Ἴδαι Stanley, Bentley: ἴδαν M   19 οὔτ᾿ . . . οὔτε Meineke:
οὐδ᾿ . . . οὐδέ M   25 ἐνετρίψατο Meineke: ἐτρίψατο M   βαλοῖσα m   27
fort. πρώκιον   οἵαν Stephanus: οἷον M   29 τι Bergk: τε M

ἔξιθ᾽, Ἀθαναία· πάρα τοι καταθύμιος ἵλα,
   παρθενικαὶ μεγάλων παῖδες Ἀρεστοριδᾶν· 165
35 ὠθάνα, φέρεται δὲ καὶ ἁ Διομήδεος ἀσπίς,
   ὡς ἔθος Ἀργείως τοῦτο παλαιοτέρως
   Εὐμήδης ἐδίδαξε, τεῖν κεχαρισμένος ἱρεύς·
   ὅς ποκα βωλευτὸν γνοὺς ἐπί οἱ θάνατον
   δᾶμον ἑτοιμάζοντα φυγᾷ τεὸν ἱρὸν ἄγαλμα 170
40 ᾤχετ᾽ ἔχων, Κρεῖον δ᾽ εἰς ὄρος ᾠκίσατο,
   Κρεῖον ὄρος· σὲ δέ, δαῖμον, ἀπορρώγεσσιν ἔθηκεν
   ἐν πέτραις, αἷς νῦν οὔνομα Παλλατίδες.
   ἔξιθ᾽, Ἀθαναία περσέπτολι, χρυσεοπήληξ,
   ἵππων καὶ σακέων ἁδομένα πατάγωι. 175
45 σάμερον, ὑδροφόροι, μὴ βάπτετε—σάμερον, Ἄργος,
   πίνετ᾽ ἀπὸ κρανᾶν μηδ᾽ ἀπὸ τῶ ποταμῶ·
   σάμερον αἱ δῶλαι τὰς κάλπιδας ἢ ᾽ς Φυσάδειαν
   ἢ ἐς Ἀμυμώναν οἴσετε τὰν Δαναῶ.
   καὶ γὰρ δὴ χρυσῶι τε καὶ ἄνθεσιν ὕδατα μείξας 180
50 ἡξεῖ φορβαίων Ἴναχος ἐξ ὀρέων
   τἀθάναι τὸ λοετρὸν ἄγων καλόν. ἀλλά, Πελασγέ,
   φράζεο μὴ οὐκ ἐθέλων τὰν βασίλειαν ἴδηις.
   ὅς κεν ἴδηι γυμνὰν τὰν Παλλάδα τὰν πολιοῦχον,
   τὦργος ἐσοψεῖται τοῦτο πανυστάτιον. 185
55 πότνι᾽ Ἀθαναία, σὺ μὲν ἔξιθι· μέστα δ᾽ ἐγώ τι
   ταῖσδ᾽ ἐρέω· μῦθος δ᾽ οὐκ ἐμός, ἀλλ᾽ ἑτέρων.

   παῖδες, Ἀθαναία νύμφαν μίαν ἔν ποκα Θήβαις
   πουλύ τι καὶ περὶ δὴ φίλατο τᾶν ἑταρᾶν,
   ματέρα Τειρεσίαο, καὶ οὔποκα χωρὶς ἔγεντο· 190
60 ἀλλὰ καὶ ἀρχαιᾶν εὖτ᾽ ἐπὶ Θεσπιέων
   —∪∪—∪∪—∪ ἢ εἰς Ἁλίαρτον ἐλαύνοι
   ἵππως, Βοιωτῶν ἔργα διερχομένα,

34 Ἀρεστοριδᾶν Valckenaer: ἀκε- M   36 Ἀργείως ... παλαιοτέρως anon.:
-ων ...-ον M   46 τῶ ποταμῶ anon.: τῶν -ῶν M   50 φορβαίων suspectum   55 μέστα Pfeiffer: μέσφα M   61 lac. ind. Wilamowitz: ἢ ᾽πὶ
κορωνείας (e u. 63)M

ἢ 'πὶ Κορωνείας, ἵνα οἱ τεθυωμένον ἄλσος
καὶ βωμοὶ ποταμῶι κεῖντ' ἐπὶ Κουραλίωι,   195
65 πολλάκις ἁ δαίμων νιν ἑῶ ἐπεβάσατο δίφρω,
οὐδ' ὄαροι νυμφᾶν οὐδὲ χοροστασίαι
ἀδεῖαι τελέθεσκον, ὅκ' οὐχ ἁγεῖτο Χαρικλώ·
ἀλλ' ἔτι καὶ τήναν δάκρυα πόλλ' ἔμενε,
καίπερ 'Αθαναίαι καταθύμιον ἔσσαν ἑταίραν.   200
70 δή ποκα γὰρ πέπλων λυσαμένα περόνας
ἵππω ἐπὶ κράναι 'Ελικωνίδι καλὰ ῥεοίσαι
λῶντο· μεσαμβρινὰ δ' εἶχ' ὄρος ἀσυχία.
ἀμφότεραι λώοντο, μεσαμβριναὶ δ' ἔσαν ὧραι,
πολλὰ δ' ἀσυχία τῆνο κατεῖχεν ὄρος.   205
75 Τειρεσίας δ' ἔτι μῶνος ἁμᾶι κυσὶν ἄρτι γένεια
περκάζων ἱερὸν χῶρον ἀνεστρέφετο·
διψάσας δ' ἄφατόν τι ποτὶ ῥόον ἤλυθε κράνας,
σχέτλιος· οὐκ ἐθέλων δ' εἶδε τὰ μὴ θεμιτά.
τὸν δὲ χολωσαμένα περ ὅμως προσέφασεν 'Αθάνα·   210
80 "τίς σε, τὸν ὀφθαλμὼς οὐκέτ' ἀποισόμενον,
ὦ Εὐηρείδα, χαλεπὰν ὁδὸν ἄγαγε δαίμων;"
ἁ μὲν ἔφα, παιδὸς δ' ὄμματα νὺξ ἔλαβεν.
ἑστάκη δ' ἄφθογγος, ἐκόλλασαν γὰρ ἀνῖαι
γώνατα καὶ φωνὰν ἔσχεν ἀμαχανία.   215
85 ἁ νύμφα δ' ἐβόασε· "τί μοι τὸν κῶρον ἔρεξας
πότνια; τοιαῦται, δαίμονες, ἐστὲ φίλαι;
ὄμματά μοι τῶ παιδὸς ἀφείλεο. τέκνον ἄλαστε,
εἶδες 'Αθαναίας στήθεα καὶ λαγόνας,
ἀλλ' οὐκ ἀέλιον πάλιν ὄψεαι. ὦ ἐμὲ δειλάν,   220
90 ὦ ὄρος, ὦ 'Ελικὼν οὐκέτι μοι παριτέ,
ἦ μεγάλ' ἀντ' ὀλίγων ἐπράξαο· δόρκας ὀλέσσας
καὶ πρόκας οὐ πολλὰς φάεα παιδὸς ἔχεις."
ἁ μὲν ἅμ' ἀμφοτέραισι φίλον περὶ παῖδα λαβοῖσα
μάτηρ μὲν γοερᾶν οἶτον ἀηδονίδων   225

82 ἔλαβεν anon.: ἔβαλεν M   83 ἑστάκη Buttmann: ἐστάθη M   93 ἅμ' suppl.
Schneider: ἁ μὲν ἀμφ- M: ἆγε μὲν … ἁ μάτηρ (μὲν² deleto) Wilamowitz

95 ἄγε βαρὺ κλαίοισα, θεὰ δ' ἐλέησεν ἑταίραν.
καί νιν 'Αθαναία πρὸς τόδ' ἔλεξεν ἔπος·
"δῖα γύναι, μετὰ πάντα βαλεῦ πάλιν ὅσσα δι' ὀργὰν
εἶπας· ἐγὼ δ' οὔ τοι τέκνον ἔθηκ' ἀλαόν.
οὐ γὰρ 'Αθαναίαι γλυκερὸν πέλει ὄμματα παίδων   230
100 ἁρπάζειν· Κρόνιοι δ' ὧδε λέγοντι νόμοι·
ὅς κε τιν' ἀθανάτων, ὅκα μὴ θεὸς αὐτὸς ἕληται,
ἀθρήσῃ, μισθῶ τοῦτον ἰδεῖν μεγάλω.
δῖα γύναι, τὸ μὲν οὐ παλινάγρετον αὖθι γένοιτο
ἔργον, ἐπεὶ Μοιρᾶν ὧδ' ἐπένησε λίνα   235
105 ἁνίκα τὸ πρᾶτόν νιν ἐγείναο· νῦν δὲ κομίζευ,
ὦ Εὐηρείδα, τέλθος ὀφειλόμενον.
πόσσα μὲν ἁ Καδμηὶς ἐς ὕστερον ἔμπυρα καυσεῖ,
πόσσα δ' 'Αρισταῖος, τὸν μόνον εὐχόμενοι
παῖδα, τὸν ἡβατὰν 'Ακταίονα, τυφλὸν ἰδέσθαι.   240
110 καὶ τῆνος μεγάλας σύνδρομος 'Αρτέμιδος
ἔσσεται· ἀλλ' οὐκ αὐτὸν ὅ τε δρόμος αἵ τ' ἐν ὄρεσσι
ῥυσεῦνται ξυναὶ τᾶμος ἑκαβολίαι,
ὁππόκα κ' οὐκ ἐθέλων περ ἴδῃ χαρίεντα λοετρὰ
δαίμονος· ἀλλ' αὐταὶ τὸν πρὶν ἄνακτα κύνες   245
115 τουτάκι δειπνησεῦντι· τὰ δ' υἱέος ὀστέα μάτηρ
λεξεῖται δρυμὼς πάντας ἐπερχομένα·
ὀλβίσταν δ' ἐρέει σε καὶ εὐαίωνα γενέσθαι
ἐξ ὀρέων ἀλαὸν παῖδ' ὑποδεξαμέναν.
ὦ ἑτάρα, τῶι μή τι μινύρεο· τῶιδε γὰρ ἄλλα   250
120 τεῦ χάριν ἐξ ἐμέθεν πολλὰ μενεῦντι γέρα,
μάντιν ἐπεὶ θησῶ νιν ἀοίδιμον ἐσσομένοισιν,
ἦ μέγα τῶν ἄλλων δή τι περισσότερον.
γνωσεῖται δ' ὄρνιχας, ὃς αἴσιος οἵ τε πέτονται
ἄλιθα καὶ ποίων οὐκ ἀγαθαὶ πτέρυγες.   255
125 πολλὰ δὲ Βοιωτοῖσι θεοπρόπα, πολλὰ δὲ Κάδμωι
χρησεῖ, καὶ μεγάλοις ὕστερα Λαβδακίδαις.

104 ἐπένησε Bentley: ἐπένευσε M   113 ὁππόκα Wilamowitz: ὁππόταν M
κ' οὐκ Bulloch: οὐκ M: κοὐκ (= καὶ οὐκ) Wilamowitz

δωσῶ καὶ μέγα βάκτρον, ὅ οἱ πόδας ἐς δέον ἀξεῖ,
   δωσῶ καὶ βιότω τέρμα πολυχρόνιον,
   καὶ μόνος, εὖτε θάνηι, πεπνυμένος ἐν νεκύεσσι   260
130 φοιτασεῖ, μεγάλωι τίμιος ᾿Αγεσίλαι.''
   ὡς φαμένα κατένευσε· τὸ δ᾿ ἐντελές, ὧι κ᾿ ἐπινεύσηι
   Παλλάς, ἐπεὶ μῶναι Ζεὺς τόγε θυγατέρων
   δῶκεν ᾿Αθαναίαι πατρώια πάντα φέρεσθαι.
   λωτροχόοι, μάτηρ δ᾿ οὔτις ἔτικτε θεάν,   265
135 ἀλλὰ Διὸς κορυφά. κορυφὰ Διὸς οὐκ ἐπινεύει
   ψεύδεα —∪‾∪‾——∪∪ ἁ θυγάτηρ.

ἔρχετ᾿ ᾿Αθαναία νῦν ἀτρεκές· ἀλλὰ δέχεσθε
   τὰν θεόν, ὦ κῶραι, τῶργον ὅσαις μέλεται,
   σύν τ᾿ εὐαγορίαι σύν τ᾿ εὔγμασι σύν τ᾿ ὀλολυγαῖς.   270
140 χαῖρε, θεά, κάδευ δ᾿ ῎Αργεος ᾿Ιναχίω.
   χαῖρε καὶ ἐξελάοισα, καὶ ἐς πάλιν αὖτις ἐλάσσαις
   ἵππως, καὶ Δαναῶν κλᾶρον ἅπαντα σάω.

IV

HYMN TO ZEUS (Hymn 1)

Ζηνὸς ἔοι τί κεν ἄλλο παρὰ σπονδῆισιν ἀείδειν
   λώιον ἢ θεὸν αὐτόν, ἀεὶ μέγαν, αἰὲν ἄνακτα,   275
   Πηλαγόνων ἐλατῆρα, δικασπόλον Οὐρανίδηισι;
   πῶς καί νιν, Δικταῖον ἀείσομεν ἠὲ Λυκαῖον;
5 ἐν δοιῆι μάλα θυμός, ἐπεὶ γένος ἀμφήριστον.
   Ζεῦ, σὲ μὲν ᾿Ιδαίοισιν ἐν οὔρεσί φασι γενέσθαι,
   Ζεῦ, σὲ δ᾿ ἐν ᾿Αρκαδίηι· πότεροι, πάτερ, ἐψεύσαντο;   280
   ''Κρῆτες ἀεὶ ψεῦσται''· καὶ γὰρ τάφον, ὦ ἄνα, σεῖο
   Κρῆτες ἐτεκτήναντο· σὺ δ᾿ οὐ θάνες, ἐσσὶ γὰρ αἰεί.

138 τῶργον Boissonade: τῶργος M

IV 3 Πηλαγόνων test.: πηλο- M

10 ἐν δέ σε Παρρασίηι Ῥείη τέκεν, ἧχι μάλιστα
   ἔσκεν ὄρος θάμνοισι περισκεπές· ἔνθεν ὁ χῶρος
   ἱερός, οὐδέ τί μιν κεχρημένον Εἰλειθυίης   285
   ἑρπετὸν οὐδὲ γυνὴ ἐπιμίσγεται, ἀλλὰ ἓ Ῥείης
   ὠγύγιον καλέουσι λεχώιον Ἀπιδανῆες.
15 ἔνθα σ' ἐπεὶ μήτηρ μεγάλων ἀπεθήκατο κόλπων,
   αὐτίκα δίζητο ῥόον ὕδατος, ὧι κε τόκοιο
   λύματα χυτλώσαιτο, τεὸν δ' ἐνὶ χρῶτα λοέσσαι.   290
   Λάδων ἀλλ' οὔπω μέγας ἔρρεεν οὐδ' Ἐρύμανθος,
   λευκότατος ποταμῶν, ἔτι δ' ἄβροχος ἦεν ἅπασα
20 Ἀζηνίς· μέλλεν δὲ μάλ' εὔυδρος καλέεσθαι
   αὖτις· ἐπεὶ τημόσδε, Ῥέη ὅτε λύσατο μίτρην,
   ἦ πολλὰς ἐφύπερθε σαρωνίδας ὑγρὸς Ἰάων   295
   ἤειρεν, πολλὰς δὲ Μέλας ὤκχησεν ἁμάξας,
   πολλὰ δὲ Καρνίωνος ἄνω διεροῦ περ ἐόντος
25 ἰλυοὺς ἐβάλοντο κινώπετα, νίσσετο δ' ἀνὴρ
   πεζὸς ὑπὲρ Κραθίν τε πολύστιόν τε Μετώπην
   διψαλέος· τὸ δὲ πολλὸν ὕδωρ ὑπὸ ποσσὶν ἔκειτο.   300
   καί ῥ' ὑπ' ἀμηχανίης σχομένη φάτο πότνια Ῥείη·
   "Γαῖα φίλη, τέκε καὶ σύ· τεαὶ δ' ὠδῖνες ἐλαφραί."
30 εἶπε καὶ ἀντανύσασα θεὴ μέγαν ὑψόθι πῆχυν
   πλῆξεν ὄρος σκήπτρωι· τὸ δέ οἱ δίχα πουλὺ διέστη,
   ἐκ δ' ἔχεεν μέγα χεῦμα· τόθι χρόα φαιδρύνασα,   305
   ὦνα, τεὸν σπείρωσε, Νέδηι δέ σε δῶκε κομίζειν
   κευθμὸν ἔσω Κρηταῖον, ἵνα κρύφα παιδεύοιο,
35 πρεσβυτάτηι Νυμφέων, αἵ μιν τότε μαιώσαντο,
   πρωτίστη γενεῆ μετά γε Στύγα τε Φιλύρην τε.
   οὐδ' ἀλίην ἀπέτεισε θεὴ χάριν, ἀλλὰ τὸ χεῦμα   310
   κεῖνο Νέδην ὀνόμηνε· τὸ μέν ποθι πουλὺ κατ' αὐτὸ
   Καυκώνων πτολίεθρον, ὃ Λέπρειον πεφάτισται,
40 συμφέρεται Νηρῆι, παλαιότατον δέ μιν ὕδωρ
   υἱωνοὶ πίνουσι Λυκαονίης ἄρκτοιο.

24 Καρνίωνος Arnaldus: καρίωνος M   33 κομίσσαι m   36 πρωτίστη γενεῆ
Schneider: -ηι…-ῆι M   γε Blomfield: τε M

εὖτε Θενὰς ἀπέλειπεν ἐπὶ Κνωσοῖο φέρουσα, 315
Ζεῦ πάτερ, ἡ Νύμφη σε (Θεναὶ δ' ἔσαν ἐγγύθι Κνωσοῦ),
τουτάκι τοι πέσε, δαῖμον, ἀπ' ὀμφαλός· ἔνθεν ἐκεῖνο
45 Ὀμφάλιον μετέπειτα πέδον καλέουσι Κύδωνες.
Ζεῦ, σὲ δὲ Κυρβάντων ἑτάραι προσεπηχύναντο
Δικταῖαι Μελίαι, σὲ δ' ἐκοίμισεν Ἀδρήστεια 320
λίκνωι ἐνὶ χρυσέωι, σὺ δ' ἐθήσαο πίονα μαζὸν
αἰγὸς Ἀμαλθείης, ἐπὶ δὲ γλυκὺ κηρίον ἔβρως.
50 γέντο γὰρ ἐξαπιναῖα Πανακρίδος ἔργα μελίσσης
Ἰδαίοις ἐν ὄρεσσι, τά τε κλείουσι Πάνακρα.
οὖλα δὲ Κούρητές σε περὶ πρύλιν ὠρχήσαντο 325
τεύχεα πεπλήγοντες, ἵνα Κρόνος οὔασιν ἠχὴν
ἀσπίδος εἰσαΐοι καὶ μή σεο κουρίζοντος.
55 καλὰ μὲν ἠέξευ, καλὰ δ' ἔτραφες, οὐράνιε Ζεῦ,
ὀξὺ δ' ἀνήβησας, ταχινοὶ δέ τοι ἦλθον ἴουλοι.
ἀλλ' ἔτι παιδνὸς ἐὼν ἐφράσσαο πάντα τέλεια· 330
τῶι τοι καὶ γνωτοὶ προτερηγενέες περ ἐόντες
οὐρανὸν οὐκ ἐμέγηραν ἔχειν ἐπιδαίσιον οἶκον.
60 δηναιοὶ δ' οὐ πάμπαν ἀληθέες ἦσαν ἀοιδοί·
φάντο πάλον Κρονίδηισι διάτριχα δώματα νεῖμαι·
τίς δέ κ' ἐπ' Οὐλύμπωι τε καὶ Ἄιδι κλῆρον ἐρύσσαι, 335
ὃς μάλα μὴ νενίηλος; ἐπ' ἰσαίηι γὰρ ἔοικε
πήλασθαι· τὰ δὲ τόσσον ὅσον διὰ πλεῖστον ἔχουσι.
65 ψευδοίμην ἀίοντος ἅ κεν πεπίθοιεν ἀκουήν.
οὔ σε θεῶν ἐσσῆνα πάλοι θέσαν, ἔργα δὲ χειρῶν,
σή τε βίη τό τε κάρτος, ὃ καὶ πέλας εἶσαο δίφρου. 340
θήκαο δ' οἰωνῶν μέγ' ὑπείροχον ἀγγελιώτην
σῶν τεράων· ἅ τ' ἐμοῖσι φίλοις ἐνδέξια φαίνοις.
70 εἵλεο δ' αἰζηῶν ὅ τι φέρτατον· οὐ σύ γε νηῶν
ἐμπεράμους, οὐκ ἄνδρα σακέσπαλον, οὐ μὲν ἀοιδόν·
ἀλλὰ τὰ μὲν μακάρεσσιν ὀλίζοσιν αὖθι παρῆκας 345
ἄλλα μέλειν ἑτέροισι, σὺ δ' ἐξέλεο πτολιάρχους
αὐτούς, ὧν ὑπὸ χεῖρα γεωμόρος, ὧν ἴδρις αἰχμῆς,

68 οἰωνῶν Stephanus: -ὸν M

75 ὦν ἐρέτης, ὦν πάντα· τί δ' οὐ κρατέοντος ὑπ' ἰσχύν;
   αὐτίκα χαλκῆας μὲν ὑδείομεν Ἡφαίστοιο,
   τευχηστὰς δ' Ἄρηος, ἐπακτῆρας δὲ Χιτώνης   350
   Ἀρτέμιδος, Φοίβου δὲ λύρης εὖ εἰδότας οἴμους·
   "ἐκ δὲ Διὸς βασιλῆες", ἐπεὶ Διὸς οὐδὲν ἀνάκτων
80 θειότερον· τῶι καί σφε τεὴν ἐκρίναο λάξιν.
   δῶκας δὲ πτολίεθρα φυλασσέμεν, ἵζεο δ' αὐτὸς
   ἄκρηισ' ἐν πολίεσσιν, ἐπόψιος οἵ τε δίκηισι   355
   λαὸν ὑπὸ σκολιῆισ' οἵ τ' ἔμπαλιν ἰθύνουσιν·
   ἐν δὲ ῥυηφενίην ἔβαλές σφισιν, ἐν δ' ἅλις ὄλβον·
85 πᾶσι μέν, οὐ μάλα δ' ἴσον. ἔοικε δὲ τεκμήρασθαι
   ἡμετέρωι μεδέοντι· περιπρὸ γὰρ εὐρὺ βέβηκεν.
   ἑσπέριος κεῖνός γε τελεῖ τά κεν ἦρι νοήσηι·   360
   ἑσπέριος τὰ μέγιστα, τὰ μείονα δ', εὖτε νοήσηι.
   οἱ δὲ τὰ μὲν πλειῶνι, τὰ δ' οὐχ ἑνί, τῶν δ' ἀπὸ πάμπαν
90 αὐτὸς ἄνην ἐκόλουσας, ἐνέκλασσας δὲ μενοινήν.
   χαῖρε μέγα, Κρονίδη πανυπέρτατε, δῶτορ ἐάων,
   δῶτορ ἀπημονίης. τεὰ δ' ἔργματα τίς κεν ἀείδοι;   365
   οὐ γένετ', οὐκ ἔσται· τίς κεν Διὸς ἔργματ' ἀείσει;
   χαῖρε, πάτερ, χαῖρ' αὖθι· δίδου δ' ἀρετήν τ' ἄφενός τε.
95 οὔτ' ἀρετῆς ἄτερ ὄλβος ἐπίσταται ἄνδρας ἀέξειν
   οὔτ' ἀρετὴ ἀφένοιο· δίδου δ' ἀρετήν τε καὶ ὄλβον.

V

CLEANTHES

HYMN TO ZEUS

Κύδιστ' ἀθανάτων, πολυώνυμε, παγκρατὲς αἰεί,   370
Ζεῦ, φύσεως ἀρχηγέ, νόμου μέτα πάντα κυβερνῶν,

79 Διὸς² suspectum   80 σφε pap., cj. Bentley: σφι M   87 ἦρι anon., Dawes:
ἠοῖ M   νοήσηι Lascaris: -σει M   93 ἀείσοι m

V Stob. *Ecl. Phys.* 1.2, 1 25 Wachsmuth

χαῖρε· σὲ γὰρ πάντεσσι θέμις θνητοῖσι προσαυδᾶν.
ἐκ σοῦ γὰρ γενόμεσθα, θεοῦ μίμημα λαχόντες
5 μοῦνοι, ὅσα ζώει τε καὶ ἕρπει θνήτ' ἐπὶ γαῖαν·
τῶ σε καθυμνήσω καὶ σὸν κράτος αἰὲν ἀείσω.   375
σοὶ δὴ πᾶς ὅδε κόσμος ἑλισσόμενος περὶ γαῖαν
πείθεται ᾗ κεν ἄγῃς, καὶ ἑκὼν ὑπὸ σεῖο κρατεῖται·
τοῖον ἔχεις ὑποεργὸν ἀνικήτοις ἐνὶ χερσὶν
10 ἀμφήκη πυρόεντα ἀειζώοντα κεραυνόν·
τοῦ γὰρ ὑπὸ πληγῆι φύσεως πάντ' ἔργα ⟨τελεῖται⟩·   380
τῶι σὺ κατευθύνεις κοινὸν λόγον, ὃς διὰ πάντων
φοιτᾶι μιγνύμενος μεγάλοις μικροῖς τε φάεσσι

†ὥς τόσσος γεγαὼς ὕπατος βασιλεὺς διὰ παντός.
15 οὐδέ τι γίγνεται ἔργον ἐπὶ χθονὶ σοῦ δίχα, δαῖμον,
οὔτε κατ' αἰθέριον θεῖον πόλον, οὔτ' ἐνὶ πόντωι,   385
πλὴν ὁπόσα ῥέζουσι κακοὶ σφετέραισιν ἀνοίαις.
ἀλλὰ σὺ καὶ τὰ περισσὰ ἐπίστασαι ἄρτια θεῖναι,
καὶ κοσμεῖν τἄκοσμα, τὰ δ' οὐ φίλα σοὶ φίλα ἐστίν.
20 ὧδε γὰρ εἰς ἓν πάντα συνήρμοκας ἐσθλὰ κακοῖσιν
ὥσθ' ἕνα γίγνεσθαι πάντων λόγον αἰὲν ἐόντα,   390
ὃν φεύγοντες ἐῶσιν ὅσοι θνητῶν κακοί εἰσι,
δύσμοροι, οἵ τ' ἀγαθῶν μὲν ἀεὶ κτῆσιν ποθέοντες
οὔτ' ἐσορῶσι θεοῦ κοινὸν νόμον οὔτε κλύουσιν,
25 ὧι κεν πειθόμενοι σὺν νῶι βίον ἐσθλὸν ἔχοιεν·
αὐτοὶ δ' αὖθ' ὁρμῶσιν ἄνευ νόου ἄλλος ἐπ' ἄλλο,   395
οἱ μὲν ὑπὲρ δόξης σπουδὴν δυσέριστον ἔχοντες,

---

3 πάντεσσι Scaliger: πᾶσι M   4 γενόμεσθα Meineke: γένος ἐσμέν M   θεοῦ Pearson: ἤχου M: σέθεν Zuntz   6 ἀείσω Ursinus: ἀίδω M   7 δὴ Scaliger: δὲ M   8 σεῖο Stephanus: σοῖο M   9 ἐνὶ Brunck: ὑπὸ M   11 πληγῆι Wilamowitz: -ῆις M   ⟨τελεῖται⟩ suppl. von Arnim: lac. in M   12 τῶι Hopkinson: ὧι M   κοινὸν λόγον Ursinus: λ. κ. M   13 μεγάλοις μικροῖς τε Brunck: μεγάλων μικροῖσι M   14 u. ad init. (et fort. ad fin.) corruptus   16 ἐνὶ Brunck: ἐπὶ M   19 τὰ δ' Hopkinson: καὶ M   21 λόγον Ursinus: -ων M   ἐόντα Brunck: -ων M   25 ὧι Ursinus: οἳ M   26 νόου Wilamowitz: κακοῦ M   ἄλλο Sauppe: ἄλλα M

οἵ δ' ἐπὶ κερδοσύνας τετραμμένοι οὐδενὶ κόσμωι,
ἄλλοι δ' εἰς ἄνεσιν καὶ σώματος ἡδέα ἔργα·
30 ⟨ἀλλὰ κακῶν ἐπέκυρσαν⟩, ἐπ' ἄλλοτε δ' ἄλλα φέρονται,
σπεύδοντες μάλα πάμπαν ἐναντία τῶνδε γενέσθαι.   400
ἀλλὰ Ζεῦ πάνδωρε κελαινεφὲς ἀρχικέραυνε
ἀνθρώπους ῥύοιο ἀπειροσύνης ἀπὸ λυγρῆς·
τὴν σύ, πάτερ, σκέδασον ψυχῆς ἄπο, δὸς δὲ κυρῆσαι
35 γνώμης, ἧι πίσυνος σὺ δίκης μέτα πάντα κυβερνᾶις,
ὄφρ' ἂν τιμηθέντες ἀμειβώμεσθά σε τιμῆι,   405
ὑμνοῦντες τὰ σὰ ἔργα διηνεκές, ὡς ἐπέοικε
θνητὸν ἐόντ', ἐπεὶ οὔτε βροτοῖς γέρας ἄλλο τι μεῖζον
οὔτε θεοῖς, ἢ κοινὸν ἀεὶ νόμον ἐν δίκηι ὑμνεῖν.

VI

ARATUS

INVOCATION TO ZEUS (*Phaenomena* 1–18)

Ἐκ Διὸς ἀρχώμεσθα, τὸν οὐδέποτ' ἄνδρες ἐῶμεν
ἄρρητον· μεσταὶ δὲ Διὸς πᾶσαι μὲν ἀγυιαί,   410
πᾶσαι δ' ἀνθρώπων ἀγοραί, μεστὴ δὲ θάλασσα
καὶ λιμένες· πάντη δὲ Διὸς κεχρήμεθα πάντες.
5 τοῦ γὰρ καὶ γένος εἰμέν· ὁ δ' ἤπιος ἀνθρώποισι
δεξιὰ σημαίνει, λαοὺς δ' ἐπὶ ἔργον ἐγείρει
μιμνήισκων βιότοιο, λέγει δ' ὅτε βῶλος ἀρίστη   415
βουσί τε καὶ μακέλησι, λέγει δ' ὅτε δεξιαὶ ὧραι
καὶ φυτὰ γυρῶσαι καὶ σπέρματα πάντα βαλέσθαι.
10 αὐτὸς γὰρ τά γε σήματ' ἐν οὐρανῶι ἐστήριξεν
ἄστρα διακρίνας, ἐσκέψατο δ' εἰς ἐνιαυτὸν

30 suppl. Dawe post von Arnim (ἀλλὰ κακοῖς ἐπ.)   φέρονται Meineke: -οντες
M   32 ἀργικέραυνε Meineke   33 ῥύοιο Brunck: ῥύου M: ῥύσασθαι
Scaliger   34 τὴν Hopkinson: ἣν M   35 ἧι Ursinus: ἣ M   38 οὔτε Scaliger
(?), Cudworth: οὗτοι M   ἄλλο τι Brunck: ἄλλοτε M

ἀστέρας οἵ κε μάλιστα τετυγμένα σημαίνοιεν   420
ἀνδράσιν ὡράων, ὄφρ᾽ ἔμπεδα πάντα φύωνται.
τῶ μιν ἀεὶ πρῶτόν τε καὶ ὕστατον ἱλάσκονται.
15 χαῖρε, πάτερ, μέγα θαῦμα, μέγ᾽ ἀνθρώποισιν ὄνειαρ,
αὐτὸς καὶ προτέρη γενεή. χαίροιτε δὲ Μοῦσαι
μειλίχιαι μάλα πᾶσαι· ἐμοί γε μὲν ἀστέρας εἰπεῖν   425
ἧι θέμις εὐχομένωι τεκμήρατε πᾶσαν ἀοιδήν.

VII

JUSTICE LEAVES THE EARTH (*Phaenomena* 96–136)

Ἀμφοτέροισι δὲ ποσσὶν ὕπο σκέπτοιο Βοώτεω
Παρθένον, ἥ ῥ᾽ ἐν χειρὶ φέρει Στάχυν αἰγλήεντα.
εἴτ᾽ οὖν Ἀστραίου κείνη γένος, ὅν ῥά τέ φασιν
ἄστρων ἀρχαῖον πατέρ᾽ ἔμμεναι, εἴτε τευ ἄλλου,   430
100 εὔκηλος φορέοιτο. λόγος γε μὲν ἐντρέχει ἄλλος
ἀνθρώποις, ὡς δῆθεν ἐπιχθονίη πάρος ἦεν,
ἤρχετο δ᾽ ἀνθρώπων κατεναντίη, οὐδέ ποτ᾽ ἀνδρῶν
οὐδέ ποτ᾽ ἀρχαίων ἠνήνατο φῦλα γυναικῶν,
ἀλλ᾽ ἀναμὶξ ἐκάθητο, καὶ ἀθανάτη περ ἐοῦσα.   435
105 καὶ ἓ Δίκην καλέεσκον· ἀγειρομένη δὲ γέροντας
ἠέ που εἰν ἀγορῆι ἢ εὐρυχόρωι ἐν ἀγυιῆι,
δημοτέρας ἤειδεν ἐπισπέρχουσα θέμιστας.
οὔπω λευγαλέου τότε νείκεος ἠπίσταντο
οὐδὲ διακρίσιος περιμεμφέος οὐδὲ κυδοιμοῦ,   440
110 αὔτως δ᾽ ἔζωον· χαλεπὴ δ᾽ ἀπέκειτο θάλασσα,
καὶ βίον οὔπω νῆες ἀπόπροθεν ἠγίνεσκον,
ἀλλὰ βόες καὶ ἄροτρα· καὶ αὐτή, πότνια λαῶν,
μυρία πάντα παρεῖχε Δίκη, δώτειρα δικαίων.
τόφρ᾽ ἦν, ὄφρ᾽ ἔτι γαῖα γένος χρύσειον ἔφερβεν·   445
115 ἀργυρέωι δ᾽ ὀλίγη τε καὶ οὐκέτι πάμπαν ἑτοίμη

VII 96 ὕπο σκέπτοιο Maass: ὑποσκέπτοιο M   99 ἀρχαῖοι Friesemann

ὡμίλει, ποθέουσα παλαιῶν ἤθεα λαῶν.
ἀλλ' ἔμπης ἔτι κεῖνο κατ' ἀργύρεον γένος ἦεν·
ἤρχετο δ' ἐξ ὀρέων ὑποδείελος ἠχηέντων
μουνάξ, οὐδέ τεωι ἐπεμίσγετο μειλιχίοισιν·   450
120 ἀλλ' ὁπότ' ἀνθρώπων μεγάλας πλήσαιτο κολώνας,
ἠπείλει δὴ ἔπειτα καθαπτομένη κακότητος,
οὐδ' ἔτ' ἔφη εἰσωπὸς ἐλεύσεσθαι καλέουσιν·
"οἵην χρύσειοι πατέρες γενεὴν ἐλίποντο
χειροτέρην· ὑμεῖς δὲ κακώτερα τεξείεσθε.   455
125 καὶ δή που πόλεμοι, καὶ δὴ καὶ ἀνάρσιον αἷμα
ἔσσεται ἀνθρώποισι, κακὸν δ' ἐπικείσεται ἄλγος."
ὣς εἰποῦσ' ὀρέων ἐπεμαίετο, τοὺς δ' ἄρα λαοὺς
εἰς αὐτὴν ἔτι πάντας ἐλίμπανε παπταίνοντας.
ἀλλ' ὅτε δὴ κἀκεῖνοι ἐτέθνασαν, οἱ δ' ἐγένοντο,   460
130 χαλκείη γενεή, προτέρων ὀλοώτεροι ἄνδρες,
οἳ πρῶτοι κακοεργὸν ἐχαλκεύσαντο μάχαιραν
εἰνοδίην, πρῶτοι δὲ βοῶν ἐπάσαντ' ἀροτήρων,
καὶ τότε μισήσασα Δίκη κείνων γένος ἀνδρῶν
ἔπταθ' ὑπουρανίη, ταύτην δ' ἄρα νάσσατο χώρην,   465
135 ἧχί περ ἐννυχίη ἔτι φαίνεται ἀνθρώποισι
Παρθένος, ἐγγὺς ἐοῦσα πολυσκέπτοιο Βοώτεω.

VIII

NICANDER

THE DIPSAS-SNAKE (*Theriaca* 334–58)

Ναὶ μὴν διψάδος εἶδος ὁμώσεται αἰὲν ἐχίδνηι
335 παυροτέρηι, θανάτου δὲ θοώτερος ἵζεται αἶσα
οἷσιν ἐνισκίμψηι βλοσυρὸν δάκος· ἤτοι ἀραιὴ   470
αἰὲν ὑποζοφόεσσα μελαίνεται ἀκρόθεν οὐρή·

---

126 κακῶν m

VIII 336 ἐνιχρίμψηι m: ἐνισκήψηι m

δάχματι δ' ἐμφλέγεται κραδίη πρόπαν, ἀμφὶ δὲ καύσωι
χείλε' ὑπ' ἀζαλέης αὐαίνεται ἄβροχα δίψης·
340 αὐτὰρ ὅγ', ἠΰτε ταῦρος ὑπὲρ ποταμοῖο νενευκώς,
χανδὸν ἀμέτρητον δέχεται ποτὸν εἰσόκε νηδὺς   475
ὀμφαλὸν ἐκρήξειε, χέοι δ' ὑπεραχθέα φόρτον.
ὠγύγιος δ' ἄρα μῦθος ἐν αἰζηοῖσι φορεῖται,
ὡς, ὁπότ' οὐρανὸν ἔσχε Κρόνου πρεσβίστατον αἷμα,
345 Ν ειμάμενος κασίεσσιν ἑκὰς περικυδέας ἀρχὰς
Ι δμοσύνηι νεότητα γέρας πόρεν ἡμερίοισι   480
Κ υδαίνων· δὴ γάρ ῥα πυρὸς ληίστορ' ἔνιπτον.
Α φρονες, οὐ μὲν τῆς γε κακοφραδίηισ' ἀπόνηντο·
Ν ωθεῖ γὰρ κάμνοντες ἀμορβεύοντο λεπάργωι
350 Δ ῶρα· πολύσκαρθμος δὲ κεκαυμένος αὐχένα δίψηι
Ρ ώετο, γωλειοῖσι δ' ἰδὼν ὁλκήρεα θῆρα   485
Ο ὑλοόν, ἐλλιτάνευε κακῆι ἐπαλαλκέμεν ἄτηι
Σ αίνων· αὐτὰρ ὁ βρῖθος ὃ δή ῥ' ἀνεδέξατο νώτοις
ἤιτεεν ἄφρονα δῶρον· ὁ δ' οὐκ ἀπανήνατο χρειώ.
355 ἐξότε γηραλέον μὲν ἀεὶ φλόον ἑρπετὰ βάλλει
ὁλκήρη, θνητοὺς δὲ κακὸν περὶ γῆρας ὀπάζει·   490
νοῦσον δ' ἀζαλέην βρωμήτορος οὐλομένη θὴρ
δέξατο, καί τε τυπῆισιν ἀμυδροτέρηισιν ἰάπτει.

IX

THEOCRITUS

THE CYCLOPS (*Idyll* 11)

Οὐδὲν πὸτ τὸν ἔρωτα πεφύκει φάρμακον ἄλλο,
Νικία, οὔτ' ἔγχριστον, ἐμὶν δοκεῖ, οὔτ' ἐπίπαστον,
ἢ ταὶ Πιερίδες· κοῦφον δέ τι τοῦτο καὶ ἁδὺ
γίνετ' ἐπ' ἀνθρώποις, εὑρεῖν δ' οὐ ῥάιδιόν ἐστι.   495

342 χέοι Bentley: χέηι m: χέει m   345 fort. ἑὰς   348 κακοφραδίηισ' Klauser
(-αις), Beazley: -ίης M   349 νωθεῖς m

IX   10 οὐδὲ ῥόδωι Ziegler: οὐδὲ ῥόδοις m: οὐδ' αὖ ῥόδωι m: οὐδ' αὖ ῥόδοις m

5 γινώσκειν δ' οἶμαί τυ καλῶς ἰατρὸν ἐόντα
   καὶ ταῖς ἐννέα δὴ πεφιλημένον ἔξοχα Μοίσαις.
   οὕτω γοῦν ῥάιστα διᾶγ' ὁ Κύκλωψ ὁ παρ' ἁμῖν,
   ὡρχαῖος Πολύφαμος, ὅκ' ἤρατο τᾶς Γαλατείας,   500
   ἄρτι γενειάσδων περὶ τὸ στόμα τὼς κροτάφως τε.
10 ἤρατο δ' οὐ μάλοις οὐδὲ ῥόδωι οὐδὲ κικίννοις,
   ἀλλ' ὀρθαῖς μανίαις, ἁγεῖτο δὲ πάντα πάρεργα.
   πολλάκι ταὶ ὄιες ποτὶ τωὔλιον αὐταὶ ἀπῆνθον
   χλωρᾶς ἐκ βοτάνας· ὁ δὲ τὰν Γαλάτειαν ἀείδων   505
   αὐτὸς ἐπ' ἀϊόνος κατετάκετο φυκιοέσσας
15 ἐξ ἀοῦς, ἔχθιστον ἔχων ὑποκάρδιον ἕλκος,
   Κύπριδος ἐκ μεγάλας τό οἱ ἥπατι πᾶξε βέλεμνον.
   ἀλλὰ τὸ φάρμακον εὗρε, καθεζόμενος δ' ἐπὶ πέτρας
   ὑψηλᾶς ἐς πόντον ὁρῶν ἄειδε τοιαῦτα·   510
     "ὦ λευκὰ Γαλάτεια, τί τὸν φιλέοντ' ἀποβάλληι,
20 λευκοτέρα πακτᾶς ποτιδεῖν, ἀπαλωτέρα ἀρνός,
   μόσχω γαυροτέρα, φιαρωτέρα ὄμφακος ὠμᾶς;
   φοιτῆις δ' αὖθ' οὕτως ὅκκα γλυκὺς ὕπνος ἔχηι με,
   οἴχηι δ' εὐθὺς ἰοῖσ' ὅκκα γλυκὺς ὕπνος ἀνῆι με,   515
   φεύγεις δ' ὥσπερ ὄις πολιὸν λύκον ἀθρήσασα;
25 ἠράσθην μὲν ἔγωγε τεοῦς, κόρα, ἁνίκα πρᾶτον
   ἦνθες ἐμᾶι σὺν ματρὶ θέλοισ' ὑακίνθινα φύλλα
   ἐξ ὄρεος δρέψασθαι, ἐγὼ δ' ὁδὸν ἁγεμόνευον.
   παύσασθαι δ' ἐσιδών τυ καὶ ὕστερον οὐδ' ἔτι παι νῦν
   ἐκ τήνω δύναμαι· τὶν δ' οὐ μέλει, οὐ μὰ Δί' οὐδέν.   520
30 γινώσκω, χαρίεσσα κόρα, τίνος οὕνεκα φεύγεις·
   οὕνεκά μοι λασία μὲν ὀφρὺς ἐπὶ παντὶ μετώπωι
   ἐξ ὠτὸς τέταται ποτὶ θώτερον ὣς μία μακρά,
   εἷς δ' ὀφθαλμὸς ὕπεστι, πλατεῖα δὲ ῥὶς ἐπὶ χείλει.   525
   ἀλλ' οὗτος τοιοῦτος ἐὼν βοτὰ χίλια βόσκω,
35 κἠκ τούτων τὸ κράτιστον ἀμελγόμενος γάλα πίνω·
   τυρὸς δ' οὐ λείπει μ' οὔτ' ἐν θέρει οὔτ' ἐν ὀπώραι,
   οὐ χειμῶνος ἄκρω· ταρσοὶ δ' ὑπεραχθέες αἰεί.

33 ὕπεστι Winsem: ἔπ- M   34 οὕτως m: ὡυτὸς m

συρίσδεν δ' ὡς οὔτις ἐπίσταμαι ὧδε Κυκλώπων,   530
τίν, τὸ φίλον γλυκύμαλον, ἁμᾶι κἠμαυτὸν ἀείδων
40 πολλάκι νυκτὸς ἀωρί. τράφω δέ τοι ἕνδεκα νεβρώς,
πάσας μαννοφόρως, καὶ σκύμνως τέσσαρας ἄρκτων.
ἀλλ' ἀφίκευσο ποθ' ἁμέ, καὶ ἐξεῖς οὐδὲν ἔλασσον,
τὰν γλαυκὰν δὲ θάλασσαν ἔα ποτὶ χέρσον ὀρεχθεῖν·   535
ἅδιον ἐν τὥντρωι παρ' ἐμὶν τὰν νύκτα διαξεῖς.
45 ἐντὶ δάφναι τηνεί, ἐντὶ ῥαδιναὶ κυπάρισσοι,
ἔστι μέλας κισσός, ἔστ' ἄμπελος ἁ γλυκύκαρπος,
ἔστι ψυχρὸν ὕδωρ, τό μοι ἁ πολυδένδρεος Αἴτνα
λευκᾶς ἐκ χιόνος ποτὸν ἀμβρόσιον προΐητι.   540
τίς κα τῶνδε θάλασσαν ἔχειν καὶ κύμαθ' ἔλοιτο;
50 αἰ δέ τοι αὐτὸς ἐγὼν δοκέω λασιώτερος ἦμεν,
ἐντὶ δρυὸς ξύλα μοι καὶ ὑπὸ σποδῷ ἀκάματον πῦρ.
καιόμενος δ' ὑπὸ τεῦς καὶ τὰν ψυχὰν ἀνεχοίμαν
καὶ τὸν ἕν' ὀφθαλμόν, τῶ μοι γλυκερώτερον οὐδέν.   545
ὤμοι ὅτ' οὐκ ἔτεκέν μ' ἁ μάτηρ βράγχι' ἔχοντα,
55 ὡς κατέδυν ποτὶ τὶν καὶ τὰν χέρα τεῦς ἐφίλησα,
αἰ μὴ τὸ στόμα λῇς, ἔφερον δέ τοι ἢ κρίνα λευκὰ
ἢ μάκων' ἀπαλὰν ἐρυθρὰ πλαταγώνι' ἔχοισαν·
ἀλλὰ τὰ μὲν θέρεος, τὰ δὲ γίνεται ἐν χειμῶνι,   550
ὥστ' οὔ κά τοι ταῦτα φέρειν ἅμα πάντ' ἐδυνάθην.
60 νῦν μάν, ὦ κόριον, νῦν αὐτίκα νεῖν γε μαθεῦμαι,
αἴ κά τις σὺν ναῖ πλέων ξένος ὧδ' ἀφίκηται,
ὡς εἰδῶ τί ποχ' ἁδὺ κατοικεῖν τὸν βυθὸν ὕμμιν.
ἐξένθοις, Γαλάτεια, καὶ ἐξενθοῖσα λάθοιο,   555
ὥσπερ ἐγὼ νῦν ὧδε καθήμενος, οἴκαδ' ἀπενθεῖν·
65 ποιμαίνειν δ' ἐθέλοις σὺν ἐμὶν ἅμα καὶ γάλ' ἀμέλγειν
καὶ τυρὸν πᾶξαι τάμισον δριμεῖαν ἐνεῖσα.
ἁ μάτηρ ἀδικεῖ με μόνα, καὶ μέμφομαι αὐτᾶι·
οὐδὲν πήποχ' ὅλως ποτὶ τὶν φίλον εἶπεν ὑπέρ μευ,   560
καὶ ταῦτ' ἆμαρ ἐπ' ἆμαρ ὀρεῦσά με λεπτύνοντα.

49 κα Brunck: κἀν m: τὰν m: ἂν m   καὶ Ahrens: ἢ M   59 κά Wilamowitz: ἂν
M   60 αὐτίκα Paley: αὐτόγα m: τόγε m   69 λεπτύνοντα Meineke: λεπτὸν
ἐόντα M

X THEOCRITUS

35

70 φασῶ τὰν κεφαλὰν καὶ τὼς πόδας ἀμφοτέρως μευ
σφύσδειν, ὡς ἀνιαθῆι ἐπεὶ κἠγὼν ἀνιῶμαι.
ὦ Κύκλωψ Κύκλωψ, πᾶι τὰς φρένας ἐκπεπότασαι;
αἴ κ᾽ ἐνθὼν ταλάρως τε πλέκοις καὶ θαλλὸν ἀμάσας   565
ταῖς ἄρνεσσι φέροις, τάχα κα πολὺ μᾶλλον ἔχοις νῶν.
75 τὰν παρεοῖσαν ἄμελγε· τί τὸν φεύγοντα διώκεις;
εὑρησεῖς Γαλάτειαν ἴσως καὶ καλλίον᾽ ἄλλαν.
πολλαὶ συμπαίσδεν με κόραι τὰν νύκτα κέλονται,
κιχλίζοντι δὲ πᾶσαι, ἐπεί κ᾽ αὐταῖς ὑπακούσω.   570
δῆλον ὅτ᾽ ἐν τᾶι γᾶι κἠγών τις φαίνομαι ἦμεν."
80 οὕτω τοι Πολύφαμος ἐποίμαινεν τὸν ἔρωτα
μουσίσδων, ῥᾷον δὲ διᾶγ᾽ ἢ εἰ χρυσὸν ἔδωκεν.

X

THE SORCERESS (Idyll 2)

Πᾶι μοι ταὶ δάφναι; φέρε, Θεστυλί. πᾶι δὲ τὰ φίλτρα;
στέψον τὰν κελέβαν φοινικέωι οἰὸς ἀώτωι,   575
ὡς τὸν ἐμὸν βαρὺν εὖντα φίλον καταδήσομαι ἄνδρα,
ὅς μοι δωδεκαταῖος ἀφ᾽ ὦ τάλας οὐδὲ ποθίκει,
5 οὐδ᾽ ἔγνω πότερον τεθνάκαμες ἢ ζοοὶ εἰμές,
οὐδὲ θύρας ἄραξεν ἀνάρσιος. ἦ ῥά οἱ ἀλλᾶι
ὤιχετ᾽ ἔχων ὅ τ᾽ Ἔρως ταχινὰς φρένας ἅ τ᾽ Ἀφροδίτα.   580
βασεῦμαι ποτὶ τὰν Τιμαγήτοιο παλαίστραν
αὔριον ὡς νιν ἴδω, καὶ μέμψομαι οἷά με ποιεῖ.
10 νῦν δέ νιν ἐκ θυέων καταδήσομαι. ἀλλά, Σελάνα,
φαῖνε καλόν· τὶν γὰρ ποταείσομαι ἄσυχα, δαῖμον,
τᾶι χθονίαι θ᾽ Ἑκάται, τὰν καὶ σκύλακες τρομέοντι   585
ἐρχομέναν νεκύων ἀνά τ᾽ ἠρία καὶ μέλαν αἷμα.
χαῖρ᾽, Ἑκάτα δασπλῆτι, καὶ ἐς τέλος ἄμμιν ὀπάδει,

74 κα Ahrens: καὶ M

X habet P.Antin.; uu. 30–2, 43–9 etiam P.Oxy. 3546   3 ἐμὸν pap., M: ἐμὶν
Valckenaer

15 φάρμακα ταῦτ᾽ ἔρδοισα χερείονα μήτε τι Κίρκας
    μήτε τι Μηδείας μήτε ξανθᾶς Περιμήδας.

    ἴυγξ, ἕλκε τὺ τῆνον ἐμὸν ποτὶ δῶμα τὸν ἄνδρα.   590

    ἄλφιτά τοι πρᾶτον πυρὶ τάκεται. ἀλλ᾽ ἐπίπασσε,
    Θεστυλί. δειλαία, πᾶ τὰς φρένας ἐκπεπότασαι;
20 ἦ ῥά γέ θην, μυσαρά, καὶ τὶν ἐπίχαρμα τέτυγμαι;
    πάσσ᾽ ἅμα καὶ λέγε ταῦτα· "τὰ Δέλφιδος ὀστία πάσσω".

    ἴυγξ, ἕλκε τὺ τῆνον ἐμὸν ποτὶ δῶμα τὸν ἄνδρα.   595

    Δέλφις ἔμ᾽ ἀνίασεν· ἐγὼ δ᾽ ἐπὶ Δέλφιδι δάφναν
    αἴθω· χὼς αὕτα λακεῖ μέγα καππυρίσαισα
25 κἠξαπίνας ἄφθη κοὐδὲ σποδὸν εἴδομες αὐτᾶς,
    οὕτω τοι καὶ Δέλφις ἐνὶ φλογὶ σάρκ᾽ ἀμαθύνοι.

27 ἴυγξ, ἕλκε τὺ τῆνον ἐμὸν ποτὶ δῶμα τὸν ἄνδρα.   600

33 νῦν θυσῶ τὰ πίτυρα. τὺ δ᾽, Ἄρτεμι, καὶ τὸν ἐν Ἅιδα
    κινήσαις ἀδάμαντα καὶ εἴ τί περ ἀσφαλὲς ἄλλο—
35 Θεστυλί, ταὶ κύνες ἄμμιν ἀνὰ πτόλιν ὠρύονται·
    ἁ θεὸς ἐν τριόδοισι· τὸ χαλκέον ὡς τάχος ἄχει.

    ἴυγξ, ἕλκε τὺ τῆνον ἐμὸν ποτὶ δῶμα τὸν ἄνδρα.   605

    ἠνίδε σιγῇ μὲν πόντος, σιγῶντι δ᾽ ἀῆται·
    ἁ δ᾽ ἐμὰ οὐ σιγῇ στέρνων ἔντοσθεν ἀνία,
40 ἀλλ᾽ ἐπὶ τήνωι πᾶσα καταίθομαι ὅς με τάλαιναν
    ἀντὶ γυναικὸς ἔθηκε κακὰν καὶ ἀπάρθενον ἦμεν.

    ἴυγξ, ἕλκε τὺ τῆνον ἐμὸν ποτὶ δῶμα τὸν ἄνδρα.   610

28 ὡς τοῦτον τὸν κηρὸν ἐγὼ σὺν δαίμονι τάκω,
29 ὣς τάκοιθ᾽ ὑπ᾽ ἔρωτος ὁ Μύνδιος αὐτίκα Δέλφις.
30 χὡς δινεῖθ᾽ ὅδε ῥόμβος ὁ χάλκεος ἐξ Ἀφροδίτας,
31 ὣς τῆνος δινοῖτο ποθ᾽ ἀμετέραισι θύραισιν.

---

18 κάεται schol. u.l.   20 θην pap.: τοι M   28–32 post 42 habent papp., m

32 Ἴυγξ, ἕλκε τὺ τῆνον ἐμὸν ποτὶ δῶμα τὸν ἄνδρα.

615

43 ἐς τρὶς ἀποσπένδω καὶ τρὶς τάδε, πότνια, φωνῶ·
εἴτε γυνὰ τήνωι παρακέκλιται εἴτε καὶ ἀνήρ,
45 τόσσον ἔχοι λάθας ὅσσον ποκὰ Θησέα φαντὶ
ἐν Δίαι λασθῆμεν ἐυπλοκάμω Ἀριάδνας.

Ἴυγξ, ἕλκε τὺ τῆνον ἐμὸν ποτὶ δῶμα τὸν ἄνδρα.

620

ἱππομανὲς φυτόν ἐστι παρ᾽ Ἀρκάσι, τῶι δ᾽ ἔπι πᾶσαι
καὶ πῶλοι μαίνονται ἀν᾽ ὤρεα καὶ θοαὶ ἵπποι·
50 ὣς καὶ Δέλφιν ἴδοιμι, καὶ ἐς τόδε δῶμα περάσαι
μαινομένωι ἴκελος λιπαρᾶς ἔκτοσθε παλαίστρας.

Ἴυγξ, ἕλκε τὺ τῆνον ἐμὸν ποτὶ δῶμα τὸν ἄνδρα.

625

τοῦτ᾽ ἀπὸ τᾶς χλαίνας τὸ κράσπεδον ὤλεσε Δέλφις,
ὠγὼ νῦν τίλλοισα κατ᾽ ἀγρίωι ἐν πυρὶ βάλλω.
55 αἰαῖ Ἔρως ἀνιαρέ, τί μευ μέλαν ἐκ χροὸς αἷμα
ἐμφὺς ὡς λιμνᾶτις ἅπαν ἐκ βδέλλα πέπωκας;

Ἴυγξ, ἕλκε τὺ τῆνον ἐμὸν ποτὶ δῶμα τὸν ἄνδρα.

630

σαύραν τοι τρίψαισα κακὸν ποτὸν αὔριον οἰσῶ.
Θεστυλί, νῦν δὲ λαβοῖσα τὺ τὰ θρόνα ταῦθ᾽ ὑπόμαξον
60 τᾶς τήνω φλιᾶς καθ᾽ ὑπέρτερον ἇς ἔτι καὶ νύξ,
62 καὶ λέγ᾽ ἐπιτρύζοισα "τὰ Δέλφιδος ὀστία μάσσω".

Ἴυγξ, ἕλκε τὺ τῆνον ἐμὸν ποτὶ δῶμα τὸν ἄνδρα.

635

νῦν δὴ μώνα ἐοῖσα πόθεν τὸν ἔρωτα δακρύσω;
65 ἐκ τίνος ἄρξωμαι; τίς μοι κακὸν ἄγαγε τοῦτο;
ἦνθ᾽ ἁ τωὐβούλοιο καναφόρος ἄμμιν Ἀναξὼ
ἄλσος ἐς Ἀρτέμιδος, τᾶι δὴ τόκα πολλὰ μὲν ἄλλα
θηρία πομπεύεσκε περισταδόν, ἐν δὲ λέαινα.

640

59 ἀπόμορξον schol. u.l.   60 ὑπέρθυρον Valckenaer   νύξ Bücheler: νῦν
pap., M   61 ἐκ θυμῶ δέδεμαι. ὃ δέ μευ λόγον οὐδένα ποιεῖ fere m: om. pap.,
m   62 ἐπιτρύζοισα pap., schol. u.l.: ἐπιφθύζοισα M   μάσσω Ahlwardt:
πάσσω M: καίω pap.   67 τόκα Casaubon: ποκα pap., M

φράζεό μευ τὸν ἔρωθ' ὅθεν ἵκετο, πότνα Σελάνα.

70 καί μ' ἀ Θευμαρίδα Θρᾶισσα τροφός, ἀ μακαρῖτις,
ἀγχίθυρος ναίοισα κατεύξατο καὶ λιτάνευσε
τὰν πομπὰν θάσασθαι· ἐγὼ δέ οἱ ἀ μεγάλοιτος
ὠμάρτευν βύσσοιο καλὸν σύροισα χιτῶνα   645
κἀμφιστειλαμένα τὰν ξυστίδα τὰν Κλεαρίστας.

75 φράζεό μευ τὸν ἔρωθ' ὅθεν ἵκετο, πότνα Σελάνα.

ἤδη δ' εὖσα μέσαν κατ' ἀμαξιτόν, ἇι τὰ Λύκωνος,
εἶδον Δέλφιν ὁμοῦ τε καὶ Εὐδάμιππον ἰόντας·
τοῖς δ' ἦς ξανθοτέρα μὲν ἑλιχρύσοιο γενειὰς   650
στήθεα δὲ στίλβοντα πολὺ πλέον ἢ τύ, Σελάνα,
80 ὡς ἀπὸ γυμνασίοιο καλὸν πόνον ἄρτι λιπόντων.

φράζεό μευ τὸν ἔρωθ' ὅθεν ἵκετο, πότνα Σελάνα.

χὠς ἴδον ὡς ἐμάνην, ὥς μοι πυρὶ θυμὸς ἰάφθη
δειλαίας, τὸ δὲ κάλλος ἐτάκετο. οὐκέτι πομπᾶς   655
τήνας ἐφρασάμαν, οὐδ' ὡς πάλιν οἴκαδ' ἀπῆνθον
85 ἔγνων, ἀλλά μέ τις καπυρὰ νόσος ἐξεσάλαξε,
κείμαν δ' ἐν κλιντῆρι δέκ' ἄματα καὶ δέκα νύκτας.

φράζεό μευ τὸν ἔρωθ' ὅθεν ἵκετο, πότνα Σελάνα.

καί μευ χρὼς μὲν ὁμοῖος ἐγίνετο πολλάκι θάψωι,   660
ἔρρευν δ' ἐκ κεφαλᾶς πᾶσαι τρίχες, αὐτὰ δὲ λοιπὰ
90 ὀστί' ἔτ' ἦς καὶ δέρμα. καὶ ἐς τίνος οὐκ ἐπέρασα
ἢ ποίας ἔλιπον γραίας δόμον ἅτις ἐπᾶιδεν;
ἀλλ' ἦς οὐδὲν ἐλαφρόν, ὁ δὲ χρόνος ἄνυτο φεύγων.

φράζεό μευ τὸν ἔρωθ' ὅθεν ἵκετο, πότνα Σελάνα.   665

χοὕτω τᾶι δώλαι τὸν ἀλαθέα μῦθον ἔλεξα·
95 "εἰ δ' ἄγε, Θεστυλί, μοι χαλεπᾶς νόσω εὗρέ τι μᾶχος.

72 μεγάλατος Maas   74 τὰν² m: τᾶς pap., m   82 μευ pap., m   πυρὶ pap.,
cj. Taylor: περὶ M   83 οὐκέτι pap.: κοὐδέ τι M   85 ἐξεσάλαξεν pap., schol.
u.l.: ἐξαλάπαξεν M

πᾶσαν ἔχει με τάλαιναν ὁ Μύνδιος· ἀλλὰ μολοῖσα
τήρησον ποτὶ τὰν Τιμαγήτοιο παλαίστραν·
τηνεὶ γὰρ φοιτῆι, τηνεὶ δέ οἱ ἀδὺ καθῆσθαι.   670

φράζεό μευ τὸν ἔρωθ' ὅθεν ἵκετο, πότνα Σελάνα.

100 κἠπεί κά νιν ἐόντα μάθηις μόνον, ἄσυχα νεῦσον,
κεῖφ' ὅτι 'Σιμαίθα τυ καλεῖ', καὶ ὑφαγέο τεῖδε".
ὣς ἐφάμαν· ἃ δ' ἦνθε καὶ ἄγαγε τὸν λιπαρόχρων
εἰς ἐμὰ δώματα Δέλφιν· ἐγὼ δέ νιν ὡς ἐνόησα   675
ἄρτι θύρας ὑπὲρ οὐδὸν ἀμειβόμενον ποδὶ κούφωι—

105 φράζεό μευ τὸν ἔρωθ' ὅθεν ἵκετο, πότνα Σελάνα—

πᾶσα μὲν ἐψύχθην χιόνος πλέον, ἐκ δὲ μετώπω
ἱδρώς μευ κοχύδεσκεν ἴσον νοτίαισιν ἐέρσαις,
οὐδέ τι φωνῆσαι δυνάμαν, οὐδ' ὅσσον ἐν ὕπνωι   680
κνυζεῦνται φωνεῦντα φίλαν ποτὶ ματέρα τέκνα·
110 ἀλλ' ἐπάγην δαγῦδι καλὸν χρόα πάντοθεν ἴσα.

φράζεό μευ τὸν ἔρωθ' ὅθεν ἵκετο, πότνα Σελάνα.

καί μ' ἐσιδὼν ὥστοργος ἐπὶ χθονὸς ὄμματα πάξας
ἕζετ' ἐπὶ κλιντῆρι καὶ ἑζόμενος φάτο μῦθον·   685
"ἦ ῥά με, Σιμαίθα, τόσον ἔφθασας, ὅσσον ἐγώ θην
115 πρᾶν ποκα τὸν χαρίεντα τράχων ἔφθασσα Φιλῖνον,
ἐς τὸ τεὸν καλέσαισα τόδε στέγος ἢ 'μὲ παρῆμεν.

φράζεό μευ τὸν ἔρωθ' ὅθεν ἵκετο, πότνα Σελάνα.

ἦνθον γάρ κεν ἐγώ, ναὶ τὸν γλυκὺν ἦνθον Ἔρωτα,   690
ἢ τρίτος ἠὲ τέταρτος ἐὼν φίλος αὐτίκα νυκτός,
120 μᾶλα μὲν ἐν κόλποισι Διωνύσοιο φυλάσσων,
κρατὶ δ' ἔχων λεύκαν, Ἡρακλέος ἱερὸν ἔρνος,
πάντοθι πορφυρέαισι περὶ ζώστραισιν ἑλικτάν.

φράζεό μευ τὸν ἔρωθ' ὅθεν ἵκετο, πότνα Σελάνα.   695

καί κ', εἰ μέν μ' ἐδέχεσθε, τάδ' ἦς φίλα (καὶ γὰρ ἐλαφρὸς

124 κ'...μ' hoc ordine pap., cj. Ahrens: μ'...κ' M

125 καὶ καλὸς πάντεσσι μετ᾽ ἀϊθέοισι καλεῦμαι),
εὕδόν τ᾽ εἴ κε μόνον τὸ καλὸν στόμα τεῦς ἐφίλησα·
εἰ δ᾽ ἄλλαι μ᾽ ὠθεῖτε καὶ ἁ θύρα εἴχετο μοχλῷ,
πάντως κα πελέκεις καὶ λαμπάδες ἦνθον ἐφ᾽ ὑμέας.   700

φράζεό μευ τὸν ἔρωθ᾽ ὅθεν ἵκετο, πότνα Σελάνα.

130 νῦν δὲ χάριν μὲν ἔφαν τᾷ Κύπριδι πρᾶτον ὀφείλειν,
καὶ μετὰ τὰν Κύπριν τύ με δευτέρα ἐκ πυρὸς εἵλευ,
ὦ γύναι, ἐσκαλέσαισα τεὸν ποτὶ τοῦτο μέλαθρον
αὕτως ἡμίφλεκτον· Ἔρως δ᾽ ἄρα καὶ Λιπαραίω   705
πολλάκις Ἀφαίστοιο σέλας φλογερώτερον αἴθει·

135 φράζεό μευ τὸν ἔρωθ᾽ ὅθεν ἵκετο, πότνα Σελάνα.

σὺν δὲ κακαῖς μανίαις καὶ παρθένον ἐκ θαλάμοιο
καὶ νύμφαν ἐφόβησ᾽ ἔτι δέμνια θερμὰ λιποῖσαν
ἀνέρος᾽᾽. ὣς ὁ μὲν εἶπεν· ἐγὼ δέ νιν ἁ ταχυπειθὴς   710
χειρὸς ἐφαψαμένα μαλακῶν ἔκλιν᾽ ἐπὶ λέκτρων·
140 καὶ ταχὺ χρὼς ἐπὶ χρωτὶ πεπαίνετο, καὶ τὰ πρόσωπα
θερμότερ᾽ ἦς ἢ πρόσθε, καὶ ἐψιθυρίσδομες ἁδύ.
ὡς καί τοι μὴ μακρὰ φίλα θρυλέοιμι Σελάνα,
ἐπράχθη τὰ μέγιστα καὶ ἐς πόθον ἤνθομες ἄμφω.
κοὔτε τι τῆνος ἐμὶν ἀπεμέμψατο μέσφα τό γ᾽ ἐχθές,   715
145 οὔτ᾽ ἐγὼ αὖ τήνωι. ἀλλ᾽ ἦνθέ μοι ἅ τε Φιλίστας
μάτηρ τᾶς ἁμᾶς αὐλητρίδος ἅ τε Μελιξοῦς
σάμερον, ἁνίκα πέρ τε ποτ᾽ ὠρανὸν ἔτραχον ἵπποι
Ἀῶ τὰν ῥοδόεσσαν ἀπ᾽ ὠκεανοῖο φέροισαι,
κεἶπέ μοι ἄλλα τε πολλὰ καὶ ὡς ἄρα Δέλφις ἔραται.   720
150 κεῖτε νιν αὖτε γυναικὸς ἔχει πόθος εἴτε καὶ ἀνδρός,
οὐκ ἔφατ᾽ ἀτρεκὲς ἴδμεν, ἀτὰρ τόσον· αἰὲν Ἔρωτος
ἀκράτω ἐπεχεῖτο καὶ ἐς τέλος ᾤχετο φεύγων,
καὶ φάτο οἱ στεφάνοισι τὰ δώματα τῆνα πυκαξεῖν.   725

128 κα Ahrens: καὶ pap., M   138 νιν Gow: μιν pap.: οἱ M   142 ὡς pap., m:
χὼς m   καί m: κα m: κεν pap.   θρυλέοιμι M: θρέοιμ᾽ ω pap.: θρυλέωμι
Hermann   148 ῥοδοεσσαν pap.: ῥοδόπαχυν M   153 πυκαξεῖν Edmonds:
-άσδεν M: -ασθην pap.

ταῦτά μοι ἁ ξείνα μυθήσατο, ἔστι δ' ἀλαθής.
155 ἦ γάρ μοι καὶ τρὶς καὶ τετράκις ἄλλοκ' ἐφοίτη,
καὶ παρ' ἐμὶν ἐτίθει τὰν Δωρίδα πολλάκις ὄλπαν·
νῦν δέ τε δωδεκαταῖος ἀφ' ὧτέ νιν οὐδὲ ποτεῖδον.
ἦ ῥ' οὐκ ἄλλο τι τερπνὸν ἔχει, ἁμῶν δὲ λέλασται;   730
νῦν μὰν τοῖς φίλτροις καταδήσομαι· αἰ δ' ἔτι κά με
160 λυπῆι, τὰν Ἀίδαο πύλαν, ναὶ Μοίρας, ἀραξεῖ·
τοῖά οἱ ἐν κίσται κακὰ φάρμακα φαμὶ φυλάσσειν,
Ἀσσυρίω, δέσποινα, παρὰ ξείνοιο μαθοῖσα.
ἀλλὰ τὺ μὲν χαίροισα ποτ' ὠκεανὸν τρέπε πώλως,   735
πότνι'· ἐγὼ δ' οἰσῶ τὸν ἐμὸν πόθον ὥσπερ ὑπέσταν.
165 χαῖρε, Σελαναία λιπαρόθρονε, χαίρετε δ' ἄλλοι
ἀστέρες, εὐκάλοιο κατ' ἄντυγα Νυκτὸς ὀπαδοί.

XI

THE REAPERS *(Idyll 10)*

ΜΙΛΩΝ ΒΟΥΚΑΙΟΣ

ΜΙ. Ἐργατίνα Βουκαῖε, τί νῦν, ὠιζυρέ, πεπόνθεις;
οὔτε τὸν ὄγμον ἄγειν ὀρθὸν δύναι, ὡς τὸ πρὶν ἆγες,   740
οὔθ' ἅμα λαιοτομεῖς τῶι πλατίον, ἀλλ' ἀπολείπηι,
ὥσπερ ὄις ποίμνας ἇς τὸν πόδα κάκτος ἔτυψε.
5 ποῖός τις δείλαν τὺ καὶ ἐκ μέσω ἄματος ἐσσῆι,
ὃς νῦν ἀρχόμενος τᾶς αὔλακος οὐκ ἀποτρώγεις;
ΒΟ. Μίλων ὀψαμᾶτα, πέτρας ἀπόκομμ' ἀτεράμνω,   745
οὐδαμά τοι συνέβα ποθέσαι τινὰ τῶν ἀπεόντων;
ΜΙ. οὐδαμά. τίς δὲ πόθος τῶν ἔκτοθεν ἐργάται ἀνδρί;
10 ΒΟ. οὐδαμά νυν συνέβα τοι ἀγρυπνῆσαι δι' ἔρωτα;
ΜΙ. μηδέ γε συμβαίη· χαλεπὸν χορίω κύνα γεῦσαι.
ΒΟ. ἀλλ' ἐγώ, ὦ Μίλων, ἔραμαι σχεδὸν ἐνδεκαταῖος.   750

159 μὰν pap., m: μὲν m   κα με pap., cj. Ahrens: κἠμὲ M   164 πόθον pap., m:
πόνον m

XI   uu. 53–8 habet *P.Antin.*, uu. 45–56 *P.Oxy.* 3549   3 ὑπολείπηι m

MI. ἐκ πίθω ἀντλεῖς, δῆλον· ἐγὼ δ' ἔχω οὐδ' ἅλις ὄξος.

BO. τοιγὰρ τὰ πρὸ θυρᾶν μοι ἀπὸ σπόρω ἄσκαλα πάντα.

15 MI. τίς δέ τυ τᾶν παίδων λυμαίνεται; BO. ἁ Πολυβώτα,

ἁ πρᾶν ἀμάντεσσι παρ' Ἱπποκίωνι ποταύλει.

MI. εὗρε θεὸς τὸν ἀλιτρόν· ἔχεις πάλαι ὧν ἐπεθύμεις·   755

μάντις τοι τὰν νύκτα χροϊξεῖται καλαμαία.

BO. μωμᾶσθαί μ' ἄρχηι τύ· τυφλὸς δ' οὐκ αὐτὸς ὁ Πλοῦτος,

20 ἀλλὰ καὶ ὠφρόντιστος Ἔρως. μὴ δὴ μέγα μυθεῦ.

MI. οὐ μέγα μυθεῦμαι· τὺ μόνον κατάβαλλε τὸ λᾶιον,

καί τι κόρας φιλικὸν μέλος ἀμβάλευ. ἅδιον οὕτως   760

ἐργαξῆι. καὶ μὰν πρότερόν ποκα μουσικὸς ἦσθα.

BO. Μοῖσαι Πιερίδες, συναείσατε τὰν ῥαδινάν μοι

25 παῖδ'· ὧν γάρ χ' ἄψησθε, θεαί, καλὰ πάντα ποεῖτε.

Βομβύκα χαρίεσσα, Σύραν καλέοντί τυ πάντες,

ἰσχνάν, ἁλιόκαυστον, ἐγὼ δὲ μόνος μελίχλωρον.   765

καὶ τὸ ἴον μέλαν ἐστί, καὶ ἁ γραπτὰ ὑάκινθος·

ἀλλ' ἔμπας ἐν τοῖς στεφάνοις τὰ πρᾶτα λέγονται.

30 ἁ αἲξ τὰν κύτισον, ὁ λύκος τὰν αἶγα διώκει,

ἁ γέρανος τὤροτρον· ἐγὼ δ' ἐπὶ τὶν μεμάνημαι.

αἴθε μοι ἦς ὅσσα Κροῖσόν ποκα φαντὶ πεπᾶσθαι·   770

χρύσεοι ἀμφότεροί κ' ἀνεκείμεθα τᾷ 'Αφροδίται,

τώς αὐλὼς μὲν ἔχοισα καὶ ἢ ῥόδον ἢ τύγε μᾶλον,

35 σχῆμα δ' ἐγὼ καὶ καινὰς ἐπ' ἀμφοτέροισιν ἀμύκλας.

Βομβύκα χαρίεσσ', οἱ μὲν πόδες ἀστράγαλοί τευς,

ἁ φωνὰ δὲ τρύχνος· τὸν μὰν τρόπον οὐκ ἔχω εἰπεῖν.   775

MI. ἦ καλὰς ἄμμε ποῶν ἐλελάθει Βοῦκος ἀοιδάς·

ὡς εὖ τὰν ἰδέαν τᾶς ἁρμονίας ἐμέτρησεν.

40 ὤμοι τῶ πώγωνος, ὃν ἀλιθίως ἀνέφυσα.

θᾶσαι δὴ καὶ ταῦτα τὰ τῶ θείω Λιτυέρσα.

Δάματερ πολύκαρπε πολύσταχυ, τοῦτο τὸ λᾶιον   780

εὔεργόν τ' εἴη καὶ κάρπιμον ὅττι μάλιστα.

σφίγγετ', ἀμαλλοδέται, τὰ δράγματα, μὴ παριών τις
45 εἴπηι, "σύκινοι ἄνδρες· ἀπώλετο χοὖτος ὁ μισθός".
ἐς βορέαν ἄνεμον τᾶς κόρθυος ἁ τομὰ ὔμμιν
ἢ ζέφυρον βλεπέτω· πιαίνεται ὁ στάχυς οὔτως.   785
σῖτον ἀλοιῶντας φεύγειν τὸ μεσαμβρινὸν ὕπνον·
ἐκ καλάμας ἄχυρον τελέθει τημόσδε μάλιστα.
50 ἄρχεσθαι δ' ἀμῶντας ἐγειρομένω κορυδαλλῶ
καὶ λήγειν εὔδοντος, ἐλινῦσαι δὲ τὸ καῦμα.
εὐκτὸς ὁ τῶ βατράχω, παῖδες, βίος· οὐ μελεδαίνει   790
τὸν τὸ πιεῖν ἐγχεῦντα, πάρεστι γὰρ ἄφθονον αὐτῶι.
κάλλιον, ὦ 'πιμελητὰ φιλάργυρε, τὸν φακὸν ἕψειν,
55 μὴ 'πιτάμηις τὰν χεῖρα καταπρίων τὸ κύμινον.

ταῦτα χρὴ μόχθεντας ἐν ἁλίωι ἄνδρας ἀείδειν,
τὸν δὲ τεόν, Βουκαῖε, πρέπει λιμηρὸν ἔρωτα   795
μυθίσδεν τᾶι ματρὶ κατ' εὐνὰν ὀρθρευοίσαι.

XII

THE DISTAFF (*Idyll* 28)

Γλαύκας, ὦ φιλέριθ' ἀλακάτα, δῶρον 'Αθανάας
γύναιξιν νόος οἰκωφελίας αἷσιν ἐπάβολος,
θέρσεισ' ἄμμιν ὑμάρτη πόλιν ἐς Νήλεος ἀγλάαν,
ὅππα Κύπριδος ἷρον καλάμω χλῶρον ὑπ' ἀππάλω.   800
5 τύιδε γὰρ πλόον εὐάνεμον αἰτήμεθα πὰρ Δίος
ὅππως ξέννον ἔμον τέρψομ' ἴδων κἀντιφιληθέω,
Νικίαν, Χαρίτων ἱμεροφώνων ἵερον φύτον,
καὶ σὲ τὰν ἐλέφαντος πολυμόχθω γεγενημέναν
δῶρον Νικιάας εἰς ἀλόχω χέρρας ὀπάσσομεν,   805
10 σὺν τᾶι πόλλα μὲν ἔργ' ἐκτελέσεις ἀνδρείοις πέπλοις,

45 ὤνδρες Edmonds   55 μὴ 'πιτάμηις pap., test., m: μή τι τάμηις m   56
μοχθεντας pap.: μοχθεῦντας pap., M

XII uu. 1–19 habet *P.Oxy.* 3551   5 τύιδε pap., cj. Hermann: τὺ δὲ M
6 κἀντιφιληθέω Lobel: -λήσω M

πόλλα δ' οἷα γύναικες φορέοισ' ὑδάτινα βράκη.
δὶς γὰρ μάτερες ἄρνων μαλάκοις ἐν βοτάναι πόκοις
πέξαιντ' αὐτοέτει, Θευγένιδός γ' ἔννεκ' εὐσφύρω·
οὕτως ἀννυσίεργος, φιλέει δ' ὅσσα σαόφρονες.   810
15 οὐ γὰρ εἰς ἀκίρας οὐδ' ἐς ἀέργω κεν ἐβολλόμαν
ὅπασσαί σε δόμοις, ἀμμετέρας ἔσσαν ἀπὺ χθόνος.
καὶ γάρ τοι πάτρις ἂν ὡς 'Εφύρας κτίσσε ποτ' 'Αρχίας,
νάσω Τρινακρίας μύελον, ἀνδρῶν δοκίμων πόλιν.
νῦν μὰν οἶκον ἔχοισ' ἄνερος ὃς πόλλ' ἐδάη σόφα   815
20 ἀνθρώποισι νόσοις φάρμακα λύγραις ἀπαλάλκεμεν,
οἰκήσεις κατὰ Μίλλατον ἐράνναν πεδ' 'Ιαόνων,
ὡς εὐαλάκατος Θεύγενις ἐν δαμότισιν πέληι,
καί οἱ μνᾶστιν ἄει τὼ φιλαοίδω παρέχηις ξένω.
κῆνο γάρ τις ἔρει τὤπος ἴδων σ'· "ἦ μεγάλα χάρις   820
25 δώρωι σὺν ὀλίγωι· πάντα δὲ τίματα τὰ πὰρ φίλων".

24 τὤπος ἴδων Ahrens: τῶ ποσείδων fere M

XIII

SIMIAS

THE WINGS OF EROS

Λεῦσσέ με τὸν Γᾶς τε βαθυστέρνου ἄνακτ', 'Ακμονίδαν τ' ἄλλυδις ἐδράσαντα,
μηδὲ τρέσηις, εἰ τόσος ὢν δάσκια βέβριθα λάχναι γένεια·
τᾶμος ἐγὼ γὰρ γενόμαν, ἁνίκ' ἔκραιν' 'Ανάγκα,
πάντα δὲ τᾶς εἶκε φραδαῖσι λυγραῖς
5 ἑρπετά, †πάνθ' ὅσ' ἕρπει†   825
δι' Αἴθρας
Χάους τε.
οὔτι γε Κύπριδος παῖς
ὠκυπέτας ἠδ' "Αρεος καλεῦμαι,   830
10 οὔτι γὰρ ἔκρανα βίαι, πραϋνόωι δὲ πειθοῖ·
εἶκε δέ μοι γαῖα, θαλάσσας τε μυχοί, χάλκεος οὐρανός τε·
τῶν δ' ἐγὼ ἐκνοσφισάμαν ὠγύγιον σκᾶπτρον, ἔκρινον δὲ θεοῖς θέμιστας.

XIV

PHANOCLES

THE DEATH OF ORPHEUS

Ἦ ὡς Οἰάγροιο πάις Θρηίκιος Ὀρφεὺς
ἐκ θυμοῦ Κάλαϊν στέρξε Βορηιάδην,   835
πολλάκι δὲ σκιεροῖσιν ἐν ἄλσεσιν ἕζετ' ἀείδων
ὃν πόθον, οὐδ' ἦν οἱ θυμὸς ἐν ἡσυχίηι,
5 ἀλλ' αἰεί μιν ἄγρυπνοι ὑπὸ ψυχῆι μελεδῶναι
ἔτρυχον, θαλερὸν δερκομένου Κάλαϊν.
τὸν μὲν Βιστονίδες κακομήχανοι ἀμφιχυθεῖσαι   840
ἔκτανον, εὐήκη φάσγανα θηξάμεναι,
οὕνεκα πρῶτος ἔδειξεν ἐνὶ Θρήικεσσιν ἔρωτας
10 ἄρρενας, οὐδὲ πόθους ἤινεσε θηλυτέρων.
τοῦ δ' ἀπὸ μὲν κεφαλὴν χαλκῶι τάμον, αὐτίκα δ' αὐτὴν
εἰς ἅλα Θρηικίηι ῥῖψαν ὁμοῦ χέλυϊ   845
ἥλωι καρτύνασαι, ἵν' ἐμφορέοιντο θαλάσσηι
ἄμφω ἅμα, γλαυκοῖς τεγγόμεναι ῥοθίοις.
15 τὰς δ' ἱερῆι Λέσβωι πολιὴ ἐπέκελσε θάλασσα·

. . . .
. . . .

ἠχὴ δ' ὡς λιγυρῆς πόντον ἐπέσχε λύρης,

XIII *AP* 15.24; Theocriti codd. *GK*   2 βέβριθα λάχναι Salmasius: βεβριθότα λαγνᾶι fere M   3 ἔκραιν' Salmasius: ἔκριν' M   4 δὲ τᾶς εἶκε Powell: δ' ἐκ τᾶς εἶκε m: δ' ἐκτάσει καὶ m: δὲ Γᾶς εἶκε ex schol. Salmasius   7 δέ Bergk, qui post Αἴθρας distinxit   9 ἠδ' Powell: δ' M: οὐδ' Wilamowitz   Ἄρεος Callierges: ἀέρος m: ἀέριος m   10 ἔκρανα Salmasius: ἔκρινα M   βίαι Stephanus: βίας M   πραΰνόωι Bergk: πραΰνω M   12 ἔκρινον Salmasius: ἔκραινον M

XIV Stob. *Ecl.* 20.2.47, IV 461–2 Hense   4 οὐδέ οἱ ἦν Bergk   9 πρῶτος ἔδειξεν Brunck: πρῶτον δεῖξεν M   12 Θρηικίηι Bergk: -ίην M   15 post h.u. lac. statuit Dawe

νήσους τ' αἰγιαλούς θ' ἁλιμυρέας · ἔνθα λίγειαν   850
   ἀνέρες 'Ορφείην ἐκτέρισαν κεφαλήν,
ἐν δὲ χέλυν τύμβωι λιγυρὴν θέσαν, ἣ καὶ ἀναύδους
20 πέτρας καὶ Φόρκου στυγνὸν ἔπειθεν ὕδωρ.
   ἐκ κείνου μολπαί τε καὶ ἱμερτὴ κιθαριστὺς
   νῆσον ἔχει, πασέων δ' ἐστὶν ἀοιδοτάτη.   855
   Θρῆικες δ' ὡς ἐδάησαν ἀρήιοι ἔργα γυναικῶν
   ἄγρια καὶ πάντας δεινὸν ἐσῆλθεν ἄχος,
25 ἃς ἀλόχους ἔστιζον, ἵν' ἐν χροΐ σήματ' ἔχουσαι
   κυάνεα στυγεροῦ μὴ λελάθοιντο φόνου·
   ποινὰς δ' 'Ορφῆϊ κταμένωι στίζουσι γυναῖκας   860
   εἰσέτι νῦν κείνης εἵνεκεν ἀμπλακίης.

XV

APOLLONIUS

THE ARGO SETS SAIL *(Argonautica* 1.536-58)

Οἱ δ', ὥστ' ἠίθεοι Φοίβωι χορὸν ἢ ἐνὶ Πυθοῖ
ἤ που ἐν 'Ορτυγίηι ἢ ἐφ' ὕδασιν 'Ισμηνοῖο
στησάμενοι, φόρμιγγος ὑπαὶ περὶ βωμὸν ὁμαρτῆι
ἐμμελέως κραιπνοῖσι πέδον ῥήσσωσι πόδεσσιν·   865
540 ὣς οἱ ὑπ' 'Ορφῆος κιθάρηι πέπληγον ἐρετμοῖς
   πόντου λάβρον ὕδωρ, ἐπὶ δὲ ῥόθια κλύζοντο·
   ἀφρῶι δ' ἔνθα καὶ ἔνθα κελαινὴ κήκιεν ἅλμη
   δεινὸν μορμύρουσα ἐρισθενέων μένει ἀνδρῶν.
   στράπτε δ' ὑπ' ἠελίωι φλογὶ εἴκελα νηὸς ἰούσης   870
545 τεύχεα· μακραὶ δ' αἰὲν ἐλευκαίνοντο κέλευθοι,
   ἀτραπὸς ὣς χλοεροῖο διειδομένη πεδίοιο.
   πάντες δ' οὐρανόθεν λεῦσσον θεοὶ ἤματι κείνωι
   νῆα καὶ ἡμιθέων ἀνδρῶν γένος, οἳ τότ' ἄριστοι
   πόντον ἐπιπλώεσκον· ἐπ' ἀκροτάτηισι δὲ νύμφαι   875
550 Πηλιάδες κορυφῆισιν ἐθάμβεον εἰσορόωσαι

XV   548 μένος m   550 κορυφῆισιν Μ: σκοπιῆισιν test.

ἔργον Ἀθηναίης Ἰτωνίδος, ἠδὲ καὶ αὐτοὺς
ἥρωας χείρεσσιν ἐπικραδάοντας ἐρετμά.
αὐτὰρ ὄγ' ἐξ ὑπάτου ὄρεος κίεν ἄγχι θαλάσσης
Χείρων Φιλλυρίδης, πολιῆι δ' ἐπὶ κύματος ἀγῆι   880
555 τέγγε πόδας, καὶ πολλὰ βαρείηι χειρὶ κελεύων
νόστον ἐπευφήμησεν ἀπηρέα νισομένοισι.
σὺν καί οἱ παράκοιτις ἐπωλένιον φορέουσα
Πηλεΐδην Ἀχιλῆα, φίλωι δειδίσκετο πατρί.

XVI

HERACLES BREAKS HIS OAR (*Argonautica* 1. 1153–71)

Ἔνθ' ἔρις ἄνδρα ἕκαστον ἀριστήων ὀρόθυνεν,   885
ὅστις ἀπολλήξειε πανύστατος· ἀμφὶ γὰρ αἰθὴρ
155 νήνεμος ἐστόρεσεν δίνας, κατὰ δ' εὔνασε πόντον.
οἱ δὲ γαληναίηι πίσυνοι ἐλάασκον ἐπιπρὸ
νῆα βίηι· τὴν δ' οὔ κε διὲξ ἁλὸς ἀίσσουσαν
οὐδὲ Ποσειδάωνος ἀελλόποδες κίχον ἵπποι.   890
ἔμπης δ' ἐγρομένοιο σάλου ζαχρηέσιν αὔραις
160 αἳ νέον ἐκ ποταμῶν ὑπὸ δείελον ἠερέθονται,
τειρόμενοι καμάτωι μετελώφεον· αὐτὰρ ὁ τούσγε
πασσυδίηι μογέοντας ἐφέλκετο κάρτεϊ χειρῶν
Ἡρακλέης, ἐτίνασσε δ' ἀρηρότα δούρατα νηός.   895
ἀλλ' ὅτε δὴ Μυσῶν λελιημένοι ἠπείροιο
165 Ῥυνδακίδας προχοὰς μέγα τ' ἠρίον Αἰγαίωνος
τυτθὸν ὑπὲκ Φρυγίης παρεμέτρεον εἰσορόωντες,
δὴ τότ' ἀνοχλίζων τετρηχότος οἴδματος ὁλκοὺς
μεσσόθεν ἄξεν ἐρετμόν · ἀτὰρ τρύφος ἄλλο μὲν αὐτὸς   900
ἄμφω χερσὶν ἔχων πέσε δόχμιος, ἄλλο δὲ πόντος
170 κλύζε παλιρροθίοισι φέρων. ἀνὰ δ' ἕζετο σιγῆι
παπταίνων · χεῖρες γὰρ ἀήθεσον ἠρεμέουσαι.

556 ἀπηρέα test.: ἀκηδέα M

XVI 1161 καμάτωι test.: καὶ δὴ M   1165 τε ῥίον schol. u.l.

XVII

MEDEA'S DILEMMA (*Argonautica* 3.744–824)

Νὺξ μὲν ἔπειτ' ἐπὶ γαῖαν ἄγεν κνέφας· οἱ δ' ἐνὶ πόντωι
745 ναυτίλοι εἰς Ἑλίκην τε καὶ ἀστέρας Ὠρίωνος   905
ἔδρακον ἐκ νηῶν· ὕπνοιο δὲ καί τις ὁδίτης
ἤδη καὶ πυλαωρὸς ἐέλδετο, καί τινα παίδων
μητέρα τεθνεώτων ἀδινὸν περὶ κῶμ' ἐκάλυπτεν·
οὐδὲ κυνῶν ὑλακὴ ἔτ' ἀνὰ πτόλιν, οὐ θρόος ἦεν
750 ἠχήεις· σιγὴ δὲ μελαινομένην ἔχεν ὄρφνην.   910
ἀλλὰ μάλ' οὐ Μήδειαν ἐπὶ γλυκερὸς λάβεν ὕπνος.
πολλὰ γὰρ Αἰσονίδαο πόθωι μελεδήματ' ἔγειρε
δειδυῖαν ταύρων κρατερὸν μένος, οἷσιν ἔμελλε
φθίσθαι ἀεικελίηι μοίρηι κατὰ νειὸν Ἄρηος.
755 πυκνὰ δέ οἱ κραδίη στηθέων ἔντοσθεν ἔθυιεν,   915
ἠελίου ὥς τίς τε δόμοις ἐνιπάλλεται αἴγλη,
ὕδατος ἐξανιοῦσα τὸ δὴ νέον ἠὲ λέβητι
ἠέ που ἐν γαυλῶι κέχυται· ἡ δ' ἔνθα καὶ ἔνθα
ὠκείηι στροφάλιγγι τινάσσεται ἀίσσουσα·
760 ὣς δὲ καὶ ἐν στήθεσσι κέαρ ἐλελίζετο κούρης.   920
δάκρυ δ' ἀπ' ὀφθαλμῶν ἐλέωι ῥέεν· ἔνδοθι δ' αἰεὶ
τεῖρ' ὀδύνη σμύχουσα διὰ χροός, ἀμφί τ' ἀραιὰς
ἶνας καὶ κεφαλῆς ὑπὸ νείατον ἰνίον ἄχρις,
ἔνθ' ἀλεγεινότατον δύνει ἄχος, ὁππότ' ἀνίας
765 ἀκάματοι πραπίδεσσιν ἐνισκίμψωσιν ἔρωτες.   925
φῆ δέ οἱ ἄλλοτε μὲν θελκτήρια φάρμακα ταύρων
δωσέμεν· ἄλλοτε δ' οὔ τι, καταφθίσθαι δὲ καὶ αὐτή·
αὐτίκα δ' οὔτ' αὐτὴ θανέειν, οὐ φάρμακα δώσειν,
ἀλλ' αὔτως εὔκηλος ἐὴν ὀτλησέμεν ἄτην.
770 ἑζομένη δὴ ἔπειτα δοάσσατο, φώνησέν τε·   930
"δειλὴ ἐγώ, νῦν ἔνθα κακῶν ἢ ἔνθα γένωμαι
πάντηι μοι φρένες εἰσὶν ἀμήχανοι· οὐδέ τις ἀλκὴ

XVII   uu. 744–5 habet *P.Oxy.* 690   745 ναυτίλοι pap., cj. Porson: ναῦται M
755–60 post 765 transposuit Fränkel   765 ἐνιχρίμψωσιν m (cf. *470*)

πήματος, ἀλλ' αὔτως φλέγει ἔμπεδον. ὡς ὄφελόν γε
Ἀρτέμιδος κραιπνοῖσι πάρος βελέεσσι δαμῆναι,
775 πρὶν τόνγ' εἰσιδέειν, πρὶν Ἀχαιίδα γαῖαν ἱκέσθαι   935
Χαλκιόπης υἷας. τοὺς μὲν θεὸς ἤ τις Ἐρινὺς
ἄμμι πολυκλαύτους δεῦρ' ἤγαγε κεῖθεν ἀνίας.
φθίσθω ἀεθλεύων, εἴ οἱ κατὰ νειὸν ὀλέσθαι
μοῖρα πέλει. πῶς γάρ κεν ἐμοὺς λελάθοιμι τοκῆας
780 φάρμακα μησαμένη; ποῖον δ' ἐπὶ μῦθον ἐνίψω;   940
τίς δὲ δόλος, τίς μῆτις ἐπίκλοπος ἔσσετ' ἀρωγῆς;
ἦ μιν ἄνευθ' ἑτάρων προσπτύξομαι οἶον ἰδοῦσα;
δύσμορος· οὐ μὲν ἔολπα καταφθιμένοιό περ ἔμπης
λωφήσειν ἀχέων· τότε δ' ἂν κακὸν ἄμμι πέλοιτο,
785 κεῖνος ὅτε ζωῆς ἀπαμείρεται. ἐρρέτω αἰδώς,   945
ἐρρέτω ἀγλαΐη· ὁ δ' ἐμῆι ἰότητι σαωθεὶς
ἀσκηθής, ἵνα οἱ θυμῶι φίλον, ἔνθα νέοιτο.
αὐτὰρ ἐγὼν αὐτῆμαρ, ὅτ' ἐξανύσειεν ἄεθλον,
τεθναίην, ἢ λαιμὸν ἀναρτήσασα μελάθρωι,
790 ἢ καὶ πασσαμένη ῥαιστήρια φάρμακα θυμοῦ.   950
ἀλλὰ καὶ ὣς φθιμένηι μοι ἐπιλλίξουσιν ὀπίσσω
κερτομίας, τηλοῦ δὲ πόλις περὶ πᾶσα βοήσει
πότμον ἐμόν· καί κέν με διὰ στόματος φορέουσαι
Κολχίδες ἄλλυδις ἄλλαι ἀεικέα μωμήσονται,
795 ἥτις κηδομένη τόσον ἀνέρος ἀλλοδαποῖο   955
κάτθανεν, ἥτις δῶμα καὶ οὓς ἤισχυνε τοκῆας,
μαργοσύνηι εἴξασα. τί δ' οὐκ ἐμὸν ἔσσεται αἶσχος;
ὤ μοι ἐμῆς ἄτης. ἦ τ' ἂν πολὺ κέρδιον εἴη
τῆιδ' αὐτῆι ἐν νυκτὶ λιπεῖν βίον ἐν θαλάμοισι
800 πότμωι ἀνωίστωι, κάκ' ἐλέγχεα πάντα φυγοῦσαν,   960
πρὶν τάδε λωβήεντα καὶ οὐκ ὀνομαστὰ τελέσσαι.''
ἦ, καὶ φωριαμὸν μετεκίαθεν, ἧι ἔνι πολλὰ
φάρμακά οἱ, τὰ μὲν ἐσθλά, τὰ δὲ ῥαιστήρι', ἔκειτο.
ἐνθεμένη δ' ἐπὶ γούνατ' ὀδύρετο, δεῦε δὲ κόλπους

775 νῆα κομίσσαι Fränkel· γαῖαν κομίσσαι schol. u.l.   782 ἰοῦσα Platt   789
μελάθρου m   794 ἄλληι m

50   XVIII APOLLONIUS

805 ἄλληκτον δακρύοισι, τὰ δ' ἔρρεεν ἀσταγὲς αὔτως,   965
    αἴν' ὀλοφυρομένης τὸν ἑὸν μόρον. ἵετο δ' ἦγε
    φάρμακα λέξασθαι θυμοφθόρα, τόφρα πάσαιτο.
    ἤδη καὶ δεσμοὺς ἀνελύετο φωριαμοῖο,
    ἐξελέειν μεμαυῖα, δυσάμμορος. ἀλλά οἱ ἄφνω
810 δεῖμ' ὀλοὸν στυγεροῖο κατὰ φρένας ἦλθ' Ἀίδαο·   970
    ἔσχετο δ' ἀμφασίηι δηρὸν χρόνον, ἀμφὶ δὲ πᾶσαι
    θυμηδεῖς βιότοιο μεληδόνες ἰνδάλλοντο.
    μνήσατο μὲν τερπνῶν, ὅσ' ἐνὶ ζωοῖσι πέλονται,
    μνήσαθ' ὁμηλικίης περιγηθέος, οἷά τε κούρη·
815 καί τέ οἱ ἥλιος γλυκίων γένετ' εἰσοράασθαι   975
    ἢ πάρος, εἰ ἐτεόν γε νόωι ἐπεμαίεθ' ἕκαστα.
    καὶ τὴν μέν ῥα πάλιν σφετέρων ἀποκάτθετο γούνων,
    Ἥρης ἐννεσίηισι μετάτροπος, οὐδ' ἔτι βουλὰς
    ἄλληι δοιάζεσκεν· ἐέλδετο δ' αἶψα φανῆναι
820 ἠῶ τελλομένην, ἵνα οἱ θελκτήρια δοίη   980
    φάρμακα συνθεσίηισι, καὶ ἀντήσειεν ἐς ὠπήν.
    πυκνὰ δ' ἀνὰ κληῖδας ἑῶν λύεσκε θυράων,
    αἴγλην σκεπτομένη· τῆι δ' ἀσπάσιον βάλε φέγγος
    Ἠριγενής, κίνυντο δ' ἀνὰ πτολίεθρον ἕκαστοι.

XVIII

TALOS (Argonautica 4. 1629–88)

    Ἦμος δ' ἥλιος μὲν ἔδυ, ἀνὰ δ' ἤλυθεν ἀστὴρ   985
1630 αὔλιος, ὅς τ' ἀνέπαυσεν ὀιζυροὺς ἀροτῆρας,
    δὴ τότ' ἔπειτ', ἀνέμοιο κελαινῆι νυκτὶ λιπόντος,
    ἱστία λυσάμενοι περιμήκεά τε κλίναντες
    ἱστόν, ἐυξέστηισιν ἐπερρώοντ' ἐλάτηισι
    παννύχιοι καὶ ἐπ' ἦμαρ, ἐπ' ἤματι δ' αὖτις ἰοῦσαν   990
1635 νύχθ' ἑτέρην. ὑπέδεκτο δ' ἀπόπροθι παιπαλόεσσα
    Κάρπαθος. ἔνθεν δ' οἵγε περαιώσεσθαι ἔμελλον
    Κρήτην, ἥ τ' ἄλλων ὑπερέπλετο εἰν ἁλὶ νήσων.
    τοὺς δὲ Τάλως χάλκειος, ἀπὸ στιβαροῦ σκοπέλοιο

ῥηγνύμενος πέτρας, εἶργε χθονὶ πείσματ' ἀνάψαι 995
540 Δικταίην ὅρμοιο κατερχομένους ἐπιωγήν.
τὸν μέν, χαλκείης μελιηγενέων ἀνθρώπων
ῥίζης λοιπὸν ἐόντα μετ' ἀνδράσιν ἡμιθέοισιν,
Εὐρώπηι Κρονίδης νήσου πόρεν ἔμμεναι οὖρον,
τρὶς περὶ χαλκείοις Κρήτην ποσὶ δινεύοντα. 1000
545 ἀλλ' ἤτοι τὸ μὲν ἄλλο δέμας καὶ γυῖα τέτυκτο
χάλκεος ἠδ' ἄρρηκτος, ὑπαὶ δέ οἱ ἔσκε τένοντος
σῦριγξ αἱματόεσσα κατὰ σφυρόν · ἀμφ' ἄρα τήνγε
λεπτὸς ὑμὴν ζωῆς ἔχε πείρατα καὶ θανάτοιο.
οἱ δέ, δύηι μάλα περ δεδμημένοι, αἶψ' ἀπὸ χέρσου 1005
550 νῆα περιδδείσαντες ἀνακρούεσκον ἐρετμοῖς.
καί νύ κ' ἐπισμυγερῶς Κρήτης ἑκὰς ἠέρθησαν,
ἀμφότερον δίψηι τε καὶ ἄλγεσι μοχθίζοντες,
εἰ μή σφιν Μήδεια λιαζομένοις ἀγόρευσε ·
"κέκλυτέ μευ · μούνη γὰρ ὀίομαι ὔμμι δαμάσσειν 1010
555 ἄνδρα τόν, ὅστις ὅδ' ἐστί, καὶ εἰ παγχάλκεον ἴσχει
ὃν δέμας, ὁππότε μή οἱ ἐπ' ἀκάματος πέλοι αἰών.
ἀλλ' ἔχετ' αὐτοῦ νῆα θελήμονες ἐκτὸς ἐρωῆς
πετράων, εἴως κεν ἐμοὶ εἴξειε δαμῆναι."
ὣς ἄρ' ἔφη · καὶ τοὶ μὲν ὑπὲκ βελέων ἐρύσαντο 1015
560 νῆ' ἐπ' ἐρετμοῖσιν, δεδοκημένοι ἥντινα ῥέξει
μῆτιν ἀνωίστως. ἡ δὲ πτύχα πορφυρέοιο
προσχομένη πέπλοιο παρειάων ἑκάτερθεν
βήσατ' ἐπ' ἰκριόφιν · χειρὸς δέ ἑ χειρὶ μεμαρπὼς
Αἰσονίδης ἐκόμιζε διὰ κληῖδας ἰοῦσαν. 1020
565 ἔνθα δ' ἀοιδῆισιν μειλίσσετο θέλγε τε Κῆρας
θυμοβόρους, Ἀίδαο θοὰς κύνας, αἳ περὶ πᾶσαν
ἠέρα δινεύουσαι ἐπὶ ζωοῖσιν ἄγονται.
τὰς γουναζομένη τρὶς μὲν παρεκέκλετ' ἀοιδαῖς,
τρὶς δὲ λιταῖς · θεμένη δὲ κακὸν νόον, ἐχθοδοποῖσιν 1025

XVIII 1644 Κρήτην ποσὶ M: ποσὶν ἥματι Fränkel   1647 ἀμφ' ἄρα Fränkel:
αὐτὰρ ὁ M   1659 ἐρύοντο m   1664 κληῖδας Brunck: -δος M   1665 μέλπε
m τε Wellauer: δὲ M

1670 ὄμμασι χαλκείοιο Τάλω ἐμέγηρεν ὀπωπάς·
λευγαλέον δ' ἐπί οἱ πρῖεν χόλον, ἐκ δ' ἀίδηλα
δείκηλα προΐαλλεν, ἐπιζάφελον κοτέουσα.
Ζεῦ πάτερ, ἦ μέγα δή μοι ἐνὶ φρεσὶ θάμβος ἄηται,
εἰ δὴ μὴ νούσοισι τυπῆισί τε μοῦνον ὄλεθρος   103
1675 ἀντιάει, καὶ δή τις ἀπόπροθεν ἄμμε χαλέπτοι,
ὡς ὅγε, χάλκειός περ ἐών, ὑπόειξε δαμῆναι
Μηδείης βρίμηι πολυφαρμάκου. ἂν δὲ βαρείας
ὀχλίζων λάιγγας ἐρυκέμεν ὅρμον ἱκέσθαι,
πετραίωι στόνυχι χρίμψε σφυρόν · ἐκ δέ οἱ ἰχὼρ   103
1680 τηκομένωι ἴκελος μολίβωι ῥέεν. οὐδ' ἔτι δηρὸν
εἱστήκει προβλῆτος ἐπεμβεβαὼς σκοπέλοιο ·
ἀλλ' ὥς τίς τ' ἐν ὄρεσσι πελωρίη ὑψόθι πεύκη,
τήν τε θοοῖς πελέκεσσιν ἔθ' ἡμιπλῆγα λιπόντες
ὑλοτόμοι δρυμοῖο κατήλυθον, ἡ δ' ὑπὸ νυκτὶ   104
1685 ῥιπῆισιν μὲν πρῶτα τινάσσεται, ὕστερον αὖτε
πρυμνόθεν ἐξαγεῖσα κατήριπεν · ὡς ὅγε ποσσὶν
ἀκαμάτοις τείως μὲν ἐπισταδὸν ἠωρεῖτο,
ὕστερον αὖτ' ἀμενηνὸς ἀπείρονι κάππεσε δούπωι.

XIX

MOSCHUS

EUROPA

Εὐρώπηι ποτὲ Κύπρις ἐπὶ γλυκὺν ἧκεν ὄνειρον·   104
νυκτὸς ὅτε τρίτατον λάχος ἵσταται, ἐγγύθι δ' ἠώς,
ὕπνος ὅτε γλυκίων μέλιτος βλεφάροισιν ἐφίζων
λυσιμελὴς πεδάαι μαλακῶι κατὰ φάεα δεσμῶι,
5 εὖτε καὶ ἀτρεκέων ποιμαίνεται ἔθνος ὀνείρων·
τῆμος ὑπωροφίοισιν ἐνὶ κνώσσουσα δόμοισι   105
Φοίνικος θυγάτηρ ἔτι παρθένος Εὐρώπεια
ὠίσατ' ἠπείρους δοιὰς περὶ εἷο μάχεσθαι,

1675 χαλέπτει m   1680 οὐδ' ἔτι Brunck: οὐδέ τι M

Ἀσίδα τ' ἀντιπέρην τε· φυὴν δ' ἔχον οἷα γυναῖκες.
10 τῶν δ' ἡ μὲν ξείνης μορφὴν ἔχεν, ἡ δ' ἄρ' ἐῴκει
ἐνδαπίηι, καὶ μᾶλλον ἑῆς περιίσχετο κούρης,   1055
φάσκεν δ' ὥς μιν ἔτικτε καὶ ὡς ἀτίτηλέ μιν αὐτή.
ἡ δ' ἑτέρη κρατερῆισι βιωομένη παλάμηισιν
εἴρυεν οὐκ ἀέκουσαν, ἐπεὶ φάτο μόρσιμον εἶο
15 ἐκ Διὸς αἰγιόχου γέρας ἔμμεναι Εὐρώπειαν.
ἡ δ' ἀπὸ μὲν στρωτῶν λεχέων θόρε δειμαίνουσα,   1060
παλλομένη κραδίην· τὸ γὰρ ὡς ὕπαρ εἶδεν ὄνειρον.
ἑζομένη δ' ἐπὶ δηρὸν ἀκὴν ἔχεν, ἀμφοτέρας δὲ
εἰσέτι πεπταμένοισιν ἐν ὄμμασιν εἶχε γυναῖκας.
20 ὀψὲ δὲ δειμαλέην ἀνενείκατο παρθένος αὐδήν·
"τίς μοι τοιάδε φάσματ' ἐπουρανίων προΐηλε;   1065
ποῖοί με στρωτῶν λεχέων ὕπερ ἐν θαλάμοισιν
ἡδὺ μάλα κνώσσουσαν ἀνεπτοίησαν ὄνειροι;
τίς δ' ἦν ἡ ξείνη τὴν εἴσιδον ὑπνώουσα;
25 ὥς μ' ἔλαβε κραδίην κείνης πόθος, ὥς με καὶ αὐτὴ
ἀσπασίως ὑπέδεκτο καὶ ὡς σφετέρην ἴδε παῖδα.   1070
ἀλλά μοι εἰς ἀγαθὸν μάκαρες κρήνειαν ὄνειρον".
   ὣς εἰποῦσ' ἀνόρουσε, φίλας δ' ἐπεδίζεθ' ἑταίρας
ἥλικας οἰέτεας θυμήρεας εὐπατερείας,
30 τῆισιν ἀεὶ συνάθυρεν ὅτ' ἐς χορὸν ἐντύναιτο
ἢ ὅτε φαιδρύνοιτο χρόα προχοῆισιν ἀναύρων   1075
ἢ ὁπότ' ἐκ λειμῶνος ἐύπνοα λείρι' ἀμέργοι.
αἱ δέ οἱ αἶψα φάανθεν, ἔχον δ' ἐν χερσὶν ἑκάστη
ἀνθοδόκον τάλαρον· ποτὶ δὲ λειμῶνας ἔβαινον
35 ἀγχιάλους, ὅθι τ' αἰὲν ὁμιλαδὸν ἡγερέθοντο
τερπόμεναι ῥοδέηι τε φυῆι καὶ κύματος ἠχῆι.   1080
αὐτὴ δὲ χρύσεον τάλαρον φέρεν Εὐρώπεια
θηητόν, μέγα θαῦμα, μέγαν πόνον Ἡφαίστοιο,
ὃν Λιβύηι πόρε δῶρον ὅτ' ἐς λέχος Ἐννοσιγαίου
40 ἤιεν· ἡ δὲ πόρεν περικαλλέι Τηλεφαάσσηι,

ἦτε οἱ αἵματος ἔσκεν· ἀνύμφωι δ' Εὐρωπείηι   10ξ
μήτηρ Τηλεφάασσα περικλυτὸν ὤπασε δῶρον.
ἐν τῶι δαίδαλα πολλὰ τετεύχατο μαρμαίροντα·
ἐν μὲν ἔην χρυσοῖο τετυγμένη Ἰναχὶς Ἰὼ
45 εἰσέτι πόρτις ἐοῦσα, φυὴν δ' οὐκ εἶχε γυναίην.
φοιταλέη δὲ πόδεσσιν ἐφ' ἁλμυρὰ βαῖνε κέλευθα   10ς
νηχομένηι ἰκέλη, κυάνου δ' ἐτέτυκτο θάλασσα·
δοιοῦ δ' ἕστασαν ὑψοῦ ἐπ' ὀφρύσιν αἰγιαλοῖο
φῶτες ἀολλήδην, θηεῦντο δὲ ποντοπόρον βοῦν.
50 ἐν δ' ἦν Ζεὺς Κρονίδης ἐπαφώμενος ἠρέμα χερσὶ
πόρτιος Ἰναχίης· τὴν δ' ἑπταπόρωι παρὰ Νείλωι   109
ἐκ βοὸς εὐκεράοιο πάλιν μετάμειβε γυναῖκα.
ἀργύρεος μὲν ἔην Νείλου ῥόος, ἡ δ' ἄρα πόρτις
χαλκείη, χρυσοῦ δὲ τετυγμένος αὐτὸς ἔην Ζεύς.
55 ἀμφὶ δέ, δινήεντος ὑπὸ στεφάνην ταλάροιο,
Ἑρμείης ἤσκητο, πέλας δέ οἱ ἐκτετάνυστο   110
Ἄργος ἀκοιμήτοισι κεκασμένος ὀφθαλμοῖσι.
τοῖο δὲ φοινήεντος ἀφ' αἵματος ἐξανέτελλεν
ὄρνις ἀγαλλόμενος πτερύγων πολυανθέι χροιῆι,
60 τὰς ὅγ' ἀναπλώσας ὡσεί τέ τις ὠκύαλος νηῦς
χρυσείου ταλάροιο περίσκεπε χείλεα ταρσοῖς.   110
τοῖος ἔην τάλαρος περικαλλέος Εὐρωπείης.
    αἱ δ' ἐπεὶ οὖν λειμῶνας ἐς ἀνθεμόεντας ἵκανον,
ἄλλη ἐπ' ἀλλοίοισι τότ' ἄνθεσι θυμὸν ἔτερπον.
65 τῶν ἡ μὲν νάρκισσον εὔπνοον, ἡ δ' ὑάκινθον,
ἡ δ' ἴον, ἡ δ' ἕρπυλλον ἀπαίνυτο· πολλὰ δ' ἔραζε   111
λειμώνων ἐαροτρεφέων θαλέθεσκε πέταλα.
αἱ δ' αὖτε ξανθοῖο κρόκου θυόεσσαν ἔθειραν
δρέπτον ἐριδμαίνουσαι· ἀτὰρ μέσσηισιν ἄνασσα
70 ἀγλαΐην πυρσοῖο ῥόδου χείρεσσι λέγουσα
οἷά περ ἐν Χαρίτεσσι διέπρεπεν Ἀφρογένεια.   111
    οὐ μὲν δηρὸν ἔμελλεν ἐπ' ἄνθεσι θυμὸν ἰαίνειν,

41 ἦ θ' ἑοῦ Gow   47 κυάνου Meineke: -νὴ M   48 δοιοῦ Hermann: -οὶ M
ὀφρύσιν m, cj. Hermann: -ύι m: -ύος m   51 Ἰναχίης· τὴν Pierson: εἰναλίης τὴν
m: εἶναι ληιστὴν m: ἐς καλλίστην m   60 τὰς ὅγ' Maas: ταρσὸν M

οὐδ' ἄρα παρθενίην μίτρην ἄχραντον ἔρυσθαι.
ἦ γὰρ δὴ Κρονίδης ὥς μιν φράσαθ' ὣς ἐόλητο
75 θυμὸν ἀνωίστοισιν ὑποδμηθεὶς βελέεσσι
Κύπριδος, ἣ μούνη δύναται καὶ Ζῆνα δαμάσσαι.   1120
δὴ γὰρ ἀλευόμενός τε χόλον ζηλήμονος Ἥρης
παρθενικῆς τ' ἐθέλων ἀταλὸν νόον ἐξαπατῆσαι
κρύψε θεὸν καὶ τρέψε δέμας καὶ γίνετο ταῦρος,
80 οὐχ οἷος σταθμοῖς ἔνι φέρβεται, οὐδὲ μὲν οἷος
ὦλκα διατμήγει σύρων εὐκαμπὲς ἄροτρον,   1125
οὐδ' οἷος ποίμνηις ἔπι βόσκεται, οὐδὲ μὲν οἷος
μάστι ὑποδμηθεὶς ἐρύει πολύφορτον ἀπήνην.
τοῦ δ' ἤτοι τὸ μὲν ἄλλο δέμας ξανθόχροον ἔσκε,
85 κύκλος δ' ἀργύφεος μέσσωι μάρμαιρε μετώπωι,
ὄσσε δ' ὑπογλαύσσεσκε καὶ ἵμερον ἀστράπτεσκεν.   1130
ἴσά τ' ἐπ' ἀλλήλοισι κέρα ἀνέτελλε καρήνου
ἄντυγος ἡμιτόμου κεραῆς ἅτε κύκλα σελήνης.
ἤλυθε δ' ἐς λειμῶνα καὶ οὐκ ἐφόβησε φαανθεὶς
90 παρθενικάς, πάσηισι δ' ἔρως γένετ' ἐγγὺς ἱκέσθαι
ψαῦσαί θ' ἱμερτοῖο βοὸς τοῦ τ' ἄμβροτος ὀδμὴ   1135
τηλόθι καὶ λειμῶνος ἐκαίνυτο λαρὸν ἀυτμήν.
στῆ δὲ ποδῶν προπάροιθεν ἀμύμονος Εὐρωπείης
καί οἱ λιχμάζεσκε δέρην, κατέθελγε δὲ κούρην.
95 ἡ δέ μιν ἀμφαφάασκε καὶ ἠρέμα χείρεσιν ἀφρὸν
πολλὸν ἀπὸ στομάτων ἀπομόργνυτο καὶ κύσε ταῦρον.   1140
αὐτὰρ ὁ μειλίχιον μυκήσατο· φαῖό κεν αὐλοῦ
Μυγδονίου γλυκὺν ἦχον ἀνηπύοντος ἀκούειν·
ὤκλασε δὲ πρὸ ποδοῖιν, ἐδέρκετο δ' Εὐρώπειαν
100 αὐχέν' ἐπιστρέψας καί οἱ πλατὺ δείκνυε νῶτον.
ἡ δὲ βαθυπλοκάμοισι μετέννεπε παρθενικῆισι·   1145
"δεῦθ', ἑτάραι φίλιαι καὶ ὁμήλικες, ὄφρ' ἐπὶ τῶιδε
ἑζόμεναι ταύρωι τερπώμεθα· δὴ γὰρ ἀπάσας

83 μάστι Ahrens: ὅστις M: ζεύγληι Bühler: αὐχέν' Jacobs   88 ἄντυγ' ἐς
ἡμίτομον Dawe   91 τ' Gow: δ' m: γ' m: om. m   97 φαῖό Meineke: φαῖέ m:
φαίης m

νῶτον ὑποστορέσας ἀναδέξεται, οἷά τ' ἐνηὴς
105 πρηΰς τ' εἰσιδέειν καὶ μείλιχος· οὐδέ τι ταύροις
ἄλλοισι προσέοικε, νόος δέ οἱ ἠΰτε φωτὸς   115
αἴσιμος ἀμφιθέει, μούνης δ' ἐπιδεύεται αὐδῆς".
ὣς φαμένη νώτοισιν ἐφίζανε μειδιόωσα,
αἱ δ' ἄλλαι μέλλεσκον, ἄφαρ δ' ἀνεπήλατο ταῦρος,
110 ἣν θέλεν ἁρπάξας, ὠκὺς δ' ἐπὶ πόντον ἵκανεν.
ἡ δέ μεταστρεφθεῖσα φίλας καλέεσκεν ἑταίρας   115
χεῖρας ὀρεγνυμένη, ταὶ δ' οὐκ ἐδύναντο κιχάνειν.
ἀκτάων δ' ἐπιβὰς πρόσσω θέεν ἠΰτε δελφὶς
χηλαῖς ἀβρέκτοισιν ἐπ' εὐρέα κύματα βαίνων.
115 ἡ δὲ τότ' ἐρχομένοιο γαληνιάασκε θάλασσα,
κήτεα δ' ἀμφὶς ἄταλλε Διὸς προπάροιθε ποδοῖιν,   116
γηθόσυνος δ' ὑπὲρ οἶδμα κυβίστεε βυσσόθε δελφίς.
Νηρεΐδες δ' ἀνέδυσαν ὑπὲξ ἁλός, αἱ δ' ἄρα πᾶσαι
κητείοις νώτοισιν ἐφήμεναι ἐστιχόωντο.
120 καὶ δ' αὐτὸς βαρύδουπος ὑπεὶρ ἁλὸς Ἐννοσίγαιος
κῦμα κατιθύνων ἁλίης ἡγεῖτο κελεύθου
αὐτοκασιγνήτωι· τοὶ δ' ἀμφὶ μιν ἠγερέθοντο   116
Τρίτωνες, πόντοιο βαρύθροοι αὐλητῆρες,
κόχλοισιν ταναοῖς γάμιον μέλος ἠπύοντες.
125 ἡ δ' ἄρ' ἐφεζομένη Ζηνὸς βοέοις ἐπὶ νώτοις
τῆι μὲν ἔχεν ταύρου δολιχὸν κέρας, ἐν χερὶ δ' ἄλληι   117
εἴρυε πορφυρέας πέπλου πτύχας, ὄφρα κε μή μιν
δεύοι ἐφελκόμενον πολιῆς ἁλὸς ἄσπετον ὕδωρ.
κολπώθη δ' ὤμοισι πέπλος βαθὺς Εὐρωπείης
130 ἱστίον οἷά τε νηός, ἐλαφρίζεσκε δὲ κούρην.
ἡ δ' ὅτε δὴ γαίης ἄπο πατρίδος ἦεν ἄνευθεν,   117
φαίνετο δ' οὔτ' ἀκτή τις ἁλίρροθος οὔτ' ὄρος αἰπύ,
ἀλλ' ἀὴρ μὲν ὕπερθεν ἔνερθε δὲ πόντος ἀπείρων,
ἀμφί ἑ παπτήνασα τόσην ἀνενείκατο φωνήν·
135 "πῆι με φέρεις θεόταυρε; τίς ἔπλεο; πῶς δὲ κέλευθα
ἀργαλέ' εἰλιπόδεσσι διέρχεαι οὐδὲ θάλασσαν   118

120 ἅλα m   127 πέπλου Bühler: κόλπου M   129 ἀνέμοισι Salmasius
136 ἀργαλέ' εἰλιπόδεσσι Ahrens: ἀργαλέοισι πόδεσσι m: -έην π. m

δειμαίνεις; νηυσὶν γὰρ ἐπίδρομός ἐστι θάλασσα
ὠκυάλοις, ταῦροι δ' ἁλίην τρομέουσιν ἀταρπόν.
ποῖόν σοι ποτὸν ἡδύ; τίς ἐξ ἁλὸς ἔσσετ' ἐδωδή;
40 ἦ ἄρα τις θεὸς ἐσσί; θεοῖς γ' ἐπεοικότα ῥέζεις.
οὔθ' ἅλιοι δελφῖνες ἐπὶ χθονὸς οὔτε τι ταῦροι   1185
ἐν πόντωι στιχόωσι, σὺ δὲ χθόνα καὶ κατὰ πόντον
ἄτρομος ἀίσσεις, χηλαὶ δέ τοί εἰσιν ἐρετμά.
ἦ τάχα καὶ γλαυκῆς ὑπὲρ ἠέρος ὑψόσ' ἀερθεὶς
45 εἴκελος αἰψηροῖσι ποτήσεαι οἰωνοῖσιν.
ὤμοι ἐγὼ μέγα δή τι δυσάμμορος, ἥ ῥά τε δῶμα   1190
πατρὸς ἀποπρολιποῦσα καὶ ἐσπομένη βοῒ τῶιδε
ξείνην ναυτιλίην ἐφέπω καὶ πλάζομαι οἴη.
ἀλλὰ σύ μοι, μεδέων πολιῆς ἁλὸς Ἐννοσίγαιε,
50 ἵλαος ἀντιάσειας, ὃν ἔλπομαι εἰσοράασθαι
τόνδε κατιθύνοντα πλόον προκέλευθον ἐμεῖο·   1195
οὐκ ἀθεεὶ γὰρ ταῦτα διέρχομαι ὑγρὰ κέλευθα".
    ὣς φάτο· τὴν δ' ὧδε προσεφώνεεν ἠύκερως βοῦς·
"θάρσει παρθενική· μὴ δείδιθι πόντιον οἶδμα.
55 αὐτός τοι Ζεύς εἰμι, κεἰ ἐγγύθεν εἴδομαι εἶναι
ταῦρος, ἐπεὶ δύναμαί γε φανήμεναι ὅττι θέλοιμι.   1200
σὸς δὲ πόθος μ' ἀνέηκε τόσην ἅλα μετρήσασθαι
ταύρωι ἐειδόμενον. Κρήτη δέ σε δέξεται ἤδη
ἥ μ' ἔθρεψε καὶ αὐτόν, ὅπηι νυμφήια σεῖο
60 ἔσσεται· ἐξ ἐμέθεν δὲ κλυτοὺς φιτύσεαι υἷας
οἳ σκηπτοῦχοι ἅπαντες ἐπιχθονίοισιν ἔσονται".   1205
    ὣς φάτο· καὶ τετέλεστο τά περ φάτο. φαίνετο μὲν δὴ
Κρήτη, Ζεὺς δὲ πάλιν σφετέρην ἀνελάζετο μορφήν,
λῦσε δέ οἱ μίτρην, καί οἱ λέχος ἔντυον Ὧραι.
65 ἡ δὲ πάρος κούρη Ζηνὸς γένετ' αὐτίκα νύμφη,
καὶ Κρονίδηι τέκε τέκνα καὶ αὐτίκα γίνετο μήτηρ.   1210

---

140 γ' Edmonds: δ' M   150 ἀντήσειας m   155 κεἰ Wakefield: καὶ M   156
ὅττι θέλωμι Hermann   166 καὶ αὐ. γ. μ. del. Wilamowitz ut interpolatoris
manu confecta; idem lac. post h.u. indicauit

XX

BION

EROS AND THE FOWLER (fr. 13)

Ἰξευτὰς ἔτι κῶρος ἐν ἄλσεϊ δενδράεντι
ὄρνεα θηρεύων τὸν ὑπόπτερον εἶδεν Ἔρωτα
ἑσδόμενον πύξοιο ποτὶ κλάδον· ὡς δὲ νόησε,
χαίρων ὥνεκα δὴ μέγα φαίνετο τὤρνεον αὐτῶι,
5 τὼς καλάμως ἅμα πάντας ἐπ' ἀλλάλοισι συνάπτων   121
τᾶι καὶ τᾶι τὸν Ἔρωτα μετάλμενον ἀμφεδόκευε.
χὠ παῖς, ἀσχαλάων ὅκα οἱ τέλος οὐδὲν ἀπάντη,
τὼς καλάμως ῥίψας ποτ' ἀροτρέα πρέσβυν ἵκανεν
ὅς νιν τάνδε τέχναν ἐδιδάξατο, καὶ λέγεν αὐτῶι
10 καί οἱ δεῖξεν Ἔρωτα καθήμενον. αὐτὰρ ὁ πρέσβυς   122
μειδιάων κίνησε κάρη καὶ ἀμείβετο παῖδα·
"φείδεο τᾶς θήρας, μηδ' ἐς τόδε τὤρνεον ἔρχευ.
φεῦγε μακράν· κακόν ἐντι τὸ θηρίον. ὄλβιος ἐσσῆι
εἰσόκε μή νιν ἕλης· ἢν δ' ἀνέρος ἐς μέτρον ἔλθηις
15 οὗτος ὁ νῦν φεύγων καὶ ἀπάλμενος αὐτὸς ἀφ' αὑτῶ   122
ἐλθὼν ἐξαπίνας κεφαλὰν ἔπι σεῖο καθιξεῖ".

XXI

THE LAMENT FOR ADONIS

Αἰάζω τὸν Ἄδωνιν, "ἀπώλετο καλὸς Ἄδωνις"·
"ὤλετο καλὸς Ἄδωνις", ἐπαιάζουσιν Ἔρωτες.

μηκέτι πορφυρέοις ἐνὶ φάρεσι Κύπρι κάθευδε·
ἔγρεο, δειλαία, κυανόστολα καὶ πλατάγησον   123
5 στήθεα καὶ λέγε πᾶσιν, "ἀπώλετο καλὸς Ἄδωνις".

XX Stob. *Ecl.* 20.2.57, IV 464–5 Hense   2 τὸν ὑπόπτερον Briggs: τὸν
ἀπότροπον M: fort. τανυσίπτερον uel ταναόπτερον   7 ὅκα Porson: οὔνεχα M

XXI 4 κυανόστολα Wilamowitz: -στόλε M

αἰάζω τὸν Ἄδωνιν· ἐπαιάζουσιν Ἔρωτες.

κεῖται καλὸς Ἄδωνις ἐν ὤρεσι μηρὸν ὀδόντι,
λευκῶι λευκὸν ὀδόντι τυπείς, καὶ Κύπριν ἀνιῆι
λεπτὸν ἀποψύχων· τὸ δέ οἱ μέλαν εἴβεται αἷμα   1235
10 χιονέας κατὰ σαρκός, ὑπ' ὀφρύσι δ' ὄμματα ναρκῆι,
καὶ τὸ ῥόδον φεύγει τῶ χείλεος· ἀμφὶ δὲ τήνωι
θνάισκει καὶ τὸ φίλημα, τὸ μήποτε Κύπρις ἀποισεῖ.
Κύπριδι μὲν τὸ φίλημα καὶ οὐ ζώοντος ἀρέσκει,
ἀλλ' οὐκ οἶδεν Ἄδωνις ὅ νιν θνάισκοντα φίλησεν.   1240

15 αἰάζω τὸν Ἄδωνιν· ἐπαιάζουσιν Ἔρωτες.

ἄγριον ἄγριον ἕλκος ἔχει κατὰ μηρὸν Ἄδωνις,
μεῖζον δ' ἁ Κυθέρεια φέρει ποτικάρδιον ἕλκος.
τῆνον μὲν περὶ παῖδα φίλοι κύνες ὠρύονται
καὶ Νύμφαι κλαίουσιν Ὀρειάδες· ἁ δ' Ἀφροδίτα   1245
20 λυσαμένα πλοκαμῖδας ἀνὰ δρυμὼς ἀλάληται
πενθαλέα νήπλεκτος ἀσάνδαλος, αἱ δὲ βάτοι νιν
ἐρχομέναν κείροντι καὶ ἱερὸν αἷμα δρέπονται·
ὀξὺ δὲ κωκύοισα δι' ἄγκεα μακρὰ φορεῖται
Ἀσσύριον βοόωσα πόσιν καὶ πολλὰ καλεῦσα.   1250
25 ἀμφὶ δέ νιν μέλαν αἷμα παρ' ὀμφαλὸν ἀιωρεῖτο,
στήθεα δ' ἐκ μηρῶν φοινίσσετο, τοὶ δ' ὑπὸ μαζοὶ
χιόνεοι τὸ πάροιθεν Ἀδώνιδι πορφύροντο.

"αἰαῖ τὰν Κυθέρειαν", ἐπαιάζουσιν Ἔρωτες.

ὤλεσε τὸν καλὸν ἄνδρα, σὺν ὤλεσεν ἱερὸν εἶδος.   1255
30 Κύπριδι μὲν καλὸν εἶδος ὅτε ζώεσκεν Ἄδωνις,
κάτθανε δ' ἁ μορφὰ σὺν Ἀδώνιδι. "τὰν Κύπριν αἰαῖ"
ὤρεα πάντα λέγοντι, καὶ αἱ δρύες "αἲ τὸν Ἄδωνιν"·
καὶ ποταμοὶ κλαίοντι τὰ πένθεα τᾶς Ἀφροδίτας,

---

7 ἐν Ameis: ἐπ' M   18 fort. μὰν (cf. Theoc. 1.71)   ὠρύονται Hermann:
ὠδύραντο M   24 πολλὰ Hermann: παῖδα M: post βοόωσα punct. Thomson,
παῖδα recepto   25 ἀιωρεῖτο suspectum: ἠρωεῖτο Fantuzzi   26 πληγῶν
Rossbach   32 "αἲ" δρύες Ameis, Bergk

καὶ παγαὶ τὸν Ἄδωνιν ἐν ὤρεσι δακρύοντι,　　　　　　126ο

35　ἄνθεα δ' ἐξ ὀδύνας ἐρυθαίνεται, ἁ δὲ Κυθήρα

　　πάντας ἀνὰ κναμώς, ἀνὰ πᾶν νάπος οἰκτρὸν ἀείδει,

　　"αἰαῖ τὰν Κυθέρειαν· ἀπώλετο καλὸς Ἄδωνις"·

　　Ἀχὼ δ' ἀντεβόασεν, "ἀπώλετο καλὸς Ἄδωνις".

　　Κύπριδος αἰνὸν ἔρωτα τίς οὐκ ἔκλαυσεν ἂν αἰαῖ;　　126ϛ

40　ὡς ἴδεν, ὡς ἐνόησεν Ἀδώνιδος ἄσχετον ἕλκος,

　　ὡς ἴδε φοίνιον αἷμα μαραινομένωι περὶ μηρῶι,

　　πάχεας ἀμπετάσασα κινύρετο, "μεῖνον Ἄδωνι,

　　δύσποτμε μεῖνον Ἄδωνι, πανύστατον ὥς σε κιχείω,

　　ὥς σε περιπτύξω καὶ χείλεα χείλεσι μίξω.　　　　　127ο

45　ἔγρεο τυτθόν, Ἄδωνι, τὸ δ' αὖ πύματόν με φίλησον,

　　τοσσοῦτόν με φίλησον ὅσον ζώει τὸ φίλημα,

　　ἄχρις ἀποψύχηις ἐς ἐμὸν στόμα, κεἰς ἐμὸν ἧπαρ

　　πνεῦμα τεὸν ῥεύσηι, τὸ δέ σευ γλυκὺ φίλτρον ἀμέλξω,

　　ἐκ δὲ πίω τὸν ἔρωτα· φίλημα δὲ τοῦτο φυλαξῶ　　127ϛ

50　ὡς αὐτὸν τὸν Ἄδωνιν, ἐπεὶ σύ με, δύσμορε, φεύγεις.

　　φεύγεις μακρόν, Ἄδωνι, καὶ ἔρχεαι εἰς Ἀχέροντα

　　πὰρ στυγνὸν βασιλῆα καὶ ἄγριον· ἁ δὲ τάλαινα

　　ζώω καὶ θεός ἐμμι καὶ οὐ δύναμαί σε διώκειν.

　　λάμβανε, Περσεφόνα, τὸν ἐμὸν πόσιν· ἐσσὶ γὰρ αὐτὰ　　128ο

55　πολλὸν ἐμεῦ κρέσσων, τὸ δὲ πᾶν καλὸν ἐς σὲ καταρρεῖ.

　　ἐμμὶ δ' ἐγὼ πανάποτμος, ἔχω δ' ἀκόρεστον ἀνίαν,

　　καὶ κλαίω τὸν Ἄδωνιν, ὅ μοι θάνε, καί σε φοβεῦμαι.

　　θνάισκεις, ὦ τριπόθητε, πόθος δέ μοι ὡς ὄναρ ἔπτα,

　　χήρα δ' ἁ Κυθέρεια, κενοὶ δ' ἀνὰ δώματ' Ἔρωτες,　　128ϛ

60　σοὶ δ' ἅμα κεστὸς ὄλωλε. τί γάρ, τολμηρέ, κυνάγεις;

　　καλὸς ἐὼν τί τοσοῦτον ἐμήναο θηρὶ παλαίειν;"

　　ὧδ' ὀλοφύρατο Κύπρις· ἐπαιάζουσιν Ἔρωτες,

　　"αἰαῖ τὰν Κυθέρειαν, ἀπώλετο καλὸς Ἄδωνις".　　　129ο

36 ἀνὰ πᾶν νάπος οἰκτρὸν Wakefield: ἀνάπαλιν ἀποσοικτρὰν M　　39 ἐν αἴαι
Ludwich　　52 πὰρ Ameis: καὶ M　　55 καταρρεῖ Stephanus: καὶ ἄρρει M
61 τί τοσοῦτον Köchly: τοσοῦτον M　　ἐμήναο Brunck: ἔμηνας M

δάκρυον ἁ Παφία τόσσον χέει ὅσσον Ἄδωνις   1290
65 αἷμα χέει, τὰ δὲ πάντα ποτὶ χθονὶ γίνεται ἄνθη·
αἷμα ῥόδον τίκτει, τὰ δὲ δάκρυα τὰν ἀνεμώναν.

αἰάζω τὸν Ἄδωνιν, "ἀπώλετο καλὸς Ἄδωνις".

μηκέτ' ἐνὶ δρυμοῖσι τὸν ἀνέρα μύρεο, Κύπρι·
οὐκ ἀγαθὰ στιβάς ἐστιν 'Αδώνιδι φυλλὰς ἐρήμα.   1295
70 λέκτρον ἔχοι, Κυθέρεια, τὸ σὸν νῦν νεκρὸς Ἄδωνις·
καὶ νέκυς ὢν καλός ἐστι, καλὸς νέκυς, οἷα καθεύδων.
κάτθεό νιν μαλακοῖς ἐνὶ φάρεσιν οἷς ἐνίαυεν
ὡς μετὰ τεῦς ἀνὰ νύκτα τὸν ἱερὸν ὕπνον ἐμόχθει·
παγχρυσέωι κλιντῆρι πόθες καὶ στυγνὸν Ἄδωνιν,   1300
75 βάλλε δέ νιν στεφάνοισι καὶ ἄνθεσι· πάντα σὺν αὐτῶι·
ὡς τῆνος τέθνακε καὶ ἄνθεα πάντ' ἐμαράνθη.
ῥαῖνε δέ νιν Συρίοισιν ἀλείφασι, ῥαῖνε μύροισιν·
ὀλλύσθω μύρα πάντα· τὸ σὸν μύρον ὤλετ' Ἄδωνις.

κέκλιται ἁβρὸς Ἄδωνις ἐν εἵμασι πορφυρέοισιν,   1305
80 ἀμφὶ δέ νιν κλαίοντες ἀναστενάχουσιν Ἔρωτες
κειράμενοι χαίτας ἐπ' 'Αδώνιδι· χὢ μὲν ὀιστώς,
ὃς δ' ἐπὶ τόξον ἔβαλλεν, ὃ δὲ πτερόν, ὃς δὲ φαρέτραν·
χὢ μὲν ἔλυσε πέδιλον 'Αδώνιδος, οἳ δὲ λέβητι
χρυσείωι φορέοισιν ὕδωρ, ὃ δὲ μηρία λούει,   1310
85 ὃς δ' ὄπιθεν πτερύγεσσιν ἀναψύχει τὸν Ἄδωνιν.

"αἰαῖ τὰν Κυθέρειαν", ἐπαιάζουσιν Ἔρωτες.

ἔσβεσε λαμπάδα πᾶσαν ἐπὶ φλιαῖς Ὑμέναιος
καὶ στέφος ἐξεκέδασσε γαμήλιον· οὐκέτι δ' "ὑμὴν
ὑμήν", οὐκέτ' ἄειδεν ἐὸν μέλος, ἀλλ' ἔλεγ', "αἰαῖ   1315

64 χέει d'Orville: ἐγχέει M   69 οὐκ Ahrens: ἔστ' M   70 ἔχοι Valckenaer: ἔχει
M   72 οἷς Stephanus: οἱ M   73 ὡς Bücheler: τοῖς M   τεῦς Wilamowitz:
σεῦ M   74 παγχρυσέωι Wilamowitz: -σωι M   πόθες Platt: πόθει m: ποθεῖ
m   75 δέ νιν Wassenbergh: δ' ἐνὶ M   77 Συρίοισιν Ruhnken: μύροισιν M
82 ἔβαλλεν ὃ Wilamowitz (ἔβαλλ' ὃς iam Könnecke): ἔβαιν' ὃς M   83 οἳ
Graefe: ὃς M   86 αἰαῖ Lennep: αὐτὰν M   88 ἐξεκέδασσε Pierson:
ἐξεπέτασσε M   89 ἄειδεν ἐὸν Köchly: ἀειδονέος M   ἀλλ' ἔλεγ' Maas:
ἄλλεται M

90 αἰαῖ", καὶ "τὸν Ἄδωνιν" ἔτι πλέον ἢ "Ὑμέναιον".
αἱ Χάριτες κλαίοντι τὸν υἱέα τῶ Κινύραο,
"ὤλετο καλὸς Ἄδωνις" ἐν ἀλλάλαισι λέγοισαι,
"αἰαῖ" δ' ὀξὺ λέγοντι πολὺ πλέον ἢ Παιῶνα.
χαὶ Μοῖραι τὸν Ἄδωνιν ἀνακλείοισιν ἐν Ἄιδαι   1320
95 καί νιν ἐπαείδουσιν, ὁ δέ σφισιν οὐκ ἐπακούει·
οὐ μὰν οὐκ ἐθέλει, Κώρα δέ νιν οὐκ ἀπολύει.

λῆγε γόων Κυθέρεια τὸ σάμερον, ἴσχεο κομμῶν·
δεῖ σε πάλιν κλαῦσαι, πάλιν εἰς ἔτος ἄλλο δακρῦσαι.

XXII

RHIANUS

ATE

Ἦ ἄρα δὴ μάλα πάντες ἁμαρτίνοοι πελόμεσθα   1325
ἄνθρωποι, φέρομεν δὲ θεῶν ἑτερόρροπα δῶρα
ἀφραδέι κραδίηι· βιότοιο μὲν ὅς κ' ἐπιδευὴς
στρωφᾶται, μακάρεσσιν ἔπι ψόγον αἰνὸν ἰάπτει
5 ἀχνύμενος, σφετέρην δ' ἀρετὴν καὶ θυμὸν ἀτίζει,
οὐδέ τι θαρσαλέος νοέειν ἔπος οὐδέ τι ῥέξαι,   1330
ἐρριγὼς ὅθι τ' ἄνδρες ἐχεκτέανοι παρέωσι,
καί οἱ θυμὸν ἔδουσι κατηφείη καὶ ὀιζύς.
ὃς δέ κεν εὐοχθῆισι, θεὸς δ' ἐπὶ ὄλβον ὀπάζηι
10 καὶ πολυκοιρανίην, ἐπιλήθεται οὕνεκα γαῖαν
ποσσὶν ἐπιστείβει θνητοὶ δέ οἱ εἰσὶ τοκῆες,   1335
ἀλλ' ὑπεροπλίηι καὶ ἁμαρτωλῆισι νόοιο
ἴσα Διὶ βρομέει, κεφαλὴν δ' ὑπέραυχον ἀνίσχει,

90 ἢ Higt: αἲ M   93 αἰαῖ Pierson: αὐτὰν M   Παιῶνα Ahrens: τύ, Διῶνα
M   94 χαὶ Meineke: καὶ M   ἀνακλείοισιν Ahrens: -κλαί- M   ἐν Ἄιδαι
Briggs: ἄδωνιν M   97 κομμῶν Barth: κώμων M

XXII   Stob. *Flor.* 3.4.33, III 227–8 Hense   3 ἀφραδέι Brunck: -ίηι M: -ίηι
κραδίης Valckenaer   6 θαρσαλέος Turnebus: -έως M   9 ὀπάζηι Winterton:
-ζει M   13 ὑπέραυχον ἀνίσχει Meineke: ὑπὲρ αὐχένας ἴσχει M

καίπερ ἐὼν ὀλίγος, μνᾶται δ' εὔπηχυν 'Αθήνην,
15 ἠέ τιν' ἀτραπιτὸν τεκμαίρεται Οὐλυμπόνδε,
ὥς κε μετ' ἀθανάτοισιν ἀρίθμιος εἰλαπινάζηι.   1340
ἡ δ' Ἄτη ἀπαλοῖσι μετατρωχῶσα πόδεσσιν
ἄκρηις ἐν κεφαλῆισιν ἀνώιστος καὶ ἄφαντος
ἄλλοτε μὲν γραίηισι νεωτέρη, ἄλλοτε δ' αὖτε
20 ὁπλοτέρηισι γρηῦς ἐφίσταται ἀμπλακίηισι,
Ζηνὶ θεῶν κρείοντι Δίκηι τ' ἐπίηρα φέρουσα.   1345

XXIII

LYCOPHRON

CASSANDRA PROPHESIES WOE FOR THE GREEKS *(Alexandra 348-72)*

'Εγὼ δὲ τλήμων ἡ γάμους ἀρνουμένη,
ἐν παρθενῶνος λαΐνου τυκίσμασιν
350 ἄνις τεράμνων εἰς ἀνώροφον στέγην
εἱρκτῆς ἀλιβδύσασα λυγαίας δέμας,
ἡ τὸν Θοραῖον Πτῶιον Ὠρίτην θεὸν   1350
λίπτοντ' ἀλέκτρων ἐκβαλοῦσα δεμνίων,
ὡς δὴ κορείαν ἄφθιτον πεπαμένη
355 πρὸς γῆρας ἄκρον, Παλλάδος ζηλώμασι
τῆς μισονύμφου Λαφρίας Πυλάτιδος,
τῆμος βιαίως φάσσα πρὸς τόργου λέχος   1355
γαμψαῖσιν ἅρπαις οἰνὰς ἑλκυσθήσομαι,
ἡ πολλὰ δὴ Βούδειαν Αἴθυιαν Κόρην
360 ἀρωγὸν αὐδάξασα τάρροθον γάμων.
ἡ δ' εἰς τέραμνα δουρατογλύφου στέγης
γλήνας ἄνω στρέψασα χώσεται στρατῶι,   1360
ἐξ οὐρανοῦ πεσοῦσα καὶ θρόνων Διός,
ἄνακτι πάππωι χρῆμα τιμαλφέστατον.

21 κρείοντι Valckenaer: κριόεντι M

XXIII   356 Πυλάτιδος Lobeck: πυλαί- M   358 γαμψαῖσιν Scheer:
γαμφαῖσιν m: γναφαῖσιν m

365 ἑνὸς δὲ λώβης ἀντί, μυρίων τέκνων
Ἑλλὰς στενάξει πᾶσα τοὺς κενοὺς τάφους,
†οὐκ ὀστοθήκαις, χοιράδων δ' ἐφημένους,   1365
οὐδ' ὑστάτην κεύθοντας ἐκ πυρὸς τέφρην
κρωσσοῖσι ταρχυθεῖσαν, ἣ θέμις φθιτῶν,
370 ἀλλ' οὔνομ' οἰκτρὸν καὶ κενηρίων γραφὰς
θερμοῖς τεκόντων δακρύοις λελουμένας
παίδων τε καὶ θρήνοισι τοῖς ὁμευνίδων.   1370

XXIV

HERONDAS

THE PROCURESS (*Mimiamb* 1)

ΜΗΤΡΙΧΗ   ΘΡΕΙΣΣΑ   ΓΥΛΛΙΣ

ΜΗ. Θ[ρέισ]σ', ἀράσσει τὴν θύρην τις· οὐκ ὄψηι
μ[ή] τ[ις] παρ' ἡμέων ἐξ ἀγροικίης ἥκει;
ΘΡ. τίς τ[ὴν] θύρην; ΓΥ. ἐγῶδε. ΘΡ. τίς σύ; δειμαίνεις
ἆσσον προσελθεῖν; ΓΥ. ἢν ἰδού, πάρειμ' ἆσσον.
5 ΘΡ. τίς δ' εἶς σύ; ΓΥ. Γυλλίς, ἡ Φιλαινίδος μήτηρ.   1375
ἄγγειλον ἔνδον Μητρίχηι παρεῦσάν με·
κάλει. ΜΗ. τίς ἐστιν; ΘΡ. Γυλλίς. ΜΗ. ἀμμίη Γυλλίς.
στρέψον τι, δούλη. τίς σε μοῖρ' ἔπεισ' ἐλθεῖν,
Γυλλίς, πρὸς ἡμέας; τί σὺ θεὸς πρὸς ἀνθρώπους;
10 ἤδη γάρ εἰσι πέντε κου, δοκέω, μῆνες   1380
ἐξ οὗ σε, Γυλλίς, οὐδ' ὄναρ, μὰ τὰς Μοίρας,
πρὸς τὴν θύρην ἐλθοῦσαν εἶδέ τις ταύτην.
ΓΥ. μακρὴν ἀποικέω, τέκνον, ἐν δὲ τῆις λαύρηις
ὁ πηλὸς ἄχρις ἰγνύων προσέστηκεν,

367 u. nondum sanatus

XXIV *P. Lit. Lond.* 96   2 suppl. Blass   fort. e.g. παροινέων: παρ' ἡμέας
Rutherford   αποικιης pap. ante corr.   7 sermonum distributio incert-
issima

15 ἐγὼ δὲ δραίνω μυῖ᾽ ὅσον· τὸ γὰρ γῆρας   1385
ἡμέας καθέλκει κἠ σκιὴ παρέστηκε.

ΜΗ. σίγη] τε καὶ μὴ τοῦ χρόνου καταψεύδεο·
οἵη τ᾽ ἔτ᾽] εἰς γάρ, Γυλλί, κἠτέρους ἄγχειν.

ΓΥ. σίλλ[α]ινε· ταῦτα τῆις νεωτέρηις ὕμιν

20 πρόσεστιν— ἀλλ᾽ οὐ τοῦτο μή σε θερμήνηι.   1390
ἀλλ᾽, ὦ τέκνον, κόσον τιν᾽ ἤδη χηραίνεις
χρόνον μόνη τρύχουσα τὴν μίαν κοίτην.
ἐξ οὗ γὰρ εἰς Αἴγυπτον ἐστάλη Μάνδρις
δέκ᾽ εἰσὶ μῆνες, κοὐδὲ γράμμα σοι πέμπει,

25 ἀλλ᾽ ἐκλέλησται καὶ πέπωκεν ἐκ καινῆς.   1395
κεῖ δ᾽ ἐστὶν οἶκος τῆς θεοῦ· τὰ γὰρ πάντα,
ὅσσ᾽ ἔστι κου καὶ γίνετ᾽, ἔστ᾽ ἐν Αἰγύπτωι·
πλοῦτος, παλαίστρη, δύναμις, εὐδίη, δόξα,
θέαι, φιλόσοφοι, χρυσίον, νεηνίσκοι,

30 θεῶν ἀδελφῶν τέμενος, ὁ βασιλεὺς χρηστός,   1400
Μουσῆιον, οἶνος, ἀγαθὰ πάντ᾽ ὅσ᾽ ἂν χρήιζηις,
γυναῖκες, ὁκόσους οὐ μὰ τὴν Ἅιδεω Κούρην
ἀστέρας ἐνεγκεῖν οὐραν[ὸ]ς κεκαύχηται,
τὴν δ᾽ ὄψιν οἷαι πρὸς Πάριν κοτ᾽ ὥρμησαν

35 θ]ε[αὶ κρ]ιθῆναι καλλονήν—λάθοιμ᾽ αὐτὰς   1405
γρύξασ]α. κο[ί]ην οὖν τάλαιν[α] σὺ ψυχὴν
ἔ]χο[υσ]α θάλπεις τὸν δίφρον; κατ᾽ οὖν λήσεις
γηρᾶσα] καί σευ τὥριον τέφρη κάψει.
πάπτ]ηνον ἄλληι κἠμέρας μετάλλαξον

40 τὸ]ν νοῦν δύ᾽ ἢ τρεῖς, κἰλαρὴ κατάστηθι   1410
φίλον πρ]ὸς ἄλλον· νηῦς μιῆς ἐπ᾽ ἀγκύρης
οὐκ] ἀσφαλὴς ὁρμεῦσα· κεῖνος ἢν ἔλθηι,
ἐκ νερτέρω]ν [οὐ] μηδὲ εἷς ἀναστήσηι
ἡ]μέας μεταῦτις· δεινὰ δ᾽ ἄγριος χειμὼν

17 suppl. Bücheler, 18 Tucker   31 χρήιζηις Bücheler: -ηι pap.   35 suppl. Bücheler, 36 Headlam, 37-8 Rutherford, 39 Weil, 41 Bücheler, 42 Hicks, 43 Headlam   44 μεταῦτις Hopkinson ex. gr.:]μεας . . . . τοδινα pap.

45   κα[ταιγίσας ἔπνευ]σε, κοὐδὲ ε[ἴ]ς οἶδε   1415
      τὸ μέλλο]ν ἡμέων· ἄστατος γὰρ ἀνθρώποις
      δειλοῖσιν αἰών.] ἀλλὰ μήτις ἔστηκε
      σύνεγγυς ἡμῖν; ΜΗ. οὐδὲ εἷς. ΓΥ. ἄκουσον δὴ
      ἅ σοι χρε[ΐ]ζουσ᾿ ὧδ᾿ ἔβην ἀπαγγεῖλαι·
50   ὁ Ματαλίνης τῆς Παταικίου Γρύλλος,   1420
      ὁ πέντε νικέων ἆθλα, παῖς μὲν ἐν Πυθοῖ,
      δὶς δ᾿ ἐν Κορίνθωι τοὺς ἴουλον ἀνθεῦντας,
      ἄνδρας δὲ Πίσηι δὶς καθεῖλε πυκτεύσας,
      πλουτέων τὸ καλόν, οὐδὲ κάρφος ἐκ τῆς γῆς
55   κινέων, ἄθικτος ἐς Κυθηρίην σφρηγίς,   1425
      ἰδών σε καθόδωι τῆς Μίσης ἐκύμηνε
      τὰ σπλάγχν᾿ ἔρωτι καρδίην ἀνοιστρηθείς,
      καί μευ οὔτε νυκτὸς οὔτ᾿ ἐπ᾿ ἡμέρην λείπει
      τὸ δῶμα, [τέ]κνον, ἀλλά μευ κατακλαίει
60   καὶ ταταλ[ί]ζει καὶ ποθέων ἀποθνήισκει.   1430
      ἀλλ᾿, ὦ τέκνον μοι Μητρίχη, μίαν ταύτην
      ἁμαρτίην δὸς τῆι θεῶι· κατάρτησον
      σαυτήν, τὸ [γ]ῆρας μὴ λάθηι σε προσβλέψαν.
      καὶ δοιὰ πρήξεις· ἡδέω[ν] τε[υ]ξ[ῆι], κ[αί σοι
65   δοθήσεταί τι μέζον ἢ δοκεῖς· σκέψαι,   1435
      πείσθητί μευ· φιλέω σε, να[ὶ] μὰ τὰς Μοίρας.
   ΜΗ. Γυλλίς, τὰ λευκὰ τῶν τριχῶν ἀπαμβλύνει
      τὸν νοῦν· μὰ τὴν γὰρ Μάνδριος κατάπλωσιν
      καὶ τὴν φίλην Δήμητρα, ταῦτ᾿ ἐγὼ [ἐ]ξ ἄλλης
70   γυναικὸς οὐκ ἂν ἡδέως ἐπήκουσα,   1440
      χωλὴν δ᾿ ἀείδειν χώλ᾿ ἂν ἐξεπαίδευσα
      καὶ τῆς θύρης τὸν οὐδὸν ἐχθρὸν ἡγεῖσθαι.
      σὺ δ᾿ αὖτις ἔς με μηδὲ ἕνα, φίλη, τοῖον
      φέρουσα χώρει μῦθον· ὃν δὲ γρήιησι
75   πρέπει γυναιξὶ τῆις νέηις ἀπάγγελλε·   1445
      τὴν Πυθέω δὲ Μητρίχην ἔα θάλπειν

45–7 et 64 suppl. Headlam   67 Γυλλίς Rutherford, Bücheler: γυλλι pap.
73 ἕνα Blass: εν pap.

τὸν δίφρον· οὐ γὰρ ἐγγελᾶι τις εἰς Μάνδριν.
ἀλλ᾽ οὐχὶ τούτων, φασί, τῶν λόγων Γυλλὶς
δεῖται· Θρέισσα, τὴν μελαινίδ᾽ ἔκτριψον
80 κἠκτημόρους τρεῖς ἐγχέασ[α τ]οῦ ἀκρήτου   1450
καὶ ὕδωρ ἐπιστάξασα δὸς πιεῖν. ΓΥ. καλῶς.
ΜΗ. τῆ, Γυλλί, πῖθι. ΓΥ. δεῖξον· οὐ [παραλλάσσειν
πείσουσά σ᾽ ἦλθον, ἀλλ᾽ ἔκητι τῶν ἱρῶν·
ὧν οὕνεκέν μοι—ΜΗ. Γυλλί, ὦνα᾽ [οὐδ᾽ ὅσσον.
85 ὥς σοι εὖ γένοιτο. ΓΥ. μᾶ, τέκνον, π[ροπίνεις μοι·   1455
ἡδύς γε· ναὶ Δήμητρα, Μητρ[ί]χη, τούτου
ἡδίον᾽ οἶνον Γυλλὶς οὐ πέ[π]ωκέν [κω.
σὺ δ᾽ εὐτύχει μοι, τέκνον, ἀσ[φα]λίζευ [δὲ
σαυτήν· ἐμοὶ δὲ Μυρτάλη τε κ[αὶ] Σίμη
90 νέαι μένοιεν, ἔστ᾽ ἂν ἐμπνέηι Γυλλίς.   1460

XXV

MACHON

PHILOXENUS THE GLUTTON

Ὑπερβολῆι λέγουσι τὸν Φιλόξενον
τῶν διθυράμβων τὸν ποιητὴν γεγονέναι
ὀψοφάγον. εἶτα πουλύποδα πηχῶν δυεῖν
ἐν ταῖς Συρακούσαις ποτ᾽ αὐτὸν ἀγοράσαι
5 καὶ σκευάσαντα καταφαγεῖν ὅλον σχεδὸν   1465
πλὴν τῆς κεφαλῆς. ἁλόντα δ᾽ ὑπὸ δυσπεψίας
κακῶς σφόδρα σχεῖν· εἶτα δ᾽ ἰατροῦ τινος
πρὸς αὐτὸν εἰσελθόντος, ὃς φαύλως πάνυ
ὁρῶν φερόμενον αὐτὸν εἶπεν· "εἴ τί σοι
10 ἀνοικονόμητόν ἐστι διατίθου ταχύ,   1470

---

82 suppl. Nairn, 84 Knox   85 ὥς σοι εὖ Headlam: οσσου pap.   fin. suppl.
Headlam post Rutherford   88 suppl. Headlam

XXV Athenaeus 8.341a–d; 9 Gow   7 σχεῖν Meineke: ἔχειν M   δ᾽ add.
Grotius: εἶτ᾽ ἰα- fere M   9 ὁρῶν φερόμενον Grotius: φ. ὁ. M

Φιλόξεν'· ἀποθανῆι· γὰρ ὥρας ἑβδόμης."
κἀκεῖνος εἶπε· "τέλος ἔχει τὰ πάντα μοι,
ἰατρέ," φησί, "καὶ δεδιώικηται πάλαι·
τοὺς διθυράμβους σὺν θεοῖς καταλιμπάνω
15 ἠνδρωμένους καὶ πάντας ἐστεφανωμένους·   1475
οὓς ἀνατίθημι ταῖς ἐμαυτοῦ συντρόφοις
Μούσαις Ἀφροδίτην καὶ Διόνυσον ἐπιτρόπους—
ταῦθ' αἱ διαθῆκαι διασαφοῦσιν. ἀλλ' ἐπεὶ
ὁ Τιμοθέου Χάρων σχολάζειν οὐκ ἐᾶι
20 οὐκ τῆς Νιόβης, χωρεῖν δὲ πορθμίδ' ἀναβοᾶι,   1480
καλεῖ δὲ μοῖρα νύχιος, ἧς κλύειν χρεών,
ἵν' ἔχων ἀποτρέχω πάντα τἀμαυτοῦ κάτω,
τοῦ πουλύποδος μοι τὸ κατάλοιπον ἀπόδοτε."

XXVI

EPIGRAMS

A. FUNERARY

Callimachus   1

Τῆιδε Σάων ὁ Δίκωνος Ἀκάνθιος ἱερὸν ὕπνον
κοιμᾶται—θνήισκειν μὴ λέγε τοὺς ἀγαθούς.   1485

Callimachus   2

Δωδεκέτη τὸν παῖδα πατὴρ ἀπέθηκε Φίλιππος
ἐνθάδε, τὴν πολλὴν ἐλπίδα, Νικοτέλην.

17 lac. post Μούσαις ind. Meineke   20 πορθμίδ' Casaubon, Meineke: πορθμὸν
M

XXVI **1** *AP* 7.451; *HE* 1231–2 (=Call. 41); 9 Pfeiffer; *OCT* 1336–7
2 *AP* 7.453; *HE* 1249–50 (=Call. 46); 19 Pfeiffer; *OCT* 1354–5

Heraclitus 3

Ἁ κόνις ἀρτίσκαπτος, ἐπὶ στάλας δὲ μετώπωι
σείονται φύλλων ἡμιθαλεῖς στέφανοι.
γράμμα διακρίναντες, ὁδοιπόρε, πέτρον ἴδωμεν,   1490
λευρὰ περιστέλλειν ὀστέα φατὶ τίνος.
5 "ξεῖν᾽, Ἀρετημιάς εἰμι· πάτρα Κνίδος· Εὔφρονος ἦλθον
ἐς λέχος· ὠδίνων οὐκ ἄμορος γενόμαν,
δισσὰ δ᾽ ὁμοῦ τίκτουσα τὸ μὲν λίπον ἀνδρὶ ποδαγὸν
γήρως, ἓν δ᾽ ἀπάγω μναμόσυνον πόσιος."   1495

Callimachus 4

Εἶπέ τις, Ἡράκλειτε, τεὸν μόρον, ἐς δέ με δάκρυ
ἤγαγεν, ἐμνήσθην δ᾽ ὁσσάκις ἀμφότεροι
ἠέλιον λέσχηι κατεδύσαμεν· ἀλλὰ σὺ μέν που,
ξεῖν᾽ Ἁλικαρνησεῦ, τετράπαλαι σποδιή·
5 αἱ δὲ τεαὶ ζώουσιν ἀηδόνες, ἧισιν ὁ πάντων   1500
ἁρπακτὴς Ἀίδης οὐκ ἐπὶ χεῖρα βαλεῖ.

Meleager 5

Δάκρυά σοι καὶ νέρθε διὰ χθονός, Ἡλιοδώρα,
δωροῦμαι, στοργᾶς λείψανον εἰς Ἀίδαν,
δάκρυα δυσδάκρυτα· πολυκλαύτωι δ᾽ ἐπὶ τύμβωι
σπένδω μνᾶμα πόθων, μνᾶμα φιλοφροσύνας.   1505
5 οἰκτρὰ γὰρ οἰκτρὰ φίλαν σε καὶ ἐν φθιμένοις Μελέαγρος
αἰάζω, κενεὰν εἰς Ἀχέροντα χάριν.
αἰαῖ ποῦ τὸ ποθεινὸν ἐμοὶ θάλος; ἅρπασεν Ἅιδας,
ἅρπασεν, ἀκμαῖον δ᾽ ἄνθος ἔφυρε κόνις.
ἀλλά σε γουνοῦμαι, Γᾶ παντρόφε, τὰν πανόδυρτον   1510
10   ἠρέμα σοῖς κόλποις, μᾶτερ, ἐναγκάλισαι.

3 AP 7.465; HE 1935–42 (=Heracl. 1); OCT 1522–9   1 μετώπων m
4 λευκὰ m: λυγρὰ m   8 ἓν Jacobs: ὃν M
4 AP 7.80; HE 1203–8 (=Call. 34); 2 Pfeiffer; OCT 1308–13   3 ἥλιον ἐν m
5 AP 7.476; HE 4282–91 (=Mel. 56); OCT 4326–35

Meleager   6

Οὐ γάμον ἀλλ' Ἀίδαν ἐπινυμφίδιον Κλεαρίστα
δέξατο παρθενίας ἄμματα λυομένα.
ἄρτι γὰρ ἑσπέριοι νύμφας ἐπὶ δικλίσιν ἄχευν
λωτοί, καὶ θαλάμων ἐπλαταγεῦντο θύραι.   1515
5 ἀῷοι δ' ὀλολυγμὸν ἀνέκραγον, ἐκ δ' Ὑμέναιος
σιγαθεὶς γοερὸν φθέγμα μεθαρμόσατο.
αἱ δ' αὐταὶ καὶ φέγγος ἐδαιδούχουν περὶ παστῶι
πεῦκαι καὶ φθιμέναι νέρθεν ἔφαινον ὁδόν.

Leonidas   7

Ἠχήεσσα θάλασσα, τί τὸν Τιμάρεος οὕτως   1520
πλώοντ' οὐ πολλῆι νηὶ Τελευταγόρην
ἄγρια χειμήνασα καταπρηνώσαο πόντωι
σὺν φόρτωι, λάβρον κῦμ' ἐπιχευαμένη;
5 χὠ μέν που καύηξιν ἢ ἰχθυβόροις λαρίδεσσι
τεθρήνητ' ἄπνους εὐρεῖ ἐν αἰγιαλῶι,   1525
Τιμάρης δὲ κενὸν τέκνου κεκλαυμένον ἀθρῶν
τύμβον δακρύει παῖδα Τελευταγόρην.

Leonidas   8

Ποιμένες οἳ ταύτην ὄρεος ῥάχιν οἰοπολεῖτε
αἶγας κεὐείρους ἐμβοτέοντες ὄις,
Κλειταγόρηι, πρὸς Γῆς, ὀλίγην χάριν ἀλλὰ προσηνῆ   1530
τίνοιτε χθονίης εἵνεκα Φερσεφόνης.
5 βληχήσαιντ' ὄιές μοι, ἐπ' ἀξέστοιο δὲ ποιμὴν

6 *AP* 7.182; *HE* 4680–7 (= Mel. 123); *OCT* 4724–31   5 ἀῷοι Graefe (ἠῷοι-):
ἠῷιον M
7 *AP* 7.652; *HE* 2040–7 (= Leon. 15); *OCT* 2029–36
8 *AP* 7.657; *HE* 2062–73 (= Leon. 19); *OCT* 2051–62   2 κεὐείρους Salmasius: κεὐήρους m: κεὐμάλους m   ἐμβοτέοντες Scaliger: ἐμβατ- M

πέτρης συρίζοι πρηέα βοσκομέναις·
εἴαρι δὲ πρώτωι λειμώνιον ἄνθος ἀμέρξας
χωρίτης στεφέτω τύμβον ἐμὸν στεφάνωι· 1535
καί τις ἀπ' εὐάρνοιο καταχραίνοιτο γάλακτι
10 οἰὸς ἀμολγαῖον μαστὸν ἀνασχόμενος,
κρηπῖδ' ὑγραίνων ἐπιτύμβιον. εἰσὶ θανόντων,
εἰσὶν ἀμοιβαῖαι κἂν φθιμένοις χάριτες.

Anyte   9

Οὐκέτι μ' ὡς τὸ πάρος πυκιναῖς πτερύγεσσιν ἐρέσσων 1540
ὄρσεις ἐξ εὐνᾶς ὄρθριος ἐγρόμενος·
ἦ γάρ σ' ὑπνώοντα σίνις λαθρηδὸν ἐπελθὼν
ἔκτεινεν λαιμῶι ῥίμφα καθεὶς ὄνυχα.

Alcaeus   10

Δίζημαι κατὰ θυμὸν ὅτου χάριν, ὦ παροδῖτα,
δισσάκι φεῖ μοῦνον γράμμα λέλογχε λίθος 1545
λαοτύποις σμίλαις κεκολαμμένον· ἦ ῥα γυναικὶ
τᾶι χθονὶ κευθομέναι Χιλιὰς ἦν ὄνομα;
5 τοῦτο γὰρ ἀγγέλλει κορυφούμενος εἰς ἓν ἀριθμός.
ἦ τὸ μὲν εἰς ὀρθὰν ἀτραπὸν οὐκ ἔμολεν,
ἁ δ' οἰκτρὸν ναίουσα τόδ' ἠρίον ἔπλετο Φειδίς; 1550
νῦν Σφιγγὸς γρίφους Οἰδίπος ἐφρασάμαν.
αἰνετὸς οὐκ δισσοῖο καμὼν αἴνιγμα τύποιο,
10 φέγγος μὲν ξυνετοῖς ἀξυνέτοις δ' ἔρεβος.

7 ἀμέρξας Scaliger: ἀμέρσας M
9 AP 7.202; HE 704–7 (=Anyte 11); OCT 716–19
10 AP 7.429; HE 96–105 (=Alc. 16); OCT 3256–65   1 ὦ Hermann: ὁ m: ἁ m
παροδῖτα Hermann: -τας m: -της m: -τις m   2 πέτρος m   3 ἄρα m

Asclepiades   11

Ἀρχεάνασσαν ἔχω, τὰν ἐκ Κολοφῶνος ἑταίραν,
     ἇς ἐπὶ καὶ ῥυτίδων ὁ γλυκὺς ἕζετ' Ἔρως.   1555
ἇ νέον ἥβης ἄνθος ἀποδρέψαντες ἐρασταὶ
     πρωτόβολοι, δι' ὅσης ἤλθετε πυρκαϊῆς.

Leonidas or Meleager   12

Παρθενικὴν νεάοιδον ἐν ὑμνοπόλοισι μέλισσαν
     Ἤρινναν Μουσέων ἄνθεα δρεπτομένην
Ἄιδας εἰς ὑμέναιον ἀνάρπασεν· ἦ ῥα τόδ' ἔμφρων   1560
     εἶπ' ἐτύμως ἁ παῖς, "βάσκανος ἔσσ', Ἀΐδα".

Antipater   13

Παυροεπὴς Ἤριννα καὶ οὐ πολύμυθος ἀοιδαῖς,
     ἀλλ' ἔλαχεν Μούσας τοῦτο τὸ βαιὸν ἔπος.
τοιγάρτοι μνήμης οὐκ ἤμβροτεν, οὐδὲ μελαίνης
     νυκτὸς ὑπὸ σκιερῇ κωλύεται πτέρυγι·   1565
5 αἱ δ' ἀναρίθμητοι νεαρῶν σωρηδὸν ἀοιδῶν
     μυριάδες λήθῃ, ξεῖνε, μαραινόμεθα.
λωΐτερος κύκνου μικρὸς θρόος ἠὲ κολοιῶν
     κρωγμὸς ἐν εἰαριναῖς κιδνάμενος νεφέλαις.

Meleager   14

Νᾶσος ἐμὰ θρέπτειρα Τύρος, πάτρα δέ με τεκνοῖ   1570
     Ἀτθὶς ἐν Ἀσσυρίοις ναιομένα Γάδαρα·

11   AP 7.217; HE 1002–5 (=Ascl. 41); OCT 1123–6   3 ἇς Jacobs: ἇς m: ἦν m
4 πρωτοβόλου m: -πλόου m
12   AP 7.13; HE 2563–6 (=Leon. 98); OCT 2552–5
13   AP 7.713; HE 560–7 (=Antip. 58); OCT 3722–9   4 καδδύεται Reiske
8 αἰθερίαις Stadtmüller
14   AP 7.417; HE 3984–93 (=Mel. 2); OCT 4028–37   2 Γάδαρα Hecker:
-ροις M

Εὐκρατέω δ' ἔβλαστον ὁ σὺν Μούσαις Μελέαγρος,
πρῶτα Μενιππείοις συντροχάσας χάρισιν.
5 εἰ δὲ Σύρος, τί τὸ θαῦμα; μίαν, ξένε, πατρίδα κόσμον
ναίομεν, ἓν θνατοὺς πάντας ἔτικτε Χάος.
πουλυετὴς δ' ἐχάραξα τάδ' ἐν δέλτοισι πρὸ τύμβου·
γῆρας γὰρ γείτων ἐγγύθεν Ἀίδεω.
ἀλλά με τὸν λαλιὸν καὶ πρεσβύτην πάρος εἰπὼν
10 χαίρειν, εἰς γῆρας καὐτὸς ἵκοιο λάλον.

1575

B. AMATORY

Asclepiades   15

Ἡδὺ θέρους διψῶντι χιὼν ποτόν, ἡδὺ δὲ ναύταις   1580
ἐκ χειμῶνος ἰδεῖν εἰαρινὸν Στέφανον·
ἥδιον δ' ὁπόταν κρύψηι μία τοὺς φιλέοντας
χλαῖνα, καὶ αἰνῆται Κύπρις ὑπ' ἀμφοτέρων.

Asclepiades   16

Νεῖφε, χαλαζοβόλει, ποίει σκότος, αἴθε κεραυνούς,
πάντα τὰ πορφύροντ' ἐν χθονὶ σεῖε νέφη·
ἢν γάρ με κτείνηις, τότε παύσομαι· ἢν δέ μ' ἀφῆις ζῆν,   1585
κἂν διαθῆις τούτων χείρονα, κωμάσομαι·
5 ἕλκει γάρ μ' ὁ κρατῶν καὶ σοῦ θεός, ὧι ποτε πεισθείς,
Ζεῦ, διὰ χαλκείων χρυσὸς ἔδυς θαλάμων.

8 γήρως m   9 πάρος εἰπὼν Peerlkamp (iam Graefe, sed cum πρεσβ.
coniunctum): προσειπὼν m: σὺ προσειπὼν m
15 AP 5.169; HE 812–15 (=Ascl. 1); OCT 967–70   3 ἥδιον Jacobs: ἡδεῖον m:
ἥδιστον m: ἡδὺ δὲ καὶ ὁπ. m
16 AP 5.64; HE 854–9 (=Ascl. 11); OCT 1009–14   1 κεραυνούς Ludwig:
κεραύνου M   4 κἂν Meineke: καὶ M   διαθεὶς m

Callimachus   17

Ἕλκος ἔχων ὁ ξεῖνος ἐλάνθανεν· ὡς ἀνιηρὸν   1590
πνεῦμα διὰ στηθέων (εἶδες;) ἀνηγάγετο,
τὸ τρίτον ἡνίκ᾽ ἔπινε, τὰ δὲ ῥόδα φυλλοβολεῦντα
τὠνδρὸς ἀπὸ στεφάνων πάντ᾽ ἐγένοντο χαμαί.
5 ὤπτηται μέγα δή τι· μὰ δαίμονας, οὐκ ἀπὸ ῥυσμοῦ
εἰκάζω, φωρὸς δ᾽ ἴχνια φὼρ ἔμαθον.   1595

Callimachus   18

Ὤμοσε Καλλίγνωτος Ἰωνίδι μήποτ᾽ ἐκείνης
ἕξειν μήτε φίλον κρέσσονα μήτε φίλην.
ὤμοσεν· ἀλλὰ λέγουσιν ἀληθέα τοὺς ἐν ἔρωτι
ὅρκους μὴ δύνειν οὔατ᾽ ἐς ἀθανάτων.
5 νῦν δ᾽ ὁ μὲν ἀρσενικῶι θέρεται πυρί, τῆς δὲ ταλαίνης   1600
νύμφης, ὡς Μεγαρέων, οὐ λόγος οὐδ᾽ ἀριθμός.

Meleager   19

Ἆ ψυχὴ βαρύμοχθε, σὺ δ᾽ ἄρτι μὲν ἐκ πυρὸς αἴθηι,
ἄρτι δ᾽ ἀναψύχεις πνεῦμ᾽ ἀναλεξαμένη.
τί κλαίεις; τὸν ἄτεγκτον ὅτ᾽ ἐν κόλποισιν Ἔρωτα
ἔτρεφες, οὐκ ἤιδεις ὡς ἐπὶ σοὶ τρέφετο;   1605
5 οὐκ ἤιδεις; νῦν γνῶθι καλῶν ἄλλαγμα τροφείων,
πῦρ ἅμα καὶ ψυχρὰν δεξαμένη χιόνα.
αὐτὴ ταῦθ᾽ εἵλου· φέρε τὸν πόνον· ἄξια πάσχεις
ὧν ἔδρας, ὀπτῶι καιομένη μέλιτι.

17 AP 12.134; HE 1103–8 (=Call. 13); 43 Pfeiffer; OCT 1208–13   3 ἡνίκ᾽
Scaliger: ηγκ M   5 ὤπτηται μέγα δή τι Bentley: ὤπτημαι μεγαλητί M
18 AP 5.6; HE 1091–6 (=Call. 11); 25 Pfeiffer; OCT 1196–1201
19 AP 12.132b; HE 4110–17 (=Mel. 22); OCT 4154–61   3 ἄτεγκτον
Ruhnken: ἄτεκνον M   4 τρέφετο Salmasius: -ται M   8 ἔδρας Graefe,
Porson: ἐδρασας M

Meleager 20

Κηρύσσω τὸν Ἔρωτα τὸν ἄγριον· ἄρτι γὰρ ἄρτι   1610
ὀρθρινὸς ἐκ κοίτας ᾤχετ' ἀποπτάμενος.
ἐστὶ δ' ὁ παῖς γλυκύδακρυς, ἀείλαλος, ὠκύς, ἀθαμβής,
σιμὰ γελῶν, πτερόεις νῶτα, φαρετροφόρος.
5 πατρὸς δ' οὐκέτ' ἔχω φράζειν τίνος· οὔτε γὰρ αἰθήρ,
οὐ χθών φησι τεκεῖν τὸν θρασύν, οὐ πέλαγος·   1615
πάντηι γὰρ καὶ πᾶσιν ἀπέχθεται· ἀλλ' ἐσορᾶτε
μή που νῦν ψυχαῖς ἄλλα τίθησι λίνα.
καίτοι κεῖνος, ἰδού, περὶ φωλεόν· οὔ με λέληθας,
10 τοξότα, Ζηνοφίλας ὄμμασι κρυπτόμενος.

'Plato' 21

Ἀστέρας εἰσαθρεῖς, ἀστὴρ ἐμός· εἴθε γενοίμην   1620
οὐρανός, ὡς πολλοῖς ὄμμασιν εἰς σὲ βλέπω.

Philodemus 22

Νυκτερινὴ δίκερως φιλοπάννυχε φαῖνε Σελήνη,
φαῖνε, δι' εὐτρήτων βαλλομένη θυρίδων·
αὔγαζε χρυσέην Καλλίστιον· ἐς τὰ φιλεύντων
ἔργα κατοπτεύειν οὐ φθόνος ἀθανάτηι.   1625
5 ὀλβίζεις καὶ τήνδε καὶ ἡμέας, οἶδα, Σελήνη·
καὶ γὰρ σὴν ψυχὴν ἔφλεγεν Ἐνδυμίων.

Meleager 23

Πταίης μοι κώνωψ, ταχὺς ἄγγελος, οὔασι δ' ἄκροις
Ζηνοφίλας ψαύσας προσψιθύριζε τάδε·

20 *AP* 5.177; *HE* 4190–9 (= Mel. 37); *OCT* 4234–43
21 *AP* 7.669; *FGE* 584–5 (= 'Plato' 1); *OCT* 511–12
22 *AP* 5.123; *GP* 3212–17 (= Philod. 9); *OCT* 4846–51
23 *AP* 5.152; *HE* 4174–81 (= Mel. 34); *OCT* 4218–25

"ἄγρυπνος μίμνει σε, σὺ δ' ὦ λήθαργε φιλούντων   1630
   εὕδεις". εἷα πέτευ, ναὶ φιλόμουσε πέτευ·
5 ἥσυχα δὲ φθέγξαι, μὴ καὶ σύγκοιτον ἐγείρας
   κινήσηις ἐπ' ἐμοὶ ζηλοτύπους ὀδύνας.
ἢν δ' ἀγάγηις τὴν παῖδα, δορᾶι στέψω σε λέοντος,
   κώνωψ, καὶ δώσω χειρὶ φέρειν ῥόπαλον.   1635

Meleager   24

'Αχήεις τέττιξ, δροσεραῖς σταγόνεσσι μεθυσθεὶς
   ἀγρονόμαν μέλπεις μοῦσαν ἐρημολάλον,
ἄκρα δ' ἐφεζόμενος πετάλοις πριονώδεσι κώλοις
   αἰθίοπι κλάζεις χρωτὶ μέλισμα λύρας·
5 ἀλλά, φίλος, φθέγγου τι νέον δενδρώδεσι Νύμφαις   1640
   παίγνιον, ἀντωιδὸν Πανὶ κρέκων κέλαδον,
ὄφρα φυγὼν τὸν Ἔρωτα μεσημβρινὸν ὕπνον ἀγρεύσω
   ἐνθάδ' ὑπὸ σκιερᾶι κεκλιμένος πλατάνωι.

C. DEDICATORY

Callimachus   25

Τίν με, λεοντάγχ' ὦνα συοκτόνε, φήγινον ὄζον
θῆκε—τίς; —'Αρχῖνος.—ποῖος; —ὁ Κρής.—δέχομαι.   1645

Callimachus   26

Κόγχος ἐγώ, Ζεφυρῖτι, παλαίτερον, ἀλλὰ σὺ νῦν με,
Κύπρι, Σεληναίης ἄνθεμα πρῶτον ἔχεις,

7 δορᾶι Pierson: -αῖς M
24   *AP* 7.196; *HE* 4066–73 (=Mel. 13); *OCT* 4110–17
25   *AP* 6.351; *HE* 1151–2 (=Call. 22); 34 Pfeiffer; *OCT* 1256–7   1 λεοντάγχ'
ὦνα Lobeck: λεοντάγχωνε M
26   Athenaeus 7.318b; *HE* 1109–20 (=Call. 14); 5 Pfeiffer; *OCT* 1214–25

ναυτίλος ὃς πελάγεσσιν ἐπέπλεον, εἰ μὲν ἀῆται,
    τείνας οἰκείων λαῖφος ἀπὸ προτόνων,
5 εἰ δὲ Γαληναίη, λιπαρὴ θεός, οὖλος ἐρέσσων   1650
    ποσσίν—ἴδ᾿ ὡς τὤργωι τοὔνομα συμφέρεται—
ἔστ᾿ ἔπεσον παρὰ θῖνας ᾿Ιουλίδος, ὄφρα γένωμαι
    σοὶ τὸ περίσκεπτον παίγνιον, ᾿Αρσινόη,
μηδέ μοι ἐν θαλάμηισιν ἔθ᾿ ὡς πάρος—εἰμὶ γὰρ ἄπλους—
10 τίκτηται νοτερῆς ὤεον ἀλκυόνος.   1655
Κλεινίου ἀλλὰ θυγατρὶ δίδου χάριν· οἶδε γὰρ ἐσθλὰ
    ῥέζειν, καὶ Σμύρνης ἐστὶν ἀπ᾿ Αἰολίδος.

Callimachus   27

Τὴν ἀλίην Εὔδημος, ἐφ᾿ ἧς ἅλα λιτὸν ἐπέσθων
    χειμῶνας μεγάλους ἐξέφυγεν δανέων,
θῆκε θεοῖς Σαμοθρᾶιξι, λέγων ὅτι τήνδε κατ᾿ εὐχήν,   1660
    ὦ λαοί, σωθεὶς ἐξ ἁλὸς ὧδε θέτο.

Posidippus or Asclepiades   28

Πορφυρέην μάστιγα καὶ ἡνία σιγαλόεντα
    Πλαγγὼν εὐίππων θῆκεν ἐπὶ προθύρων,
νικήσασα κέλητι Φιλαινίδα τὴν πολύχαρμον
    ἑσπερινῶν πώλων ἄρτι φρυασσομένων.   1665
5 Κύπρι φίλη, σὺ δὲ τῆιδε πόροις νημερτέα νίκης
    δόξαν, ἀείμνηστον τήνδε τιθεῖσα χάριν.

1 παλαίτερον Bentley: -ρος M: πάλαι τέρας Schneider   με Musurus: μοι M
3 ναυτίλος Kaibel: -λον M   6 ἴδ᾿ ὡς τὤργωι Schneider: ἰν᾿ ὡσπεργωι M
7 ᾿Ιουλίδος Casaubon: -ίδας M   8 ᾿Αρσινόη test.: -όης M   9 ἄπλους
Lobeck: ἄπνους M   10 emend. Bentley: τίκτει τ᾿ αἰνοτέρης ὤεον ἀλκυόνης M
27 AP 6.301; HE 1175-8 (=Call. 28); 47 Pfeiffer; OCT 1280-3
28 AP 5.202; HE 974-9 (=Ascl. 35); OCT 1704-9   6 τήνδε τιθεῖσα
Emperius: τήνδ᾿ ἐπιθεῖσα M

D. MISCELLANEOUS

Leonidas   29

Φεύγεθ' ὑπὲκ καλύβης, σκότιοι μύες· οὔτι πενιχρὴ
μῦς σιπύη βόσκειν οἶδε Λεωνίδεω.
αὐτάρκης ὁ πρέσβυς ἔχων ἅλα καὶ δύο κρίμνα·   1675
ἐκ πατέρων ταύτην ἠινέσαμεν βιοτήν.
5 τῶ τί μεταλλεύεις τοῦτον μυχόν, ὦ φιλόλιχνε,
οὐδ' ἀποδειπνιδίου γευόμενος σκυβάλου;
σπεύδων εἰς ἄλλους οἴκους ἴθι—τἀμὰ δὲ λιτά—
ὧν ἄπο πλειοτέρην οἴσεαι ἀρμαλιήν.   1675

Posidippus   30

—Τίς πόθεν ὁ πλάστης;—Σικυώνιος.—οὔνομα δὴ τίς;
—Λύσιππος.—σὺ δὲ τίς;—Καιρὸς ὁ πανδαμάτωρ.
—τίπτε δ' ἐπ' ἄκρα βέβηκας;—ἀεὶ τροχάω.—τί δὲ ταρσοὺς
ποσσὶν ἔχεις διφυεῖς;—ἵπταμ' ὑπηνέμιος.
5 —χειρὶ δὲ δεξιτερῆι τί φέρεις ξυρόν;—ἀνδράσι δεῖγμα   1680
ὡς ἀκμῆς πάσης ὀξύτερος τελέθω.
—ἡ δὲ κόμη τί κατ' ὄψιν;—ὑπαντιάσαντι λαβέσθαι
νὴ Δία.—τἀξόπιθεν δ' εἰς τί φαλακρὰ πέλει;
—τὸν γὰρ ἅπαξ πτηνοῖσι παραθρέξαντά με ποσσὶν
10 οὔτις ἔθ' ἱμείρων δράξεται ἐξόπιθεν.   1685
—τοὔνεχ' ὁ τεχνίτης σε διέπλασεν;—εἵνεκεν ὑμέων,
ξεῖνε, καὶ ἐν προθύροις θῆκε διδασκαλίην.

29 *AP* 6.302; *HE* 2191–8 (= Leon. 37); *OCT* 2180–7   6 γευσόμενος m
30 *A. Plan.* 275; *HE* 3154–65 (= Pos. 19); *OCT* 1662–73   10 fort. ἐφημερίων   11 τοῖον m   σε d'Orville: με M

Philodemus   31

—Χαῖρε σύ.—καὶ σύ γε χαῖρε.—τί δεῖ σε καλεῖν; —σὲ δέ;
  —μήπω
  τοῦτο φιλοσπούδει.—μηδὲ σύ.—μή τιν' ἔχεις;
—αἰεὶ τὸν φιλέοντα.—θέλεις ἅμα σήμερον ἡμῖν   1690
  δειπνεῖν; —εἰ σὺ θέλεις.—εὖ γε· πόσου παρέσηι;
5 —μηδέν μοι προδίδου.—τοῦτο ξένον.—ἀλλ' ὅσον ἄν σοι
  κοιμηθέντι δοκῆι, τοῦτο δός.—οὐκ ἀδικεῖς.
ποῦ γίνηι; πέμψω.—καταμάνθανε.—πηνίκα δ' ἥξεις;
  —ἦν σὺ θέλεις ὥρην.—εὐθὺ θέλω.—πρόαγε.   1695

Anyte   32

Ἵζευ ἅπας ὑπὸ καλὰ δάφνας εὐθαλέα φύλλα
  ὡραίου τ' ἄρυσαι νάματος ἁδὺ πόμα,
ὄφρα τοι ἀσθμαίνοντα πόνοις θέρεος φίλα γυῖα
  ἀμπαύσηις πνοίαι τυπτόμενα Ζεφύρου.

Philodemus   33

Ἰνοῦς ὦ Μελικέρτα σύ τε γλαυκοῦ μεδέουσα   1700
  Λευκοθέη πόντου, δαῖμον ἀλεξίκακε,
Νηρήιδων τε χοροὶ καὶ κύματα καὶ σύ, Πόσειδον,
  καὶ Θρήϊξ ἀνέμων πρηύτατε Ζέφυρε,
5 ἵλαοί με φέροιτε διὰ πλατὺ κῦμα, φυγόντα
  σῶιον ἐπὶ γλυκερὴν ἠιόνα Πειραέως.   1705

---

31 *AP* 5.46; *GP* 3180–7 (= Philod. 4); *OCT* 4814–21   2 φιλοσπούδει Kaibel:
-δος M   μηδὲ Dübner: μήτε M
32 *AP* 9.313; *HE* 726–9 (= Anyte 16); *OCT* 738–41   1 καλὰ: τῆσδε m
33 *AP* 6.349; *GP* 3274–9 (= Philod. 19); *OCT* 4908–13   1 γλαυκοῦ Reiske:
-κὴ M   3 κυανοχαῖτα Ποσ. F. W. Schmidt   6 γλυκερὴν post d'Orville
(-ρὰν) Kaibel: γλυκὺν M

XXVII

DRINKING-SONG

[Θ] . . . . . .
μηδ᾽ ἀδικεῖν ζήτει, μηδ᾽ ἂν ἀδι[κῆι πρ]οσερίσηις·
φεῦγε φόνους καὶ φεῦγε μάχας, φ[εῖ]σαι διαφρονε[ῖ]ν,
εἰς δ᾽ ὀλίγον πονέσεις, καὶ δεύτερον οὐ μεταμέλῃι.

5   αὔ[λει μοι.

Ἴδες ἔαρ, χειμῶνα, θέρος· ταῦτ᾽ ἐστι διόλου·   1710
ἥλιος αὐτὸς [ἔδυ], καὶ νὺξ τὰ τεταγμέν᾽ ἀπέχει·
μὴ κοπία ζητεῖν πόθεν ἥλιος ἢ πόθε[ν] ὕδωρ,
ἀλλὰ π[ό]θεν τ[ὸ] μύρον καὶ τοὺς στεφάνου[ς] ἀγοράσηις.

10   αὔλει μο[ι.

Κρήνας αὐτορύ[το]υς μέλ[ιτ]ος τρεῖς ἤθελον ἔχειν,   1715
πέντε γαλακτορύτους, οἴνου δέκα, δ[ώδε]κα μύρου,
καὶ δύο πηγαίων ὑδάτων, καὶ τρεῖς χιονέων·
παῖδα κατὰ κρήνην καὶ παρθένον ἤθελον ἔχειν.

15   αὔλει μο[ι.

Λύδιος αὐλὸς ἐμοὶ τὰ δὲ Λύδια παίγματα λύρας   1720
κα[ὶ] Φρύγ[ιο]ς κάλαμος τὰ δὲ ταύρεα τύμπανα πονεῖ·
ταῦτα ζῶν ἀισαί τ᾽ ἔραμαι καὶ ὅταν ἀποθάνω
αὐλὸν ὑπὲρ κεφαλῆς θέτε μοι παρὰ ποσσὶ δὲ λύρα[ν.

20   αὔλει μοι.

Μέτρα τί[ς] ἂν πλούτου, τίς ἀνεύρατο μέτρα πενίας   1725
ἢ τίς ἐν ἀνθρώποις χρυσοῦ πάλιν εὕρατο μέτρον;
νῦν γὰρ ὁ χρήματ᾽ ἔχων ἔτι πλε[ί]ονα χρήματα θέλει,
πλούσιος ὢν δ᾽ ὁ τάλας βασανίζεται ὥσπερ ὁ πένης.

25   αὔλ[ει μοι.

XXVII *P. Oxy.* 1795; suppl. Hunt   5 ταῦτ᾽ Gow: ταῦτ᾽ edd.   7 ἐπέχει
Dawe (cf. LSJ s.v. VI.2)   18 ἔραμαι Hunt: ἐρο- pap.   21 τις² Hunt: παλι (e
u. seq.) pap.

Νεκρὸν ἐάν ποθ' ἴδηις καὶ μνήματα κωφὰ παράγηις   1730
κοινὸν ἔσοπτρον ὁρᾶις· ὁ θανὼν οὕτως προσεδόκα.
ὁ χρό[ν]ος ἐστὶ δάνος, τὸ ζῆν πικρός ἐσθ' ὁ δανίσας,
κἂν τότ' ἀπαιτῆσαί σε θέληι, κλαίων [ἀ]ποδιδοῖς.

30   αὔλει μοι.

Ξέρξης ἦν βασιλε[ὺ]ς ὁ λέγων Διὶ πάντα μερίσαι,   1735
ὃς δυσὶ πηδαλ[ί]ο[ι]ς μόνος ἔσχισε Λήμνιον ὕδωρ.
ὄλβιος ἦν ὁ Μίδας, τρὶς δ' ὄλβιος ἦν ὁ [Κ]ινύρ[α]ς,
ἀλλὰ τίς εἰς 'Αίδα ὀβολοῦ πλέον ἤλυθεν ἔχων;

35   αὔλει μοι.

29 ποτ' Hunt

COMMENTARY

I–IV

Callimachus

Callimachus (c. 305–c. 240 B.C.), son of Battus, most innovative, most polemical, and historically most important of the Hellenistic poets, was born in Cyrene and moved as a young man to Alexandria, where he took a post as schoolmaster. Later he gained employment in the Library (p. 5–6) and produced the Πίνακες, a 120-volume list of the holdings in prose and verse (Pfeiffer, *HCS* 127–34). It seems likely that this huge work was more than a mere catalogue: Callimachus probably concerned himself with writers' biographies and with problems of authenticity, and this in turn must have entailed the use of stylistic and other criteria to form an authoritative judgement of a work's date and authorship. By-products of Callimachus' omnivorous reading in connection with the Πίνακες were various prose treatises (all now lost), including *On games, On winds, Non-Greek customs, Local nomenclature,* Παράδοξα (a collection of astounding facts), *Local month-names, Foundations of islands and cities and their changes of name, On nymphs* and *On birds* (frr. 403–59). At the same time as he was compiling these classificatory works on topography, ethnography, natural history, language and etymology, Callimachus maintained a varied and startlingly original poetic output. By reviving and 'modernizing' old types of poetry and metrical forms long obsolete; by using his immense erudition to cast new light on the mythical and historical subjects which he treated; and by experimenting with novel combinations of metre, dialect and subject-matter – by these means he succeeded in producing a novel, witty, complex, self-consciously 'literary' type of verse in which poetry and learning were inextricably linked. His major works comprised:

Aetia (frr. 1–190; *SH* 238–77), an epic-length elegiac poem in four books on the 'causes'/'origins' of names, customs, rites, etc.: see p. 85–6.

Iambi (frr. 191–225), a collection of 13 poems in various metres (iambic, choliambic, epodic) creatively adapted from the work of Hipponax, a sixth-century Ionian writer of scurrilous anecdote and lampoon (see p. 233–4). The subject-matter, length and dialect of these poems is varied, and the overall impression is of an informal medley. Topics include fable, lampoon, epinician and a description of Phidias' statue of Zeus at Olympia; the collection began and ended with polemical poems on literary matters (see p. 88). Substantial fragments of the *Iambi* survive on papyrus.

Hymns, six in number, Callimachus' only large-scale works to survive complete: see p. 111.

Lyric poems (frr. 226–9), including the *Deification of Arsinoe*, a consolatory court poem in the archebulean metre written after the death of Ptolemy's wife in 270 B.C.

Hecale (frr. 230–377; *SH* 280–91), a hexameter poem of about a thousand lines which gave a new slant to an old tale. Theseus, on his way to slay the savage Marathonian bull, sheltered from the rain in the hut of a poor old woman, Hecale. Returning to thank her after completing his task, he discovered that she had died; in her honour he founded the Attic deme of Hecale and set up a sanctuary to Zeus Hecaleus. The poem thus closed with an αἴτιον; but it seems that the chief emphasis lay neither on that nor on Theseus' heroic struggle with the bull, but on his overnight stay with Hecale – the simple meal which she prepared for him and her garrulous conversation. Considerable fragments of the poem survive, but not enough to establish the details of Callimachus' treatment. The pseudo-Virgilian *Moretum* and Ovid's Baucis and Philemon episode (*Met.* 8.624–724), both directly inspired by the *Hecale*, provide some impression of what must have been the general tone.

Ibis (frr. 381–2), a short vituperative poem, perhaps written in elegiacs, wittily execrating an enemy called by the pseudonym Ibis (after the bird of that name, notorious for its filthy habits). The extant *Ibis* of Ovid seems to be an imitation rather than a translation.

Σωσιβίου νίκη (fr. 384), a victory-ode written in elegiacs, a novel combination.

Epigrams, in various metres – see p. 244–5.

Tragedies, comedies and satyr-plays. Not a single fragment of these survives.

Bibl.: Text: R. Pfeiffer, *Callimachus* (2 vols, Oxford, 1948–53). Gen.: Pfeiffer, *HCS* 123–52; Fraser *passim*; *CHCL* 1 549–70, 815–17; John Ferguson, *Callimachus* (Boston, 1980).

I

The *Aetia*, Callimachus' longest and in ancient times most famous poem, dealt discursively with the 'causes' or 'origins' of various aspects of custom, ritual and nomenclature from all over the Greek world – a complete fusion of poetry and learning. It was an epic-length poem (? 4000–6000 lines) written in elegiacs, a 'single song' which was neither heroic in theme nor 'continuous' (*3–4*), but episodic. Considerable papyrus fragments survive, most of them badly damaged; the poem can be reconstructed only in broad outline. At the beginning of Book I Callimachus made clear his literary affiliations by creatively adapting Hesiod's encounter with the Muses at the start of the *Theogony*. Callimachus pictured himself transported in a dream from his native Libya to Mt Helicon, and Books I and 2 consisted of a dialogue between himself and the learned Heliconian Muses, who replied at length to his antiquarian enquiries. Books 3 and 4 dispensed with the question-and-answer format. This pair of books was framed by references to Berenice, wife of Ptolemy III Euergetes, who acceded to the throne in 246 B.C. Book 3 opened with an elegy commemorating a win at the Nemean Games by Berenice's chariot (*SH* 254–69). This subject led into an αἴτιον of the founding of the games: after he had overcome the Nemean lion Heracles was told to institute them by Athena. Before he set out against the lion Heracles lodged with a poor peasant named Molorchus; and juxtaposed with Heracles' slaying of the lion was a description of Molorchus' attempt to slay his own troublesome beasts, the mice, by the invention of the mousetrap. This unlikely 'aetiology' of a household object was told in counterpoint to the narrative of Heracles' heroic exploit – a witty juxtaposition probably typical for the *Aetia* as a whole. The final αἴτιον of Book 4 was the famous *Lock of Berenice* (Βερενίκης Πλόκαμος), which told how a lock of hair dedicated by the queen (cf. p. 265) was translated to heaven as a star-cluster. Some fragments of this section survive (fr. 110), together with a version by Catullus (poem 66).

We can only guess at the overall effect of the *Aetia*. Propertius' fourth Book and the *Fasti* of Ovid are both directly inspired by the poem; but Ovid's *Metamorphoses* perhaps provides a closer general impression. That work, too, is made up of highly diverse episodes linked by a common theme; and this diversity means that each section can be read in contrast or counterpoint to preceding and following sections. The overall effect is thus one of complex organic unity rather than of unstructured chaos. The most challenging of all Latin poems is also the most thoroughly 'Callimachean'.

Quite how the *Aetia* was published is not clear. The *Coma* seems at one time to have circulated as a separate poem; and it may be that before the final arrangement other αἴτια from Books 3–4 did so too. It is virtually certain that these two books were published later than Books 1–2, perhaps considerably later. At the same time (or possibly later still) Callimachus appears to have revised the *Aetia* and *Iambi*, and perhaps other of his works, for publication in a Collected Edition. At the end of *Aetia* 4 he placed an epilogue to introduce the transition from elegiacs to the Μουσέων πεζὸν ... νομόν, 'the pedestrian pasture of the Muses' (fr. 112.9), a reference to the less 'pretentious' iambic genre (cf. Horace's *Musa pedestris*, *Sat.* 2.6.17). Prefixed to the collection of *Aetia*, *Iambi* and perhaps other works was the *Reply to the Telchines*. This polemical preface is often referred to as 'the prologue to the *Aetia*'; but its content suggests that it was also designed to stand by way of introduction to or apologia for Callimachus' entire poetic oeuvre.

Callimachean poetry and literary polemic. Nowhere is the 'self-conscious' aspect of Callimachus' work more apparent than in his numerous polemical references to the theory and practice of poetry. We know that he wrote a prose treatise *Against Praxiphanes*, a Peripatetic philosopher and literary theorist in the Aristotelian mould. The *Reply*, which is the fullest surviving expression of Callimachus' poetic stance, uses vivid metaphor and imagery to advocate short, sweet, 'naive', refined verse and to deny that length is a valid yardstick for measuring talent. Several other passages throw light on Callimachus' attitude to poetry:

AP 12.43; *HE* 1041–6 (= Call. 2); Pfeiffer 28; *OCT* 1146–51. In this epigram Callimachus expresses his dislike of 'cyclic' epic, i.e. neo-'Homeric' epic on traditional mythological themes:

> Ἐχθαίρω τὸ ποίημα τὸ κυκλικόν, οὐδὲ κελεύθωι
> χαίρω τὶς πολλοὺς ὧδε καὶ ὧδε φέρει·
> μισέω καὶ περίφοιτον ἐρώμενον, οὐδ' ἀπὸ κρήνης
> πίνω· σικχαίνω πάντα τὰ δημόσια.
> Λυσανίη, σὺ δὲ ναίχι καλὸς καλός· ἀλλὰ πρὶν εἰπεῖν
> τοῦτο σαφῶς, Ἠχώ φησί τις "ἄλλος ἔχει".

'I detest the cyclic poem, I do not like the path that carries many to and fro; I hate too the roaming lover, I do not drink at the fountain – I loathe all common things. Lysanias, yes fair you are, how fair – the words are scarcely out, says an echo "he's another's affair" ' – trans. A. W. Bulloch). The joke seems to be that "ἄλλος ἔχει" sounds like an echo of ναίχι καλός; but more important for our purposes is the imagery used here for the well worn themes of cyclic epic: the public road (cf. *25–8*), the promiscuous boy and the public spring. This latter image is related to that of the cicada's diet of dew at *33–4*. In another passage Callimachus further elaborates poetic water-imagery:

> Ὁ Φθόνος Ἀπόλλωνος ἐπ᾽ οὔατα λάθριος εἶπεν·
> "οὐκ ἄγαμαι τὸν ἀοιδὸν ὃς οὐδ᾽ ὅσα πόντος ἀείδει."
> τὸν Φθόνον ὡπόλλων ποδί τ᾽ ἤλασεν ὧδέ τ᾽ ἔειπεν·
> "Ἀσσυρίου ποταμοῖο μέγας ῥόος, ἀλλὰ τὰ πολλὰ
> λύματα γῆς καὶ πολλὸν ἐφ᾽ ὕδατι συρφετὸν ἕλκει.
> Δηοῖ δ᾽ οὐκ ἀπὸ παντὸς ὕδωρ φορέουσι μέλισσαι,
> ἀλλ᾽ ἥτις καθαρή τε καὶ ἀχράαντος ἀνέρπει
> πίδακος ἐξ ἱερῆς ὀλίγη λιβὰς ἄκρον ἄωτον."
>
> *Hymn to Apollo* 105–12

('Envy spoke secretly in Apollo's ear: "I do not admire the poet who does not sing even as much as the sea". Apollo gave Envy a kick with his foot and spoke as follows: "Great is the stream of the Assyrian river, but for much of its course it drags along on its waters filth from the land and much refuse. For Demeter the bees do not bring water from every source, but a small trickle (ὀλίγη λιβάς) which, pure and unsullied, comes up from a holy fountain".') These lines have given rise to much conjecture, and the function of πόντος in the comparison is still debated (see Williams ad loc. for details and bibliography). The basic comparison, however, is between the huge but polluted Euphrates (length, unity, magnitude, access for all and sundry; cf. ἓν ἄεισμα διηνεκές) and individual droplets from the purest spring (polish, refinement, exclusivity, *dis*continuity). This passage has other similarities to the *Reply*: Apollo appears in both, and Φθόνος is reminiscent of the Βασκανίης ὀλοὸν γένος of Callimachus' detractors (*17*).

Fr. 398. In a lost epigram Callimachus referred to Antimachus' *Lyde* using terminology similar to that of *23–4*: Λύδη καὶ παχὺ γράμμα καὶ οὐ τορόν ('*Lyde*, a gross and obscure book'): books, like girls, are better slim (cf. the anecdote about Philetas' λεπτότης, p. 9). For the *Lyde* as canon of taste see *1* and *9–12* nn. and p. 8–9.

Fr. 465 Καλλίμαχος ὁ γραμματικὸς τὸ μέγα βιβλίον ἴσον ἔλεγεν εἶναι τῶι μεγάλωι κακῶι. This *bon mot* ('a big book is a big evil') is unfortunately quoted out of context; but it seems likely that Callimachus was punning, *qua* librarian, on the physical clumsiness of a long papyrus roll and the artistic clumsiness of a long 'cyclic' poem.

Iambus 13 (fr. 203). In this poem Callimachus defended himself against the charge of πολυείδεια, i.e. of writing many different kinds (εἴδη) of poetry. He quoted the example of Ion of Chios, a fifth-century tragedian whose work covered a similarly wide range; and he made the point that a workman is not criticized for producing many different artefacts.

Sources of Callimachus' imagery. The *Reply* and the coda of the *Hymn to Apollo* both introduce vaguely defined malicious objectors (Τελχῖνες, Φθόνος) whose criticisms are triumphantly dismissed. This defensive/ offensive stance owes something to the interest in praise and blame, and the self-consciousness about composition and performance, of earlier lyric poetry. Pindar in his epinicia is much concerned to mention and set aside the spiteful jealousy of those envious of his victors; and, since Pindar is as pre-eminent in his own sphere as his victors are in theirs, it is not surprising that we find him using imagery and simile to refer to the challenges and challengers of his poetry. Particularly suggestive is Pindar's emphasis on brevity, conciseness and compression. Here are a few relevant passages (trans. of the *Odes* by F. J. Nisetich):

Nemean 4.33–41 'But the laws of song and the passing time forbid dwelling on a theme at length (τὰ μακρὰ... ἐξενέπειν)... Come then! though the deep salt sea grip your waist, fight against conspiracy! Mightily will we seem to enter the lists, in daylight, superior to our foes, while another fellow looks about him with envy in his eye (φθονερὰ... βλέπων), fumbling in darkness at an empty thought that tumbles to the ground.'

Nemean 8.19–22 'I stand on light feet now, catching breath before I speak. For there are songs in every style, but to put a new one (νεαρὰ δ' ἐξευρόντα) to the touchstone for testing is all danger. Words are a morsel to the envious (φθονεροῖσιν), and their envy always fastens on the noble, but leaves the base alone.'

Olympian 2.83–9 'There are in my quiver many swift arrows, striking to the wise (συνετοῖσιν), but the crowd need interpreters (or rather, 'there is an absolute need for interpreters'). The man of discernment (σοφός) knows much by nature. Let those who have acquired their knowledge chatter in vain, unruly jackdaws bickering at the majestic eagle of Zeus (κόρακες ὡς ἄκραντα γαρυέτων | Διὸς πρὸς ὄρνιχα θεῖον). It is time we took aim, my heart...' Ancient commentators believed the 'jackdaws' to be Pindar's rivals Simonides and Bacchylides. The bird-imagery here is analogous to *13–14, 29 ff.*

Paean 7 b 10–14 κελαδήσαθ' ὕμνους, Ὁμήρου [δὲ μὴ τρι]πτὸν κατ' ἀμαξιτὸν | ἰόντες, ἀ[λλ' ἀλ]λοτρίαις ἀν' ἵπποις, | ἐπεὶ αὐ[τοὶ ἐς π]τανὸν ἅρμα | Μοισα[ῖον ἀνέβα]μεν. ('Sound forth your songs, travelling not on Homer's well worn path, but with a different horse-team, since we ourselves(?) have mounted the winged chariot of the Muses.') Cf. the passage of Choerilus quoted on p. 1 and *25–8*, where the chariot is driven by the poet.

Pythian 4.247–8 μακρά μοι νεῖσθαι κατ' ἀμαξιτόν· ὥρα | γὰρ συνάπτει καί τινα | οἶμον ἴσαμι βραχύν· πολ- | λοῖσι δ' ἄγημαι σοφίας ἑτέροις ('But it's a long way by the main road, and time presses. I know a certain short cut, for I am a guide to many in the turns of song.') Here the 'main road' represents not trite subject-matter but long-winded narrative; the poet knows the right time to stop. Imagery and vocabulary are closely akin to *25–8*; and σοφία includes the notion of 'poetic skill' as at *18*. It seems, therefore, that Callimachus' polemical stance and his concern with brevity both have precedent in Pindaric lyric. That is not surprising, given his interest in lyric poetry (see p. 84) and his adoption in the *Aetia* and *Hymns* of an allusive, discontinuous form of narrative which has much in common with Pindar's presentation of myth. See further Newman 45–8.

Other metaphors can be paralleled from an unexpected source. The contest between Aeschylus and Euripides in Aristophanes' *Frogs* uses some of the terminology which in the *Reply* might seem most characteristically 'Hellenistic'. Compare, for instance, the bombastic-cum-'sophistic' choral ode which precedes the appearance of the two rival poets (814–29): 'Terrible wrath will the loud-roarer (ἐριβρεμέτης, = Aeschylus) have within him when he sees his rival artificer whetting his chatterbox tusks!... There will be helmet-glancing struggles of horsehaircrest arguments and splinterings near the axle when the fine-chisel-wielder tries to ward off the horse-prancing phrases (ῥήμαθ' ἱπποβάμονα, 821) of the mind-builder! Raising the bristly hair of his shaggy neck, frowning ferociously and bellowing, he will shoot forth phrases fastened with bolts, tearing them up like ship's timbers with gigantic blast of lungs (γηγενεῖ φυσήματι, 825). Then the mouth-worker, the tester of phrases, the smooth tongue, unrolling itself, shaking the bridle of envy (φθονερούς κινοῦσα χαλινούς, 827), will dissect and splinter (καταλεπτολογήσει, 828) the phrases, the large labour of his lungs.' Here both poets are caricatured – Aeschylus as bombastic and ponderous, Euripides as light and subtle. Aeschylus roars and bellows (cf. *19–20*); he is associated with the paraphernalia of war (cf. *3–5*); and he produces a resounding noise (cf. *19*). Euripides is characterized as glib and hair-splitting, a finicky artisan of words who dissects his phrases κατὰ λεπτόν (cf. *11*). The 'catch-word' λεπτός is used of Euripides' techniques also at 876 λεπτολόγους ξυνετὰς φρένας and 956 λεπτῶν... κανόνων εἰσβολάς. It seems probable that λεπτός was first used by the sophists in the sense 'intellectually refined': in the *Clouds* it is applied to Socrates and his pupils, and Euripides himself has it at *Medea* 529 and elsewhere. Cf. p. 137.

Callimachus' humorous concretization of λεπτότης, his 'lean Muse' (*24*), is similar in concept to *Frogs* 939–43, where Euripides describes how he took over the tragic τέχνη from Aeschylus and, treating it like a diseased patient, reduced its 'swelling': 'When I first took over the art from you, swollen with bombast and weighty phrases, I first reduced (ἴσχνανα) her and got rid of her weight with little words (ἐπυλλίοις) and exercise and beetroot [a laxative], administering an infusion of chatter-someness distilled from books'. ἴσχνανα probably alludes to the ἰσχνὸς χαρακτήρ or 'unadorned style' of rhetoric, which used plain words and uncontrived syntax.

There are several other verbal parallels between the two passages. At *Frogs* 785–6 we learn that there is to be a κρίσις... τῆς τέχνης; at 882 the contest is called ἀγὼν σοφίας; and at 799 are mentioned κανόνας... καὶ πήχεις ἐπῶν, 'rulers and measuring-tapes for phrases': cf. *17–18* αὖθι δὲ τέχνηι | κρίνετε,] μὴ σχοίνωι Περσίδι τὴν σοφίην. Further points of resemblance are discussed by F. Cairns, *Tibullus* (Cambridge, 1979) 8–10.

Pfeiffer (*HCS* 137–8) has argued that these similarities are the result of direct borrowing by Callimachus from Aristophanes; and this seems more likely than the assumption that both writers were dependent on sophistic treatises or handbooks of rhetoric. If Pfeiffer is right on this point, Callimachus has appropriated terminology used to satirize

Euripides and, by combining it with the polemical voice of early lyric, has created a wittily triumphant apologia for the 'new poetics'.

The text. The *Reply* survives on a damaged papyrus, which was first published in 1927; but several lines were already known from quotations by ancient grammarians, and others can be supplemented from the fragmentary notes of two papyrus commentaries. In the text printed here half-square brackets (⌊ ⌋) indicate that, although the papyrus is missing or illegible, the text can be certainly supplemented from one of these other sources; full square brackets ([ ]) mark conjectures by modern scholars, many of whom have expended much ingenuity in attempting to provide convincing supplements. Supplementation of an author so unpredictable and so fond of recherché vocabulary is a hazardous business, and it is likely that most of these modern conjectures represent the spirit rather than the letter of what Callimachus wrote. Except at *9–12* (see n.) and *39–40*, however, the sense of the argument seems clear.

Bibl.: *Aetia* in general: Fraser I 718–33, II 1052–8; *CHCL* I 553–9, 815–17; P. J. Parsons, 'Callimachus: Victoria Berenices', *ZPE* 25(1977)1–50 (structure). *Reply*: V. J. Matthews, 'Antimachos in the *Aitia* prologue', *Mnemosyne* ser. 4, 32 (1979) 128–37.

1–7 [1–7] The Telchines ignorantly complain that although Call. is now advanced in years he has not produced a long poem on a single epic / heroic theme in thousands of verses – in other words, although he is a poet of high reputation he has not written a 'major work'. The *Aetia* was indeed thousands of lines long and dealt incidentally with 'the deeds of kings and heroes of old' (3–5, if that is the right supplement); but it was written in elegiacs, it concentrated on aspects other than the 'heroic', and it consisted of a *dis*continuous series of episodes linked thematically rather than chronologically.

1[1] Τελχῖνες: a race of sorcerers generally said to have been inhabitants of Rhodes. As well as being the inventors of metal-working they were said to be spiteful wizards who possessed the evil eye (*oculos . . . uitiantes omnia uisu* Ovid, *Met.* 7.366; cf. *1017–28*n.): they are variously described as βάσκανοι (cf. 17), γόητες (cf. 118), φαρμακεῖς, πανοῦργοι, πονηροί and φθονεροί. For their role in the *Reply* cf. Φθόνος / Μῶμος at *Hymn to Apollo* 105–12 (p. 87); on their fate see *118–23* n. The word Τελχίς was thought to be derived either from θέλγειν, 'bewitch', or from τήκειν, which can be used both of (s)melting metals and of causing someone to pine away (cf. *612*). There is an allusion to this latter ambiguous etymology in line 8. A papyrus commentary puts names to the Telchines and includes amongst them the epigrammatists Asclepiades and Posidippus (both of whom are known to have approved of Antimachus' *Lyde* – see 9-12 n.) and Praxiphanes of Mitylene, against whom Call. published a prose work (p. 86). Asclepiades, however, was almost certainly dead by the time the *Reply* was written; and it seems highly probable that the supposed list of Telchines is in fact a list of writers with whom Call. had disagreed during his long and polemical career. **ἐπιτρύζουσιν** 'mutter at'. The implication is that they spitefully mumble malicious spells; cf. *634*. τρύζειν is a Homeric *hapax* (*Il.* 9.311). **μοι . . . ἀοιδῆι**: it seems most likely that μοι is governed by ἐπι- ('the Telchines mutter at me for my song'); but possibly ἐπι- governs ἀοιδῆι and μοι is a loosely constructed dat. of interest ('the Telchines mutter at my song').

3[3] εἵνεκεν 'because'. Two ancient grammarians cite this line as a solecism: they argue that ἕνεκα is a preposition meaning 'on account of', and that the corresponding conjunction is οὕνεκα, 'on account of the fact that'. However, papyrus and manuscript evidence suggests that both ἕνεκα and οὕνεκα were used for both meanings. For ἕνεκα as a conjunction cf. Hes. fr. 180.10, *Hom. Hymn to Aphrodite* 199, Ap.Rh. 4.1523, Call. *60* and fr. 6. **διηνεκές**, lit. 'continuous', probably implies a single theme treated with smooth narrative progression. Ovid alludes to this concept in his wittily ambiguous description of the *Metamorphoses* as a *perpetuum . . . carmen* (1.4).

3-5[3-5] βασιλ[ήων | πρήξι]ας and **προτέρ]ους ἥρωας** are (if the supplements are right) in apposition to ἓν ἄεισμα διηνεκές.

5[5] ἔπος δ᾽ ἐπὶ τυτθὸν ἐλ[ίσσω seems to mean 'I roll forth my poetry little by little', i.e. on a small scale or episodically. τυτθός is often used of young children, and here looks forward to the simile παῖς ἅτε; thus qualified, the whole phrase can be seen in retrospect to mean, 'I speak in small, childlike sentences'.

7-20[7-20] Call.'s reply to his detractors. Short, highly worked pieces are best; length and bombast are no criteria for poetry.

7[7] καί: in epic καί is sometimes used to introduce words of reply, apparently with the meaning 'in turn': cf. *Il.* 2.336 τοῖσι δὲ καὶ μετέειπε . . . **ἀ[κανθές** 'prickly' – an uncertain conjectural restoration by Pfeiffer. The word is found only in Hesychius, a fifth-century A.D.

lexicographer, who may possibly have drawn his citation from here; but the fact that Antiphanes, a first-century A.D. epigrammatist, calls carping grammarians ἀκανθοβάται, 'treaders on thorns' (*AP* 11.322.2), lends some support to Pfeiffer's supplement. Other derogatory words (e.g. ἄμουσον, ἀλιτρόν, ἄιδρι, ἀηνές) are equally possible.

8[8] See 1 n. The legendary Telchines were named after their ability to (s)melt metals; Call.'s detractors can 'melt' nothing but their own hearts (sc. with impotent jealousy). **ἧπαρ:** lit. 'liver'; often of the seat of passions in Greek poetry = Eng. 'heart' (cf. *508, 1273–4*).

9–12 [9–12] '... of few lines; but bountiful Demeter far outweighs the long...; and of the two the fine-spun..., not the large woman, have taught that Mimnermus is a sweet poet.' The papyrus commentary says that Call. here mentions short poems by Mimnermus (the sixth-century 'inventor' of amatory elegy) and Philetas, but it does not resolve the problems of the passage. Most critics have favoured one or other of the following lines of approach: (1) Short poems by Mimnermus and Philetas are judged superior to their long poems. In this case ὄμπνια Θεσμοφόρος must refer to Philetas' famous *Demeter* (p. 9), and a reference to a long Philetan poem should be supplied at the beginning of line 10. No likely candidate is known; but Maas's conjecture γρηῦν] ('the long old woman') assumes a long elegy on the death of Bittis, Philetas' mistress. On this hypothesis αἱ κατὰ λεπτὸν | ῥήσιες] would refer to Mimnermus' shorter, 'slender' poems and ἡ μεγάλη γυνή to a long elegy, perhaps the famous Nanno, named after his mistress. τοῖν δὲ] δυοῖν would refer to these two classes of Mimnermus' poetry. (2) Short poems by Philetas and Mimnermus are judged superior to long poems by *other* poets. In this case γρηῦν] might refer to Antimachus' *Lyde* (p. 8–9); or e.g. θεῦν] might be supplied, referring to the same author's *Artemis* (fr. 75 Wyss). ὄμπνια Θεσμοφόρος would still refer to Philetas' *Demeter*; in line 12 e.g. Κώιαι] would have to be supplied, referring to Philetas' 'slender' Coan poems, characterized as slim girls in contrast to 'the large woman' of (?again) Antimachus' *Lyde*, which Call. elsewhere described as a 'fat book' (fr. 398 – see p. 87). τοῖν δὲ] δυοῖν would then mean 'of the two ⟨poets⟩', i.e. of these two (Philetas and Antimachus), both of whom wrote in the elegiac tradition of Mimnermus, it was Philetas who taught how 'sweet' Mimnerman poetry could be.

Further uncertainties: (1) We cannot be sure that ὀλιγόστιχος refers to Call., since ἔην (if that is the right reading) could be third rather than first person singular. It might, for instance, refer to Philetas, the subject of the next sentence: Κῷος δὴ γὰρ] ἔην has been suggested. But the egocentric tone of the poem so far tells against this. (2) Housman's conjecture δρῦν] in line 10 raises another possibility: 'Bountiful Demeter far outweighs the tall oak tree' could be the first in the series of metaphors and images describing long and short poems which takes up much of the rest of the *Reply*. Call. might be saying 'My poems are indeed short; but Demeter's harvest is far better than acorns, even if they are the fruit of an impressively tall tree'. In this case the comparison between long and short poems by Mimnermus and Philetas, or between Philetas and Antimachus as followers of Mimnermus – (1) and (2) above – would be restricted to lines 11–12. Alternatively, ὄμπνια Θεσμοφόρος might still refer to Philetas' *Demeter* and δρῦν ... μακρήν to some long poem of his of which no mention has survived.

The text printed here is based on hypothesis (1), which at least has the advantage of simplicity; but the evidence does not permit of a definite conclusion. For a fuller discussion see V. J. Matthews, art. cit. (p. 91).

9[9] ὀλιγόστιχος: if this word does indeed refer to Call. (see previous n.), what does it mean? How can he describe himself as 'of few lines' in a poem prefixed to the *Aetia*, which amounted to at least 4000 verses? The answer may be that the *Aetia* consisted of many sections, each in itself brief and condensed; but this is not a very satisfactory explanation.

10[10] ὄμπνια: a cult epithet of Demeter (ὄμπη = 'corn'). **Θεσ-μοφόρος:** Demeter was supposedly so-called either because she set up laws (θεσμοί) after introducing agriculture or because inscribed bronze tablets recording the law were set up (τιθέναι) in her temple. The true etymology may be connected with the fact that at Thesmophoric festivals pig-meat was deposited (τιθέναι) in pits and carried (φορεῖν) in procession.

13–16[13–16] 'Let the crane, delighting in the Pygmies' blood, fly far from Egypt to the Thracians, and let the Massagetae shoot far at the Mede; but poems are sweeter *this* (i.e. *my*) way.' The emphasis is on length (μακρόν 13(?), 15); and, if Housman's ἁ[ηδονίδες] is right, the contrast is between on the one hand the far-flying cranes and arrows and on the other Call.'s delicate 'nightingales' (cf. p.249 on ἀηδόνες). Homer refers to the battle of the cranes and Pygmies, comparing the birds' noisy migratory formation to the oncoming Trojan battle-line (*Il.* 3.3–7). The origin of the legend is not known. The Massagetae were a tribe of archer-warriors living east of the Caspian Sea; they defeated and killed Cyrus, king of the Medes and Persians, in battle; cf. Herod. 1.204–16.

15[15] καί: postponed. In Classical literature it is extremely rare for καί = 'and' not to be first word in its clause (Denniston, *GP* 325–7); but with Hellenistic poets its postponement is something of an affectation (cf. *55*, *714*, *883*, *1049*(?), *1230*).

17[17] ἔλλετε: this is presumably intended to be a variant form of ἔρρετε, 'begone!'; but -ρρ- and -λλ- are not interchangeable elsewhere in Greek, and other verbs of stem ἐλλ- are cognate with ἱλάσκομαι: see LSJ s.v. *ῖλημι. At fr. 7.13 Call. has ἔλλατε = 'be gracious!'; but that meaning is hardly suitable here. **Βασκανίης:** ι n. **αὖθι:** Call. uses this word with the meaning '(t)hereafter': see LSJ s.v. αὖθις II.3.

18[18] σχοίνωι Περσίδι 'the Persian chain', a land-measure used in Egypt (probably about 6–7 miles). **τὴν σοφίην:** poetic skill. Cf. Pind. *Ol.* 1.116, *Pyth.* 4.247–8 (p. 89), 6.49, etc.

19[19] διφᾶτε 'expect to find'. διφᾶν is an Ionic verb implying diligent search; it is a Homeric *hapax* (*Il.* 16.747).

21–8[21–8] Apollo advised the young Call. to keep his Muse lean and to follow untrodden paths.

21[21] δέλτον: it is interesting that Call. describes himself as composing stylus-in-hand, wax tablet on his knees: not for him the affectation of vatic inspiration. Cf. *131* n. **ἐπὶ . . . ἔθηκα:** tmesis.

22[22] Ἀπόλλων εἶπεν ὅ μοι Λύκιος: by placing the pronoun between def. art. and adj. Call. is perhaps stressing the intimate link between himself and 'my Lycian Apollo', who, according to one aetiology of the epithet, turned himself into a wolf (λύκος) and mated with Cyrene, the eponymous nymph of Call.'s native city. Usually the words are taken to = Ἀπόλλων ὁ Λύκιος εἶπέ μοι; but the displacement here cannot be classed with the regular attraction of enclitic pronouns to *second* place in a sentence (for which cf. 25(?), *283* ἐν δέ σε Παρρασίηι Ῥείη τέκεν).

24[24] ὠγαθέ 'my good fellow' – an affectionate address often used in Platonic dialogues to introduce a gentle remonstrance or imperative. **λεπταλέην:** at its only occurrence in Homer this word describes a 'delicate' voice (*Il.* 18.571).

25[25] πρός: adv., 'in addition'. **μή:** the normal negative word for the indicative in indefinite relative clauses ('whatever ground there may be over which...'): Goodwin, *GMT* § 525. **πατέουσιν** 'trample': elsewhere only of humans or animals. Call. has probably used this word here because in its metaphorical senses it represents what is trite (*tritum* < *tero*), ground which has been 'gone over' many times: in later Greek τὸ πεπατημένον = 'a hackneyed expression', and already in Aristophanes (*Birds* 471) οὐδ' Αἴσωπον πεπάτηκας = 'your copy of Aesop isn't well thumbed'.

26[26] καθ' ὁμά: lit. 'along the same', here used prepositionally + acc. ἴχνια, 'along the tracks of others'.

27[27] ἀλλὰ κελεύθους: i.e. ἀλλὰ ⟨δίφρον ἐλᾶν ἀνά⟩ κελεύθους ἀτρίπτους.

28[28] εἰ καί 'even though': LSJ s.v. καί B.8. **στεινοτέρην:** sc. κέλευθον: acc. of extent, with ἐλάσεις intrans.

29–36[29–36] Call. wishes to be like the delicate, tuneful cicada, favourite of the Muses (Plato, *Phaedrus* 259 b–d), which was believed to feed only on air and / or dew (see Gow on Theoc. 4.16) and to shed old age together with its skin. Call.'s literary opponents are characterized as braying asses. A fable of Aesop (278 Chambry) told how a foolish ass, aspiring to a voice as sweet as the cicada's, pined away and died on a diet of dew.

29–30[29–30] οἳ . . . ὄνων: the construction is similar to that in 11–12: ἐφίλησαν is to be supplied in the first clause from οὐκ ἐφίλησαν in the second.

30[30] θόρυβον: elsewhere always of *human* uproar, tumult and confusion: cf. on 25 πατέουσιν. **ἐφίλησαν:** Greek sometimes uses the aor. to describe a state resulting from a specific past action: cf. *Il.* 3.415 τὼς δέ σ' ἀπεχθήρω ὡς νῦν ἔκπαγλ' ἐφίλησα, 5.423.

31[31] πανείκελον 'altogether like', here adverbial. **ὀγκήσαιτο:** the spondaic fifth foot creates a dragging effect, reproducing the ass's clumsy bray. There is probably a pun on ὄγκος, which is Greek for a lofty or bombastic style.

32[32] οὐλ[α]χύς = ὁ ἐλαχύς.

33[33] ἃ πάντως 'yes indeed!', lit. 'ah! entirely'.

33–5[33–5] The syntax of this fervent wish is confused. We have in effect two ἵνα-clauses, probably not parallel in construction. The objects of the participle ἔδων and the verb ἐκδύοιμι are stated first (γῆρας, δρόσον), then resumed in reverse order by demonstrative pronouns (ἥν (for τήν), τό), so that the sense is ἵνα ἀείδω ἔδων τὴν μὲν δρόσον, πρώκιον εἶδαρ, ἐκ δίης ἠέρος, ἵνα δὲ τὸ γῆρας αὖθι ἐκδύοιμι. (The alternation of subj. and opt. in final clauses is found in Homer and elsewhere: K.–G. II 387–8.) On this reading ἀείδω is absolute and δρόσον is the object of ἔδων, πρώκιον εἶδαρ being in apposition to δρόσον; ἐκ δίης ἠέρος is to be taken with either ἔδων or εἶδαρ. It might be objected that both natural word-order and parallelism between the two clauses should lead us to read δρόσον as object of ἀείδω; and the notion of 'singing dew', i.e. singing finely and purely like dew, gains some support (1) from Call.'s poetic image of the fine spray (ὀλίγη λιβάς) from the pure spring at *Hymn to Apollo* 112 (p. 87), and (2) from e.g. Persius, *prol.* 13–14 *coruos poetas et poetridas picas | cantare credas Pegaseium nectar.* But *cantare nectar* is a more readily intelligible expression than δρόσον ἀείδω; and on the whole this explanation seems less likely.

34[34] ἐκ δίης ἠέρος: a variation on the Homeric phrase αἰθέρος ἐκ δίης (*Il.* 16.365).

35[35] αὖθι 'forthwith', a meaning not given by LSJ. Cf. *345.* **ὅσσον** is displaced from its natural position at the beginning of 36.

35–6[35–6] Enceladus, a giant who joined in battle against the gods, was struck down by Zeus's thunderbolt and buried under Sicily: see Virg. *Aen.* 3.578–82. Call.'s lines are inspired by Eur. *H.F.* 637 ff. ἄχθος δὲ τὸ γῆρας αἰεὶ βαρύτερον Αἴτνας σκοπέλων ἐπὶ κρατὶ κεῖται . . .

36[36] τριγλώχιν 'three-cornered', nom. Ancient grammarians often vouch for the existence of alternative nom. forms in -ιν for nouns and adjs. in -ις; but very few are actually attested in surviving texts.

37–8[37–8] 'But never mind! ⟨sc. about being old⟩. For those they looked on not-askance as children the Muses do not reject as friends when they are old.' Call. may not have the cicada's ability to shed old age, but he is still favoured with poetic inspiration. These lines echo the opening of the poem (Μοῦσαι ~ 2 Μούσηις, παῖδας ~ 6 παῖς ἅτε, φίλους ~ 2 φίλοι). They are based on Hesiod's description of the good king, whom the Muses make persuasive speech: ὅντινα τιμήσουσι Διὸς κοῦραι μεγάλοιο | γεινόμενόν τε ἴδωσι . . . (*Theog.* 81–2). 'Just as the evil eye harms, so the eye of a favourable deity directed upon a man, especially at his birth, brings him fortune' (West ad loc.). The Muses' look of favour thus contrasts with the βασκανίη of Call.'s detractors (17); and the echo of Hesiod looks forward to his appearance at the beginning of the *Aetia* proper (fr. 2). Cf. Horace, *Odes* 4.3.

37[37] οὐ νέμεσις 'never mind!', lit. 'not a cause for anger'. **ὄθματι:** an Aeolic form of ὄμμα used several times elsewhere by Call.

38[38] μή: the regular negative for nouns and adjs. in generic statements: LSJ s.v. B.7. **λοξῶι**: often of sidelong glances of disfavour, suspicion, anger, etc. (cf. the Homeric ὑπόδρα ἰδών). **ἀπέθεντο**: gnomic aor. **φίλους** really belongs with ὅσους.

39–40[39–40] These lines are very badly damaged, and even the sense is uncertain. The text printed here assumes an allusion to the 'swansong' of Apollo's sacred bird, which was reputed to sing most beautifully and vigorously just before its death.

The Reply and Latin programmatic poetry. It is beyond the scope of this book to investigate the influence of 'Alexandrianism' on Roman poetry, an influence clearly visible at least as early as Ennius, who was writing some 40 years after Callimachus' death. Catullus emphatically states his allegiance in the opening lines of his dedicatory poem: *cui dono lepidum nouum libellum | arida modo pumice expolitum?* His book is new / original (*nouum*) and small (*libellum*, diminutive), freshly (*modo*) 'polished up' both literally and metaphorically; and it seems likely that *lepidum* has been chosen because its l-p-d consonant sequence is reminiscent of the word λεπτόν.

More specifically, the *Reply* and the coda of the *Hymn to Apollo* (p. 87) are, directly or indirectly, sources for much 'programmatic' imagery in Augustan poetry; and the *Reply* in particular lies behind the Roman poets' *recusationes*. Opinions differ over the extent to which Virgil, Horace and Propertius were under pressure to extol in epic verse the great achievements of Augustus. It is possible to read their *recusationes* primarily as ingenious variations on a theme – a theme which does however reflect general expectation of a great poem on Roman affairs. More recently some scholars have begun to emphasize the influence which Maecenas may have been able to exert on Horace and Propertius. Callimachus, too, relied on patronage and wrote what might be termed 'court poetry' (cf. p. 84 on the *Deification of Arsinoe*, p. 85 on the *Lock of Berenice*, *352–63*, *1646–57*). The kings whose deeds he declines to describe are probably the kings of myth, and his objections are directed not at the subject-matter as such, but at the way it is treated in contemporary poetry. For Augustan poets, on the other hand, *proelia* meant primarily historical events of the recent past. They adapted Callimachean terminology accordingly:

Virgil, *Ecl.* 6.3–5 *cum canerem reges et proelia, Cynthius aurem | uellit et* admonuit: 'pastorem, Tityre, pingues|pascere oportet ouis, deductum dicere carmen'. Virgil declines to celebrate Varus' military exploits, saying that Apollo has advised him to compose a 'fine-spun song'. These lines owe something to the shepherd Hesiod's encounter with the Muses on Mt Helicon (*Theog.* 22–34); but in expression they are a direct adaptation of *3–4* and *21–4* (*deductum* = λεπταλέην). Callimachus' unspecified 'sacrificial victim' (θύος, *23*) becomes the pastoral *ouis*. (The contrast between slender Muse and fat victim lies behind the concluding lines of the *Eclogues* (10.70–7), where 70 *haec sat erit, diuae, uestrum cecinisse poetam* contrasts with 77 *ite domum saturae, uenit Hesperus, ite capellae*: by ending here the Eclogue-book remains λεπτός, though the goats are by now fed fat. Still more clearly 'programmatic' is the close of the third *Eclogue* (111) *claudite iam riuos, pueri: sat prata biberunt.*)

Horace, *Sat.* 1.10.31–9. Horace says that Quirinus appeared to him *cum Graecos facerem . . . uersiculos* (cf. Virgil's *cum canerem reges et proelia, Ecl.* 6.3) and advised him not to 'bring wood to the forest' (the opposite of originality). Horace refers to his own poetry as 'play' and makes a slighting reference to long poems by M. Furius Bibaculus ('Alpinus') on Caesar's Gallic campaign and on Ethiopia: *turgidus Alpinus iugulat dum Memnona dumque|defingit Rheni luteum caput, haec ego ludo* (36–7) – great deeds and a muddied river are contrasted with 'slight' poetry. A poet should be *contentus paucis lectoribus* (74). Horace writes for the discriminating few (76–92).

Horace, *Sat.* 2.1.10–20. The jurist Trebatius advises Horace to abandon satire and *Caesaris inuicti res dicere* (11); but the poet evasively replies that he will treat such subjects *cum res ipsa feret* (18).

Horace, *Odes* 1.6. Horace professes himself unable to sing of Agrippa's victories and says that Varius is better equipped to write such a poem in Homeric vein.

Horace, *Odes* 2.12. Horace recommends Maecenas to write a prose history of Augustus' achievements; his own muse is fit to tell only the violence of love, not the violence of war.

Horace, *Odes* 4.2. This poem characterizes Pindar as the swan, sublime in subject-matter and expression, who *deos regesque canit* (13); Horace himself is like a bee which labours painstakingly on a small scale: *operosa paruus|carmina fingo* (31–2). The conquests of Augustus are not material for such a slight talent. (Pindar had already compared his own poetry to a flitting bee, and in Horace's poem the contrast is not to Pindar's disadvantage; but the way in which it is presented is reminiscent of Callimachus' contrast between ass and cicada, large-scale and small-scale verse.)

Horace, *Epist.* 2.1.245–70. Horace apologizes to Augustus for not being able to write about *res... gestas* (251) and other 'bombastic' topics: Virgil and Varius, he says, are better equipped for such a task. Were he to try himself, the result would be a miserable failure.

Propertius 2.1. In the opening elegy of Book 2 Propertius addresses Maecenas and says that if he were capable of writing epic he would sing not mythological themes but *bellaque resque... Caesaris* (25). But, he goes on, *neque Phlegraeos Iouis Enceladique tumultus* (cf. *35–6*) | *intonet* (cf. *20* βροντᾶν) *angusto* (= λεπτῶι) *pectore Callimachus,| nec mea conueniunt duro praecordia uersu | Caesaris in Phrygios condere nomen auos* (39–42). Callimachus' *pectus* is *angustum* in the sense that, being slender, it is not capable of a μέγα ψοφέουσαν ἀοιδήν (*19*). In the following lines Propertius further exploits this metaphor: *nos contra angusto uersamus proelia lecto* (45): his 'battles' take place in a 'narrow bed', 'narrow' in part because the poetry in which he describes his bed-campaigning is itself λεπτός.

Propertius 2.10. Propertius affects to be about to abandon love-poetry and to write a *magni ... oris opus* (12) about *tumultus* and *bella* (7–8) and the achievements of Augustus. At line 19, however, the poem moves into the future tense, and it transpires that these *will* be his subjects when his poetic powers are strong enough to sustain them. For the moment, he says, *pauperibus sacris uilia tura damus* (24).

Propertius 3.1. Propertius declares his allegiance to the *Callimachi manes et Coi sacra Philitae* (1) and uses more Callimachean programmatic imagery: 3 *puro de fonte sacerdos*, 5 *carmen tenuastis*, 8 *exactus tenui pumice uersus eat* (< Cat. 1.1–2), 14 *non datur ad Musas currere lata uia*, 18 *intacta ... uia*, 21 *inuida turba*, 38 *Lycio uota probante deo* (<22). In a tone of triumphant self-confidence he rejects Roman themes (15–16) and prophesies the future fame of his own poetry.

Propertius 3.3. Propertius says he dreamt that he was about to apply his lips to the large fountain from which Ennius had drunk in order to write epic on Roman themes; but that just in time Apollo warned him off. The idea of the dream is derived from the opening lines of *Aetia* Book I (see p. 85), imitated by Ennius at the beginning of his *Annals*; and Apollo's speech is full of Callimachean imagery: *quid tibi cum tali, demens, est flumine?* (15), *mollia sunt paruis prata terenda rotis* (18). Apollo points out to the poet a *noua... semita* (26); and the Muse Calliope, after warning him against epic subjects, symbolically wets his lips with *Philitea ... aqua* (52).

Propertius 3.9. Propertius says that he is willing to venture outside his usual poetic range and to write on mythological and patriotic subjects – provided that Maecenas, who is urging him to such a course, will venture outside his own *tenues ... umbras* (29), within which at present he leads a life free from the cares of state. Otherwise, says Propertius, *inter Callimachi sat erit placuisse libellos | et cecinisse modis, Coe poeta, tuis* (43–4).

Propertius 4.1. In the opening elegy of Book 4 Propertius announces his intention to sing Roman themes and earn an immortal name: *exiguo quodcumque e pectore riui | fluxerit, hoc patriae seruiet omne meae ... ut nostris tumefacta superbiat Vmbria libris, | Vmbria Romani patria Callimachi* (59–60, 63–4); his subjects will be similar to those of the *Aetia*: *sacra deosque* (*diesque* MSS) *canam et cognomina prisca locorum* (69). At this point he is interrupted by the astrologer Horus, who reminds him that when he was a youth confined within *tenues ... lares* (128) Apollo gave him good advice: *tum tibi pauca suo de carmine dictat Apollo | et uetat insano uerba tonare foro* (133–4). The advice was that Propertius should write about the *militia Veneris* (137).

Ovid, *Amores* 1.1 Ovid introduces the first book of his *Amores* with a witty parody of the *recusatio*: he was, he says, preparing to sing of *arma ... uiolentaque bella* (1), but Cupid stole away a foot, making his verse the non-heroic elegiac couplet. After a mock-indignant protestation the poet can only exclaim *ferrea cum uestris bella ualete modis* (28).

Ovid, *Amores* 3.1. In the introductory elegy of Book 3 Ovid elaborates the idea of 'odd feet': a lame Elegia competes for the poet's attentions with grave Tragoedia. Elegy wears a *uestis tenuissima* (9), and her odd feet make her particularly attractive. Tragedy is stately in appearance and advises *cane facta uirorum* (25); Ovid's muse has 'played' long enough (27). Ovid intervenes. He feels Tragedy inspiring him with *magnus in ore sonus* (64); but he respectfully asks for, and is granted, a short time longer for elegy: the line *tu labor aeternus; quod petit illa, breue est* (68) plays on the meanings 'short in duration' and 'short in length'.

Bibl.: Newman *passim*; W. Clausen, 'Callimachus and Roman poetry', *G.R.B.S.* 5 (1964) 181–96.

II

Better preserved than most *Aetia*-fragments are two sections from the story of Acontius and Cydippe, which formed a substantial part of Book 3. Missing portions can be supplemented from a prose summary by the fifth-century A.D. epistolographer Aristaenetus. No αἴτιον seems to have been pointed explicitly (cf., however, *105–6*): this is an elegant and allusive love-story of a type perhaps pioneered by Philetas (p. 9). Callimachus tells how the desirable Cean youth Acontius fell in love with the Naxian Cydippe, daughter of Ceyx, when he saw her at a Delian festival. Acontius had himself rejected many male suitors; now he felt what it was to experience ἔρως. At the Delian temple of Artemis he contrived to throw in front of Cydippe an apple (traditional Greek love-token) in which he had cut the words 'I swear by Artemis to marry Acontius'. Cydippe read out the inscription and threw the apple away, realizing that she had bound herself unwittingly with an oath. Back home in Naxos Ceyx arranged a marriage for her; but three times she was taken violently ill just before the wedding day. Ceyx learned the cause of her illness from the Delphic oracle. On Apollo's advice he sent for Acontius, who had been wandering disconsolately through the Cean countryside, and allowed Cydippe to fulfil her vow of marriage.

Such is the basic story; but a bare summary gives no impression of Callimachus' narrative, which is constantly moving away from the romantic details of the tale to points of genealogy, topography, science and myth (*51–4*, *58–63*, *67*, *76–9*, *84–5*, *88–91*, *98–101*); and the section closes with a discursive treatment of early Cean history summarized from the historian Xenomedes (*107–31*), whom Callimachus openly acknowledges as his source. The overall effect, therefore, is one of an irrepressibly exuberant and self-consciously learned narrator who is constantly playing (παῖς ἄτε, *6*) with his reader, challenging him to keep pace along allusive and difficult by-ways (*27–8*). It is highly appropriate that lines *76–91*, an elaborate tissue of recondite allusions, should be spoken by Apollo, god of poetry, prime advocate of Callimachean poetics (cf. *23–30*, *Hymn to Apollo* fin., p. 87).

Bibl.: F. Cairns, *Tibullus* (Cambridge, 1979) 115–20; E. J. Kenney, 'Virgil and the elegiac sensibility', *I.C.S.* 8.1 (1983) 44–59.
> Cf. Ovid, *Heroides* 20–1.

1–4[41–4] Love always finds a way (a reference to the trick with the apple). Acontius was a παῖς, hence inexperienced.

2[42] παῖς ἐπὶ παρθενικῆι: dat. of the object *upon* which his blazing love was concentrated. The prep. is displaced from its natural position before καλῆι to emphasize by juxtaposition the youth of boy and girl.

3[43] τέχνην: with ἐδίδαξεν (double acc.). ἔσκε: epic imperf. form of εἰμί (cf. *284, 1085*). πολύκροτος 'a trickster', lit. 'much wrought' – a controversial word, since some ancient scholars read πολύκροτον for πολύτροπον in the first line of the *Odyssey*.

3–4[43–4] ὄφρα . . . κουρίδιον: this whole sentence is awkward, and it may well be corrupt. One would expect the sense to be 'so that for his ⟨whole⟩ life he might be called "wedded husband" ⟨sc. of Cydippe⟩'; but then nom. κουρίδιος would be needed. It seems just possible that λέγο[ιτο (not a certain reading) means 'choose' rather than 'be called': 'so that he might choose for himself (i.e. gain) for his ⟨whole⟩ life this name: "wedded husband"'. Neither of these explanations is very convincing.

5–6[45–6] ἄναξ . . . Κύνθιε: Apollo, who was born on Mt Cynthus in Delos.

5[45] Ἰουλίδος: Iulis was one of the four major Cean towns (see *124–8*). ἀπό: the prep. governs both nouns: cf. *1186* χθόνα καὶ κατὰ πόντον.

6[46] Δήλωι: Ceos is about 50 miles NW of Delos, Naxos about 25 miles SE. An international festival (πανηγυρίς) with sacrifices (βουφονίη) and celebrations was periodically held there in honour of Apollo. Festivals provided a rare opportunity for young women to appear in public and hence for young men to fall in love: cf. Theoc. 2.66 (= *638*) with Gow's n., *1426*. Many plots of the New Comedy were based on such encounters.

7[47] αἷμα τὸ μέν: αἷμα is sometimes used for a descendant or blood relation (cf. *478*). The expected word-order would be τὸ μὲν αἷμα (Acontius) ⟨ἦν⟩ γεν. Εὐξ., τὸ δὲ (Cydippe) Προμηθίς; but for the second element Call. reverts to natural gender. γενεῆς Εὐξαντίδος: when the gods destroyed Ceos in order to punish the hybristic Telchines (*118–23* n.) only Macelo and her daughter Dexithea survived. Dexithea later married Minos and bore him Euxantius, who recolonized the island. Προμηθίς 'a descendant of Promethus', who fled Athens and settled in Naxos after killing his brother Damasichthon. The pair were sons of Codrus, king of Athens: hence Κοδρείδης in *86*.

8[48] ἀστέρες: Greek, like English, uses 'star' of a person of outstanding beauty or talent: cf. *155–6* n., *1620–1*.

9[49] ὀλίγην ἔτι 'while she was still a small girl'.

10[50] ἐδνῆστιν 'bride for whom a dowry (ἕδνον) must be paid' – not found elsewhere. They promised dowries of 'horned oxen'.

11–14[51–4] 'For no other girl with a face (ῥέθος acc. of respect) more like dawn than she (κείνης) came to the moist rock of hairy old Silenus.' Nothing is known of Silenus' Rock; it was presumably honoured in some way by the girls of Naxos.

11[51] γάρ: it is a mannerism of Call. to postpone particles: cf. *24*, *66*, *84*, *90* and *15* n. **ἐπὶ λασ-**: such lengthening of a short final vowel before a liquid consonant in the next word is familiar from Homer, but very rare in Hellenistic elegiacs (West, *GM* 157).

12[52] Σιληνοῦ: an ugly old satyr-like figure, not associated particularly with Naxos. See Coleman on Virg. *Ecl.* 6.13–14 for a discussion of his magical powers, etc. **πιδυλίδα**: attested only in the glossary of Hesychius, who defines it as πέτρα ἐξ ἧς ὕδωρ ῥεῖ (πιδύω = 'gush forth'). The word is a conjectural restoration by Pfeiffer for the papyrus' πηγυλίδα, 'frost'.

13[53] μάλιον: Ionic form of μᾶλλον.

13–14[53–4] Ἀριήδης ... | εὐδούσης: Ariede is a Cretan form of the name Ariadne: another philologically controversial word (cf. πολύκροτος, *43* n.), since Zenodotus wished to read Ἀριήδηι for Ἀριάδνηι at *Il.* 18.592. Ariadne, daughter of Minos, accompanied Theseus from Crete after he had killed with her assistance her half-brother, the Minotaur; but he abandoned her as she slept on the seashore at Naxos. These circumstances, and her subsequent rescue by Dionysus, were no doubt celebrated in the χορός referred to here. Cf. Cat. 64.50–264.

14[54] ἐς χορόν: with ἔθηκε πόδα.

After a few badly damaged lines the papyrus breaks off; the narrative of Acontius falling in love and his trick with the apple is lost. A fragment of another papyrus begins with Cydippe at home in Naxos on the eve of her arranged marriage.

1–3[55–7] 'The maiden had already slept with the boy ...': εὐνάζομαι, lit. 'go to bed', is sometimes used in epic as a euphemism for sexual intercourse; and we assume that κούρωι refers to Cydippe's intended husband (cf. κουρίδιον, *44*). Only a reader learned in Naxian marriage-ritual would avoid this momentary false alarm: κούρωι means '*a* boy', not '*the* boy', and the reference is to a custom (τέθμιον ... προνύμφιον) which required a girl to sleep on the night before her wedding with a boy under the age of puberty both of whose parents were living (ἀμφιθαλεῖ, lit. 'flourishing on both sides').

2[56] τέθμιον: Ionic for θέσμιον.

3[57] τᾶλιν: an originally Aeolic word for 'bride', found only here and at Soph. *Ant.* 629.

4–9[58–63] The Naxians explained their custom as a reminiscence of the premarital intercourse of Zeus and Hera (*Il.* 14.294–6 & schol.). The claim to know 'even how Zeus married Hera' seems to have been proverbial for a know-all in Greece (Theoc. 15.64); but Call.'s researches have revealed details of greater intimacy still. Just as he is about to relate this αἴτιον, however, the poet pulls himself up short in mock horror at his lack of discretion (for the technique cf. Pind. *Ol.* 1.52). Knowledge is a dangerous thing when combined with garrulity. The problem is when to stop, what to leave unsaid. The *Aetia* is a poem whose raison d'être is to provide answers; but some things are best left unexplained.

4[58] Ἥρην γάρ κοτέ φασι- 'for they say that once upon a time Hera−': for the learned reader these words are of course enough to suggest the suppressed αἴτιον. **κύον, κύον:** a common insult, implying 'shamelessness or audacity' (LSJ s.v. II).

5[59] τά περ οὐχ ὁσίη 'what it is not right ⟨to sing⟩'.

6[60] ὤναο κάρθ' 'very lucky for you', lit. 'you have great profit' (aor. mid. of ὀνίνημι). **ἕνεκ'** 'because': see *3* n. **θεῆς . . . ἱερὰ φρικτῆς:** the mysteries of Demeter held at Eleusis in Attica. Initiates were forbidden to reveal the rites. **φρικτῆς:** lit. 'to be shuddered at' (<φρίσσω).

7[61] 'Since you would have spewed forth the story of those, too' – **ἐξ . . . ἤρυγες** (tmesis) is aor. of ἐξερυγγάνω; in poetry the cognate verb (ἐξ)ἐρεύγομαι is commoner.

8[62] ὅστις: translate 'for the man who...' – a slight anacoluthon of a type regular in Classical prose and verse. **ἀκαρτεῖ:** Ionic form of ἀκρατεῖ, 'has no control of...' (+gen.). A play on κάρθ' (*60*).

9[63] ὡς . . . ἔχει 'really such a person is a child with a knife', lit. 'how truly this child has a knife' – a reference to the proverb μὴ παιδὶ μάχαιραν (sc. δίδου). **μαῦλιν:** a recherché synonym for μάχαιραν.

10–21[64–75] Back to the main story. Three times preparations were made for the wedding; three times Cydippe fell ill, with epilepsy, a fever and a chill. Her father consulted the Delphic oracle.

10–11[64–5] 'The oxen were about to rend their hearts at dawn, seeing the sharp knife in the water.' Before being sacrificed the victim was sprinkled with lustral water from a bowl (χέρνιψ); here the oxen are imagined as glimpsing the reflection of the knife in the water. **ἐν ὕδατι** is therefore to be taken with δερκόμενοι (cf. Ovid, *Fasti* 1.327 *praeuisos in aqua timet hostia cultros*).

10[64] ἠῶιοι: Greek often uses an adj. where Eng. requires a temporal adv.: cf. *66*, *1514*. **θυμὸν ἀμύξειν:** Homer has this phrase of Achilles 'tearing his heart' in rage and grief (*Il.* 1.243); here, less naturally, of fear. Perhaps the expression looks forward to the δορίς (< δέρω, 'flay'), which will literally 'tear' the victim.

12[66] τήν: Cydippe.

12–14[67–9] νοῦσος . . . φημίζομεν: epilepsy, 'the sacred disease'. The formula κατ' αἶγας ἀγρίας, 'to the wild goats', was uttered as an attempt to exorcize it (ἀποπέμπειν). **ψευδόμενοι:** Call. reflects the best medical opinion, which denied that epilepsy was sacred: see Hippocrates, Περὶ ἱερῆς νούσου 1–5, who says that doctors called the disease 'sacred' as an insurance against their failure to cure it.

14[68] ἥ: relative. **ἀνιγρή** 'grievous', a rare by-form of ἀνιαρός.

15[69] 'Αΐδεω . . . δόμων 'wasted her ⟨away⟩ right to the Halls of Hades', i.e. she was 'at Death's door'. The notion of wasting perhaps implies a series of fits or a long period of unconsciousness.

16[70] ἐστόρνυντο τὰ κλισμία: probably mid. verb, acc. noun; but possibly pass. verb, nom. noun (n. pl. nouns do sometimes govern a pl. verb: cf. *337*, *680–1*, *867*, *1087*). κλισμίον, not found elsewhere, is a diminutive of fem. κλισμία, 'couch'; pl. perhaps by analogy with δέμνια. **δεύτερον** (and τὸ τρίτον in *72*) point the recurrence of illness in general, not the specific symptoms, which are different each time.

17[71] τεταρταίωι . . . πυρί 'with a quartan fever', that is a fever which recurs critically every third day (every fourth day in ancient inclusive reckoning). **ἐμνήσαντο γάμου κάτα** 'bethought themselves (aor. of μνάομαι) of the marriage'. For κατά = 'concerning' see LSJ s.v. A.II.7.

20[74] ἄρας 'setting out', intrans.: LSJ s.v. ἀείρω I.5.

21[75] ἐννύχιον: presumably Ceyx slept in the temple and was visited by Apollo in a dream.

22–37[76–91] The speech of Apollo. With a wealth of mythological and genealogical references he tells Ceyx that Artemis was resident in her temple at Delos when Cydippe made her vow, and advises him to unite two distinguished families by immediately performing the marriage.

22[75] 'A weighty oath by Artemis is frustrating marriage for your child.' For ἐνικλᾶν cf. *363*.

23[77] Λύγδαμιν: king of the Cimmerians from S. Russia, who swept through Ionia in the seventh cent. B.C. and burnt the temple of Artemis at Ephesus. Their army was eventually destroyed, perhaps by the Assyrians; here it is assumed that Artemis herself brought about their ruin (ἔκηδε). Call. treats the story at greater length in his *Hymn to Artemis* 251–8.

24[78] ἐν 'Αμυκλαίωι 'in her temple at Amyclae', a town on the banks of the Eurotas in Laconia. Temple-names often end in -αῖον or -εῖον (e.g. Μουσεῖον). θρύον ἔπλεκεν 'was plaiting rushes' – presumably for a garland. θρύον is a Homeric *hapax* (*Il.* 21.351).

25[79] Παρθενίωι: a river which flowed through Paphlagonia to the south coast of the Black Sea; so named because it was associated with Artemis, the virgin huntress.

28[82] συμφράδμονα 'counsellor' – a Homeric *hapax* (*Il.* 2.372).

30–1[84–5] The union of Cydippe and Acontius will not be an unequal match (silver with lead); rather each family will add lustre to the other (gold with electrum, a precious gold-and-silver alloy).

32[86] Κοδρείδης 'descendant of Codrus': see *47* n. ἄνωθεν: Eng. uses the opposite metaphor, 'by descent'.

32–7[86–91] 'And the Cean bridegroom ⟨is sprung⟩ from the priests of Zeus Aristaeus the Icmian, whose task it is on the mountain crests to mollify stern Maera as she rises, and to entreat from Zeus the wind by which many quail are dashed into the linen nets.' Aristaeus, son of Apollo and Cyrene, came to the aid of the Ceans when the Dog-Star's heat was causing a drought or plague: he built an altar on a mountaintop to Zeus Icmaeus ('Moist') and to Sirius, and prayed for cooling winds. Zeus in return ever after made the Etesian winds blow for the 40 days following the rise of Sirius. The Euxantiadae, Acontius' family, were hereditary priests of the cult, and sacrificed annually to appease Sirius and invoke the winds (Schol. Ap. Rh. 2.498–527). After his philanthropic intervention Aristaeus' name was linked in worship with that of Zeus.

34[88] ἀμβώνεσσι: ἀμβών is a rare word for 'mountain crest'. Diogenes, a grammarian of uncertain date, thought that ἀμβώνεσσι should be read for ἂμ βωμοῖσι at *Il.* 8.441; but whether the variant was current in Call.'s time is not known.

35[89] Μαῖραν: the Dog-Star, otherwise known as Σείριος; cognate with the redupl. pres. μαρμαίρω, 'glitter'.

36[90] αἰτεῖσθαι: Call. points to the popular derivation of Ἐτησίαι from αἰτεῖν (Hyginus, *Poet. astr.* 2.4). ὧι τε: referring to ἄημα. θαμεινοί: a rarer equivalent of πυκνοί, 'close-set', i.e. in large numbers.

37[91] ὄρτυγες: quails migrated from the direction of the NW Etesian winds. Call. wrote prose-works Περὶ ἀνέμων (fr. 404) and Περὶ ὀρνέων (frr. 414–28): cf. p. 83. νεφέλαις: nets of a particularly fine texture.

39[93] ἀν' . . . ἐκάλυψεν 'disclosed' (tmesis). ἐτῶς 'truly'; = ἐτεόν adv., as in *63*.

40[94] κἠν αὖ σῶς 'and she was well again'.

40–1[94–5] 'And what (ὅ neut. rel.) remained ⟨for you⟩, Acontius, ⟨was⟩ to go to Dionysias to fetch your ⟨σεῖο⟩ wife': a sudden vocative characteristic of Call.'s style. **μετελθεῖν** often means 'go to seek'. **Διονυσιάδα:** another name for Naxos. Dionysus was said to have been brought up on the island, just as was Zeus on Crete.

42–9[96–103] The marriage is not even described; instead we are given a list, complementary to the negative clauses of *77–9*, of what advantages Acontius would *not* have accepted in exchange for his wedding night.

42–3[96–7] 'And Artemis was sworn well by (i.e. the oath sworn in her name was fulfilled) and the girls of Cydippe's own age straightaway sang their companion's wedding song, which was not delayed.'

44–8[98–9] The construction is probably οὔ σε δοκέω ἀντὶ νυκτὸς ἐκείνης δέξασθαί κε οὐ σφυρὸν . . . οὐδ' . . . Pfeiffer takes ἀντὶ . . . δέξ. as a compound verb in tmesis and νυκτὸς ἐκείνης alone as meaning 'in return for that night'; but this hardly seems reconcilable with the position of τῆι . . . παρθενίης.

44[98] τημοῦτος = τῆμος, 'then'.

46[100] Iphicles son of Phylacus, a hero of the generation before the Trojan War, was proverbial for his fleetness of foot: he could run over a field of corn without damaging the ears (Hes. fr. 62). **ἀσταχύεσσιν:** a Homeric *hapax* (*Il.* 2.148).

47[101] Κελαινίτης . . . Μίδης: Midas of the golden touch was from Celaenae in Phrygia.

48–9[102–3] 'And whichever men are not ignorant of the harsh god [Eros] would be corroborators of my judgement.'

50–74[104–28] From this union sprang the famous Acontiadae of Ceos. Call. acknowledges the chronicler Xenomedes (fl. c. 450 B.C.) as his source, and goes on to mention some notable events in the island's early history.

51[105] ὑμέτερον: occasionally in epic verse ὑμέτερος is used for σός.

52[106] πουλύ τι καὶ περίτιμον 'prominently (or perhaps 'in great numbers') and honoured' – both adverbial phrases. τι is often used to qualify adverbs: cf. *Bath of Pallas* 58 (= *189*) with Bulloch's n., *1190*.

53[107] Κεῖε: Acontius; another abrupt vocative (cf. *94–5* n.).

53–4[107–8] τεὸν . . . ἵμερον . . . | τόνδε 'this love of yours'.

55[109] μνήμηι . . . μυθολόγωι 'in a mythological record'.

56–8[110–12] Ceos was first inhabited by water-nymphs who had been driven from the Corycian cave on Mt Parnassus by a huge lion; hence the island's old name of Hydrussa (< ὕδωρ).

56[110] ἄρχμενος ὡς 'beginning with how . . .', a formula used twice elsewhere by Call. at the start of a narrative (fr. 7.25, *Hymn to Artemis* 4) and perhaps borrowed by him from earlier epic. The irreg. form ἄρχμενος is only found in this expression.

58–9[112–13] An obscure couplet. Κιρώ[δης seems to be the only known word which will fit the damaged traces in the papyrus; but no one of that name is known to have been connected with Ceos. There were towns named Caryae in Laconia, Arcadia and Lycia; perhaps Cirodes (?) left Ceos and moved to one of these.

60–3[114–17] The next inhabitants of Ceos were Carians and Leleges, who spread across the Aegean from the coast of Asia Minor. Call. refers to their custom of sounding trumpets as they sacrificed to Zeus of the War Cry (Ἀλαλάξιος).

60[114] ἐννάσσαντο: 3rd pl. aor. mid. of ἐνναίω. τέων: Ionic for τινῶν. Here the indef. pronoun is used as a relative: '⟨those people⟩ whose sacrifices are received', etc.: see LSJ s.v. τις B.II.d.

61[115] ἐπὶ σαλπίγγων . . . βοῆι 'to the accompaniment of a blast of trumpets'.

62–3[116–17] 'And how Ceos, son of Phoebus and Melia, caused it to be changed (μετ' . . . βαλέσθαι, tmesis) ⟨to⟩ another name', i.e. from Hydrussa to Ceos. Call. wrote a prose treatise entitled Κτίσεις νήσων καὶ πόλεων καὶ μετονομασίαι (fr. 412): see p. 83.

63[117] ἶνις: a rare word for 'offspring' found only in tragedy before the Hellenistic period.

64–9[118–23] On the Telchines see *I* n. Xenomedes apparently made them inhabitants not of Rhodes, as was usually related, but of Ceos (cf. Pind. *Paean* 4.42–5). The story presupposed here is that the wizard Telchines offended the gods, who destroyed with bolts of lightning the whole population of the island except for Macelo, wife of Demonax, and Dexithea (*47* n.), who had once provided Zeus and Apollo with hospitality.

64[118] ἐν . . . ἐν . . . : looking forward to ἐνεθήκατο δέλτοις (*120*).

66[120] ἠλεά 'foolishly': n. pl. as adverb. **γέρων:** Xenomedes.

70–4[124–8] The four chief towns of Ceos: Carthaea was founded by Megacles, Iulis by Eupylus son of Chryso, Poiessa by Acaeus, Coressia by Aphrastus. Of these founders nothing is known; but much κτίσις-literature, both prose and verse, was written in the Hellenistic period (cf. *116–17* n. on Call. fr. 412).

70[124] τέσσαρας . . . πόληας: the four towns are later itemized; **τείχισσε** (a Homeric *hapax*, *Il.* 7.449) governs their names and also the preceding appositional phrase.

74–7[128–31] round off both the Xenomedes digression (πρέσβυς *130* ∼ ἀρχαίου *108*, μῦθος *131* ∼ μυθολόγωι *109*) and the Acontius story as a whole (ἔρωτα *129* ∼ Ἔρως *41*, παιδός *130* ∼ παῖς *42*). Call. is concerned to stress the reliability of his source: cf. fr. 612 ἀμάρτυρον οὐδὲν ἀείδω.

75[129] ξυγκραθέντ' ἀνίαις 'he told of your powerful love mixed with pain'. The papyrus reads αὐταῖς, which, if sound, must refer to πόληας (*124*) – Xenomedes mingled with the cities (i.e. with his narrative of them) the story of Acontius. But the fem. pronoun sounds both weak and forced after so many lines.

76[130] ἐτητυμίηι μεμελημένος 'concerned for truth'. The dat. is much less common than the gen. with this verb.

77[131] ἡμετέρην . . . Καλλιόπην: the allotment of particular arts to particular Muses is later than the third century. Call. perhaps singles out Calliope here because of the etymology of her name ('my fair-voiced Muse') or because, according to Hes. *Theog.* 79, she is προφερεστάτη amongst her sisters. Call. humorously presents his Muse as a highly literate lady who has eagerly scanned the works of an obscure fifth-century historian. She helps the poet not with pure inspiration, but by being well read.

III

The hymn. The hexameter hymn was a traditional Greek poetic mode. Thirty-three so-called 'Homeric' Hymns survive, of greatly varying date and length. The four longest, to Demeter, Apollo, Hermes and Aphrodite, probably belong to the seventh century. Basic constituents of these and of the shorter hymns are naming of the god (cult-titles, etc.), recital of his / her deeds with more or less narrative development, and a closing prayer. Callimachus adopts this basic framework for his own six hymns. *Hymns* 3 and 4, to Artemis and Delos, are closer in length and presentation to the longer 'Homeric' models; but the others (1 to Zeus, 2 to Apollo, 5 to Athena, 6 to Demeter) mark a distinctively new departure. All six probably owe much in narrative technique, tone and presentation to hymns written in lyric metre by poets of the sixth and fifth centuries (cf. e.g. Pind. frs. 29–51).

The fifth hymn, to Athena, is entitled in our medieval MSS Εἰς λουτρὰ τῆς Παλλάδος, *The Bath of Pallas*. This is the only one of the six to be written in elegiacs. ἔλεγος can mean 'lament'; but it seems unlikely that Chariclo's sad story motivates the choice of metre. Callimachus' desire for experiment and variety may be sufficient explanation.

The setting. The poem is 'mimetic', creating as it were incidentally through the words of a narrating voice the opening moments of an Argive ceremony. It purports to be an address to women celebrants as they wait to carry out their ritual bathing of Athena's statue, the Palladion, in the river Inachus. So convincing is the poem's present-ation, and so subtly are we 'fed' information by the narrator, that many scholars have felt that the hymn was composed for actual delivery at the ceremony itself. This is almost certainly not so: the poet's skill consists in creating verbally the *illusion* of 'being there'. Similar attempts at 'realism' are to be found in the mimiambi of Herondas, in Bion's *Lament for Adonis* (*1227–1324*), and in many of Theocritus' *Idylls*.

Callimachus is our only source for the details of this Argive ceremony. The Athenian Πλυντήρια provide a parallel: the goddess's statue was stripped, washed, anointed and given a new robe, and processed through the city on a wagon. The statue at Argos is said to be that which Diomedes brought back from Troy – now the safety of his city depends on its talismanic protection (53 πολιοῦχον). Throughout the poem the Palladion is spoken of as if it is the goddess herself – in other words, its appearance on a horse-drawn wagon will be for the putative celebrants a divine epiphany. The poem creates a mood of urgency and expectation, and closes at the very moment of the goddess's appearance.

Argos had two temples of Athena, at one of which she had the cult-title Ὀξυδερκής, 'Sharp-sighted'. This (*pace* Bulloch) can hardly be coincidental, given the importance of sight and blindness in the Tiresias narrative.

Tiresias. Set within this ritual framework is the story of Tiresias (57–136), adduced by the narrator as a warning to the men of Argos not to look at the Palladion – Tiresias was struck blind when he accidentally glimpsed Athena as she bathed naked in the Eurotas. Hymns often narrate a divinity's triumph over his or her enemies; but the tone of *this* narrative is in striking contrast to its ostensible purpose. Tiresias himself never speaks. After his blinding, attention is concentrated on the reaction of his mother Chariclo, whose despairing address to the goddess points the distance between human and divine. Tiresias receives compensatory gifts of prophetic 'insight', long life and consciousness after death; but for his mother, struck with incomprehension at the undiscriminating nature of divine retribution, these things can neither explain nor relieve her cause for grief. The Tiresias narrative is thus in counterpoint to the ritual frame and to the reader's hymnic expectations, and provides a surprisingly qualified view of the relations between god and man.

Sources. (1) For details of the cult Callimachus is indebted to the Ἀργολικά of Agias and Dercylus (*FGH* 305 F 1–9). (2) For his unusual version of the Tiresias story his source was probably Pherecydes (*FGH* 3 F 92), a fifth-century Athenian mythographer. (The common version tells how Tiresias was blinded by Hera when, having been both man and woman, he adjudged that women derive nine times more pleasure from the sexual act than men.) (3) Callimachus is the first known author to make Actaeon's death a consequence of his accidentally intruding on Artemis as she bathed (earlier versions have him attempting rape or boasting to be a better hunter than the goddess – cf. Bulloch on 107–18). It seems possible that Callimachus has himself adapted the story so that it resembles the Tiresias narrative more closely.

Dialect. The poem is written in predominantly epic language but in Doric dialect. There are several possible explanations. (1) Argos was a Doric-speaking area. There is, however, no comparable explanation for the sixth hymn, also written in Doric. (2) A genuine cult-hymn would have been written in lyric metre, which traditionally employed language with a Doric coloration. This does not account for the similarly 'mimetic' *Hymn* 2 which is in regular epic/Ionic dialect. (3) Call. wished to point *Hymns* 5 and 6 as a complementary pair, and did so with a typical piece of Hellenistic dialectal experimentation (cf. Theocritus' Doric, Herondas' Ionic, etc.).

The MSS are not reliable in matters of dialect, and many Doric forms in this poem are uncertain conjectural restorations.

Bibl.: A. W. Bulloch, *Callimachus: the fifth hymn* (Cambridge, 1985).

> Cf. Ovid, *Met.* 3.138–252 (Actaeon).

1–32[132–63] Exhortation to the celebrants to leave their homes and assemble. Anaphora, repetition, interjections and vivid description create an atmosphere of excitement and expectation.

1[132] ὅσσαι: sc. ἐστέ.

2–3[133–4] τᾶν . . . τᾶν: all males are taboo at this ceremony. Free use of the def. art. here (cf. 47, 51, 53) gives an effect of immediacy, as if pointing out the objects which we are to imagine present before the participants.

2[133] ἄρτι: really with ἐσάκουσα. This type of displacement is common with several adverbs: see Goodwin, *GMT* §858 and cf. *676* n.

3[134] ἕρπεν = -ειν (App.C.8). Doric uses ἕρπω for ἔρχομαι.

4[135] σῶσθε = σοῦσθε, irreg. imper. mid. of σεύω. **Πελασγιάδες** 'Pelasgian women', synonym for Ἀργεῖαι (cf. 51 n.). Argos was believed to have been colonized by Pelasgians from NW Greece.

5–12[136–43] Athena's care for her horses after the Battle of Gods and Giants. It seems that this section is an implicit αἴτιον for the ritual cleansing of the horses which are to draw her statue.

5[136] μεγάλως = -ους.

6[137] ἐξελάσαι: vigorous metaphor, vigorous goddess.

8[139] γαγενέων: the Giants, born from Earth.

10[141] παγαῖς: in verse πηγαί often = simply 'water'.

11[142] ῥαθάμιγγας: probably 'particles' of dirt: cf. *Il.* 23.502 κονίης ῥαθάμιγγες.

12[143] χαλινοφάγων: found only here.

13–32[144–63] Having mentioned Athena's warlike qualities the narrator now stresses her femininity. It is rather surprising to find mention of the Judgement of Paris, since Athena was not the winner; but the contest is so described that Aphrodite is disparaged, Athena praised. Simple unguents and a comb (29–32) were used in the bathing ceremony.

13[144] Ἀχαιιάδες: a synonym for Πελασγιάδες (4) with philological point: some ancient grammarians believed that the Homeric phrases Ἄργος Ἀχαιικόν and Πελασγικὸν Ἄργος denoted different places. Call. implicitly disagrees. **ἀλαβάστρως**: jars of alabaster for holding perfumes.

14[145] 'I hear from under the axle the sound of the wheel-hubs', which creak as the wagon begins to move. But Schneider's ὑπ᾿ ἀξονίων ('a sound from the axle-naves') may well be right.

16[147] μεικτά: mixed effeminately with scent.

17[148] ἀεὶ καλὸν ὄμμα τὸ τήνας: ambiguous: 'her appearance/eye is always fair'. 'Eye' might tie in with the cult-title Ὀξυδερκής (see p. 112) and ironically foreshadow Tiresias' fate of blindness.

18[149] Φρύξ: Phrygian Paris. The word has contemptuous overtones.

19[150] ὀρείχαλκον: a romantic-sounding precious metal mentioned in archaic poetry (LSJ s.v.); here of a polished metal mirror. **Σιμοῦντος**: the Trojan river Simois, which is not in fact situated near Mt Ida.

20[151] δίναν: the word is often used with no notion of turbulence.

21[152] διαυγέα 'bright', not 'translucent'.

22[153] κόμαν 'lock', a rare use (cf. Lat. *coma*) for πλόκαμος (as in 32).

23[154] δὶς ἑξήκοντα διαύλως: about 30 miles. δίαυλος = two stades, i.e. one lap of the stadium. A pointed contrast with Aphrodite's δὶς μετέθηκε κόμαν (22).

24–5[155–6] Λακεδαιμόνιοι | ἀστέρες: the Dioscuri. 'Star' is a common metaphor for famous men (cf. *48*); but here there is added point, since Castor and Pollux were thought to be the constellation Gemini.

25[156] ἐμπεράμως 'skilfully' (= ἐμπείρως). Cf. *344*.

26[157] ἰδίας: the olive was Athena's gift to men. **φυταλιᾶς** 'plant' ('garden' or 'orchard' in Homer).

27[158] τὸ δ᾿ ἔρευθος ἀνέδραμε 'a healthy glow suffused her'.

27–8[158–9] πρώιον . . . ῥόδον 'a spring (lit. early) rose', symbolic of freshness. But perhaps we should rather read πρώκιον, 'dewy' (cf. *34*): cf. Theoc. 20.16 φοινίχθην ὑπὸ τὠλγεος ὡς ῥόδον ἔρσαι.

28[159] The double simile appropriates two of Aphrodite's cult-attributes, rose and pomegranate (Attic σίδη); i.e. Athena can rival Aphrodite in beauty on Aphrodite's own terms.

29[160] τῶι 'therefore' (cf. 119): common in Homer. **μῶνον:** adverb. **ἄρσεν τι . . . ἔλαιον:** the wild olive was thought to be a male plant. It is therefore suitable for anointing manly, active persons.

30[161] ὧι καὶ χρίεται Ἡρακλέης: i.e. ὧι καὶ 'Ηρ. χρ. The anaphora ὧι . . . ὧι suggests that after Castor will be mentioned his brother Pollux; but instead we find Heracles, paragon of manly prowess.

31–2[162–3] Verbal reminiscence of *Il.* 14.175–6 (Hera beautifies herself to seduce Zeus) τῶι ῥ' ἥγε χρόα καλὸν ἀλειψαμένη ἰδὲ χαίτας | πεξαμένη χερσὶ πλοκάμους ἔπλεξε φαεινούς. The allusion perhaps functions like the similes in line 28, appropriating to Athena words applied to a rival goddess. **ἀπὸ . . . πέξηται** 'comb out'.

32[163] λιπαρόν: predicative: her hair became 'shining' after she had anointed it.

33–56[164–87] The celebrants are imagined as having assembled in answer to the summons of 1–32. There follows an invocation to the goddess herself, including aetiological details of cult practice.

33[164] πάρα τοι = πάρεστί σοι.

34[165] 'Αρεστοριδᾶν: Arestor was an Argive hero. There may be an etymological play on ἀρεστός ('pleasing') and καταθύμιος (33).

35–42[166–73] Diomedes brought the Palladion from Troy. At a later time Eumedes, priest of Athena, took the statue with him when he fled the usurper Eurystheus and joined the Heraclidae, who were about to reclaim their right to kingship in Argos. The reference in 36–7 is obscure: perhaps Diomedes appeared in epiphany to protect with his shield the fleeing Eumedes (Bulloch).

36–7[167–8] 'In the way that Eumedes taught the Argives of old ⟨what has since become⟩ the custom.'

36[167] παλαιοτέρως: the 'contrastive' comparative, the contrast being here implicit with 'the Argives of today'.

37[168] τεῖν = σοί, Homeric dat. sing.

38–9[169–70] The word-order gives the emphasis 'realizing the threat of death, that the people were arranging for him . . .'.

40[171–2] Nothing is known of the Κρεῖον ὄρος; but the fact that the name is repeated may mean that Call. is stressing a particular version of the story.

40[171] ὠικίσατο: he must have set up a rival temple.

43[174] περσέπτολι: she has the power both to protect (53) and to destroy cities.

44[175] σακέων . . . πατάγωι: perhaps we are to imagine shields being clashed during the procession.

45–6[176–7] Today the river Inachus is dedicated to holy purposes, and citizens must not drink from it.

45[176] βάπτετε: this verb is sometimes used of drawing by dipping (= ἀντλεῖν).

47–8[178–9] Φυσάδειαν . . . 'Αμυμώναν: springs near Argos. Poseidon once dried up all the region's water. Danaus sent out his 50 daughters to search; Amymone gave herself to Poseidon and was rewarded with the spring subsequently named after her.

49–50[180–1] χρυσῶι . . . ἄνθεσιν: perhaps a reference to golden vessels used in bathing Athena's statue, and to ritual scattering of flowers; but the narrator speaks as if the river will miraculously beautify himself with gold and flowers to honour the goddess.

50[181] φορβαίων 'giving pasture' (LSJ). The word occurs only here, and may be corrupt: the context leads one to expect a proper name.

51–6[182–7] Lead-in to the story of Tiresias, who saw Athena naked and was blinded.

51[182] Πελασγέ: every Argive man; cf. 4 n.

52[183] οὐκ qualifies ἐθέλων, 'unintentionally'.

54[185] τὠργος = τὸ Ἄργος.

55[186] μέστα: μέσφα, for which this is the Doric form, is elsewhere a conj. or prep., 'until'; only here adverbial, 'meanwhile'.

56[187] μῦθος δ' οὐκ ἐμός, ἀλλ' ἑτέρων: such disclaimers are traditional at the beginning of narratives; but in a work by Call., who insisted on adherence to 'fact' (fr. 612 ἀμάρτυρον οὐδὲν ἀείδω), the words gain added point. The ἕτεροι are in fact Agias and Dercylus (see p. 112).

57–69[188–200] The friendship and inseparability of Athena and Chariclo, mother of Tiresias.

57[188] ἔν ποκα Θήβαις 'once upon a time in . . .'. ποτέ is often found within the locative phrase which it qualifies: cf. the opening line of the *Hecale* Ἀκταίη τις ἔναιεν Ἐρεχθέος ἔν ποτε γουνῶι (fr. 230).

58[189] πουλύ τι καὶ περὶ δή: very strong emphasis: 'a great deal and exceedingly'. **περί** is probably adverbial; construe πουλύ τι καὶ περὶ δὴ φίλατο νύμφαν μίαν τᾶν ἑταρᾶν ('companions'), κτλ.

59[190] ματέρα Τειρεσίαο: the unlearned reader must wait until line 67 to discover Chariclo's name. **ἔγεντο:** an alternative to ἐγένετο found in Hesiod and later poetry.

60–4[191–5] Thespiae, Haliartus and Coronea, Boeotian towns in the area of Mt Helicon, all had temples of Athena.

61[192] At the beginning of this line the MSS read ἢ 'πὶ Κορωνείας; but the words are probably an intrusion from 63 – the repetition would be odd and pointless.

62[193] ἔργα 'worked land', a regular use.

65[196] πολλάκις . . . ἐπεβάσατο: one would expect the verb to be imperf. (as τελέθεσκον, 67); but the aor. is sometimes found with πολλάκις, suggesting many single instances (K.–G. II 450).

66[197] ὄαροι: friendly, sportive gatherings.

68[199] ἔτι καὶ τήναν 'even her'.

69[200] ἔσσαν: App. C.10.

70–84[201–15] A famous passage, describing with carefully controlled repetition and anaphora the stillness of mid-day, the charmed and dangerous hour when gods are traditionally abroad. Tiresias breaks into the silent landscape: he sees the goddess naked, and is blinded.

70[201] λυσαμένα: fem. dual.

71[202] ἵππω . . . κράναι: Hippocrene, created by a blow from Pegasus' hoof. **καλά:** n. pl. adv.

72–3[203–4] λῶντο . . . λώοντο: alternative epic forms: λῶντο from λοέω, λώοντο from λούω. For similar self-conscious variation cf. *275, 315–16, 328, 367, 1560–1*.

72[203] ἀσυχία: it is a fact that Greek mountainsides become quiet in the hottest part of the day; but nature's silence tends to accompany epiphanies. See Dodds on Eur. *Bacchae* 1084–5.

75[206] ἔτι: with ἀνεστρέφετο (76). **ἀμᾶι** 'together with' (+dat.). The Doric form of ἅμα has a long final syllable and, if the MSS are to be trusted, an iota (cf. λάθραι, εἰκῆι, etc.); cf. *531*.

75–6[206–7] ἄρτι γένεια | περκάζων 'his beard just darkening' (cf. *501*). The metaphor is from ripening grapes. Pl. γένεια means not 'cheeks' but 'beard'.

77[208] ἄφατόν τι: for adverbial τι cf. 58 n.

78[209] εἶδε τὰ μὴ θεμιτά: what he saw is not described, and the narrative moves on swiftly.

79[210] τὸν δὲ χολωσαμένα: τόν/τήν + part. + verb of saying is a common way of introducing direct speech in epic. περ ὅμως: concessive, though ὅμως really belongs to the second part of the sentence. For other examples see LSJ s.v. ὅμως ΙΙ.1.

81[212] ὦ Εὐηρείδα: Tiresias was son of Eueres. A grave and weighty phrase. ὁδόν: internal acc.

82[213] μέν . . . δ᾽: does she blind him herself? Call. does not *quite* say so. The point is further blurred by mention of the (non-personal) δαίμων in 81. ὄμματα νὺξ ἔλαβεν 'night occupied his eyes'. Again the description does not dwell on detail. The words are reminiscent of Homeric death (ὄσσε . . . νὺξ ἐκάλυψε): cf. 89, 111–14 nn.

83[214] ἐστάκη: Doric pluperf., = Attic ἐστήκει. The MSS read ἐστάθη, which is unmetrical. ἄφθογγος: Tiresias never speaks. ἐκόλλασαν: 'glued'. πήγνυμι is commoner.

84–136[215–67] Focus shifts from Tiresias to his mother, who utters a speech of shock and pathos. She blames Athena directly for what has happened. Athena replies that divine law made the result inescapable. She cites the example of Actaeon, who will die for a similar offence; and she foretells the powers Tiresias will have by way of compensation. The narrator adds that Athena always keeps her promises.

87[218] τέκνον ἄλαστε: neut. noun, masc. adj.: a common form of attraction (cf. *Il.* 22.84 φίλε τέκνον, K.–G. I 53–4). ἄλαστος| 'wretched', 'ill-starred'.

89[220] οὐκ ἀέλιον πάλιν ὄψεαι: 'to look upon the sun' usually = 'be alive': cf. 82 n. ὦ ἐμὲ δειλάν: the rare exclamatory acc. is found only in ritual laments (cf. *1254*, etc.). The next line has the more common voc.

90[221] οὐκέτι μοι παριτέ: she will never again be able to bear to visit Helicon. παριτός is not found elsewhere.

91[222] ἐπράξαο: πράττω, act. or mid., is often used of exacting payment. δόρκας . . . φάεα: there may be word-play here: δόρξ/δορκάς was derived by later grammarians from δέρκομαι. φάεα = 'eyes' (as occasionally in Homer), extinguished by νύξ (82).

93–4[224–5] ἁ μέν . . . μάτηρ μέν: ἁ is really demonstrative, not def. art.: 'she . . . being, as she was, his mother' (Bulloch). The repeated

(?resumptive) μέν within a single clause is not easy to parallel, and the text may be corrupt: see app. crit.

93[224] ἀμφοτέραισι: sc. χερσί. περί . . . λαβοῖσα: tmesis.

94[225] οἶτον: here and occasionally elsewhere = 'lament' (perhaps by confusion with οἶκτος); usually = 'fate' or 'doom'.

95[226] ἄγε 'kept up'. ἐλέησεν: aor., i.e. she felt a sudden surge of pity.

96[227] Construe καὶ 'Αθ. πρός νιν ἔλεξεν τόδ' ἔπος.

97[228] δῖα γύναι: a stately combination of the Homeric voc. δῖα θεά and the nom. formula δῖα γυναικῶν, 'noble⟨st⟩ among women'. μετά . . . βαλεῦ 'reconsider' rather than 'take back': μεταβάλλεσθαι = 'change one's mind'.

98[229] ἀλαόν: used of Tiresias at *Od.* 10.493 = 12.267.

100[231] Κρόνιοι . . . νόμοι: laws of great antiquity first laid down under the rule of Cronus.

101[232] ἔληται 'chooses ⟨to be seen⟩'.

102[233] μίσθω . . . μεγάλω 'at great cost⟨to himself⟩', gen. of price.

103–4[234–5] τὸ μὲν . . . ἔργον: cf. 93–4 n.

103[234] οὐ παλινάγρετον: metrically anomalous, since the caesura falls between the proclitic negative and its adj. Ap. Rh. has the licence occasionally, Call. nowhere else. Cf. *427–8* n. γένοιτο: the potential opt. is occasionally found without ἄν/κε: cf. *544*, *602*, Goodwin, *GMT* § 240. αὖθι: originally a shortened form of αὐτόθι; but the Hell. poets use it as a by-form of αὖθις/αὖτις, by analogy with the dispensable ς of e.g. πολλάκι(ς): cf *17*, *35* nn.

104–5[235–6] There is an allusion to *Il.* 24.209–10 (Hecuba on the dead Hector) τῶι δ' ὥς ποθι Μοῖρα κραταιὴ | γιγνομένωι ἐπένησε λίνωι, ὅτε μιν τέκον αὐτή. What the Fates' spinning foreshadows cannot be altered.

105[236] κομίζευ 'take for yourself', 'receive': LSJ ii.2.

106[237] τέλθος: Doric form of τέλος: 'payment, i.e. punishment, ⟨for what you have done⟩'.

107–18[238–49] The consolatory and prophetic *exemplum* of Actaeon.

107–8[238–9] πόσσα . . . πόσσα: for ὅσσα . . . ὅσσα, perhaps by analogy with e.g. *Il.* 4.350 ποῖόν σε ἔπος φύγεν ἕρκος ὀδόντων, which modern editors punctuate as a question, not an exclamation. Interchange between πόσος and ὅσος, πῶς and ὡς, etc. is a feature of κοινή-Greek.

107[238] ἁ **Καδμηΐς**: Autonoe, daughter of Cadmus, mother of Actaeon.

109[240] τυφλὸν ἰδέσθαι: a pathetic juxtaposition. ἰδέσθαι depends on εὐχόμενοι.

110[241] καὶ τῆνος 'he too'. The parallel is not logically exact, since Chariclo, not Tiresias, is Athena's companion.

111–14[242–5] These lines are reminiscent of *Il.* 5.53–5 (death of Scamandrius, a favourite of Artemis) ἀλλ' οὔ οἱ τότε γε χραῖσμ' Ἄρτεμις ἰοχέαιρα, | οὐδὲ ἑκηβολίαι, ᾗσιν τὸ πρίν γ' ἐκέκαστο, | ἀλλά…

112[243] ξυναί 'which they shared'. **τᾶμος**: points forward to ὁππόκα.

113[244] οὐκ ἐθέλων: third occurrence (cf. 52, 78). Divine law takes no account of intention.

115[246] δειπνησεῦντι 'will dine on' – elsewhere almost always of human meals.

115–16[246–7] ὀστέα … λεξεῖται: conventional vocabulary emphasizes the unnaturalness of his death: bones are usually 'gathered up' after cremation.

119[250] τῶι: see 29 n.

120[251] τεῦ χάριν 'for your sake': τεῦ = σοῦ. **μενεῦντι**: Doric fut. Gifts in store as compensation for the δάκρυα πολλά which awaited (ἔμενε) Chariclo at line 68.

121[252] ἀοίδιμον ἐσσομένοισιν: < *Il.* 6.358.

122[253] μέγα … δή τι 'greatly', a common adverbial phrase in Hell. verse; cf. *1190*.

123–4[254–5] ὅς … οἵ … ποίων: cf. *355* n. We should expect ὁποίων. For a Homeric parallel cf. *Il.* 5.85 οὐκ ἂν γνοίης ποτέροισι μετείη (Bulloch); but see also 107–8 n. on possible κοινή influence. Note the 'rising tricolon', each element longer than the last, and the studied variation of expression (adj.; vb. + adv.; noun + adj.).

124[255] ἄλιθα 'without significance'. In Homer the word means 'exceedingly'; but Hell. poets sometimes use it as if it were the adverbial n. pl. of ἠλίθιος, 'vain'. **οὐκ ἀγαθαί** 'ill-omened'.

125[256] θεοπρόπα 'oracles'.

126[257] ὕστερα: adverb. **Λαβδακίδαις** 'descendants of Labdacus', grandson of Cadmus.

128[259] πολυχρόνιον: probably 'coming after a long time' (Bulloch), since τέρμα means 'term' in the sense of 'end', not 'duration'.

129–30[260–1] Allusion to *Od.* 10.493–5, where Persephone grants to Tiresias τεθνηῶτι . . . | οἴωι πεπνῦσθαι ('be conscious').

130[261] ᾿Αγεσίλαι 'leader of the peoples', a rare title of Hades. The underworld was proverbially well populated.

131–6[262–7] That to which Zeus nods assent is irrevocable and binding: cf. *Il.* 1.524–7.

131–3[262–4] 'That thing (τό, demonstr.) to which Pallas nods assent is as good as done (ἐντελές, lit. accomplished); for Zeus granted to Athena alone of his daughters to take for herself all the attributes / powers of her father.' τόγε is antecedent to πατρώια πάντα φέρεσθαι.

136–7[267–8] Athena's birth from the head of Zeus. The fact that she neither has nor is a mother is perhaps significant for the emotional distance between herself and Chariclo.

136[267] All our MSS are deficient here. A. W. Mair's supplement probably conveys the sense of the original: ψεύδεα, κοὐδὲ Διὸς ψεύδεται ἁ θυγάτηρ.

137–42[268–73] The cautionary tale of Tiresias is made conveniently to end just as the goddess is at last about to appear. The traditional coda thus serves a dual purpose – χαῖρε (140, 141) is both 'hail' (to Athena in person) and 'farewell' (because the poem is ending).

137[268] ἀτρεκές 'really'.

138[269] τὥργον ὅσαις μέλεται: those concerned with the task of greeting (δέχεσθε) the goddess.

139[270] εὐαγορίαι 'fair speech', i.e. words of good omen (= εὐφημίαι).

140[271] ᾿Ιναχίω: since Athena is to be bathed in the Inachus, the adj. points the celebrants' particular claim to her protection.

141[272] πάλιν: at the close of hymns πάλιν usu. implies 'next year'; but here it = 'back from the river'. ἐς . . . ἐλάσσαις: 2nd pers. aor. opt. act. of ἐσελάω, with epic doubling of -σσ-.

142[273] κλᾶρον 'estate', i.e. territory. σάω: (Homeric σάου): imper. mid. of σαόω (= σώιζω).

IV

The first hymn is to Zeus, first of the gods. It probably dates from early in Callimachus' career (? c. 280 B.C. – see 55–67 n.); but we observe here already the main characteristics of his· writing – wit, erudition, allusiveness, literary self-consciousness. The poem's movement is novel and interesting. After a resounding start (1–3) the tone changes to one of doubt – who tells the true story about Zeus's birth? This doubt is dispelled in a surprising and witty manner, and we hear next of Zeus's birth and his secret rearing in Crete (10–54). This passage is full of geographical allusions and aetiologies which implicitly 'prove' the truth of Callimachus' version of events by an appeal to names and places still in existence. Next comes the story, again polemically presented, of the division between Zeus and Hades of heaven and the underworld, and a section on kings, the particular objects of Zeus's patronage. The poem thus builds up to a climactic reference to Ptolemy, pre-eminent amongst the favourites of Zeus and Zeus-like himself in his omnipotence (85–90). Finally there is a coda structured on traditional lines but strikingly novel in effect.

Throughout the hymn there can be sensed a contrast between the poet's ingenuous stance as praiser of the god and the sophisticated and allusive nature of his presentation (4–9, 5, 8, 29, 42–54, 55–67, 79, 91–6 nn.); between, that is, the religious and the literary. Alternations of mood and tone, of lightness and gravity, produce a complex whole, a poem constantly drawing attention to its innovatory status. It is not possible to form any idea of Callimachus' own religious views from these hymns. What one can say is that the poem captures the imagination chiefly because of the fascinating way in which it adapts, modifies and wittily exploits basic constituents of the hymn-genre.

Bibl.: G. R. McLennan, *Callimachus: Hymn to Zeus* (Rome, 1977); N. Hopkinson, 'Callimachus' *Hymn to Zeus*', *C.Q.* n.s. 34 (1984) 139–48.

1[274] Ζηνὸς . . . παρὰ σπονδῇσιν: these 'libations to Zeus' suggest that the poem is to be imagined as sung before a symposium, when it was the custom to pour three libations (to Olympian Zeus, the Heroes and Zeus Soter) and sing a hymn to a pipe accompaniment. The poem contains no further reference to such a setting. **Ζηνός:** in Homeric hymns the god's name is often first word. The first of the gods here begins the first poem of Call.'s collection. Cf. *409* n. **ἔοι:** epic form of εἴη.

1–2[274–5] ἀείδειν | λώιον 'better to sing', infin. depending on the adj. (Goodwin, *GMT* § 759).

2[275] ἀεί . . . αἰέν: a third form, αἰεί, occurs in line 9 (cf. *51* n.). There is word-play between ἀεί and ἀείδειν, hinting at immortality through song (cf. *375*, *819* n., *1500*, Theoc. 16.1–4).

3[276] A resounding four-word line, chiastically constructed. **Πηλαγόνων**: the MSS all read Πηλογόνων, 'the Mud-born Ones' (i.e. the Giants born from Γῆ), which gives a neat contrast with the Heavenly Ones at line-end. But independent sources which quote the line have Πηλαγόνων 'Pelagonians', which is said by Strabo to be another name for the Titans. Choice between these two readings is very difficult.

4–9[277–82] The usual account told how Zeus was born in a cave on Mt Dicte (or Mt Ida) in Crete; but Call. is to propound an alternative version in which he is born on Mt Lycaeum in Arcadia and transported to Crete soon afterwards; cf. 42–54 n. (Call. is our earliest source for this Arcadian version.) Choice between many possibilities is a standard technique at the beginning of hymns. Here the apparently serious inquiry after fact is wittily sidestepped in lines 8–9.

4[277] πῶς καί: for this emphatic use of καί following an interrogative see Denniston, *GP* 312–16. **νιν**: Call. occasionally uses Doric forms of pronouns, so that we cannot with certainty emend to epic μιν. **ἀείσομεν**: the doubting tone of line 5 suggests that this verb is not fut. but deliberative aor. subj. with 'epic' short vowel (= ἀείσωμεν); cf. e.g. Aesch. *Choe.* 997 τί νιν προσείπω;

5[278] This line is generally thought to be adapted from a hymn to Eros by Antagoras of Rhodes, a contemporary of Call.: ἐν δοιῆι μοι θυμός, ὅ τοι γένος ἀμφίσβητον (fr. 1.1, *CA* p. 120). But it is hardly certain who borrowed from whom. **ἐν δοιῆι** 'in two minds'.

6[279] Ἰδαίοισιν: Cretan, not Trojan, Ida.

6–7[279–80] σὲ μὲν . . . σὲ δ᾽: μέν and δέ here serve a dual purpose: (1) to reinforce the anaphora, a common use even where no contrast is involved (Denniston, *GP* 370); (2) to point the contrast between Idaean and Arcadian.

7[280] πάτερ: piquant in a discussion of his birth (cf. 43, Hes. *Theog.* 468).

8[281] "Κρῆτες ἀεὶ ψεῦσται": Cretans were proverbial liars. These words are a well known quotation from Epimenides, a sixth-cent. Cretan poet and wise man. (The full line, which is modelled on Hes. *Theog.* 26 and was perhaps addressed to Epimenides by the Muses, reads Κρῆτες ἀεὶ ψεῦσται, κακὰ θηρία, γαστέρες ἀργαί.) Whether these words constitute Zeus's reply or the poet's own statement is left ambiguous.

9–10[282–3] τάφον . . . ἐτεκτήναντο: like Eng. 'forge' and 'fabricate' τεκταίνομαι can refer to construction and deceit. Here both meanings are appropriate: they deceitfully built the tomb. In Crete

Zeus seems originally to have been a nature-god like Adonis, who died and was reborn each year (see p. 217). Zeus's tomb was shown in various places on the island.

9[282] αἰεί: pointedly contrasting with ἀεί in line 8: Zeus lives 'for ever'; so the Cretans are 'ever' liars.

10[283] Παρρασίηι: an area in S. Arcadia. **μάλιστα** qualifies θάμνοισι περισκεπές.

11[284] περισκεπές 'covered all round' (σκέπας = 'shelter' in Homer). **ἔνθεν** 'for that reason', pointing an αἴτιον: cf. 44.

12–13[285–6] οὐδέ . . . μιν . . . ἐπιμίσγεται: because giving birth is an unclean act forbidden in holy places. ἐπιμίσγομαι often denotes sexual intercourse; its use here of women 'in need of the goddess of childbirth' perhaps plays on that meaning. Elsewhere this verb takes the dat.; acc. μιν perhaps because motion is implied. Cf. *Il.* 15.32–3 φιλότης τε καὶ εὐνή, | ἦν ἐμίγης (though ἦν is there an internal acc.).

13[286] ἑρπετόν: any animal, not just a creeping one. A Homeric *hapax* (*Od.* 4.418).

14[287] Ἀπιδανῆες 'Peloponnesians', named after the mythical king Apis. The sequel shows that Call. is hinting at derivation from ἀ + πιεῖν, i.e. 'non-drinkers': cf. 19–20, 41 nn.

15[288] μεγάλων . . . κόλπων: she was 'big' with child. The basic meaning of κόλπος was perhaps 'inlet-like space'; it is used as a poetic euphemism for 'womb'.

16[289] ῥόον ὕδατος: probably a play on the etymology of ῾Ρείη / ῾Ρέη, which some derived from ῥεῖν (cf. 18, 21). Despite being named after flowing water she cannot find even a spring. See *J.H.S.* 104 (1984) 176–7.

17[290] λύματα χυτλώσαιτο: both literal cleansing and ritual purification after childbirth. χυτλόομαι is found once in Homer (*Od.* 6.80), meaning 'anoint oneself', intrans. **λοέσσαι:** 3rd sing. aor. opt. of λοέω.

18–41[291–314] Arcadia and its rivers, which flowed underground until Zeus's birth; Zeus is tended by the nymph Neda. Call.'s prose works Περὶ νυμφῶν and Περὶ ποταμῶν (frr. 413, 457–9) probably dealt with these stories in detail.

19[292] λευκότατος: λευκὸν ὕδωρ is a stock phrase for clear, translucent water.

19–20[292–3] ἄβροχος . . . ᾿Αζηνίς: probably pointing the derivation from ἄζα, 'dryness'; but McLennan may be right to see a further word-play, ἀ-Ζην- = 'Zeus-less'. Azania = N. Arcadia.

20[293] μέλλεν 'was destined to . . .'.

21[294] αὖτις 'thereafter'. **λύσατο μίτρην**: another poetic euphemism for giving birth.

22[295] σαρωνίδας 'oak-trees', a very rare word not attested before the Hellenistic period.

23[296] ἤειρεν: it was as yet underground. **Μέλας**: complement to λευκότατος (19). **ὤκχησεν**: ὀκχέω, by-form of ὀχέω, is first attested in Pindar (*Ol.* 2.67). Wagons usually carry things; but here a river bears wagons.

24[297] ἄνω: prep. + gen., a rare use. **διεροῦ περ ἐόντος**: it was 'wet' but hidden under the ground. Some ancient grammarians derived διερός from Δι-, because it is Zeus who rains.

25[298] ἰλυούς 'lairs', places which enclose (εἰλύω) animals. **ἐβάλοντο**: i.e. 'placed', 'made': cf. LSJ s.v. βάλλω A.II.6 for similar meanings. **κινώπετα** 'reptiles', first here.

26[299] πολύστιον: στῖον = 'pebble'.

29[302] Γαῖα φίλη, τέκε καὶ σύ: at *Il.* 21.106 Achilles, about to kill Lycaon, says ἀλλά, φίλος, θάνε καὶ σύ; he strikes him with his sword, ἐκ δ' αἷμα μέλαν ῥέε, δεῦε δὲ γαῖαν (119). Call.'s allusion contrasts pointedly with the Homeric context, birth vs death. Rhea strikes the earth a blow (31), and from the 'wound' flows not blood, but water (32). **Γαῖα φίλη** is a rhyming adaptation of Odysseus' address to his old nurse, μαῖα φίλη (*Od.* 20.129, etc.). **τεαὶ δ' ὠδῖνες ἐλαφραί**: oxymoronic: '*your* birth-pangs are light', i.e. you give birth easily. Γῆ is unlimitedly fecund, mother of all.

30[303] ἀντανύσασα = ἀνατανύσασα; in epic some preps. can lose their final vowel, e.g. πάρ, κάτ; cf. *493* n. τανύω is an epic equivalent of τείνω.

31[304] πουλύ: adv.; cf. 38, *189*.

32[305] ἔχεεν: probably aor., an epic alternative to ἔχευε; but possibly imperf., 'began to pour'. **χρόα φαιδρύνασα**: <Hes. *WD* 753.

33[306] ὦνα: = ὦ ἄνα (contrast 8). **σπείρωσε** 'swaddled'. σπειρόω is a very rare alternative to σπαργανόω.

34[307] κευθμόν 'hiding-place' (the Cretan cave): a Homeric *hapax* (*Il.* 13.28), 3rd decl. κευθμών, -ῶνος being the commoner form.

35[308] Νυμφέων: according to Pausanias 8.38.3 the others were

Theisoa and Hagno. **μαιώσαντο** 'acted as midwives'. μαιόομαι = μαιεύομαι, the commoner form.

36[309] πρωτίστη γενεή: the nymphs (nom. in apposition to αἵ) who attended Rhea were of the oldest 'race' of nymphs, junior only to Styx (the eldest daughter of Ocean – Hes. *Theog.* 775–7) and Philyra (mother of Chiron by Cronus). **τὲ Φιλ-**: Homer often allows a short vowel to stand in the first half of the foot before a single consonant, and Hellenistic poets reproduce the precious anomaly: see West, *GM* 156.

37[310] ἀλίην 'vain', 'useless', i.e. it was not a useless favour that Hera repaid Neda for her care. The word is no doubt chosen for the sake of a pun on ἅλιος, 'of the sea', because of the watery context: see LSJ s.v. ἅλιος (A) and (B). For a similar pun cf. on *1658–61*.

38–9[311–12] ποθι . . . κατ' αὐτὸ | . . . πτολίεθρον 'somewhere right by the city'.

39[312] Καυκώνων . . . Λέπρειον: the ancient nation of the Caucones was based on Lepreum in southern Elis. The town was actually several miles inland from the spot where Neda joined the sea (hence ποθι). **πεφάτισται** 'is called', a Hellenistic use of φατίζω.

40[313] Νηρῆϊ: metonymic for the sea, a personification complementary to that of Neda. **παλαιότατον**: because it was Arcadia's first visible river. The nymph/river is πρεσβυτάτη (35).

41[314] υἱωνοί . . . Λυκαονίης ἄρκτοιο: Callisto, daughter of Lycaon, was raped by Zeus and changed by him into a bear (cf. Io, *1088–1105* n.) to escape the notice of Hera. Hera persuaded Artemis to shoot her; Zeus turned her into the constellation of the Bear and rescued her unborn child, calling it Arcas (<ἄρκτος), after whom the Arcadians, Callisto's descendants (υἱωνοί), were named. There is a verbal paradox in the expression Λυκαονίης ἄρκτοιο, wolf ∼ bear. The Arcadian section ends with a line of spondaic rhythm; cf. 54, end of the Cretan section. **πίνουσι**: referring back to the etymology of Ἀπιδανῆες in 14: the Arcadians, formerly 'non-drinkers', now drink the waters of Neda.

42–54[315–27] Zeus's upbringing in Crete. The transition from Arcadia to Crete, which reconciles the two main versions of Zeus's birth (4–9 n.), was made at 33–4; here topographical sleight-of-hand unites the two places: towns called Thenae existed in both.

42–3[315–16] ἐπὶ Κνωσοῖο . . . ἐγγύθι Κνωσοῦ: whilst alluding to the two towns named Thenae Call. presents two forms of the gen. of Cnossus, and in addition varies the prosody before each.

43[316] Ζεῦ πάτερ: cf. 7 n. **(Θεναὶ δ' ἔσαν ἐγγύθι Κνωσοῦ):** perhaps translate 'it was the Thenae near Cnossus' – i.e. not, as the reader might have imagined, Thenae in Arcadia.

44[317] πέσε . . . ἄπ': = ἀπέπεσε ('anastrophic tmesis', in which the prep. follows the verb from which it is disjoined).

45[318] Κύδωνες 'Cretans'. Cydonia strictly = NW Crete.

46–7[319–20] Κυρβάντων ἑτάραι . . . Δικταῖαι Μελίαι 'ash-tree nymphs of Mt Dicte, companions of the Corybants' (Κυρβ- shortened form of Κορυβ-). The Corybants were youths attendant on the Phrygian goddess Cybele, the Curetes youths attendant on Cretan Rhea. Similarities between the two cults led to Corybants and Curetes being treated as virtual synonyms (cf. 52).

47[320] 'Αδρήστεια: a nymph, sister of the Curetes.

48[321] λίκνωι ἐνὶ χρυσέωι: gods' attributes are conventionally golden (cf. *180–1* n.). The λίκνον was a scoop-shaped winnowing-basket suitable for use as a cradle: see J. E. Harrison, 'Mystica vannus Iacchi', *J.H.S.* 23 (1903) 292–324. **ἐθήσαο:** from θῆσθαι, 'suck'.

49[322] αἰγὸς 'Αμαλθείης: according to Diodorus 5.70 this was the origin of Zeus's epithet αἰγίοχος. Other accounts made Amalthea a nymph. **ἐπὶ . . . ἔβρως:** 2nd aor. act. of ἐπιβιβρώσκω, 'eat in addition'.

50[323] γέντο: *190* n. **ἐξαπιναῖα:** gods brook no delay: cf. 56, 57 n., 87–8. **ἔργα:** probably = 'products', i.e. honey.

51[324] κλείουσι = καλέουσι, as often in Hellenistic poetry; in Homer = 'celebrate'. καλέουσι itself occurs at 45; cf. 2 n.

52[325] 'The Curetes vigorously (?) danced you a war-dance', σε obj. of περιωρχήσαντο (tmesis), πρύλιν internal acc. **οὖλα:** a word of many meanings – 'in quick tempo.' (LSJ), 'vigorously' and 'intensely' are possibilities here. **πρύλιν:** Cretan word for the πυρρίχη or dance in armour.

53[326] πεπλήγοντες: perf. part. with pres. ending, a sporadically occurring Aeolic feature of Homeric language; or possibly a redupl. aor. Participial πεπλήγων is found at *Il.* 2.264, though some ancient scholars preferred to write πεπληγώς: Call. alludes to a controversial point of philology.

54[327] καὶ μή: i.e. καὶ ἵνα μὴ εἰσαῖοι. **κουρίζοντος:** elsewhere this verb means 'be a youth/child'; here 'uttering babyish cries'. Call. is making an etymological point: cf. Strabo 10.3.19 τὸν Δία κουροτροφή-σαντας Κούρητας ὀνομασθῆναι.

55–67[328–40] The young Zeus grew swiftly and gained heaven as his habitation. According to Homer Zeus was the elder brother (*Il.* 13.355, 15.166) and was apportioned heaven by lot (*Il.* 15.187–93); Hesiod made him the youngest (*Theog.* 478), gaining power by the gods' universal consent (*Theog.* 881–5). Call. adopts in outline this latter version, probably in order to point the parallel with Ptolemy Philadelphus, youngest of Soter's five sons.

55[328] κᾱλά . . . κᾰλά: adverbial. A prosodic preciosity, alternative epic scansions of the same word within the same line. Cf. *203–4* n., *Glotta* 60 (1982) 162–78. ἠέξευ: 2nd pers. imperf. mid. of ἀέξω, 'increase'. ἔτραφες: this 2nd aor. act. of τρέφω is used almost as a passive in Homer. οὐράνιε: pointing the subject of the next section, Zeus's acquisition of the οὐρανός.

56[329] ἀνήβησας: usually 'grow young again'; here 'grow up'. ἴουλοι 'down', a Homeric *hapax* (*Od.* 11.319).

57[330] τέλεια: literally 'full-grown': there was nothing childish about his plans. Τέλειος, 'fulfiller', was a title of Zeus. Immediate fulfilment of intention is a characteristic of gods: see Nisbet & Hubbard on Horace, *Odes* 1.12.31. Cf. 87 n.

58[331] τῶι: *160* n. τοι = σοι; dat. with ἐμέγηραν (59), 'begrudge ⟨to⟩ you'. γνωτοί 'brothers', a Homeric word.

59[332] ἐπιδαίσιον 'apportioned' (ἐπιδαίομαι = 'distribute').

60[333] δηναιοὶ . . . ἀοιδοί: Homer, specifically (55–67 n.), and Pindar (*Ol.* 7.54 ff.). δηναιός is found once in Homer (*Il.* 5.407), = 'long-lived'; here 'living long ago'.

61[334] διάτριχα 'three ways' (=τρίχα). νεῖμαι: aor. inf. act. of νέμω.

62[335] κλῆρον ἐρύσσαι 'would draw a lot' (aor. opt.).

63[336] μή: *38* n. νενίηλος 'silly'; not found elsewhere. ἐπ' ἰσαίηι 'on equal terms' or 'for equal shares'. Probably a neologism. ἔοικε 'it is reasonable', = εἰκός ἐστι; cf. 85. πήλασθαι: aor. inf. mid. of πάλλομαι, 'draw lots'.

64[337] τά: heaven and underworld. τόσσον ὅσον . . . πλεῖστον: a rather redundant expression, lit. 'so much as very greatly'. διά . . . ἔχουσι: tmesis. For the pl. cf. *70* n.

65[338] The liar-theme again (cf. 7–8, 60). The line is open to two interpretations, hypothetical and actual: either 'If *I* lie, I hope to be more persuasive than that!' or 'May *my* lies (i.e. *my* poetry) be more convincing than that!' Poets do not always tell the truth; but a more important criterion is the success of the illusion. Cf. *Od.* 19.203–4, Hes. *Theog.* 27–8 (the Muses) ἴδμεν ψεύδεα πολλὰ λέγειν ἐτύμοισιν ὅμοια, | ἴδμεν δ', εὖτ' ἐθέλωμεν, ἀληθέα γηρύσασθαι. **πεπίθοιεν**: redupl. aor. opt. act. of πείθω.

66[339] ἐσσῆνα 'king', perhaps lit. 'leader of the swarm' (ἐσμός).

67–90[340–63] The attributes of Zeus – he is patron of the eagle, king of birds, and of earthly rulers. Other occupations he leaves to the lesser gods; but kings belong to Zeus, and Ptolemy is pre-eminent amongst them.

67[340] σή τε βίη τό τε κάρτος: traditional attributes of Zeus, sometimes depicted as separate deities (cf. Hes. *Theog.* 385–8 . . . αἰεὶ πὰρ Ζηνὶ βαρυκτύπωι ἑδριόωνται, [Aesch.] *Prom.* 1). Here the two aspects seem to be merged: σή suggests an abstract attribute, while the position of κάρτος and βίη next to the throne suggests deities on hand to fulfil Zeus's commands. **ὅ** = διό, 'for which reason'. **εἴσαο**: aor. mid. of ἵζω, 'place'.

68–9[341–2] 'You made far the most eminent of birds the messenger of your portents.' Appearance of the eagle was considered a sign from Zeus.

69[342] ἐνδέξια: omens on the observer's right were thought propitious (δεξιός). The poet prays for good fortune for unspecified 'friends'.

70[343] ὅ τι: vaguer than ὅν τινα. **οὐ**: *sc.* εἷλεο.

71[344] ἐμπεράμους: 'skilled in' + gen.; cf. *156*n. **σακέσπαλον**: lit. 'shield-wielder', a Homeric *hapax* (*Il.* 5.126). **οὐ μὲν ἀοιδόν** 'nor, again, the poet' – ironic self-depreciation. For uses of οὐ μέν see Denniston, *GP* 362.

72[345] ὀλίζοσιν: comparative of ὀλίγος, found only once in Homer (*Il.* 18.519) but attested in Attic inscriptions. **αὖθι** 'forthwith'; *35* n.

74[347] ὧν ἴδρις αἰχμῆς: sc. ὑπὸ χεῖρά ἐστι.

76[349] αὐτίκα 'for example', a meaning rare in verse. **χαλκῆας** 'blacksmiths', acc. pl. of χαλκεύς. **ὑδείομεν**: ὑδε(ι)ω, 'sing', is not found in extant literature before the Hellenistic period. **Ἡφαίστοιο** 'as belonging to Hephaestus'.

77[350] ἐπακτῆρας 'huntsmen', who ἐπάγουσι the dogs. **Χιτώνης**: probably 'she who wears the χιτών' or hunting-tunic.

78[351] λύρης . . . οἴμους 'the pathways of song': cf. p. 89.

78–80[352–3] ' "But *kings* are from Zeus", since there is nothing more

holy than Zeus's kings; and for that reason you chose them as your lot.'
I.e. kings are the most worshipful of mortals and are therefore adopted
by Zeus, most worshipful of gods. The sense would be clearer if the
second Διός were removed ('kings belong to Zeus because no one is more
worshipful than they'); but it can perhaps stand as emphasizing the
supervisory nature of Zeus's patronage.

79[352] **"ἐκ δὲ Διὸς βασιλῆες"**: a quotation from *Theog.* 96, part of a
passage where Hesiod describes the powers of persuasion which the
Muses bestow on good kings and on poets (cf. 78).

80[353] **λάξιν**: Ionic form of λῆξις, '(allotted) portion'.

81[354] **δῶκας**: sc. βασιλεῦσι.

82–3[355–6] 'Keeping watch to see who ⟨misdirect⟩ the people with
crooked laws and who, conversely, direct them ⟨with good laws⟩': a
zeugma with an element of paradox, crooked and straight; adapted
from *Il.* 16.387 σκολιὰς κρίνωσι θέμιστας. Straight and crooked judgements are mentioned at e.g. *Il.* 16.386–8, Hes. *WD* 256–64; and note
particularly *Theog.* 84–6 οἱ δέ τε λαοὶ | πάντες ἐς αὐτὸν (the good king; cf.
79 n.) ὁρῶσι διακρίνοντα θέμιστας | ἰθείησι δίκησι.

82[355] **ἄκρησ' ἐν πολίεσσιν**: i.e. ἐν ἀκροπόλεσι. **ἐπόψιος** 'keeping
watch', not (as in Homer) 'conspicuous'. For syntactical purposes here
ἐπόψιος = ἐφορῶν, introducing the direct interrogative clauses οἵ
τε…οἵ τε: cf. e.g. *Il.* 2.365–6 γνώσηι…ὅς θ' ἡγεμόνων κακός, ὅς τέ νυ
λαῶν, | ἠδ' ὅς κ' ἐσθλὸς ἔηισι, *254–5*.

84[357] **ῥυηφενίην** 'wealth', perhaps coined by Call. on the model of
Homeric εὐηφενής, 'wealthy' (εὐ + ἄφενος with 'metrical lengthening')
with reference to the phrase ῥυδὸν ἀφνειοῖο, '⟨over⟩flowingly rich'
(*Od.* 15.426). **σφισιν**: the rich.

85[358] **ἔοικε**: 63 n. **τεκμήρασθαι** 'judge by', + dat.

86[359] **εὐρὺ βέβηκεν**: an unusual expression, presumably = 'he has
gained power far and wide', 'he is widely established' – cf. the Homeric
phrase εὐρὺ κρείων and Herod. 7.164 τυραννίδα… εὖ βεβηκυῖαν, 'firmly
established'.

87[360] Ptolemy is Zeus-like in immediately fulfilling his intentions:
cf. 57 ἐφράσσαο πάντα τέλεια & n.

88[361] **εὖτε** 'at the very moment when…'.

89[362] **οἱ … τῶν**: less fortunate rulers. **πλειῶνι** 'a full year', a rare
word found earlier only at Hes. *WD* 617.

89–90[362–3] **ἀπό … ἄνην ἐκόλουσας** 'you cut off their fulfilment', i.e. frustrate their intentions (gnomic aor.). ἄνη is found elsewhere only at Alcman fr. 1.83 and Aesch. *Septem* 713.

90[363] ἐνέκλασσας δὲ μενοινήν 'you thwart their desire'. μενοινή is not found before the Hellenistic period. For ἐνικλᾶν cf. *76*.

91–6[364–9] All the Homeric hymns close with a coda of farewell to the god. In these lines Call. uses anaphora and parallelism to great effect in a final prayer for wealth and virtue. It would be rash to assume that this is a plea for Ptolemaic patronage early in the poet's career: his prayer is for general prosperity for the king and his people. *Homeric Hymns* 15 and 20 end δίδου δ' ἀρετήν τε καὶ ὄλβον; and it is by presenting variations on this theme, and by finally closing with these very words (*96*), that Call. points his own similarities to and differences from traditional hexameter hymns.

91[364] πανυπέρτατε: a Homeric *hapax* (*Od.* 9.25). **δῶτορ ἐάων** 'giver of good things' (*Od.* 8.335), irreg. gen. pl. of ἐΰς.

92[365] ἀπημονίης 'freedom from harm (πῆμα)'; not found elsewhere.

92–3[365–6] Zeus's deeds are too great for poetry. We realize why Call. has stressed the γοναί of Zeus, but not his ἔργα, in this poem.

93[366] τίς κεν Διὸς ἔργματ' ἀείσει;: κε/ἄν + fut. indic. is found in Homer (Goodwin, *GMT* § 196) – not in sentences of this kind, but in statements of what is likely to happen (cf. *95:3–4*). Perhaps the more regular optative (ἀείσαι or ἀείδοι) should be restored here.

94[367] ἄφενος: 3rd decl. neut.; in 96 2nd decl. masc.; in 84 1st decl. fem. (compounded): another aspect of self-conscious variation (cf. *2*, *51* nn.).

95–6[368–9] Wealth and virtue are traditionally linked: cf. e.g. Hes. *WD* 313 πλούτωι δ' ἀρετὴ καὶ κῦδος ὀπηδεῖ, with West's n.

95[368] ἀέξειν 'increase in repute', i.e. exalt.

96[369] ἀφένοιο: sc. ἄτερ.

V

Cleanthes

Cleanthes (331–232 B.C.), inspired by Stoic teachers, moved to Athens from his home town of Assos near Troy and became a disciple of Zeno, the founder of Stoicism, whom he eventually succeeded as head of the school in 263. He seems to have adorned his prose philosophical works with passages of hexameter and iambic verse, which he considered more suitable to convey the grandeur of divinity (Seneca, *Epist.* 108.10). This hymn is his only complete poem of any length to survive. It makes for an interesting comparison with Callimachus' *Hymn to Zeus* (*274–369*). Whereas Callimachus is concerned with adaptation of traditional hymnic features for a self-consciously literary effect, Cleanthes adapts and modifies the basic format of the hexameter hymn (invocation, ἀρεταί of the god, prayer and farewell) in rather rough-hewn verse (e.g. harsh hiatus at 10, 18 and ?33) for a philosophical purpose (1–6, 7–31 nn.), subsuming the standard poetic Zeus and his conventional attributes and epithets into the new Stoic cosmology. The poem is full of allusions to Heraclitus, whose world-view was seen by Cleanthes as reinforcing Zeno's Stoic ideas: cf. 2 with Her. frr. 35 and 41 Diels–Kranz; 10–12 ~ frr. 3, 64; 18–19 ~ frr. 10, 51; 20–1 ~ frr. 1, 2, 50; 24–6 ~ frr. 34, 114; 30–1 ~ fr. 110; 34–5 ~ fr. 41, and see Long, art. cit.

Bibl.: Frr. in *CA* pp. 227–31. Gen.: A. W. James, 'The Zeus hymns of Cleanthes and Aratus', *Antichthon* 6 (1972) 28–38; A. A. Long, 'Heraclitus and Stoicism', ΦΙΛΟΣΟΦΙΑ 5–6 (1975–6) 133–53; F. H. Sandbach, *The Stoics* (London, 1975).

1–6[370–5] Proem. The universal god/νόμος directs all things and deserves our praise. Cl. uses largely Homeric vocabulary with new meaning (1, 2, 5 nn.). His invocation is traditionally structured (address to the god, epithets, repetition of 2nd pers. pronoun, reason for singing); cf. Call.'s more experimental opening. Lines 1 and 2 are both tricola, the second a 'rising' tricolon in which each sense unit is longer than the last. End-stopped lines and sonorous epithets (1–2; cf. 32) increase the effect of stateliness and solemnity.

1[370] κύδιστ': from the Homeric voc. phrase Ζεῦ κύδιστε μέγιστε (*Il.* 2.412, etc.). **πολυώνυμε:** in traditional religious contexts this word refers to a god's many cult-titles; but here it is applied to the Stoic god, who is λόγος / νόμος / φύσις, πρόνοια, εἱμαρμένη, etc. (The Stoic 'god', unlike the Judaeo-Christian god, is not over and above the universe he creates and rules, but is identical with it.) Perhaps there is also an allusion to the Stoic idea that the names of the different Olympians are in fact all names for different parts or aspects of the single φύσις.

2[371] φύσεως ἀρχηγέ 'first cause of nature'. For Stoics god and nature are one and the same – see 1 n. ἀρχηγός, a poetic word for 'chief' or 'leader', is here used as a Stoic technical term. φύσις, 'the nature of things', gives each thing in the world its own individual nature and controls the processes of change and decay. **νόμου μέτα**: all things are directed by divine law in accordance with Reason, λόγος.

4[373] θεοῦ μίμημα: mortals are created in god's image in the sense that they alone of living things have the faculty of reason and are thus in touch with the divine Reason which underlies the universe.

5[374] A reminiscence of *Il.* 17.447 = *Od.* 18.131 ('there is nothing feebler / more wretched than man') πάντων ὅσσα τε γαῖαν ἔπι πνείει τε καὶ ἕρπει; but Cl.'s Stoic philosophy is more optimistic than this. The antecedent to ὅσα is omitted.

7–31[376–400] As fiery principle in the universe the Zeus / λόγος directs all things. The Stoic world-view is rigidly deterministic – every single thing which happens is foreordained and takes place in accordance with the divine plan / λόγος, which works always for the good. Fools no less than the wise act out their part in this divine plan; but whereas the wise play their part willingly, fools vainly struggle against what is fated. (This deterministic view involved Stoics in insoluble problems in discussing free will: is not the fool's folly fated, too?) In these lines the stately end-stopped rhythm continues, reinforced by frequent anaphora and repetition (11/12, 15/16, 19, 24, 27/8, 26/30), another traditional hymnic device (cf. *364–9* n.).

7[376] ἐλισσόμενος περὶ γαῖαν: the celestial sphere was seen to revolve around the earth, and Stoics believed in a geocentric universe.

8[377] ἑκών: emphatic, contrasting with the foolish men of 17–31, who vainly struggle against the λόγος.

9[378] ὑποεργόν 'assisting you', i.e. 'as your instrument'.

10–11[379–80] The Stoics, following Heraclitus, saw pure ethereal fire (πῦρ ἀείζωον, Her. fr. 30) as the guiding principle of the universe (τὰ δὲ πάντα οἰακίζει κεραυνός, fr. 64). They believed that a 'tension', τόνος, held together both the universe as a whole and each individual thing in it (cf. Her.'s παλίντροπος ἁρμονίη ὅκωσπερ τόξου καὶ λύρης, fr. 51); this tension was brought about by the πληγὴ πυρός, the directive stroke of fire.

10[379] ἀμφήκη 'forked'.

12[381] κοινὸν λόγον: Reason / Order, which pervades the whole universe. **διά**: there may be a reference to the etymologizing of Δία as διά (cf. Hes. *WD* 3–4, *410*n.), which Stoics approved: it is 'through' Zeus that all things happen (Chrysippus, *SVF* II 1062). (They also derived Ζῆνα from ζῆν: he is giver of life.)

13[382] μεγάλοις: the sun and moon.

After 13 there is a lacuna, probably of several lines – Cl. may have listed other things pervaded by the Zeus / λόγος.

14[383] As it stands, this line makes very poor sense. It seems likely that not only the first two words are corrupt.

15–31[384–400] These lines seem to imply two approaches to the problem of evil, or rather what non-Stoics term 'evil' or 'bad' (cf. 7–31 n.). (1) 18–21. What seems bad is so only on a narrow view. When seen in wider perspective bad things turn out to be part of the overall beneficent plan (ἕνα...λόγον, 21). (2) Men should try to discern this plan and live in accord with it, εὐκόσμως, using the reason with which they have been endowed (4 n.). Foolish (in common parlance 'wicked') men do not perceive the plan and struggle against it οὐδενὶ κόσμωι (28); but their efforts are vain, since they are not living in accord with Nature and Fate, the only truly good and fulfilled life (24–5).

16[385] πόλον: in poetry simply = 'sky', not 'pole'. **θεῖον** because Zeus / λόγος is immanent there, too.

18–19[387–8] 'You know how to bring the excessive into line and to order the disordered, and in your sight (σοί, emphatic) things 'apparentlỹ at odds with one another are reconciled': i.e. excesses are smoothed out on a wider view of things, apparent disorder turns out to contribute to the ordered nature of the universe, and things which to our limited understanding seem at odds are in fact part of the cosmic plan. For the wording cf. Solon fr. 4.32 Εὐνομίη δ' εὔκοσμα καὶ ἄρτια πάντ' ἀποφαίνει, and for the sentiment Her. frr. 67 ὁ θεὸς ἡμέρη εὐφρόνη, χειμὼν θέρος, κτλ. and 102 τῶι μὲν θεῶι πάντα καὶ ἀγαθὰ καὶ δίκαια...

19[388] τὰ δ': this seems preferable to the MSS καί: (1) καί...καί...καί implies three parallel things; but only the first two are in fact parallel. (2) The other neut. plurals have the article.

20[389] ὧδε: antecedent to ὥσθ' (21).

21[390] πάντων λόγον 'Reason which belongs to, affects, all things'.

22[391] ἐῶσιν 'dismiss'. Rather weak after the more act. φεύγοντες.

24–5[393–4] If they had the sense to perceive and obey the κοινὸς νόμος which the rest of the κόσμος follows (8 πείθεται) they would have (κεν with ἔχοιεν) a good life in Stoic terms. Cl. is alluding to Heraclitus' statement (fr. 114) that although individual cities' laws may differ, a κοινὸς νόμος underlies them all. Heraclitus puns on ξυνῶι (=κοινῶι) and ξὺν ν(o)ωι – those who 'have sense' should rely on what is 'common to all', the νόμος. Here Cl. makes a similar pun with σὺν νῶι in 25, which contrasts with ἄνευ νόου (26) as ξυνῶι would with ἄλλος ἐπ' ἄλλο.

26[395] αὖθ' 'on the contrary'.

27[396] σπουδὴν δυσέριστον 'evil competition with one another' (not 'misplaced competitiveness') – the Stoic's striving to live in accord with the divine plan is not *competitive* at all, since everyone can succeed).

28[397] κερδοσύνας: here probably = κέρδεα, 'gains' (not 'cunning', 'craft', as LSJ).

29[398] ἄνεσιν: lit. 'loosening' (< ἀνίημι), i.e. relaxation (< *laxare*), enjoyments. For Stoics not bodily pleasure, but the pursuit of it, is wrong.

30–1[399–400] The sense must be 'they strive for βίον ἐσθλόν (25) but get only its opposite'. ἄλλα cannot therefore be the antecedent of τῶνδε, since they are not striving for the opposite of inconsistency. Dawe's supplement gives the necessary antecedent, κακῶν.

30[399] ἐπ' qualifies ἄλλα: at one time they are carried towards one object, at another time towards another.

31[400] μάλα πάμπαν: perhaps qualifying ἐναντία rather than the participle: they strive for 'the complete opposite' of what they actually achieve.

32–9[401–8] It is due to god / λόγος that we live and move and have our being: praise him. A single, majestic period rounds off the hymn. There are several echoes of the proem (32 three epithets + voc. ∼ 1–2, 35 ∼ 2, 37 ∼ 3, 38 ∼ 5, 39 ∼ 1/6); and, like the proem, this concluding section turns conventional hymnic techniques to novel purpose (32 n.; cf. 1 and 2 nn.). The standard closing prayer in Greek hymns is a bargain between two unequal and dissimilar parties in which man gives god honours and receives prosperity in return. Here, however, god must act first to honour the worshipper and will then be honoured in return (36). This is an 'inward' religion in which god and man *share* Reason; only if god gives it can man use it to give proper worship.

32[401] Vocatives of one, three, four and five syllables give an impressive crescendo effect. **ἀλλά:** often used to introduce a closing prayer: cf. *735, 1071, 1193*. **κελαινεφές:** a traditional Homeric epithet of

Zeus, with no particular Stoic application. **ἀρχικέραυνε**: if this is the right reading it is a pointed Stoic variation on the Homeric ἀργικέραυνε ('with bright lightning'): Zeus is controller of the ethereal Heraclitean fire (10–11 n.). (Strictly speaking, Zeus *is* the fire; but cf. 2 φύσεως ἀρχηγέ.)

33[402] ἀπειροσύνης: the ignorance which prevents all but a handful of Stoics from discerning and living perfectly in accord with the λόγος.

38[407] θνητόν: the poet moves from the generalizing pl. to speak in his own person (cf. 4–6). **γέρας** 'prerogative' – men and gods alone have the intelligence to praise the controlling principle, and they should use it.

39[408] θεοῖς: Stoics did not rule out the existence of many gods: cf. 1 n. **ἀεί** is itself a κοινὸς λόγος, since it qualifies both ὑμνεῖν and νόμον: αἰὲν ἀείσω in line 6 and ὑμνοῦντες . . . διηνεκές in 37 suggest that it should qualify ὑμνεῖν; but the νόμος is κοινός for all people at all times. Cf. the neatly ambiguous placing of ἀεί at Her. fr. 1 τοῦ δὲ λόγου τοῦδ' ἐόντος ἀεὶ ἀξύνετοι γίγνονται ἄνθρωποι . . .

VI–VII

Aratus

Aratus (late fourth–mid third cent. B.C.) was born at Soli in Cilicia, studied in Zeno's Stoic school at Athens and spent much of his life as a member of the literary circle assembled by Antigonus Gonatas, king of Macedonia, at his court at Pella (see p. 2). He edited the *Odyssey* and composed hymns, epigrams, a collection of short pieces called Κατὰ λεπτόν, and didactic poems on pharmacology and anatomy. His only surviving work is the *Phaenomena*, which deals with the constellations and with weather-signs – how to recognize them and what they portend. Information given in the star-section (19–757) is based closely on a prose *Phaenomena* by the famous fourth-century astronomer Eudoxus; the meteorological part (758–1154) is related to the extant pseudo-Theophrastean treatise Περὶ σημείων. Several poets, including, it was believed, Hesiod ('Αστρονομία, frr. 288–93), had already written didactic works on astronomy. We might guess that Aratus' originality lay in his obvious dependence on the best modern prose-work on the subject – that is, he contrived to impart precise technical matters without resorting to technical language. Original, too, was his Stoic approach. The extent to which the *Phaenomena* is influenced by Stoic doctrine has been much debated. Apart from the proem (1–18: see below) there seems to be little that could be called specifically Stoic; and those who argue that the *Phaenomena* is a thoroughgoing attempt to show the all-pervasive nature of a beneficent deity in the ordered Stoic cosmos rely on rather flimsy evidence – Zeus is, after all, traditionally the sky-god as well as the Stoic guiding principle.

Aratus' language is basically Homeric; but in scale and conception the poem owes much to Hesiod (though we are hampered here by the loss of the pseudo-Hesiodic Ἀστρονομία). The *Phaenomena* might be characterized as an attempt to revive and update Hesiodic verse. It presents itself as a utilitarian treatise for sailors and farmers, and in succeeding centuries it enjoyed great success as a practical handbook of astronomy (witness the large number of surviving ancient commentaries). Yet it may be doubted whether Aratus' aim was to produce such a handbook. Verse had long since been replaced by prose as the medium for technical works. It seems more likely that the *Phaenomena* is another Hellenistic attempt at the 'modernization' of an older genre, parallel in this respect with, for example, Callimachus' treatment of the hymn and Apollonius' of the epic. The poem is indeed ostensibly utilitarian, resembling in tone the 'didactic' sections of the *Works and Days*; Aratus' metrical practice has been shown to have significant similarities to that of Hesiod; and the poet's persona – grave, 'mantic', exhortatory, solicitous for the reader's welfare – is reminiscent of the *Works and Days*. But these 'Hesiodic' features serve only to emphasize the differences between the literary milieux of the two poets. Aratus is a modern writing in a self-consciously archaic style; and there is a corresponding contrast between the poem's ostensible audience of sailors and farmers and the sophisticated literati for whom it is actually intended. Aratus is quite explicit about his literary affiliations. Included in the *Phaenomena* is an acrostic spelling out the word λεπτή (783–7). (For λεπτός as a key term of 'Callimachean' aesthetics see pp. 9, 90; and cf. Aratus' collection Κατὰ λεπτόν). In an epigram Callimachus praises the *Phaenomena* as Hesiodic in manner, and ends with the words χαίρετε, λεπταὶ | ῥήσιες, Ἀρήτου σύμβολον ἀγρυπνίης, 'Hail, subtle expressions, evidence of Aratus' sleeplessness' – a witty ambiguity, since Aratus' ἀγρυπνίη was spent not in observing the stars but in 'burning the midnight oil' as he polished up his subtle poem (*AP* 9.507; *HE* 1297–1300 = Call. 56; 27 Pf.; *OCT* 1402–5).

Many modern readers find the *Phaenomena* unexciting. Ancient readers regarded the poem as a masterpiece of elegant exposition. Two factors, one applicable to didactic poetry in general and the other to astronomy in particular, help to explain these different reactions. (1) Ancient readers enjoyed and appreciated for their own sake formal aspects of the art of poetry – elegant versification, elegant expression, elegant solutions to difficult problems of presentation. Aratus composed a lucid and polished poem on a technically difficult subject. (2) In the absence of clocks and artificial light ordinary people were far more aware of the endless mutations of the heavenly bodies. In ancient times men told the time by the sun, navigated by the stars, and arranged their journeys to coincide with a full moon. The heavens were a matter of importance and a source of continual fascination.

Large fragments of a hexameter translation of the *Phaenomena* by Cicero, and complete versions by Germanicus (first cent. A.D.) and Avienius (fourth cent. A.D.), survive. In his *Georgics* Virgil is largely indebted to Aratus, both directly (e.g. *Geo.* 1.351–460 < *Phaen.* 758–1152) and indirectly through a lost meteorological poem by Varro of Atax.

Bibl.: Edn: J. Martin (Florence, 1956). Trans.: G. R. Mair (Loeb *Callimachus: Hymns*, 1921). Gen.: W. Sale, 'The popularity of Aratus', *C.J.* 61 (1965–6) 160–4; H. N. Porter, 'Hesiod and Aratus', *T.A.Ph.A.* 77 (1946) 158–70 (metre); E. J. Kenney, *C.R.* n.s. 29 (1979) 71–3 (Stoicism).

VI

In tone this proem stands midway between Callimachus' novel and inventive approach to Zeus and the impassioned, semi-technical address of Cleanthes. (Relative dating is quite uncertain, but Cl. is probably the earliest.) Aratus describes the all-pervasive nature of the Stoic Zeus/πρόνοια/λόγος (*370–408* nn.) in general terms, with clear reminiscences of Hesiod's proem in the *Works and Days*. Hesiod had invoked the Muses first, asking them to sing of Zeus; Aratus pointedly reverses the order, describing the all-motivating Zeus first and invoking the Muses only later (16–18). A less harsh, more philanthropic Zeus presides over Aratus' world: compare *WD* 42ff. (the gods keep man's livelihood hidden) with lines 5–6, and note the telling contrast between *WD* 101 and *Phaen.* 2–4 (see n.).

Bibl.: A. W. James, 'The Zeus hymns of Cleanthes and Aratus', *Antichthon* 6 (1972) 28–38.

1[409] ἐκ Διὸς ἀρχώμεσθα: the same words begin Theoc.'s 17th *Idyll*; possibly both poets are borrowing from some lost Zeus-hymn. Cf. Virg. *Ecl.* 3.60 *ab Ioue principium, Musae: Iouis omnia plena*, Pind. *Nem.* 2. 1–3.

2[410] ἄρρητον: an echo of *WD* 3–4 (Zeus) ὅν τε διὰ βροτοὶ ἄνδρες ὁμῶς ἄφατοί τε φατοί τε | ῥητοί τ' ἄρρητοί τε Διὸς μεγάλοιο ἕκητι. There is probably a play on the name Ἄρητος.

2–4[410–12] Cf. *WD* 101 πλείη μὲν γὰρ γαῖα κακῶν, πλείη δὲ θάλασσα. When seen in terms of the Stoic Zeus the world seems a friendlier place.

5[413] τοῦ γὰρ καὶ γένος εἰμέν: not only is Zeus all-pervasive – he also (καί) brought us into existence. Cf. Cleanthes *373* ἐκ σοῦ γὰρ γενόμεσθα (ἐκ σοῦ γὰρ γένος ἐσμέν MSS). These words are quoted by St Paul at *Acts* 17.28. **ἤπιος ἀνθρώποισι:** < Hes. *Theog.* 407.

6[414] ἐπὶ ἔργον ἐγείρει: < Hes. *WD* 20.

9[417] φυτὰ γυρῶσαι: digging round vines and olives in a ring (γῦρος) to loosen the earth.

10–13[418–21] Cf. Virg. *Geo.* 1.351–5.

10[418] γε: emphasizing the poem's main theme.

11[419] ἄστρα διακρίνας 'making distinct the constellations'.

11–13[419–21] ἐσκέψατο . . . ὡράων: a rather obscure passage. The most likely meaning is 'and for the ⟨whole⟩ year he provided (LSJ s.v. σκέπτομαι II.3) stars which might particularly show men the fore-ordained times of the seasons'; this seems less complicated than Martin's construction of ὡράων with σημαίνοιεν ('give signs of the seasons') and τετυγμένα as acc. of respect.

13[421] ἔμπεδα: the word implies both sureness and continuance.

14[422] πρῶτόν τε καὶ ὕστατον: the words are appropriated to Zeus from a Hesiodic reference to the Muses: *Theog.* 34 (μ' ἐκέλοντο) σφᾶς δ' αὐτὰς πρῶτόν τε καὶ ὕστατον αἰὲν ἀείδειν.

16[424] προτέρη γενεή 'the earlier generation', a phrase of uncertain meaning. Hesiod uses the words of the Heroic Age, 'the race before ours' (*WD* 160); but perhaps Aratus means here 'the race before you', i.e. the Golden Race which flourished under Zeus's father Cronus. Some think the reference is to earlier astronomers, who benefited mankind by discovering the information which Ar. is about to impart. *Alii alia*. See D. A. Kidd, *C.Q.* n.s. 31 (1981) 355-7.

17[425] μειλίχιαι 'gracious'.

17–18[425–6]: cf. Cleanthes *406–8*.

18[426] ἦι θέμις: sc. ἐστί. The words are ambiguously placed, and might qualify εἰπεῖν ('to give a right account of the stars') or εὐχομένωι ('praying as is right ⟨at the beginning of a poem⟩') or τεκμήρατε (sc. 'I am not praying to be told things which are οὐ θέμις').

VII

Aratus' longest 'digression' from his celestial theme, a nostalgic aetiology of the constellation Virgo, is placed prominently near the beginning of the poem. Virgo is Justice, who dwelt on earth during the Golden and Silver Ages but fled to heaven when she could no longer bear men's wicked ways. The passage is creatively adapted from Hesiod. At *WD* 256 Dike is called παρθένος; but in Hesiod it is Aidos and Nemesis, not Dike, who flee in disgust to heaven (*WD* 197–201). Their flight occurs as the culmination of the Myth of Ages (*WD* 106–201), which Aratus simplifies (by omitting the Age of Heroes) and adapts: in his Golden Age the earth does not provide food αὐτομάτη (*WD* 117–18), but is worked by men living in organized communities (106). Like his vision of Zeus in the proem, Aratus' picture of the Golden Age is more 'civilized' than that of his archaic source.

> Cf. Catullus 64.384–408.

96–7[427–8] The order is ὑπὸ ἀμφ. ποσσὶν Βοώτεω Παρθένον σκέπτοιο (opt. for imper.: K.–G. 1 229–30). ὑπό coheres closely with its noun ποσσίν, and the caesura is considerably weakened. Cf. *1124*, *1126*, *1328*(?); there is ample Homeric precedent.

96[427] Βοώτεω: the constellation whose most prominent member is Arcturus.

97[428] Στάχυν: Spica, the most prominent star in Virgo.

98–9[429–30] These lines seem to be an attempt to bridge the Hesiodic and Aratean stories. In Hesiod it is Aidos and Nemesis who flee the earth; and another name for Nemesis is Astraea, which Ar. here implies might be an alternative title of Dike because she is daughter of Astraeus. The Hesiodic version, that Dike is daughter of Zeus (*WD* 256,

Theog. 901–2), is referred to only vaguely as an alternative account (εἴτε τευ (=τινὸς) ἄλλου, 99). εἴτ' οὖν … εἴτε: οὖν in this combination implies that the alternatives are not important for the main point at issue: cf. Denniston, *GP* 418–19.

100[431] εὔκηλος φορέοιτο 'may she have an untroubled course!'. ἐντρέχει 'is current'. For a similar metaphor cf. *131*.

102[433] ἤρχετο: the imperf. of ἔρχομαι is rarely found uncompounded. Cf. 118. **κατεναντίη** 'face-to-face'.

103[434] ἀρχαίων: with both ἀνδρῶν and γυναικῶν.

105[436] γέροντας: the city's elders.

107[438] δημοτέρας 'for the people' – not a comparative in sense. ἤειδεν: apparently 'uttered solemnly' rather than 'sang'; ἀείδω can be used of oracular pronouncements (e.g. Eur. *Ion* 92). **ἐπισπέρχουσα** 'urging ⟨the elders⟩ on'. **θέμιστας** presumably means 'decrees' rather than 'judgements', since we are about to learn that men in those days knew no form of contention.

108[439] νείκεος ἠπίσταντο: ἐπίσταμαι occasionally takes the gen. in epic ('have knowledge of…').

109[440] διακρίσιος: lit. 'separation', i.e. disagreement, strife.

110[441] αὔτως 'just as they were', i.e. in a state of innocence.

110–11[441–2] Crossing the sea in ships was regarded as an act of hybris characteristic of later, degenerate ages. Cf. Hes. *WD* 236–7.

110[441] ἀπέκειτο 'was far off ⟨from their thoughts⟩' (not in physical distance).

111–12[442–3] 'And ships did not yet bring them livelihood from afar, but oxen and ploughs ⟨brought it⟩': ἀπόπροθεν applies only to the first element of the sentence. For the zeugma cf. *355–6* n.

113[444] μυρία πάντα: an idiomatic expression for abundance. **δώτειρα δικαίων**: modelled on the Homeric δωτῆρες ἐάων, 'givers of good things' (*Od.* 8.325; cf. *364*).

114[445] τόφρ' ἦν seems to be impersonal, 'that was as long as…'; but possibly it is personal, = παρῆν, 'she was around' (as, apparently, at 117).

115[446] ὀλίγη '⟨only⟩ a little'.

118[449] ὑποδείελος 'towards evening' – first here.

119[450] μουνάξ: i.e. she no longer ἀναμὶξ ἐκάθητο (104). **μειλιχίοισιν** 'with friendly words', a Homeric use.

120[451] ἀνθρώπων … πλήσαιτο 'filled with her audience'.

κολώνας: presumably not the ὅρη of 118 and 127, but lower hills on whose slopes men could sit to listen to Δίκη.

121[452] καθαπτομένη 'upbraiding them for...'.

122[453] εἰσωπός 'face-to-face' – a Homeric *hapax* (*Il.* 15.653) of uncertain etymology; Ar. obviously derives it from ὤψ, 'face'. **καλέουσιν**: dat. pl. part.

123[454–5] Cf. Horace, *Odes* 3.6.46–8 *aetas parentum peior auis tulit | nos nequiores, mox daturos | progeniem uitiosiorem.*

124[455] τεξείεσθε: an unparalleled fut. of τίκτω – perhaps a false archaism, perhaps found by Ar. in some lost poem, perhaps corrupt.

126[457] ἐπικείσεται: sc. αὐτοῖς.

127[458] ὀρέων ἐπεμαίετο 'she would make for the hills'.

128[459] ἐλίμπανε: this verb is a by-form of λείπω found almost exclusively in prose.

131[462] κακοεργόν: a Homeric *hapax* (*Od.* 18.54).

132[463] εἰνοδίην 'by the road-side', i.e. belonging to 'highwaymen' who ambush travellers. **βοῶν ἐπάσαντ' ἀροτήρων**: in archaic times laws expressly forbade men to eat oxen which had helped work their land. Cf. Virg. *Geo.* 2.536–7 *ante | impia quam caesis gens est epulata iuuencis.*

136[467] The 'digression' is formally rounded off with an echo of 96–7; the adj. πολυσκέπτοιο ('conspicuous'), which is not found elsewhere, picks up the verb σκέπτοιο (96).

VIII

Nicander

Nicander probably lived in the second century B.C. He was born in Colophon, the birthplace of Homer (according to one account), Mimnermus, Xenophanes and Antimachus; the town produced several poets in the Hellenistic period, including Hermesianax and Phoenix. Like Aratus he was a metaphrast, converting into epic verse prose treatises of whose subjects he had no specialist knowledge. Only his Θηριακά (958 lines on poisonous creatures and remedies for their bites) and Ἀλεξιφάρμακα (630 lines on antidotes to poisons) survive complete. Works no longer extant exerted considerable influence on Latin poetry: he wrote Γεωργικά and Μελισσουργικά, used by Virgil in his *Georgics*, and Ἑτεροιούμενα ('Things changed into other things'), which supplied

Ovid with material for his *Metamorphoses*. Scanty fragments survive of poems on geography and local history.

The Θηριακά is a poetical version of the Περὶ θηρίων of Apollodorus, a third-century expert on poisons. The poem is ostensibly an aid to those suffering from the bites of noxious animals; but the poet's solicitous professions of concern for his 'patients' should fool no one. His real aim is to astonish the reader with a mixture of highly incongruous basic ingredients, viz. epic language and the technical vocabulary of zoology and clinical medicine. This he attempts to do by elegant presentation of his unlikely subject-matter: 'didactic' sections are complemented by brief digressions; moods and tenses are constantly varied; Apollodorus' objective 'textbook' description of symptoms gives way to striking metaphor and simile; and over the whole broods a lurid atmosphere of danger and horror, as the disgusting effects of each lurking creature's bite are described in terms at once loathsome and ingenious. This contrast between subject-matter and presentation, 'science' and poetry, is the driving force behind the poem. Cf. on Aratus, p. 137.

Nicander was a grammarian as well as a poet, and he published a prose work on rare words (Γλῶσσαι). His poetical vocabulary is highly recondite, including many Homeric *hapax legomena* (in the present passage αὐαίνω, λήϊστωρ, νωθής, πολύσκαρθμος, τυπή, χανδόν), medical terms and new coinages and compounds (ὀλκήρης, περικυδής, περιοπάζω, ὑποζοψόεις); and his manner of expression is strained on both semantic and syntactical levels (see 334, 335, 336, 347 nn.). He has many allusions to earlier poetry, especially to Callimachus (349 n.).

This passage, the most elaborate in the whole poem, tells a curious myth as an αἴτιον for the burning thirst which is a symptom of the dipsas-snake's bite. Zeus had given men eternal youth in return for their denunciation of Prometheus; but they foolishly entrusted their precious gift to an ass for carriage. Burning with thirst, the ass ran off and implored a snake to help; the snake promised its aid in return for the ass's burden. Thus the dipsas acquired eternal youth, and sloughs off old age together with its skin. It inherited, too, the ass's thirst, which it passes on to creatures which it bites.

Incorporated into this 'purple passage' is an acrostic of the poet's name. According to Cicero (*De diuin.* 2.112) Ennius 'signed' one of his poems in this way; and the device later became very popular in both pagan and Christian poetry. For a more interesting acrostic in Aratus see p. 137.

Bibl.: Edn: A. S. F. Gow & A. F. Scholfield (Cambridge, 1953).

> Lucan 9.737–60.

334[468] ναὶ μήν: literally 'verily, indeed'; but Nic. often uses these words simply as a mark of transition to a new topic. **ὁμώσεται** = ὁμοιώσεται. ὁμωθῆναι is a Homeric *hapax* (*Il.* 14.209), but with the meaning 'unite'. Greek uses the fut. for generalizations as well as the pres. and aor. (K.–G. 1 171–2); this is also an Eng. idiom, e.g. 'a dog will always fight a cat'.

334–5[468–9] ἐχίδνηι | παυροτέρηι 'a smallish viper'. For this use of the comparative cf. 358.

335[469] θοώτερος: it would be easy to emend to the adverb θοώτερον; but this is by no means the only instance in Nic. of a fem. noun being qualified by an adj. of masc. ending.

336[470] ἐνισκίμψηι . . . δάκος: it seems best to take δάκος as acc., 'bite', and ἐνισκ. as transitive. Usually δάκος = 'biting animal'; and it is possible that βλοσυρὸν δάκος is nom., ἐνισκίμψηι (unusually) intransitive, 'those whom the fearful biter assails'.

338[472] κραδίη: sc. of the victim. **ἀμφί** seems to mean no more than 'in'. **καύσωι**: a technical term in medicine for a burning fever.

339[473] A variant (AbaB) of the 'Golden Line' – elegant presentation, horrible subject, piquant contrast.

341[475] χανδόν 'greedily', adverb from χανδάνω, 'hold', 'contain'. **εἰσόκε** is found once with the opt. in Homer (*Il.* 15.70–1); usually + subj. (*1224* n.).

343–58[477–92] This story of how men lost eternal youth was told by, amongst others, Ibycus (*PMG* 342) and Sophocles (in a play entitled Κωφοὶ Σάτυροι, fr. 362).

343[477] ὠγύγιος . . . αἰζηοῖσι: there is a verbal contrast here: αἰζηός has overtones of 'young and lusty'.

344–5[478–9] Nic. follows the version which makes Zeus eldest of the three brothers, allotting Poseidon and Hades their realms after his murder of their father Cronus. See *328–40* n.

344[478] ὁπότ' . . . ἔσχε: this is the common Homeric use of ὁπ(π)ότε + indic. referring to a particular time in the past, i.e. 'when', not 'whenever'. **πρεσβίστατον**: a 'double superlative', the usual form being πρεσβύτατος. Call. has τερπνίστατα and μαλκίστατον (frr. 93.3,

348), Nic. elsewhere κυδίστατε (*Ther.* 3). The model for these Hellenistic coinages, if such they are, is not known. **αἷμα**: for this word used metaphorically of a lineal descendant cf. *47*.

345[479] ἑκάς: heaven, sea and underworld are each far distant from the other two.

347[481] πυρὸς ληίστορ': Zeus denied fire to men, but Prometheus stole some for them from heaven. No other known version of the story tells that mankind betrayed him. **ἔνιπτον**: in Homer ἐνίπτω usually = 'reprove'. In later poetry it is confused with ἐνέπω, 'tell'; and here Nic. seems to be extending slightly this latter meaning: 'tell' / 'announce', hence 'inform on' / 'denounce'.

348[382] κακοφραδίηισ': the MSS read -ίης, agreeing with τῆς, 'they got no good of their imprudence' (Gow); but it was from the gift of youth, not from their denunciation, that they derived no benefit; and their imprudence lay not so much in denouncing Prometheus as in entrusting their precious gift to the ass. Both these difficulties are remedied by the minimal correction to -ίηισ' (cf. *2* app. crit.), dat. pl. used adverbially, = 'in their folly'; τῆς then refers to the gift of νεότης: cf. *Il.* 17.25 ἧς ἥβης ἀπόνητο. κακοφραδίηισι νόοιο is a variant reading at *Od.* 2.236; cf. *Hom. Hymn to Dem.* 227.

349[483] νωθεῖ: this adj. is found once in Homer, of an ass (*Il.* 11.559), and its meaning there is 'slow', 'sluggish'. Here 'sluggish' would accord badly with πολύσκαρθμος, 'skittish', in the next line; the rarer meaning 'stupid' (for which cf. [Aesch.] *Prom.* 62) seems more suitable, preparatory to ἄφρονα in 354. Some MSS read νωθεῖς, in agreement with 'mankind'; but that gives a less elegant distribution of adjs. within the line, and seems less likely in view of the *Iliad* passage. **ἀμορβεύοντο λεπάργωι**: a pointed imitation-cum-variation of a line from Callimachus, σὺν δ' ἡμῖν ὁ πελαργὸς ἀμορβεύεσκεν ἀλοίτης, 'the revenging stork accompanied us' (fr. 271): Nic. has transposed the first two consonants of πελαργός to give a different animal. **ἀμορβεύοντο**: the verb ἀμορβεύω is not found outside Call. and Nic. The act. means 'follow'; but the mid. here must = 'hand over to be carried by an attendant', i.e. by the ass. λέπαργος (< λέπος 'outer coat' + ἀργός 'white') is here used as a 'kenning'-type noun (cf. Hesiod's φερέοικος = snail, etc.): cf. Gow on Theoc. 4.44f.

351–3[485–7] With a typical Hellenistic ellipse Nic. leaves us to understand (or remember) that the snake is guardian of a spring.

351[485] γωλειοῖσι: Nic. uses both γωλε(ι)ός and φωλε(ι)ός for 'lair'. Neither word is attested before Aristotle.

355[489] ἐξότε = ἐξ οὗ. **φλόον** = φλοιόν.

356[490] περὶ . . . ὀπάζει: literally 'attends around'. The verb is found only once elsewhere, Nic. *Alex.* 270, of the husk surrounding a nut. Here it extends the φλόον-image of 355: the snake casts its old skin, but mortals are encased in wrinkled age. For the wording(only) cf. *Il.* 8.103 (Diomedes to Nestor) σὴ δὲ βίη λέλυται, χαλεπὸν δέ σε γῆρας ὀπάζει.

357[491] βρωμήτοροs: another 'kenning' (cf. 349 n.). **οὐλομένη θήρ**: at 353 the θήρ was masc.; but here, towards the end of the αἴτιον, its gender is assimilated to that of the διψάς.

358[492] ἀμυδροτέρηισιν 'rather weak', with no real comparative force. Cf. 334–5 n. **ἰάπτει**: lit. 'sends ⟨it⟩ forth' into the victim.

IX–XII

Theocritus

Of Theocritus' life hardly anything is certainly known. He was born in Syracuse in Sicily, perhaps c. 300 B.C.; he may have lived for some time on the Aegean island of Cos; and he seems to have benefited from the patronage of Ptolemy Philadelphus whilst resident either on Cos (Ptolemy's birthplace) or in Alexandria itself. His few datable works are from the 270s B.C. Unlike most poets of the time, he seems not to have been a professional scholar or critic. It is clear that he was one of the foremost exponents of the short, highly finished poem.

In addition to twenty-seven epigrams and the curious Σῦριγξ (see p. 176), thirty so-called *Idylls* (εἰδύλλια – a term of obscure origin) are attributed to Theocritus in medieval manuscripts. Of these, eight are generally considered spurious (nos. 8, 9, 19, 20, 21, 23, 25 and 27). Three of the genuine poems are written in Aeolic metre and dialect in imitation of Sappho and Alcaeus (see p. 172). The remaining nineteen are relatively short hexameter pieces (between 37 and 223 lines) written for the most part in Doric dialect. Four are 'epyllia' (see p. 200) on mythical themes, dealing in brief compass and novel presentation with stories from the past; two of these polemically re-work contiguous episodes from Apollonius' *Argonautica* (*Id.* 13 ∼ *Arg.* 1.1187–357; *Id.* 22.27–134 ∼ *Arg.* 2.1–97). Two of the *Idylls* are encomia (16 on

Hiero II of Syracuse, 17 on Ptolemy Philadelphus). For the rest generalizations are of limited use, since the poems are deliberately varied in structure, tone, subject-matter and setting. A considerable number are 'mimetic' (see p. 111), presenting monologues, songs and conversations. Most of them deal with country people: they are the so-called 'pastoral' (or 'bucolic') idylls, which form a highly diverse sub-group within Theocritus' oeuvre.

Theocritus is best known as the inventor of pastoral. (Scholars unwilling to credit his great originality have not succeeded in identifying literary predecessors of any significance.) Song features largely in all the pastorals, and it is probable that Theocritus set out to represent in hexameters some of the formal characteristics of real shepherds' songs (e.g. symmetrical repetition and 'capping' response). Although his literary Doric dialect is an artificial amalgam of forms and not an attempt to reproduce the speech of any one place, Theocritus may have been inspired to use it because Doric was spoken by real Sicilian shepherds. Another possibility is that he was influenced by the Doric mimes of the fifth-century Sicilian Sophron (see p. 233). Certainly the pastorals have little affinity with types of verse which were conventionally written in Doric (e.g. choral lyric). Some of Theocritus' poems are written in a more 'realistically' broad dialect than others.

The great king Ptolemy is said to have expressed regret that he could never enjoy the simple pleasures of some Egyptians whom he saw reclining at their ease on a river bank (Phylarchus, *FGH* 81 F 40). Theocritus' pastorals exploit similar feelings. Usually set in a timeless rural landscape, they are selectively idealized representations of the lives, loves and songs of country people; most might be said to provide reflections on the relation between desire and song, man and nature. The poems are written for a sophisticated audience of city-dwellers capable of savouring the piquant combination of rustic simplicity and highly self-conscious presentation. Literary critics speak of the 'ironic distance' between naive characters and superior reader.

Bibl.: Edn: *Bucolici Graeci*, ed. A. S. F. Gow (*OCT*, 1952). Comm.: A. S. F. Gow (2 vols, 2nd edn, Cambridge, 1952); K. J. Dover (1971). Gen.: *CHCL* I 570–86; S. Walker, *Theocritus* (Boston, 1980); C. P. Segal, *Poetry and myth in ancient pastoral* (Princeton, 1981); F. T. Griffiths, *Theocritus at court = Mnemosyne* suppl. 55 (1979); G. Fabiano, 'Fluctuation in Theocritus's style', *G.R.B.S.* 12 (1971) 517–37. Virgil and later pastoral:

R. Coleman, *Vergil. Eclogues* (Cambridge, 1977) 21–36; T. G. Rosen-
meyer, *The green cabinet* (Berkeley / Los Angeles, 1969).

IX

Summary. The main part of the poem is a love-song of the Cyclops
Polyphemus; it was with songs such as this, we are told, that he used to
console himself in his hopeless longing for the sea-nymph Galatea. The
poem is framed by an address to the doctor Nicias which humorously
suggests that song provides a better (and cheaper) φάρμακον for ἔρως
than conventional medicine.

Nicias. This poem and *Id.* 13 are addressed to Nicias; *Id.* 28
(*797–821*) is a compliment to his wife Theugenis. Nicias was a doctor and
poet from Miletus; eight of his epigrams survive (*HE* 2755–86). Lines
1–7 of this poem may imply that Nicias is himself in love; the opening of
Id. 13 suggests the same. Nicias is known to have written a poem in reply
to this idyll; two lines of it are extant (*SH* 566).

Polyphemus and Galatea. Polyphemus' first and best known appearance in Greek literature is at *Od.* 9.105–564. He is there portrayed
as a savage and solitary cannibal, who devours Odysseus' companions
when they become trapped in his cave. Odysseus offers him wine, which
he has never tasted; and while he lies in a drunken stupor Odysseus and
his remaining companions burn out his single eye with a red-hot stake.
Odysseus has told Polyphemus that his name is Οὖτις; when his
neighbours hear his cries and ask what is wrong, he shouts "ὦ φίλοι,
Οὖτις με κτείνει δόλωι οὐδὲ βίηφιν", and his neighbours retire in
puzzlement. Odysseus and his companions escape through the cave-
entrance, which Polyphemus is guarding, by hanging underneath his
sheep as they are let out to pasture. Theocritus' poem has several verbal
reminiscences of this episode from the *Odyssey* (22, 27, 45, 51, 61 nn.).

We find a rather more 'refined' Polyphemus in the *Cyclops* of
Euripides, a satyr-play which further exploits the humorous potential of
Homer's narrative: see R. Seaford, *Euripides. Cyclops* (Oxford, 1984)
51–9.

In about 400 B.C. the lyric poet Philoxenus was imprisoned by
Dionysius I of Syracuse, because he had tried to seduce the tyrant's
mistress Galatea. In revenge Philoxenus composed a satirical dithyramb in which he depicted Dionysius as the unperceptive Sicilian

monster Polyphemus, Galatea as the sea-nymph of that name, and himself as the wily Odysseus. This famous poem, now lost (see *PMG* 815–24), was the first literary treatment of the Cyclops in love, and it provided Theocritus with his basic approach both in this poem and in *Id.* 6 (a singing-contest between two herdsmen in which one reproves Polyphemus for being backward in love and the other replies in the character of the Cyclops himself). In particular the Cyclops' monody as an attempt to cure his love is derived from Philoxenus (cf. *PMG* 821–2).

Theocritus' treatment.   Nowhere in Theocritus is the 'ironic distance' greater than in this poem. By framing the song with an address to Nicias Theocritus contrives to import a sophisticated reader-figure into the poem itself; and Polyphemus, the one-eyed Odyssean pastoralist, is presented as a quintessentially naive and rustic character. Theocritus concentrates on a re-working of Philoxenus' love-song episode: Galatea is tantalizingly absent, and Odysseus is present only through heavy irony and Homeric verbal allusion (29, 38, 51, 61 nn.). In this version sight and insight are of central importance: the Cyclops' single eye presents to him only a partial view of the world. He sees himself and his own attractions in a much more favourable light than we do; he sees his song as a tour-de-force of persuasion, whereas we see a humorous incongruity in the rustic nature of his similes and enticements; where he sees flirtatious encouragement we see mockery (77–8); in what he sees as a harmless wish we foresee his doom (60–2). But Polyphemus is not simply risible. Just as our image of him wavers between a cannibalistic and godless monster (as we know him from the *Odyssey*) and a lovestruck adolescent shepherd with an unfortunate cast of features (the aspect emphasized by himself), so the tone of his song wavers between pathos and bathos, between lyricism and a childlike self-indulgence.

Song: symptom or cure?   The beginning and end of the introductory address to Nicias tell us that the only φάρμακον for ἔρως is song, and the last two lines of the poem recapitulate this idea. At 13–16, however, Polyphemus' singing is said to be not a cure for ἔρως, but a symptom of it. How are these two statements to be reconciled? Gow argued that lines 1–7, 17–18 and 80–1 were added later when Theocritus decided to make Nicias the addressee of an already completed Cyclops poem. This is a very violent solution to the problem, and assumes that Theocritus had not the wit to notice any difficulty. Dover more plausibly suggests that the Cyclops sang (unsuccessfully at first) and kept singing until at last he

10 COMMENTARY: IX THEOCRITUS: 493–6
found the 'cure' for his love. This seems a possible solution, despite the
fact that no word for 'at last' is present in the text in lines 17–18. A
development of this view might run as follows: φάρμακον does not mean
'cure' but 'antidote': he discovered at last the sort of thing (18 τοιαῦτα)
which he could sing each time (18 ἄειδε, 81 διᾶγ', both imperf.) he felt
the pangs of ἔρως. In this way 'he used to look after' (80 ἐποίμαινεν) his
love by song, and he fared better than he would have done by paying a
doctor. Another interpretation is offered by Goldhill (see bibl.), who
argues that the relation of frame to poem brings out the dual nature of
φάρμακον as both 'cure' and 'love-philtre': song, in other words, can be
seen as both cause and cure of ἔρως.

Bibl.: E. B. Holtsmark, 'Poetry as self-enlightenment: Theocritus 11',
T.A.Ph.A. 97 (1966) 253–9; E. W. Spofford, 'Theocritus and Polyphemus', *A.J.Ph.* 90 (1969) 22–35; A. Brooke, 'Theocritus' Idyll 11: a
study in pastoral', *Arethusa* 4 (1971) 73–81; S. D. Goldhill, 'Desire and
the figure of fun: glossing Theocritus 11' in *Beyond Aporia?*, ed. A.
Benjamin (forthcoming); I. M. le M. Du Quesnay, 'From Polyphemus
to Corydon' in *Creative imitation in Latin literature*, eds. D. West & T.
Woodman (Cambridge, 1979) 35–69.

>Ovid, *Met.* 13.749–897 (esp. 789–869). Cf. Virg. *Ecl.* 2, Call. *AP*
12.150 = *HE* 1047–56 (= Call. 3) = 46 Pf. = *OCT* 1152–61.

1–18[493–510] Address to Nicias, himself perhaps in love. There is no
better φάρμακον against desire than song, but to find the right song is not
easy. (Nicias is well qualified to confirm this, being both doctor and
poet.) Polyphemus is a good example of this statement: he kept singing
disconsolately of Galatea; but he found the φάρμακον, and eventually
sang / kept singing like this...

1[493] πότ: in broader literary Doric ποτί sometimes loses its -ί; cf.
epic πάρ for παρά, κάτ for κατά, etc.

2[494] οὔτ' ἔγχριστον . . . οὔτ' ἐπίπαστον 'neither ointment
smeared on (χρίω) nor a remedy sprinkled on (πάσσω)': external
applications for an open wound (cf. 15 ὑποκάρδιον ἕλκος).

3[495] Πιερίδες: the Muses, who came from Pieria near Mt
Olympus. **κοῦφον . . . τι** 'a gentle thing', as opposed to more painful
remedies.

4[496] γίνετ(αι): elision of -αι is rare in Hellenistic epic and elegiac
verse; cf. *802* n. **ἐπ' ἀνθρώποις** 'among men'. **εὑρεῖν:** like a rare herb,
picking up the imagery in πεφύκει (1).

6[498] ταῖς ἐννέα δή 'all nine', implying not that Nicias is a polymath (see *131* n.), but that he is an exceptionally inspired poet (cf. 81 μουσίσδων = 'singing').

7[499] ῥάιστα: ῥάιων is used in medicine of a patient being 'easier' (LSJ s.v. ῥάιδιος II.2). There is a contrast with οὐ ῥάιδιον in line 4. διᾶγ' 'got on', intrans. ὁ παρ' ἀμῖν 'my neighbour'. According to post-Homeric writers Polyphemus was a Sicilian.

10[502] μάλοις . . . ῥόδωι . . . κικίννοις: apples (cf. p. 102), roses and locks of hair were all used as love-tokens. Alternation of sing. and pl. is not unusual in poetic lists.

11[503] ὀρθαῖς μανίαις 'with real frenzy', an ironic antonym of ὀρθὴ φρήν, a standard phrase for 'sound mind'. Cf. *708*. πάντα: i.e. πάντα τὰ ἄλλα.

12[504] τωὔλιον = τὸ αὔλιον. αὐταί 'of their own accord'; or perhaps 'alone', paralleling αὐτός of the Cyclops in 14. The Homeric Cyclops treats his sheep with care and affection.

14[506] κατετάκετο: cf. *655*.

15[507] The subject is βέλεμνον; τό (= ἕλκος) is the object of πᾶξε: 'the wound which a shaft from great Aphrodite had fixed in his liver'. For ἧπαρ see *8* n.

20–3[512–15] The fourfold rustic simile of 20–1 and the repeated half-lines at 22–3 may characterize the Cyclops' composition as rather clumsy. Cf. 28–9 n.

20[512] λευκοτέρα πακτᾶς ποτιδεῖν 'fairer than cream-cheese to behold' (πήγνυμι is used of 'setting' cheese): an amusingly rustic comparison. For women a fair complexion was desirable; Galatea's lives up to her milky name.

21[513] φιαρωτέρα ὄμφακος ὠμᾶς 'sleeker than an unripe grape' – her skin is smooth and unwrinkled.

22[514] δ': continuing the thought of τί τὸν φιλέοντ' ἀποβάλληι; (19). αὐθ(ι) 'at once'. οὕτως 'without more ado'. γλυκὺς ὕπνος: a Homeric phrase, used of Polyphemus at *Od.* 9.333 (the time for blinding) ὅτε τὸν γλυκὺς ὕπνος ἱκάνοι.

23[515] ἀνῆι: aor. subj. of ἀνίημι, 'let go', often used of sleep.

26[518] ματρί: Polyphemus was the son of Poseidon and the sea-nymph Thoösa. φύλλα: sometimes the word φύλλον includes flower and stalk as well as leaves.

27[519] ἐγὼ δ' ὁδὸν ἀγεμόνευον: < *Od.* 6.261.

28–9[520–1] 'And having seen you, from that time forth (ἐκ τήνω) I cannot afterwards even now at all (παι) cease ⟨from love⟩' – a rather redundant, perhaps intentionally clumsy, sentence.

29[521] οὐ μὰ Δί': in the *Odyssey*, by contrast, Polyphemus dismisses Zeus with contempt (9.275–8).

32[524] θώτερον = τὸ ἕτερον. **ὥς** = οὕς.

33[525] ὕπεστι: sc. τῆι ὀφρύι.

34–51[526–43] A list of mostly respectable pastoral enticements for one's beloved; but the words take on a grotesque incongruity when we remember that the speaker is a young monster and his habitation a cave.

34[526] οὗτος τοιοῦτος ἐών 'although my appearance is as you see', lit. 'I, here, being such'.

35–7[527–9] These lines are suggested by *Od.* 9.244–9, where Polyphemus milks his ewes and portions out the milk for cheese-making and drinking.

36[528] οὐ λείπει μ' 'does not fail me'. **οὔτ' ἐν θέρει οὔτ' ἐν ὀπώραι:** < *Od.* 12.76.

37[529] χειμῶνος ἄκρω 'at the end of winter', when stocks are at their lowest. **ταρσοί:** *1105* n.

38[530] 'I know how to pipe like no ⟨other⟩ of the Cyclopes hereabouts.' **οὖτις:** it is tempting to see in this word an ironic reference to Odysseus' assumed name Οὖτις, which proves the undoing of Polyphemus at *Od.* 9.366–408; cf. 79, where the Cyclops claims not to be a 'nobody', and 61.

39[531] τίν: acc., as in 55 and 68, not dat. as in 29. **γλυκύμαλον** 'sweet girl' (lit. a cross between apple and quince). **ἁμᾶι:** *206* n.

40[532] νυκτὸς ἀωρί 'at dead of night'. **τράφω:** Doric form of τρέφω.

41[533] μαννοφόρως 'wearing collars' – a humorous touch.

42[534] ἀφίκευσο: the -σο imper. ending is usually found with -μι verbs. Theoc. may be imitating a lost Doric literary source. **ἐξεῖς οὐδὲν ἔλασσον** 'you will be no worse off' (sc. than at present).

45[537] δάφναι: cf. Odysseus' description of the Cyclops' cave, *Od.* 9.182–3 ἔνθα δ' ἐπ' ἐσχατιῆι σπέος εἴδομεν ἄγχι θαλάσσης | ὑψηλὸν δάφνηισι κατηρεφές.

46–8[538–40] The Cyclops is an uncivilized milk-drinker (35), and he sees only decorative attraction in his 'sweet-fruited vine'. In the *Od.* wine is his downfall: at 9.359 he describes the drink given him by Odysseus as ἀμβροσίης ... ἀπόρρωξ, echoed by Theoc. in ποτὸν ἀμβρόσιον (48). Ice-cold water tempers wine at 'civilized' symposia: *1717* n.

49[541] τῶνδε 'rather than these things'. In the construction αἱρεῖσθαι Χ μᾶλλον ἢ Υ the word μᾶλλον is sometimes omitted; the gen. here is perhaps an alternative to this ἤ.

50[542] αἰ 'even if', 'granted that'. **λασιώτερος** 'too hairy'.

51[543] ὑπὸ σποδῷ: a covert reference to *Od.* 9.375, where Odysseus thrusts into the fire the stake he will use for blinding Polyphemus: καὶ τότ᾽ ἐγὼ τὸν μόχλον ὑπὸ σποδοῦ ἤλασα πολλῆς, | εἷος θερμαίνοιτο. The irony is heightened in 52–3. **ἀκάματον πῦρ** 'undying, lit. untiring, fire': a Homeric phrase.

52[544] ἀνεχοίμαν 'I would offer up'. See *234* n.

54[545] ὅτ᾽ = ὅτι, a very rare elision (cf. *79*).

55–6[546–7] ὡς κατέδυν . . . ἐφίλησα . . . ἔφερον 'so that I might have descended . . .': the indic. is regular in secondary tenses 'to denote that the purpose is dependent upon some unaccomplished action . . . and therefore . . . was not attained' (Goodwin, *GMT* § 333).

56[548] λῇς: sc. με φιλεῖν. λῶ is a Doric equivalent of ἐθέλω.

57[549] πλαταγώνι᾽ 'petals', so named because lovers took omens from smacking (πλαταγέω) a poppy-petal laid on the arm, observing either the mark made on the skin or the sound produced by the blow.

58–9[550–1] He is sorry that κρίνα and poppies flower at different seasons, so that he cannot bring her a varied bouquet. Another example of Polyphemus' amusing pedantry.

60[552] μαθεῦμαι: apparently a Doric fut. form (App. C. 4), perhaps by analogy with -ε- stem futures such as βασεῦμαι (= βησέομαι).

61[553] τις . . . ξένος: ξεῖνε is the Cyclops' word of address to Odysseus in Homer (cf. *Od.* 9.252, 267–71, 273, 369–70); the 'stranger' is not τις but Οὖτις. **ὧδ᾽** 'hither': cf. 38, 64 (both 'here').

62[554] ποχ᾽: < ποκα (= ποτε). **ἀδύ:** *sc.* ἐστί. **ὕμμιν:** sea-nymphs in general.

66[558] πᾶξαι: aor. infin. of πήγνυμι. Cf. 20 n. **τάμισον:** a coagulant used for setting cheese – probably rennet, curdled milk from the stomach of a young animal. **δριμεῖαν** 'acidic'.

67–8[559–60] In real urban life the sexes were segregated, and mothers could act as go-betweens for their sons. Here Polyphemus' mother performs a similar function: as a sea-nymph (26 n.) she has ample opportunity to meet Galatea in her own element.

67[559] 'It's all my mother's fault, and it's her I blame' (sc. not you).

68[560] οὐδὲν ... ὅλως 'absolutely nothing'. **πήποχ'** = πώποτε.

69[561] καὶ ταῦτ': adv., 'despite the fact that...'. Cf. LSJ s.v. οὗτος c.VIII.2.

71[563] ἀνιαθῆι: sc. ἡ μήτηρ.

72–9[564–71] Critics differ over these lines. Some see 72 as the turning-point of Polyphemus' 'talking-cure': it is here, they argue, that he finally resigns himself to the impossibility of attaining Galatea. Others (e.g. Gow on line 13) feel that the tone is not so positive: in 72–3, for instance, Polyphemus says 'you *would* do better if you *were* to do something practical'. It does seem, however, that by the end of this song the Cyclops has attained a state of mind more cheerful than he had at the start, and to that extent his singing has proved an antidote (φάρμακον) to ἔρως; perhaps the treatment had to be repeated (cf. p. 150). *We* may well suspect that the girls' flirtatious behaviour is mocking, not enticing; but the important fact is that Polyphemus himself takes it at face value and derives consolation from it.

72[564] πᾶι τὰς φρένας ἐκπεπότασαι; 'where have your wits flown?' (=592). Cf. Theognis 1053 τῶν γὰρ μαινομένων πέτεται θυμός τε νόος τε.

73–4[565–6] αἴ κ' ... πέκοις ... φέροις: this use of ἄν / κε + opt. in conditional clauses is found in Homer (Goodwin, *GMT* §460), but seems also to have occurred in Doric.

73[565] ἐνθών 'going ⟨away from here⟩'. **ταλάρως:** baskets for draining cheese or curd. **θαλλὸν ἀμάσας** 'cutting young branches'.

75[567] τὰν παρεοῖσαν: sc. ὄιν or αἶγα. **τὸν φεύγοντα:** masc. because this is a proverbial expression. Cf. 746 n.

76[568] ἴσως: probably with εὑρησεῖς rather than with καὶ καλλίον'.

77[569] συμπαίσδεν: sc. sexually.

78[570] ὑπακούσω: probably 'reply' rather than 'give heed to'.

79[571] ἐν τᾶι γᾶι 'on land'. **τις** 'a somebody'. Cf. 38 n.

80[572] ἐποίμαινεν: he neglected his sheep (12–13) and 'shepherded' his love instead (cf. 65).

81[573] ἢ εἰ χρυσὸν ἔδωκεν: sc. ἰατρῶι: a humorous allusion to Nicias' job as a doctor – he usually supplies φάρμακα for a fee. Poetry is free – and more effective.

X

Summary. This is a 'mimetic' poem (cf. pp. 111, 218): the reader is left to deduce the situation from a speaker's words. Simaetha is a young woman who lives alone with a single servant called Thestylis. (Her social status and the reason for her unusual lack of a legal guardian are not made clear.) She has been abandoned by her lover Delphis, a socially superior athlete. In the first section of the poem (1–63) she performs various magical rites, partly in order to draw him back to her house. In the second section (64–162), having sent away Thestylis, she tells the Moon the story of her passion – how she was sickening with desire for Delphis, how she summoned him to her house, his smooth talk, their lovemaking, and his ultimate betrayal of her. In the final four lines (163–6) she bids farewell to the Moon in a tone of quiet resignation.

Source. The scholia tell us that the name Thestylis and her mission with the herbs (59–62) are borrowed from a mime of Sophron (see p. 233). It is possible, but by no means certain, that this was the mime entitled Ταὶ γυναῖκες αἳ τὰν θεόν φαντι ἐξελᾶν ('The Female Exorcists'), and that Theocritus derived inspiration for his magical scene from that poem.

Theocritus' treatment. We have seen that in the Cyclops-poem Theocritus took a character familiar from the *Odyssey* and treated him (via Philoxenus) in a novel and more intimate manner. In this poem he adopts a theme familiar from fifth-century tragedy – the power of Eros and The Revenge of the Disappointed Woman – and 'downgrades' it by attributing these same feelings of anger and frustration to a contemporary young woman of humble status. Simaetha is made to draw the parallel herself with Medea, a witch of truly awesome power (16), who was abandoned by Jason (15–16 n.). In another age, in another situation, Simaetha's story might have resulted in a tragedy no less memorable than those of Medea and Phaedra, women whose revengeful passion caused the downfall of those they once loved. Instead we are presented with a girl affected by the power of Eros no less strongly than a tragic heroine, but with no weapons other than reproach (8–9) and mundane magic. (Compare *931–61*, where Apollonius' Medea, her magical powers still in the background, soliloquizes in her agony of guilt and desire.)

Magic. Anthropologists who have studied magic often observe that to the practitioner performance of the rites is just as important as any hoped-for result. When effectual action is impossible magic lessens anxiety and releases pent-up frustration: it is essentially a *substitute* for action (this is clearly pointed in lines 9–10). To distinguish between 'white' and 'black' (i.e. destructive) magic is not easy, either in literature or in life. Simaetha's emotions are compounded of anger and desire, and this is reflected in the ambiguous nature of some of her 'charms'. The iynx (17 n.) which she whirls is designed to attract Delphis to her house; but her burning of bay-leaves (23–6) and her pounding of a lizard for Delphis to drink (κακὸν ποτόν, 58; cf. 159–62) can be seen as attempts to do him physical harm.

Structure. The magic section proper (17–63) is divided into nine stanzas of four lines each by the refrain 'Magic wheel, draw that man to my house'. It seems likely that this refrain is, as Dover suggests, 'the artistic equivalent... of the monotonous repetition of words and phrases which actually characterize magical spells'. The device is continued into the next section (64ff.), which is divided into twelve stanzas of five lines each by the refrain 'Note, lady Moon, whence came my love'. This continued use of the refrain points the similar functions of magic and narrative, both of which are for Simaetha substitutes for action. (As her story moves to its climax (136–57) she drops the refrain altogether.)

Simaetha. The 'ironic distance' between character and reader, so obvious in the Cyclops-poem, operates here too. From Simaetha's own narrative we see the hopelessness of her situation: she has been abandoned by a glib-tongued and uncaring young man. To her the relationship was of enormous importance; to him it was just another casual liaison. Simaetha's words suggest that she half perceives this (112 ὥστοργος, 138 ἀ ταχυπειθής); but by the end of the poem she has achieved only resignation, which we feel will be short-lived. She still wants Delphis, and we know he will not come again.

The control of desire. This idyll has more in common with the Cyclops-poem than might at first appear. Both show unconventional characters trying to deal with helpless and hopeless desire by using song as a substitute for action. Where Polyphemus sought a (metaphorical) φάρμακον through the process of singing (*493–510* ἀείδων, etc., *572–3*), Simaetha in the first part of this poem prepares (literal) φάρμακα and chants spells (ἐπαοιδαί) in an effort to win back Delphis; in the second part she finds a similar temporary antidote in soliloquy as did Polyphemus.

Bibl.: C. Segal, 'Simaetha and the iynx (Theocritus, Idyll II)', *Q.U.C.C.* 15 (1973) 32–43 = *Poetry and Myth*... 73–84; id., 'Understanding and intertextuality: Sappho, Simaetha and Odysseus in Theocritus' Second

Idyll', *Arethusa* 17 (1984) 201–9; id., 'Space, time and imagination in Theocritus' Second Idyll', *C.S.C.A.* 16 (1985) 103–19; F. T. Griffiths, 'Poetry as *Pharmakon* in Theocritus' *Idyll* 2' in *Arktouros: Hellenic studies presented to Bernard M. W. Knox on the occasion of his 65th birthday* 1 (Berlin, 1979) 81–8; id., 'Home before lunch: the emancipated woman in Theocritus' in H. P. Foley (ed.), *Reflections of women in antiquity* (London, 1981) 247–73.

> Virg. *Ecl.* 8.64–109.

1–2[574–5] Simaetha calls for bay-leaves and orders Thestylis to encircle the bowl (to be used at 43 for a libation) with red wool. It seems likely that both bay (worn as a garland) and wool are intended to ward off any harmful powers invoked during her sorcery; but possibly the bay is that to be burnt at 23–6.

2[575] οἰὸς ἀώτωι: a Homeric phrase, usually translated 'the finest sheep's wool'. The meaning of ἄωτος is uncertain, and it was uncertain in the third cent. B.C.; but it is almost always found with associations of high quality.

3[576] 'So that I can bind fast that dear man who is troublesome to me.' ὡς . . . καταδήσομαι: occasionally in verse the subj. in final clauses is replaced by a fut. ind. (Goodwin, *GMT* § 324). καταδέω is a common term in magic for bewitching a person with spells.

4[577] '"Who ⟨is⟩ for me a twelfth-day-person from which (i.e. 'since') he... does not even come to me"' (Dover), i.e. it is eleven days since he came (the Eng. idiom has no negative). For the temporal adj. cf. *64* n. **τάλᾶς:** the final syllable is not found scanned short before the Hellenistic period. **ποθίκει:** Doric for προσήκει.

5[578] ζοοί: when a woman speaks of herself in the 1st pers. pl. she conventionally uses masc. adjs. and participles.

6[579] ἀνάρσιος: probably cognate with ἀραρίσκω; so the root meaning is perhaps 'out of joint', 'at odds with' rather than 'hostile', 'implacable' (LSJ). **ἀλλᾶι:** adv.; cf. *127*.

7[580] ταχινὰς φρένας 'his fickle heart', swift to change.

8[581] Τιμαγήτοιο: wrestling-schools were often privately owned.

9[582] οἶα = ὅτι τοῖα, an idiom found already in Homer.

10[583] ἐκ 'by means of', instrumental (LSJ s.v. III.6).

11[584] καλόν: adv.: φαίνω is sometimes used intransitively = 'shine' (cf. *1622–3*). **ἄσυχα:** of a low, muttered incantation. Cf. 62.

12[585] καὶ σκύλακες 'even dogs', which were associated with the cult of Hecate (cf. 35–6) and might therefore be expected not to fear her as much as other creatures. This seems more likely than a reference to dogs' proverbial shamelessness (for which cf. *58*).

13[586] 'As she comes among the tombs of corpses and the black blood', perhaps of sacrificial victims. The line is an echo of *Il.* 10.297–8 βάν ῥ' ἴμεν ὥς τε λέοντε δύω διὰ νύκτα μέλαιναν | ἂμ φόνον, ἂν νέκυας, διά τ' ἔντεα καὶ μέλαν αἷμα, where the scene is a battlefield.

14[587] δασπλῆτι: a Homeric *hapax* (*Od.* 15.234), apparently meaning 'dreadful'. ἐς τέλος: until the rite shall be successfully completed.

15–16[588–9] Simaetha cites Circe and Medea as arch-enchantresses; but we remember that in the end both lost their men.

15[588] 'Making these drugs not at all worse (i.e. more powerful) than ⟨those⟩ of Circe...'

16[589] ξανθᾶς Περιμήδας: apparently a reference to the powerful witch ξανθὴν Ἀγαμήδην (*Il.* 11.740). Scholars have debated whether περι- is (1) an elegant variation by Theoc., an allusion to an alternative version of the name; (2) a misremembering of the *Il.* passage by Theoc.; (3) a mistake by Simaetha, intended to characterize her as an unlearned girl overreaching herself in her attempts at ritual solemnity.

17[590] ἴυγξ: Iynx is said to have been a nymph who gained Zeus's love through magic and was turned by Hera into a bird, the wryneck, which makes strange twisting movements of its neck in the mating season. It seems that in order to attract or recapture a lover Greek magical practitioners would whirl a wooden or terracotta disc on which a wryneck was pinioned by its outstretched wings (cf. Pind. *Pyth.* 4.214–17); but since disappointed lovers were commoner than wrynecks the bird was usually dispensed with, and the word ἴυγξ came to be applied to the wheel itself. Several such wheels are shown in vase-paintings, often carried by Eros (see Gow's comm., pls. iv–v). The wheel was made to spin by alternately tightening and loosening a cord passed through two holes near the centre. Simaetha is to be imagined as whirling the iynx at the end of each 'stanza'.

18[591] The first of Simaetha's 'sympathetic' rites: crushed barley-meal (ἄλφιτα) shrivels away on the fire; just so, she hopes, Delphis will waste away, literally or metaphorically (cf. 28–9), with the fires of love. ἀλλ' 'come now', encouraging Thestylis to get on with the job (cf. 96). For this use of ἀλλά with imperatives see Denniston, *GP* 13–15.

19[592] πᾶι . . . ἐκπεπότασαι;: *564* n.

20[593] καὶ τίν 'to you, too ⟨as well as to Delphis⟩'.

23[596] ἐπί 'against' Delphis, i.e. to affect him.

24[597] λακεῖ: ληκέω = 'crackle'. καππυρίσαισα = καταπ-, 'being in the fire'. Cf. *303* n., 85 n.

26[599] σάρκ' ἀμαθύνοι 'may he waste his flesh away', consumed by the fires of love: cf. 89–90, where Simaetha says she was reduced to skin and bone.

34[602] ἀδάμαντα: the adamantine gates of Hades: cf. Virg. *Aen.* 6.552 *porta aduersa ingens solidoque adamante columnae.* κινήσαις: apparently a potential opt. without ἄν (*234* n.) – 'you can move Hell's adamant and anything else ⟨as⟩ firmly fixed ⟨–so move Delphis' heart for me⟩'. Simaetha breaks off as she hears, or affects to hear, evidence of Hecate's presence.

35[603] ἄμμιν: ethic dat. (cf. 5 μοι, 66 ἄμμιν).

35–6[603–4] κύνες . . . τριόδοισι: Hecate was goddess of the crossroads, and dogs were sacrificed to her there (cf. 12 n.).

36[604] τὸ χαλκέον . . . ἄχει: in many societies bronze is clashed to ward off evil (in Greece this was done particularly during an eclipse). Simaetha takes care to protect herself from the dangerous powers she has conjured up. ἄχει: imper. of ἠχέω.

38[606] A supernatural silence is often described as accompanying epiphanies: see *203* n.

39–40[607–8] ἀνία . . . καταίθομαι: picking up ἀνίασεν . . . αἴθω (23–4).

41[609] ἀντὶ γυναικός 'instead of his wife', which she had hoped to become. κακάν: perhaps 'disgraced ⟨in the eyes of others⟩' rather than 'wretched'.

28[611] κηρόν: perhaps a wax image of Delphis. Such images are commonly used in 'sympathetic' magic. σὺν δαίμονι 'with the goddess's aid', a Homeric phrase.

29[612] ὥς 'just so'. Μύνδιος 'from Myndia', a town on the coast of Caria, almost opposite Cos. This fact, plus the reference to πόντος (38) and the mention of Philinus, a famous Coan athlete (115), suggests that Cos may be the imagined setting for the poem.

30[613] δινεῖθ' = δινεῖται. Cf. *496* n. ῥόμβος 'bull-roarer', a piece of wood or metal which hums loudly when spun at the end of a length of cord. Its use is attested in many cultures throughout the world. Here it is probably intended, like the ἴυγξ, to attract Delphis. ἐξ: its power derives *from* Aphrodite.

31[614] δινοῖτο 'may he pace to and fro'.

43[616] ἐς τρίς: the magic number. The prep. is redundant; cf. *1324* n.

45–6[618–19] 'May he have as much ⟨of⟩ forgetfulness as they say Theseus on Dia once had of Ariadne of the fair tresses.' Dia is another name for Naxos: it was there that Theseus abandoned Ariadne, who had fled with him from Crete after helping him to kill her half-brother, the Minotaur (cf. *53–4* n., Cat. 64.76–264). The irony here is apparent: it is in his forgetfulness of Simaetha that Delphis resembles Theseus, and she herself is destined to remain abandoned like Ariadne. Cf. 15–16 n.

46[619] λασθῆμεν: aor. inf. of λανθάνομαι, with Doric inf. ending (Attic λησθῆναι). εὐπλοκάμω 'Αριάδνας: an echo with variation of *Il.* 18.592 καλλιπλοκάμωι 'Αριάδνηι.

48[621] ἱππομανές: an unidentified Arcadian plant so named because horses were thought to be madly keen for it (τῶι…ἔπι). It is not clear what ritual act Simaetha performs here.

50[623] καὶ … περάσαι 'and ⟨just so⟩ may he pass (aor. opt. of περάω) to this house'.

51[624] λιπαρᾶς 'oily' because athletes anointed themselves with oil. A 'transferred epithet'.

53–4[626–7] Simaetha shreds and burns a fringe (κράσπεδον) from Delphis' cloak. Destruction of such bodily tokens (especially hair and nails) was thought to affect by 'sympathy' the body itself.

53[626] ὤλεσε 'lost'.

54[627] ὠγώ = ὃ ἐγώ. κατ' … βάλλω: tmesis. ἐν πυρί: ἐν is sometimes used with verbs of motion 'implying both *motion to* and subsequent *position in* a place' (LSJ s.v. 1.8). Cf. *1585, 1291* n.

56[629] λιμνᾶτις … βδέλλα 'a marsh-living leech'. Love has made her pale and drawn.

58[631] The lizard-drink might be a love-potion; but κακόν sounds ominous. αὔριον: cf. 9.

59–62[632–4] Thestylis is sent off to knead gently (ὑπόμαξον) certain magic herbs (θρόνα) above Delphis' threshold (φλιᾶς) in order to make his bones ache with desire.

60[633] ἇς: Doric for ἕως; sc. ἐστί.

61 An interpolated line inserted to fill out the sense after νύξ in 60 had been corrupted to νῦν: see app. crit.

62[634] ἐπιτρύζοισα: cf. *1* n.

64[636] πόθεν: i.e. 'where should I begin the narrative?'. δακρύσω: probably deliberative aor. subj.: cf. *277* n.

65[637] τίνος: neut.

66[638] ἦνθ' 'went'. τωὐβούλοιο = τοῦ Εὐβ-; sc. θυγάτηρ. Anaxo, daughter of Eubulus, invited Simaetha to the festival of Artemis, on the way to which she fell in love at first sight with Delphis. On such encounters see *46* n.; but here the usual situation is reversed, and it is the girl who is struck by Eros. καναφόρος 'basket-bearer'. At major festivals (e.g. the Thesmophoria) virgins of spotless reputation were chosen to carry in procession baskets containing ritual objects for the sacrifice. Selection for this task was a great honour. ἄμμιν: 35 n.

67[639] τᾶι 'in whose honour', lit. 'for whom'.

68[640] πομπεύεσκε περισταδόν 'processed around', = περιεπομπεύεσκε; the -στα- element (< ἵστημι) is not operative here. The animals are for public amusement, not for sacrifice. As goddess of the hunt Artemis is particularly associated with wild beasts. ἐν δέ 'and amongst them', i.e. particularly impressive.

70[642] Θευμαρίδα 'belonging to Theumaridas'. Thracian female slaves were common. ἁ μακαρῖτις: a euphemism for 'dead' (cf. Eng. 'God bless her soul!'). This detail (and the imperf. ἐπᾷδεν in 91) suggests that Simaetha's relationship with Delphis has lasted for some time.

72[644] ἁ μεγάλοιτος 'greatly doomed'. The phrase pointedly contrasts with ἁ μακαρῖτις in the same metrical position in line 70.

73–80[645–52] Simaetha's detailed account of her dress (73–4) and her double simile describing Delphis and Eudamippus are 'epic' in structure but 'homely' in particulars.

73[645] βύσσοιο 'made of linen'. σύροισα: lit. 'trailing', i.e. wearing a garment which trails to the ground. ξυστίδα: apparently some sort of expensive outer garment. Simaetha had borrowed it for the day from her friend Clearista.

76[648] ἇι τὰ Λύκωνος 'where Lycon's place ⟨is⟩' – perhaps a farm.

77[649] ὁμοῦ: with ἰόντας.

78[650] ξανθοτέρα . . . ἐλιχρύσοιο 'more golden than helichryse', a plant with yellow flowers. γενειάς: sing. because the beard of each was golden.

80[652] ὡς ἀπὸ . . . λιπόντων: tmesis; gen. abs.: 'as they would be, having left off their fair gymnastic exercise' – probably to attend the festival.

82[654] χὠς ἴδον ὡς ἐμάνην: the rhythm and phrasing are borrowed from *Il.* 14.294 (Zeus sees Hera) ὡς δ' ἴδεν ὥς μιν Ἔρως πυκινὰς φρένας ἀμφεκάλυψεν; but Simaetha's description of her symptoms in the following lines seems, when read in conjunction with 106–8, to be an allusion to Sappho fr. 31.7 ff. ὡς γὰρ ἔς σ' ἴδω βρόχε', ὥς με φώναι-|σ' οὐδ' ἓν ἔτ' εἴκει... λέπτον|(10) δ' αὔτικα χρῶι πῦρ ὑπαδεδρόμηκεν. ('For when I look at you for a moment, I have no longer power to speak...straightaway a subtle flame has stolen beneath my flesh...' – Page). These echoes, if such they are, add to the literary texture of Simaetha's narrative: see Segal in *Arethusa*, art. cit. The ὡς...ὡς / ὥς construction has provoked much discussion: is the second ὡς exclamatory or demonstrative? In Homer (and Sappho) it is almost certainly demonstrative ('At the instant he saw her, at that instant, lit. just so, desire engulfed his mind'), and it may be also in Theoc. ('When I saw him, at that moment I became mad'); but an exclamation would make good sense ('When I saw him, how I was maddened!'). Virgil in his famous imitation (*ut uidi ut perii ut me malus abstulit error!*, *Ecl.* 8.41) seems to have taken it as exclamatory, though there too the construction is debatable. For a full discussion see S. Timpanaro, *Contributi*...(Rome, 1978) 219–87. Cf. *1118*.

82–3[654–5] μοι ... δειλαίας: a change of construction similar to τοῖς...λιπόντων above (78–80).

84[656] ἐφρασάμαν 'took notice of', + gen. Contrast 69, etc., φράζεό μευ τὸν ἔρωθ', which has the more normal acc. ὡς 'how'.

85[657] καπυρά: used only here of disease. LSJ translate 'drying', 'parching'; but probably Theoc. is alluding to a derivation from κατά + πῦρ, i.e. 'burning' (cf. καππυρίσαισα, 24): this would literalize the metaphorical πυρί of 82.

88[660] πολλάκι: as the fever came and went. θάψωι: fustic, a shrub from which yellow dye was made.

89[661] αὐτά 'alone'.

90[662] ἐς τίνος: sc. δόμον.

91[663] ἔλιπον 'omitted ⟨to visit⟩'.

92[664] ἧς οὐδὲν ἐλαφρόν: it is hardly possible to decide between the translations 'It was no light matter' and 'There was nothing alleviatory'; for the latter cf. *495* κοῦφόν τι. ἄνυτο φεύγων 'was hurrying by in flight'.

94[666] χοὔτω 'and so'.

95[667] Both εἰ δ' ἄγε and μῆχος are dignified epicisms.

96[668] ἀλλά: 18 n.

98[670] τηνεί: Doric for ἐκεῖ.

100[672] μόνον: masc., with ἐόντα. **ἄσυχα** 'discreetly'.

101[673] κεἴφ' = καὶ εἶπέ. **ὅτι:** Greek, unlike modern Eng., often uses conjunctions to introduce direct speech. **λιπαρόχρων:** cf. 51 n., 79.

104[676] ἄρτι . . . ἀμειβόμενον: cf. *133* n. The meaning is really 'as soon as I saw him crossing . . .', not 'as I saw him just crossing . . .'.

106–10[678–82] For these symptoms cf. Sappho fr. 31.9–16 (cf. 82 n.) ἀλλ' ἄκαν μὲν γλῶσσα †ἔαγε† . . . | (13) κὰδ δέ μ' ἴδρως ψῦχρος ἔχει ('my tongue is silent . . . a cold sweat holds me . . .').

107[679] κοχύδεσκεν: κοχυδέω is a reduplicated form of the root 'pour' (cf. χύδην adv. cognate with χέω). **ἴσον:** adv., 'like'.

108–9[680–1] οὐδ' ὅσσον . . . τέκνα 'not even as much as children whimper in their sleep crying to their dear mother'. For the pl. verb see *70* n.

110[682] ἐπάγην 'I became stiff': aor. pass. of πήγνυμι. **δαγῦδι** 'a wax doll' with rigid limbs and body. **ἴσα:** fem.

112[684] ὥστοργος = ὁ ἄστοργος, 'the heartless one'. στοργή = deep affection. **ἐπὶ χθονὸς ὄμματα πάξας** < *Il.* 3.217, where the words are used of Odysseus concentrating before he makes a brilliant speech. Simaetha seems to construe Delphis' action as a sign of modesty; but his speech will be all too persuasive, as she at last begins to realize (138 ταχυπειθής).

113[685] For the verse-structure cf. *555*.

114[686] τόσον . . . ὅσσον 'by ⟨only⟩ so much . . . as . . .'.

115[687] πρᾶν ποκα 'the other day'. **τράχων:** Doric form of τρέχων (cf. *Id.* 11.40 (= *532*) τράφω for τρέφω); also at 147. **Φιλῖνον:** a famous Coan athlete: cf. 29 n. The boast illustrates Delphis' conceit; cf. 121–2 n., 124–5.

116[688] ἢ 'μὲ παρῆμεν: with ἔφθασας (114), an idiom hard to render literally in English. The meaning is 'in summoning me you just anticipated my coming' (παρῆμεν Doric for παρεῖναι).

118–28[690–700] Delphis says that he would have come in a κῶμος to Simaetha's door, with apples and garlands; and that if she had rejected him and kept the door barred he and his friends would have used torches to burn it or axes to break it down. Literary sources (e.g. New Comedy and epigrams) have many references to such behaviour on the part of excluded lovers. Here, however, Delphis' allusions to the standard behaviour of male lover and reluctant female beloved serve to draw attention to his own anomalous position: it is he who is the beloved, she who is the pursuer. In making this speech Delphis goes some way towards restoring conventional roles.

119[691] ἢ τρίτος . . . φίλος 'with two or three friends'. Usually in such phrases αὐτός is expressed. αὐτίκα νυκτός: for the gen. with the temporal adv. cf. *532* νυκτὸς ἀωρί.

120[692] μᾶλα . . . Διωνύσοιο: apples are love-tokens. Perhaps they are here said to belong to Dionysus because he is patron of drinkers at the symposium.

121–2[693–4] λεύκαν . . . περὶ ζώστραισιν ἑλικτάν '⟨a garland of⟩ white poplar entwined with bands ⟨of wool⟩' (=περιελικτὰν ζώστραισι). Heracles introduced the white poplar into Greece, and this type of garland consisting of alternate strips of greenery and wool seems to be particularly associated with him (see Gow ad loc.). Delphis imagines himself, perhaps with some vanity, as wearing a garland characteristic of the patron of athletics.

124–8[696–700] ἐδέχεσθε . . . ὠθεῖτε . . . ὑμέας: the plurals refer, perhaps rather condescendingly, to Simaetha's household, which seems to consist only of herself and Thestylis. καί κ' . . . τάδ' ἦς φίλα 'that would have been nice'.

126[698] εὗδον 'I would have slept ⟨content⟩'; κε is understood from 124.

130–8[702–10] The tone of Delphis' speech becomes suspiciously high-flown. Simaetha calls her house δῶμα (17, etc., 103); Delphis has already called it στέγος (116), and he now uses the words μέλαθρον (132) and θάλαμος (136), both high poeticisms. His portentously platitudinous reflections on the effects of Eros are patently insincere.

130[702] χάριν . . . ἔφαν . . . ὀφείλειν 'I declare that I owe thanks . . .': ἔφαν is a sort of 'instantaneous' aor.

131[703] δευτέρα: because she was inspired by Cypris to summon him.

133[705] Λιπαραίω: one of the Lipari islands (NE of Sicily) was a volcano which was thought to be Hephaestus' forge.

137[709] ἐφόβησ' 'rouses' or 'startles' (with a sudden impulse) – gnomic aor. The irresistible madness of desire (cf. *503*) forces virgins shamelessly to leave their homes and married women to sneak out to meet lovers, leaving their place in bed beside their husbands still warm (ἔτι θερμά).

138[710] In hexameter verse it is extremely rare for direct speech to end after the first foot. The interruption of speech here shows the effect of Eros' madness on Simaetha: in her case Delphis' platitudes are all too true, and she cannot control herself any longer. She is quick – too quick – to believe him (ταχυπειθής, 138) and they quickly (ταχύ, 140) begin to make love.

140[712] πεπαίνετο 'grew warm'. The usual meaning of πεπαίνω is 'grow ripe', 'soften'.

142[714] 'And, that I might not chatter to you at great length, dear Moon...', i.e. 'to cut a long story short'. καί is postponed (*277* n.).

143[715] ἐπράχθη τὰ μέγιστα: a euphemism. πόθον '⟨object of⟩ desire' (cf. *1284* n.), i.e. what we both wanted.

144[716] μέσφα τό γ' ἐχθές 'until yesterday, at least'. The words really belong to the next clause, since it was yesterday that *she* had cause to blame *him*, not he to blame her. The meaning is presumably that although he has not been near her for eleven days (4, 157) she had no cause to suspect his infidelity until she heard today from the mother of Philista and Melixo that yesterday Delphis had paid attention to someone else.

146[718] ἁμᾶς: Doric for ἡμετέρας (or ἐμᾶς). In this context the word might mean 'my neighbour' or 'the one who plays for Delphis and me'. It is presumably in her capacity as flute-girl at some party that Philista has come to know of Delphis' new love.

147–8[719–20] A stately 'epic' description of dawn which looks forward to 163–6, where Simaetha tries to close her narrative in a tone of dignity and resignation. Cf. 13, 46, 73–80, 82, 95, 112 nn.

147[719] ἵπποι: Dawn, Helios, Selene (cf. 165) and Night (cf. 166) were all conceived of as travelling across the sky in horse-drawn chariots.

149[721] ἔραται: there are two middle forms of the verb 'desire', ἔραμαι and ἐράομαι. From the first one would expect 3rd pers. ἔραται; from the second Doric ἐρῆται (see App.A.3). It seems possible that ἔραται is a mistake by Theoc.; or perhaps ἐρῆται should be written.

150[722] αὖτε 'further', of the extra information which Simaetha demanded.

151[723] ἀτὰρ τόσον 'but ⟨only⟩ this much, that...'.

151–2[723–4] Ἔρωτος | ἀκράτω ἐπεχεῖτο 'he was having poured for himself (< ἐπιχέω) unmixed wine (ἀκράτω partitive gen.) ⟨in honour⟩ of Love', i.e. he kept drinking toasts to an absent person.

152[724] ᾤχετο: sc. from the party.

153[725] οἱ: dat. of interest: Delphis said he would garland the house in question (τῆνα) *for* him/her (sc. the beloved). Leaving garlands (worn during the κῶμος) at a person's door was a more common alternative to breaking and entering; cf. 118–28 n.

154[726] ἀλαθής 'truthful', i.e. what she says is true (hence γάρ, 155).

155[727] καὶ τρὶς καὶ τετράκις: sc. τῆς ἡμέρας.

156[728] παρ' ἐμὶν ἐτίθει: as a pledge of his return. **τὰν Δωρίδα . . . ὄλπαν**: the oil-flask from which he anointed himself after exercise. The adj. 'Dorian' may refer to a particular shape of flask; but since the usual word is λήκυθος, the phrase may imply 'what the Dorians call an ὄλπα'.

157–61[729–33] Various echoes of the opening lines mark the end of the poem: 157 δωδεκαταῖος ἀφ' ὧτε ~ 4, οὐδὲ ποτεῖδον ~ 4 οὐδὲ ποθίκει; 158 ἁμῶν δὲ λέλασται ~ 5 οὐδ' ἔγνω...; 159 φίλτροις ~ 1, καταδήσομαι ~ 3; 160 τὰν Ἀίδαο πύλαν... ἀραξεῖ (sc. if he will not knock at mine) ~ 6 οὐδὲ θύρας ἄραξεν; 161 κακὰ φάρμακα ~ 15 φάρμακα... χερείονα.

159[731] καταδήσομαι: the spells just completed will take effect.

159–62[731–4] Simaetha closes her narrative with a threat: if Delphis fails to obey her summons she will consign him to Hades with powerful magic. The picture which we have formed of Simaetha in the rest of the poem leads us to suspect that she could never fulfil such a threat. The delusion of power lightens her despair.

160[732] ναὶ Μοίρας: cf. *1381*. For the scansion -ᾱς see App.D.1.

161[733] οἱ 'for him', i.e. to be used against him.

162[734] Ἀσσυρίω . . . παρὰ ξείνοιο: the Assyrians were famous as practitioners of magic.

163[735] πώλως: 147 n.

164[736] ὥσπερ ὑπέσταν 'as I have undergone it ⟨hitherto⟩'.

166[738] εὐκάλοιο: cf. *431* & n. **κατ' ἄντυγα Νυκτὸς ὀπαδοί** 'attendants at the chariot of Night'. In Homer ἄντυξ means the rail around a chariot, but in later poetry it can mean the chariot itself. Cf. 147 n.

XI

Summary. The poem is a dialogue, set in a harvest field, between Milon (perhaps the foreman) and Bucaeus, a reaper who has fallen behind in his work because he is preoccupied with love for Bombyca. Encouraged by Milon, he sings a song of 14 lines in her praise. Milon sings in reply a 14-line compilation of down-to-earth rustic themes, which he says are far more suitable for a working man than Bucaeus' love-lorn encomium. The reader is left to make what he can of these two complementary responses to ἔρως.

The place of Eros. This is a 'pastoral' (strictly speaking, 'agricul-tural') poem; but its themes of song and desire are related to those of the last two idylls. We have seen that in the *Cyclops* a reader-figure, Nicias, is incorporated into the poem itself by means of the hortatory 'frame', and that Polyphemus' song gains in effect because it is addressed by way of advice to a poet-doctor who is himself perhaps in love. In this idyll a less sympathetic audience is provided for a song of love. Milon subscribes (or affects to subscribe) to the commonplace that Eros is a luxury for men with nothing better to do. Hard work is the thing (1 ἐργατίνα (first word of the poem), 9 ἐργάται ἀνδρί, 23 ἐργαξῆι, 43 εὔεργον, 56 μόχθεντας); ἔρως is only for spoilt mother's boys (13, 57–8; cf. Polyphemus' words at *564–6* 'You would be wiser to do something useful . . .'). He nevertheless acknowledges as true the assumption which underlies the last two poems, namely that song can be a palliative or antidote for desire (22–3), and he compliments Bucaeus, albeit rather ironically, on his composition (38–40). Milon's own song is of a piece with his character. In his dialogue with Bucaeus he appears as rough, cynical, and much given to proverbial expressions and clichés (11, 13, 17, 40); his song is similarly colloquial, forceful and hard-headed, reminiscent in places of Hesiod's practical advice and exhortations in the *Works and Days.* The tone of the idyll as a whole is humorous: Milon is a caricature of the bluff confidant, while Bucaeus, the pining lover, is besotted with a spindly girl of poor colour – his song only confirms his blindness to her obvious imperfections (18, 24–9). But in love he is; and by the end of the poem he has gained less relief from his desire even than did Simaetha and Polyphemus.

Bibl.: F. Cairns, 'Theocritus Idyll 10', *Hermes* 98 (1970) 38–44.

1[739] ὠιζυρέ = ὦ οἰζυρέ.

2[740] δύναι: a rare contracted form of δύνασαι.

3[741] λαιοτομεῖς 'cut the crop' (λήιος, Dor. λᾶιος). τῶι πλατίον (adv., = πλησίον) 'your neighbour', i.e. the man who should be next to you in the line of reapers. Dat. after ἅμα.

4[742] A pastoral simile: cf. *512–13.* ποίμνας: gen.: sc. ἀπολείπεται, 'separated *from*'.

5[743] δείλαν . . . καὶ ἐκ μέσω ἄματος 'during the evening, or even from (i.e. after) mid-day'.

6[744] τᾶς αὔλακος: to be taken with both ἀρχόμενος and ἀποτρώγεις. αὖλαξ usually = 'furrow'; but the basic meaning, as with ὄγμος, seems to be 'narrow, well defined strip'. **οὐκ ἀποτρώγεις** 'you're not getting your teeth into it', lit. 'not nibbling it away'.

7[745] ὀψαμᾶτα 'you who reap (ἀμάω) until late in the day (ὀψέ)'. **πέτρας ἀπόκομμ' ἀτεράμνω** 'a chip off the unyielding stone'. He knows that Milon is a hard worker and emotionally hard-headed.

8[746] ἀπεόντων: masc. (normal in generalizing expressions, even when the reference is to a girl – cf. *567*); but the unsympathetic Milon affects to understand it as neut. pl. (hence τῶν ἔκτοθεν, lit. 'things outside ⟨your work⟩', i.e. 'things not of immediate importance', in 9).

11[749] μηδέ γε συμβαίη '⟨No;⟩ and may it not happen, either!'. **χαλεπὸν χορίω κύνα γεῦσαι** 'it's bad that a dog should taste guts' (because he will find them addictive).

13[751] Milon now affects to believe that Bucaeus is happily in love. **ἐκ πίθω ἀντλεῖς** 'you draw ⟨wine⟩ from the jar', i.e. you must have ample resources and can therefore afford self-indulgence. **δῆλον:** sc. ἐστὶν ὅτι. **ὄξος:** sour dregs from the bottom of the jar.

14[752] 'For that reason (i.e. because I am in love) everything before my door has been unhoed (ἄσκαλα < σκάλλω) since the sowing' – some crop of his own which he has recently sown and subsequently neglected.

15[753] ἁ Πολυβώτα: the gen. may imply either parentage or ownership.

16[754] ἀμάντεσσι: dat. pl. pres. part. act. of ἀμάω. **παρ' Ἱπποκίωνι** 'at Hippocion's place', i.e. on his farm. **ποταύλει** = προσηύλει.

17[755] 'It serves you right: you asked for it', lit. 'God finds out (εὖρε gnomic aor.) the sinner: you've got what you've been wanting for a long time'. Milon unsympathetically implies that Bucaeus wanted to fall in love, and that he must now take the consequences.

18[756] μάντις: the praying mantis, a skinny (cf. 27 ἰσχνάν), angular and vicious creature with protruding eyes, which seizes other insects in a deadly embrace. **χροΐξεῖται:** related to χρώς, 'touch another's skin with one's own' (LSJ), i.e. embrace. **καλαμαία:** probably 'cornfield-dwelling' rather than 'thin as a stalk'.

19[757] τυφλὸς . . . ὁ Πλοῦτος: he is traditionally blind because he bestows wealth without regard for virtue or just deserts. **αὐτός** 'alone'; cf. *661*.

20[758] ὠφρόντιστος Ἔρως: Eros is 'blind' in the sense that, like Wealth, he exercises his power indiscriminately, carelessly (ἀφρόντ-ιστος) and unexpectedly on the most unsuitable people. **μὴ δὴ μέγα μυθεῦ** 'don't talk big', sc. or you may be struck down with ἔρως yourself.

21[759] λᾶιον: 3 n.

22[760] κόρας 'for the girl', objective gen. **ἀμβάλευ** (=ἀναβάλου): a play on κατάβαλλε in the last line: he should 'knock down' the crop and 'strike up' a tune.

22–3[760–1] ἄδιον οὕτως | ἐργαξῆι: the songs of Bucaeus and Milon are probably to be understood as substitutes for the rhythmical work-songs chanted by labourers (cf. 41 n.). It is perhaps for this reason that each piece falls into seven sets of end-stopped couplets.

24[762] Μοῦσαι Πιερίδες: a grand proem for a rustic song: cf. Hes. WD 1–2 Μοῦσαι Πιερίηθεν, ἀοιδῆισι κλείουσαι, | δεῦτε... On Pieria see 495 n. **συναείσατε ... μοι** 'join me in celebrating': the production of song is conceived of as a joint creative effort between Muses and poet.

26[764] Βομβύκα: she is named after the βόμβυξ, a type of flute (cf. 16, 34). **Σύραν:** because she is dark-skinned she has the nickname 'Syrian'. In women a pale complexion was admired; cf. 512 n.

27[765] μελίχλωρον 'honey-yellow', presumably a more compli-mentary synonym for ἀλιόκαυστον rather than a flat contradiction of others' judgement. Lovers are notorious for their euphemisms: cf. Plato, Rep. 474d (where μελίχλωρος is cited as an example), Lucr. 4.1153–70, Hor. Sat. 1.3. 38–67, Ovid, Ars Am. 2.657–62 (cf. Rem. Am. 325–30).

28[766] ἁ γραπτὰ ὑάκινθος: an unidentified plant (not our hyacinth) whose leaves had marks resembling the letters ΑΙ. Various myths explained them as standing for αἰαῖ or Αἴας.

29[767] τὰ πρᾶτα: adv.: 'they are chosen first, i.e. preferred, in garlands'.

31[769] ἁ γέρανος τὤροτρον: cranes, like seagulls, follow behind the plough to pick up worms and insects which it uncovers.

32–5[770–3] A wish of hopelessly maudlin sentimentality, ending in bathos with – a new pair of shoes.

32[770] 'Would that there were to me, i.e. would that I had, as many things as (ὅσσα neut. pl.) they say Croesus once possessed.' Croesus was a proverbially wealthy king of Lydia.

33[771] ἀνεκείμεθα 'we would be dedicated' (sc. as statues).

34[772] αὐλώς: cf. 16. **ῥόδον ... μᾶλον:** love-tokens: cf. 502, 692. **τύγε:** γε does not always make the pronoun emphatic (see Dawe on

Soph. *O.T.* 1101), and no emphasis is required here. The word is delayed unusually late in its clause.

35[773] σχῆμα 'clothes'. **καινάς**: to be taken with both σχῆμα and ἀμύκλας; cf. 6 n. **ἐπ' ἀμφοτέροισιν**: sc. τοῖς ποσί. **ἀμύκλας**: a type of shoe named after the Spartan town Amyclae.

36–7[774–5] Bucaeus strives for novel compliments, but succeeds only in obscuring his meaning.

36[774] ἀστράγαλοι: knucklebones can be well moulded, symmetrical, pleasingly shiny, swiftly moving. In which of these respects her feet resemble them is not made clear. **τευς**: with πόδες.

37[775] τρύχνος: an unexplained, perhaps humorously obscure, reference. τρύχνος is the name for various plants of the nightshade family, said to induce sleep or madness; so Bucaeus may mean 'your voice lulls me to sleep' or 'drives me mad with passion'. But a comic poet (*CAF* adesp. 605) has the expression μουσικώτερος τρύχνου, which suggests that τρύχνος may occasionally have meant something other than a plant. **τὸν μὰν τρόπον οὐκ ἔχω εἰπεῖν** 'I have not the power to describe your disposition'. The words ought to mean 'you are beyond all description'; but in the light of Bucaeus' naïveté and rather limited poetic talents one might prefer to understand his statement literally.

38[776] ἐλελάθει = 'and we never knew it'. **Βοῦκος**: a shorter alternative for Βουκαῖος.

39[777] ' "How well he measured the form of the mode". In other words, Bukaios chose a musical mode and imposed it upon the verses, which have a particular metrical form, in a way which produced a good song.' (Dover). The tone is ironically pompous.

40[778] Milon means that his seniority is useless because it is not matched by superiority in singing.

41[779] θᾶσαι 'consider', lit. 'behold'; aor. imper. of θᾱέομαι (= Attic θεᾱομαι) with -αε- contracted to ᾱ. **τῷ θείῳ Λιτυέρσα**: Lityerses was for the Phrygians the inventor of agriculture, and a particular work-song was named after him. Here the assumption is that he was himself a composer of songs, one of which Milon is to perform. The song is subsumed into the hexameter metre of the idyll; in real life work-songs were probably simple rhythmical chants.

42[780] πολύκαρπε πολύσταχυ: laudatory epithets in asyndeton are characteristic of addresses to divinities, especially at the beginning of hymns (cf. *276, 370–1, 401*).

43[781] εὔεργον 'easy to work', i.e. in this context 'easy to reap'.

44[782] ἀμαλλοδέται 'binders'. ἄμαλλα = 'sheaf of corn'.

45[783] σύκινοι: fig-wood was proverbially weak. χοὗτος ὁ μισθός 'these wages, too' – a disenchanted comment on the quality of hired labour nowadays.

46–7[784–5] Wheat and barley were harvested while still unripe, and were put to ripen (πιαίνομαι) in a granary.

46[784] τᾶς κόρθυος ἁ τομά 'the cut end of the sheaves' should face south or west. κόρθυς is a sheaf cut half-way down the stem rather than at the very bottom.

48[786] φεύγειν = φευγόντων, infin. for 3rd pers. imper. (Goodwin, *GMT* § 784.2).

49[787] καλάμας here seems to mean 'stalk and ear together' (usually 'stalk' alone) and ἄχυρον 'grain and chaff together' (usually 'chaff' alone). ἐκ . . . τελέθει 'is produced from'.

51[789] τὸ καῦμα '⟨during⟩ the mid-day heat', acc. of duration. This is the normal work pattern in hot climates, and is contrasted with the precept at 48–9 (hence δ' in 50).

52–3[790–1] οὐ μελεδαίνει | τὸν τὸ πιεῖν ἐγχεῦντα 'he doesn't care about someone pouring his drink'. τὸ πιεῖν is the epexegetic infin., commoner without a def. art. (Goodwin, *GMT* § 795). In sense it = ποτόν, and thus provides the subject for πάρεστι.

54[792] (ἐ)πιμελητά 'bailiff' in charge of the reapers' rations. φιλάργυρε '⟨over-⟩fond of money': he economizes by cutting down on the seasoning in his lentil soup. ἕψειν: 48 n.

55[793] 'Lest you cut your hand sawing up the cummin-seed' – a proverbial expression for niggardliness (cummin-seeds are tiny), particularly suitable here because cummin was used to season soup.

56[794] μόχθεντας: this is the reading of a papyrus; the MSS and another papyrus have the expected μοχθεῦντας (App.A.3). The practice of transferring contracted verbs to the -μι conjugation is common in Aeolic (see p. 173), but is also attested in some Doric inscriptions from Cyrene. In their Doric literary amalgam poets sometimes use forms current in only a small part of the Doric-speaking world.

57[795] πρέπει: sc. σε. λιμηρὸν ἔρωτα 'love which will make you starve (sc. because if you don't reap you will have nothing to eat), or (perhaps less likely) 'your half-starved girlfriend' (cf. 18, 27).

58[796] κατ' εὐνὰν ὀρθρευοίσαι 'as she lies in bed at dawn'. Milon implies that Bucaeus is like a small child who tells his mother his dreams each morning.

XII

This is an experimentally archaic piece in imitation of Sappho and / or Alcaeus, perhaps modelled on specific poems by them on similar themes. Theocritus is (or claims to be) about to set sail from Syracuse to Miletus, bearing with him an ivory distaff as a gift for Theugenis, the wife of his friend Nicias (see p. 148). The poem is imagined as somehow accompanying the gift, and it has several formal features in common with dedicatory epigrams (name of recipient, description of object, reason for giving); but, like most epigrams of the Hellenistic period, it is in fact an independent composition which subtly 'feeds' us information not necessary in a purely functional poem (cf. e.g. 5–9).

Addressee. Ancient writers sometimes address their own poems, exhorting them to act as representatives in the poet's business (cf. Pind. *Nem.* 5.3, Cat. 35, Hor. *Epist.* 1.20, Ovid, *Tristia* 1.1); Ovid, *Amores* 2.15 has as its addressee a ring which the poet is about to send to his mistress: 1–3 *anule, formosae digitum uincture puellae,* | *in quo censendum nil nisi dantis amor* (cf. Theoc. 24–5), | *munus eas gratum . . .* Here, however, the personification of the object serves a different purpose. The poem refers to the founder-colonist of both Miletus (3) and Syracuse (17); and Theocritus' personification of the distaff means that it, too, can be wittily described as an emigrant, setting out from Sicily to 'colonize' Miletus (21 οἰκήσεις κατὰ Μίλλατον; κατοικέω /-ίζω = 'settle'). The poem is an exotic production – it is written in Aeolic metre by a Dorian for an Ionian destination (21).

Theugenis. Nicias' wife is the 'real' addressee of the poem. By addressing the distaff Theocritus can praise her indirectly and describe her admirable ways. Her husband is presumably a man of considerable means; but this makes no difference to the role of his wife. In Greek society at all periods a woman's sphere was the management of the household (= 14 φιλέει δ' ὅσσα σαόφρονες); and wives of the wealthiest husbands were expected to direct and assist their maids in the production of clothes for the family. We should beware, therefore, of assuming that the archaic form of this poem reflects a domestic arrangement outmoded at the time it was written.

Metre. The 'Greater Asclepiad', used by Alcaeus and in Sappho's third Book: ⏑ ⏑ _ ⏑⏑ _ _ ⏑⏑ _ _ ⏑⏑ _ ⏑ ⏑ (the first two syllables are never both short together). Its naming after Asclepiades (q.v., p. 244) suggests that poems by him in this metre were well known in the third century, but no fragments survive.

Dialect. Aeolic with an admixture of epic forms, as in many poems of Alcaeus and Sappho. Distinctive features include:

A   No rough breathings ('psilosis').

B   Recessive accent, representing the pitch of Aeolic speech: 2 γύναιξιν ~ -ξίν, 4 χλῶρον ~ -όν, 23 τώ ~ τοῦ, etc. (This does not apply to prepositions.)

C   *Vowels*
   (1) Original Indo-European ᾱ is retained: ἀλακάτα = Attic ἠλακάτη.
   (2) υ for ο: 3 ὑμάρτη (ὁμάρτει), 16 ἀπύ.

D   *Consonants* are sometimes doubled, for various phonological reasons: 15 ἐβολλόμαν, 3 ἄμμιν, 6 ξέννον, 4 ὄππα, 9 χέρρας, 9 ὀπάσσομεν. (4 ἀππάλω and 14 ἀννυσίεργος, which are phonologically inexplicable, are probably by false analogy.)

E   *Verbs*
   (1) Verbs which in other dialects have vowel-stems are usually conjugated as -μι verbs in Aeolic: 3 θέρσεισ' < θέρσημι not θαρσέω, 3 ὑμάρτη < ὑμάρτημι not ὁμαρτέω, 5 αἰτήμεθα < αἴτημι not αἰτέω. (But note 11 φορέοισ', 14 φιλέει.)
   (2) 3rd pers. pl. indic. act. in -οισι: 11 φορέοισ' = φορέουσι.
   (3) Fem. pres. part. act. in -οισα: 19 ἔχοισ' = ἔχουσα.

F   *Nouns and adjectives*
   (1) Acc. pl. of 1st and 2nd decl. in -αις / -οις (12, 15–16, 20).
   (2) Dat. pl. of 1st and 2nd decl. usually in -αισι / -οισι. (But note 10 πόκοις.)
   (3) 2nd decl. gen. sing. in -ω (8, 9, 13, 23).

G   *Prepositions* suffer apocope: 5, 25 πάρ. (21 κατά is an epicism; true Aeolic would be κὰμ Μίλλατον.)

It should be noted that the MSS are not trustworthy in matters of Aeolic orthography and accentuation, and much remains uncertain. See Gow 1 lxxvii–lxxx.

Erinna. The fourth-century poetess Erinna wrote a 300-line hexameter poem entitled Ἠλακάτη, which was very popular in the Hellenistic period (cf. *AP* 11.322; *GP* 771–6 (= Antiphanes 9)). It was written in a mixture of Doric and Aeolic, and was called Ἠλακάτη because it included Erinna's memories of her childhood spinning. See M. L. West, 'Erinna', *Z.P.E.* 25 (1977) 95–119. The surviving fragments (*SH* 401) have nothing of substance in common with Theocritus' poem.

Bibl.: F. Cairns, 'The distaff of Theugenis – Theocritus *Idyll* 28', *Arca* 2 (1976) 293–305.

1[797] γλαύκας . . . 'Αθανάας: Athena, goddess of women's work, traditionally γλαυκῶπις (*Il.* 1.206, etc.); γλαύκας 'grey' for 'grey-eyed' as we say 'blonde' for 'blonde-haired'.

2[798] οἰκωφελίας: a Homeric *hapax* (*Od.* 14.223). ἐπάβολος + gen. here = 'skilled in', 'knowledgeable about' (lit. 'having attained', <ἐπιβάλλω): another Homeric *hapax* (*Od.* 2.319), popular in Hell. verse; attested, however, for Sappho (fr. 21.2).

3[799] Neleus was the legendary founder of Miletus.

4[800] Miletus was not particularly famed for this sanctuary of Aphrodite, and it is not clear why Theoc. has chosen to mention it here. Perhaps Nicias lived nearby. καλάμω χλῶρον ὑπ' ἀππάλω: the reeds make the precinct green. For this 'causal' sense of ὑπό cf. LSJ s.v. A.II.3.

5[801] τύιδε: in this word ι affects the pronunciation of δ and does not form a diphthong with υ (M. L. West, *Glotta* 48 (1970) 196–8); hence the apparently proparoxytone accent.

6[802] τέρψομ': short-vowel subj. (o for ω). Elision of -αι is common in Alcaeus and Sappho.

7[803] The Graces lend beauty and charm to any human artistic endeavour; Nicias is called their 'offspring' because his poetry is charming and beautiful (cf. *498*). The metaphor is a common one: see Gow on Theoc. 7.44. ἴερον: a variant prosody ∼ 4 ἴρον.

9[805] Νικιάας: fem. gen. sing. of Νικίαος, an adj. = 'belonging to Nicias'.

10[806–7] Much effort went into making the distaff (8 πολυμόχθω), and Nicias' wife will expend much effort in using it.

10[806] τᾶι: relative.

11[807] βράκη: i.e. Ϝράκεα. Here (uniquely?) of fine clothing ∼ usual 'rags'.

12–13[808–9] Gently humorous (cf. 15–16, 22 n.). This domestic activity is described in high-sounding 'epic' phraseology: μάτερες ἀρνῶν is a dignified periphrasis for 'sheep'; εὔσφυρος is used elsewhere of epic heroines.

12[808] μαλάκοις . . . πόκοις: acc. of respect, with πέξαιντ' mid. for passive.

13[809] Θευγένιδος: her name is the middle word of the middle line of the poem: cf. L. A. Moritz, *C.Q.* n.s. 18 (1968) 116–31 (Horace), Virg. *Ecl.* 1.42.

14[810] ἀννυσίεργος 'getting work done' (< ἀνύω). For the sentiment cf. 10.

15–16[811–12] Join εἰς . . . δόμοις (acc. pl.).

15[811] ἀκίρας 'slothful'. The ἀ- is not a negative prefix; hence the adj. is three-termination. A very rare word.

16[812] ἔσσαν = οὖσαν; also Doric (cf. *200*).

17–18[813–14] Syracuse, in the 'three-promontoried' island of Sicily, was founded in 734 B.C. by Archias from Corinth, the original name of which was Ephyra.

17[813] τοι = σοι; sc. ἐστί. ἂν ὥξ = ἦν ὁ ἐξ.

18[814] μύελον: an unusual metaphor. The marrow was prized as a toothsome titbit; hence μύελον here perhaps suggests delicacy as well as innermost vital force. For the latter sense we might say 'life-blood'.

20[816] νόσοις is acc. pl., and the infin. ἀπαλάλκεμεν depends on σόφα: 'drugs skilled at averting diseases'. Cf. Pind. *Ol.* 8.85 ὀξείας δὲ νόσους ἀπαλάλκοι.

21[817] πεδ' = μετ'.

22[818] εὐαλάκατος: a humorous epicizing coinage by Theoc., with reference to Homeric phrases such as ἐυκνήμιδες Ἀχαιοί and ἐυμμελίω Πριάμοιο: Theugenis will be as famous in the sphere of housewifery as these heroes were for their weapons of war.

23[819] The word-play ἀεί ~ ἀείδειν / ἀοιδός, hinting at immortality through poetry, is very common (see Williams on Call. *Hymn* 2.30 and cf. *275* n.). Theugenis, like the distaff, is φιλέριθος (1; cf. 14); Theoc. is φιλάοιδος. The ivory distaff will remind her of Theoc.; the poetic *Distaff* will celebrate both its recipient's industry and its donor's love.

24–5[820–1] By addressing the distaff Theoc. has contrived to praise Theugenis indirectly. Now he praises the value of his own gift indirectly by introducing an anonymous speaker. The 'someone might say'-sentiment is quite common in Greek poetry (cf. e.g. *Il.* 4.176–81, 6.479).

25[821] 'Ring-composition' ~ line 1: δώρωι ~ δῶρον, φίλων ~ φιλέριθ'. ὀλίγωι: Theoc. infects the speaker's words with his own self-disparagement: the gift is slight, but the gratitude which prompts it is great. Theoc.'s description of course belies this alleged slightness: the distaff, like *The Distaff*, is in fact precious, highly wrought and exotic in appearance.

XIII

Simias

Simias of Rhodes (fl. c. 290–270 B.C.), grammarian and poet, published three books of Γλῶσσαι ('On Rare Words') and four books of ποιήματα διάφορα, of which only small fragments survive: they included hexameter pieces entitled Ἀπόλλων and Γοργώ (?his mistress), epigrams, and poems in innovatory metres. He is the first known composer of pattern-poems (later called *Technopaegnia*), in which lines of various lengths are used to produce a particular shape on the page. *Wings*, *Axe* and *Egg* survive, all in Doric dialect. If he was the inventor of pattern-poems, Simias may have derived his idea from prose dedications inscribed on awkwardly shaped objects; but it seems unlikely that his verses were themselves intended for inscription on real axes, eggs or wings. (Pattern-poems are found also in Sanskrit literature: they include a sword, a bow, a lotus-flower and a stream of cow's urine.)

Each 'wing' has six 'feathers', i.e. lines, of decreasing length. The wings affect to belong to a grotesque statue of Eros, a bearded child, who speaks the poem in the manner of a dedicatory epigram. The poem is in fact an αἴτιον for the statue's odd appearance. The text is corrupt, and the content of Eros' speech is not clear in every detail. Its theology is partly Orphic: this is the demiurge Eros, who took over governance of the world from Uranus and Ge. The statue thus represents an amalgam of Eros' attributes – he is ancient, hence bearded, but depicted in traditional Hellenistic fashion as a winged child.

Metre. Choriambs (‿∪∪‿) followed by ∪‿ ⌣, decreasing by one choriamb per line from 5*ch* + ∪‿⌣ to ∪‿⌣ alone in the shortest 'feathers', then increasing again.

Bibl.: *OCT Bucol. Gr.* 172–9; *CA* pp. 116–20.

> George Herbert, *Easter Wings*. Theocritus composed the Σῦριγξ in the shape of a Pan-pipe (Gow I 256, II 552–7), and a certain Dosiadas wrote a Βωμός or *Altar* (*OCT Bucol. Gr.* 182–3; *CA* p. 175–6), which was imitated by Besantinus (*OCT Bucol. Gr.* 184–5) and Herbert. Cf. Herrick's *Anthem to Christ on the Cross*; *The Mouse's Tail | Tale* in *Alice in Wonderland*; G. Apollinaire, *Calligrammes*.

1[822] βαθυστέρνου: referring to the earth's deep, fertile plains; a standard expression (cf. Pind. *Nem.* 9.25 βαθύστερνον χθόνα). **'Ακμονίδαν τ' ἄλλυδις ἐδράσαντα** 'who set apart the son of Acmon'. Eros displaced Ge and Uranus, son of Acmon, as ruler of the world: cf. 11–12. **ἄλλυδις** occurs elsewhere only in combination with ἄλλος, meaning 'in different directions'; here it must = 'apart' or 'aside'.

2[823] τόσος 'of such a ⟨small⟩ size'.

3[824] ἔκραιν' 'held sway': cf. 10. **'Ανάγκα**: according to one version of the Orphic cosmogony Χρόνος and 'Ανάγκη held joint sway at the beginning of time and were parents of Χάος and Αἰθήρ (cf. 6–7). Here 'Ανάγκη must be imagined as overseer of the rule of Uranus and Ge. At Plato, *Symp.* 197b Agathon says that before the birth of Eros πολλὰ καὶ δεινά (cf. 4 λυγραῖς) θεοῖς ἐγίγνετο, ὡς λέγεται, διὰ τὴν τῆς 'Ανάγκης βασιλείαν. (This confirms that τᾶς, not Γᾶς, is the right reading in line 4.)

4[825] φραδαῖσι 'will', 'purposes', a meaning not given by LSJ.

5–7[826–8] †πάνθ' ὅσ' ἔρπει† | δι' Αἴθρας | Χάους τε: presumably a reference to the gods (Plato's θεοῖς, 3 n.), Αἴθρα being a synonym for Αἰθήρ. ἔρπει is almost certainly a corruption caused by the preceding ἑρπετά; but emending the word to a different verb (e.g. ἐμπνεῖ Kaibel) does nothing to ease the harsh lack of a conjunction in this clause.

7[828] Χάους: Hes. *Theog.* 117–22 relates how Chaos was created first, then Γαῖα, Τάρταρα and Ἔρος. Simias seems to be alluding to this tradition rather than to the Orphic cosmogony which had Eros born from an egg placed in the αἰθήρ by Χρόνος.

10[831] Eros gained power not by force (for he is not the son of Ares – 9) but by 'gentle-minded persuasion'.

11[832] μυχοί 'recesses', i.e. 'depths'. **χάλκεος οὐρανός**: a Homeric expression (*Il.* 17.425) – heaven a solid vault of bronze.

12[833] ἔκρινον δὲ θεοῖς θέμιστας: in Homer κρίνειν θέμιστας = 'give judgements'; but here perhaps 'made ordinances' or 'laid down rules' gives better sense; cf. *438* n. The imperf. is inceptive, implying 'began to…'.

XIV

Phanocles

The pseudo-Hesiodic mythological poem Γυναικῶν Κατάλογος (otherwise known as 'Ηοῖαι, because each new heroine was introduced with

the words ἢ οἵη, 'or like her...') found several imitators in the
Hellenistic period: Book 3 of Hermesianax' Λεόντιον listed famous love-
affairs (the only long surviving fragment (*CA* pp. 98–100) begins οἵην),
Nicaenetus of Samos wrote his own Γυναικῶν Κατάλογος (*CA* p. 2), and
a certain Sosicrates or Sostratus an 'Ηοῖοι (*SH* 731–4: a masculine
parody of Hesiod?). This fragment of a long poem by Phanocles is in the
same tradition (1 ἢ ὡς a variation on 'Hesiodic' ἢ οἷος). The poem's title
was Ἔρωτες (cf. Lat. *Amores*) ἢ Καλοί; and a few other exiguous
fragments (*CA* pp. 108–9) confirm that it was a catalogue of male
homosexual love-affairs.

The fragment tells an unusual version of the story of Orpheus' death:
he was torn to pieces by the jealous Thracian women as he wandered
disconsolately through the countryside thinking of his beloved Calais.
The αἴτιον-theme was clearly prominent in Phanocles' poem: in this
fragment we learn why the Thracians tattoo their women and, in
passing, who first introduced homosexuality amongst them and why
Lesbos is famous for song. The main αἴτιον is strongly signposted by the
tell-tale ἐκ κείνου (21) and εἰσέτι νῦν (28). The whole piece has a
mournful, 'elegiac' tone, which infects not only the death of Orpheus,
but also the description of his love in 1–6. The shady groves through
which he wanders (3) and the 'sleep-robbing cares' which wear him out
(5) are symbolic of unrequited love – Orpheus can captivate the natural
world with his song, but not his beloved Calais.

Of Phanocles we know nothing. Equally obscure is his source for the
tale of Orpheus and Calais. Various stories were told of Orpheus' death,
the most common being that his constant mourning for the death of
Eurydice and consequent rejection of the Thracian women led to his
murder at their hands; but no extant independent source connects him
with homosexual love. It seems not impossible that Phanocles invented
the story himself, making Calais the beloved because (1) he was a well
known fellow-Argonaut (2) he came from Thrace (cf. Ap.Rh. 1.211–23)
and (3) his name is reminiscent of the standard adjective of homosexual
admiration, καλός (hence Καλοί of the poem's title, 'Pretty Boys'). No
other independent account connects Orpheus with the origins of
tattooing.

The style of this fragment forms an interesting comparison with
Callimachus' elegiac narratives (*41–131, 132–273*). Phanocles cultivates
a studied simplicity far different from Callimachus' overwhelmingly

animated persona. The narrative moves along smoothly and is clearly pointed (7 τὸν μὲν, 11 τοῦ δ', 15 τὰς δ'), and the tone of the language is 'epic'. Much of the phraseology, and almost all of the vocabulary, can be paralleled from Homer (including several Homeric *hapax legomena*: γλαυκός, ἐμφορέω, ἱμερτός, κιθαριστύς, μελεδώνη, ῥόθιος). Many epithets are 'conventional': 6 θαλερόν, 14 γλαυκοῖς, 15 πολιή, 24 δεινόν, 26 στυγεροῦ. The sense rarely runs over without pause from one couplet to the next. There is much repetition, on both metrical and lexical levels: 4, 6, 8 and 10 all have sense-break after the first word; frequently words at the end of each half of the pentameter are in (often rhyming) agreement (2, 6, 12 cj., 14, 16, 18, 26, 28); θυμός is found at 2 & 4, πόθος 4 & 10, Κάλαϊς 2 & 6, θάλασσα 13 & 15 (both at line-end), λιγύς / λιγυρός 16 & 17 & 19, στίζειν 25 & 27, γυναῖκες 23 & 27 (both at line-end).

Bibl.: *CA* pp. 106–8. Gen.: M. Marcovich, 'Phanocles ap. Stob. 4.20.47', *A.J.Ph.* 100 (1979) 359–66; J. Stern, 'Phanocles fragment 1', *Q.U.C.C.* n.s. 3 (32) (1979) 135–43.

> Ovid, *Met.* 11.1–66.

1–2[834–5] The lines are structured chiastically: father, son; son, father.

1[834] = Ap.Rh. 4.905 (with εἰ μὴ ἄρ' for ἢ ὡς). Most critics believe that Ap. is the borrower; but there is no real evidence that Phan. wrote earlier. **Θρηΐκιος**: both Call. and Ap.Rh. vary the quantity of ι in this word. In extant pre-Hellenistic poetry only Θρηΐκιος is found, but some lost source may well have had ῑ.

2[835] ἐκ θυμοῦ . . . στέρξε: a variation on the Homeric ἐκ θυμοῦ φίλεον / -έων (*Il.* 9.343, 486). **Κάλαϊν**: Calais and Zetes were winged sons of Boreas. As members of the Argonautic expedition they saved Phineus from the Harpies (Ap.Rh. 2.240–447). According to one account they were killed by Heracles because they persuaded the Argonauts to leave him behind at Cius (Ap.Rh. 1.1298–1308).

5–6[838–9] Greek lovers conventionally waste away (τήκομαι, etc.), literally as well as metaphorically (*506, 611–12, 654–62*). ἔρως is a malignant disease with only one real cure; but song can be a palliative (cf. pp. 149–50, 156, 167).

6[839] Occasionally in both prose and verse a gen. absolute is used when the participle might be expected to agree with a pronoun in the preceding clause, here acc. μιν. Goodwin, *GMT* §850 says this is 'to make the participial clause more prominent'; but here one suspects the main reason is to avoid a double accusative. Cf. *Od.* 6.155–7 μάλα πού σφισι θυμὸς |… ἰαίνεται …| λευσσόντων and Page on Eur. *Med.* 910.

7[840] Βιστονίδες: the Bistones were a tribe in SW Thrace; but here the word is probably a recherché equivalent of 'Thracian'. **ἀμφιχυθεῖσαι:** lit. 'pouring round', i.e. surrounding him.

8[841] θηξάμεναι: the mid. for act. with this verb is found once in Hom., *Il.* 2.382.

9–10[842–3] The women abhorred him because he made them redundant. The neatly aetiological theme of 'first inventor' (πρῶτος εὑρετής) is found quite frequently in Greek poetry of all periods.

10[843] θηλυτέρων: in Homer the form is always adjectival, but Hellenistic poets used it as a noun. The acc. would have sounded flat and predictable after ἔρωτας | ἄρρενας.

11[844] Cf. *Il.* 17.126 ἔλχ᾽, ἵν᾽ ἀπ᾽ ὤμοιιν κεφαλὴν τάμοι ὀξέι χαλκῷ.

12[845] Bergk's correction is probably right: Orpheus' lyre is often called 'Thracian' (e.g. Hermesianax fr. 7.2 Θρῆισσαν στειλάμενος κιθάρην), and this position for adj. and noun in agreement is a favourite with Phanocles.

13[846] ἥλωι: no other source mentions the quaint detail of the nail. **καρτύνασαι** 'fixing it firmly', a slight extension of the usual meaning 'strengthen', 'make firm'.

15[848] Cf. *Il.* 4.248 πολιῆς ἐπὶ θινὶ θαλάσσης.

16–17[849–50] Dr R. D. Dawe has suggested the two-line lacuna after 15 and strong punctuation before ἔνθα (17). This solves three problems: (1) The text as transmitted has no mention of the famous detail of the singing head (except indirectly in 17 λίγειαν). (2) If the head's melodiousness is mentioned in the lacuna, ὥς can be translated 'likewise'. In the transmitted text ὡς / ὥς is very difficult ('in this way'? 'when … then'? 'as it were'?). (3) ἔνθα ('there', not 'then') can refer to the island of Lesbos, not to the awkward plural antecedent αἰγιαλούς.

16–19[849–52] λιγυρῆς … λίγειαν … λιγυρήν represent the ceaseless melody – the lyre was *still* playing as it was placed in the grave.

20[853] Φόρκου στυγνὸν ἔπειθεν ὕδωρ: Phorcus / -ys was a sea-god (ἁλὸς ἀτρυγέτοιο μέδοντος, *Od.* 1.72), and most commentators have taken the phrase Φόρκου … ὕδωρ to be a periphrasis for 'sea' – the lyre formerly had the power (imperf. ἔπειθεν) to charm rocks and seas. **στυγνόν** because the sea (and rocks) are proverbially unhearing and unsympathetic (cf. Page on Eur. *Med.* 28–9) – the adj. has concessive force, = στυγνόν περ ὄν.

25–8[858–61] Vase-paintings show the murderous women as already tattooed: K. Zimmermann, *J.D.A.I.* 95 (1980) 163–96. Tattooing was familiar to the Greeks from Thracian slaves, and was considered a barbarous custom. Runaway slaves seem occasionally to have been tattooed rather than branded (Headlam on Herondas 5.66).

25[858] ἅς = ἑάς. ἔστιζον 'they began the custom of tattooing', inceptive imperf.

26[859] κυάνεα: a funereal colour: cf. *1230*, Gow on Theoc. 17.49. λελάθοιντο: the 'reduplicated aorist' of λανθάνομαι is often used by Homer with no distinction in sense from the present.

27[860] ποινάς, acc. 'in apposition to the sentence' ('*as* a penalty . . .'), is elsewhere always found with the gen. (e.g. *Il.* 21.27–8 δυώδεκα λέξατο κούρους, | ποινὴν Πατρόκλοιο); but the dat. of interest seems quite acceptable here, and repetition of στιζ- from 25 neatly rounds off the aetiology.

XV–XVIII

Apollonius

Of Apollonius' life hardly anything is certainly known. Born in Alexandria, probably c. 295 B.C., he came to be called Ῥόδιος perhaps because at some stage in his life he taught rhetoric in Rhodes. He succeeded Zenodotus as head of the Alexandrian library and was tutor to the future Ptolemy III Euergetes. He wrote epigrams, poems on the foundations of various cities, and a prose work on Zenodotus' edition of Homer (see p. 9–10). As a young man he is said to have quarrelled with his former teacher, Callimachus, and to have had a poor reception when he first recited the *Argonautica* in Alexandria. We are told that he retired in pique to Rhodes, where he re-wrote the work and finally returned home to poetic fame. However, ancient biographies of poets are notoriously unreliable, and these stories may contain only the smallest grain of truth, or none at all. (It is interesting to note in this connection that the ancient commentator's list of Telchines does not contain Apollonius' name: cf. *1* n.)

Both the *Aetia* (which treated some episodes from the Argonautic saga) and the *Argonautica* itself were probably circulated or recited as 'Work in Progress' over a number of years, and numerous verbal allusions testify to their interdependence (see p. 7); *Idylls* 13 and 22 of Theocritus were written during this same period (see p. 146).

Apollonius' language, diction and phrasing are closely Homeric, and almost every line contains words and expressions quoted or adapted from the *Iliad* or *Odyssey*. The present commentary has space to record only a small proportion of such allusions; for a full list see M. Campbell, *Echoes . . .* (op. cit., below). But despite this verbal similarity to Homer, and despite the fact that it is epic in scope and theme, the *Argonautica* is a self-consciously 'Callimachean' poem. Especially noticeable are the large number of aetiologies of places and customs, and the constant allusion to topical points of Homeric philology and textual criticism. The versification is smoother than that of Homer. There are no formulae or repeated lines. The gods play a smaller role; and the human protagonists are presented in a less 'idealized' light. (ἀμήχανος is a frequent epithet.) For an epic the poem is short (four books, 5835 lines). Thus the *Argonautica* is not anti-Callimachean: it is an attempt to revivify the old epical–heroical format by bringing to it the preoccupations of the new poetry. If Callimachus appreciated any ἓν ἄεισμα διηνεκές, it must have been this one.

Bibl.: Ed.: H. Fränkel (*OCT*, 1961); F. Vian (3 vols, Budé, 1974–81). Comm.: G. W. Mooney (Dublin, 1912); Bk 3 M. M. Gillies (Cambridge, 1928), R. L. Hunter (Cambridge, forthcoming). Biog.: Fraser I 749–54, II 1055–7; Pfeiffer, *HCS* 141–8; M. R. Lefkowitz, *The lives of the Greek poets* (London, 1981) ch. 11. Crit.: *CHCL* I 586–98; C. R. Beye, *Epic and romance in the Argonautica of Apollonius* (Carbondale / Edwardsville, 1982); M. Campbell, *Studies in the third Book of Apollonius Rhodius' Argonautica* (Hildesheim, 1983). Language: M. Campbell, *Echoes and imitations of early epic in Apollonius Rhodius = Mnemosyne* suppl. 72 (1981).

XV

After a 200-line catalogue of the Argonauts, modelled on the Iliadic Catalogue of Ships, we hear of Jason's departure from home, the Argonauts' choice of leader (first Heracles, who refuses, then Jason), the preliminary sacrifices, and a quarrel between the heroes Idas and Idmon calmed by a song from Orpheus. As the weeping Jason takes a last look at his homeland the mood changes to one of joy and optimism. The harmony of the Argonauts' oar-strokes beating in time to Orpheus' lyre is compared to the feet of a happy chorus dancing in honour of Apollo; Chiron and his wife stand on the shore to display the young

Achilles, hero of a future epic, to his Argonaut father Peleus. This is an impressive passage: vivid simile and description and swift changes of visual perspective (547–52) emphasize the wondrous and exciting nature of this epic voyage.

536–9[863–6] These lines allude to *Il.* 18.567–72 (grape-harvest celebrations depicted on Achilles' shield) ἠίθεοι...|...|τοῖσιν δ' ἐν μέσσοισι πάις φόρμιγγι λιγείηι|ἱμερόεν κιθάριζε...|...τοὶ δὲ ῥήσσοντες ὁμαρτῆι|...ποσὶ σκαίροντες ἕποντο.

536–7[863–4] ἢ...ἤ που...ἤ: listing of various possibilities for a god's present location is a standard technique in religious contexts (cf. *277–82* n., *191–5*). Here the rising tricolon, each element slightly longer than the last, gives added solemnity.

536[863] Φοίβωι: as patron of music and the arts Apollo would be honoured with a choral performance of perfect rhythm and harmony. Πυθοῖ: the Delphic sanctuary of Pythian Apollo (*1421* n.).

537[864] που 'perhaps'. 'Ορτυγίηι: another name for Delos, birthplace of Apollo. ἐφ' 'near'. 'Ισμηνοῖο: on the banks of the river Ismenus near Thebes was a sanctuary of Apollo Ismenius.

538[865] στησάμενοι 'having set up', i.e. performing – normal usage. φόρμιγγος ὑπαί: ὑπό + gen. or dat. (540) is common of musical accompaniment. ὁμαρτῆι: wherever this word occurs in Homer (e.g. at *Il.* 18.571, 536–9 n.) ἁμαρτῆι is a variant reading. Ap. shows his preference.

539[866] ἐμμελέως 'harmoniously', 'in time' (ἐν + μέλος). κραιπνοῖσι...πόδεσσιν: an inversion of the common Homeric phrase ποσ(σ)ὶ κραιπνοῖσι. ῥήσσωσι: 'generalizing' subj., common in Homeric similes (Goodwin, *GMT* § 543–6).

540[867] 'Ορφῆος: one aspect of Ap.'s self-conscious approach to poetry is the prominence which he gives to Orpheus, the greatest poet of all. In the catalogue of Argonauts Orpheus has first mention (1.23–34), and his magical powers of song often benefit his companions (e.g. at 4.903–9 he out-sings the Sirens).

540[866] πέπληγον: *326* n.

541[867] ἐπὶ δὲ ῥόθια κλύζοντο 'the surge ⟨produced by the oars⟩ kept flooding on'.

542[868] κήκιεν 'seethed'. Cf. *Il.* 7.262 μέλαν δ' ἀνεκήκιεν αἷμα.

543[869] -σα ἐρι-: hiatus between the second and third elements of a dactyl is rare in Ap., whose versification in this respect is smoother than

Homer's. (Contrast Cleanthes *379, 387*.) **μένει**: the effort they put into rowing.

544[870] φλογὶ εἴκελα: a Homeric phrase. **νηὸς ἰούσης**: a Homeric clausula.

545[871] τεύχεα: shields with polished metal fittings, fastened on the sides of the ship. Cf. J. S. Morrison & R. J. Williams, *Greek oared ships* (Cambridge, 1968) 83 (pl. 10d). **μακραὶ … κέλευθοι**: the wake stretching far behind. **αἰέν**: they never stopped. **ἐλευκαίνοντο**: a Homeric *hapax* (*Od*. 12.172).

546[872] πεδίοιο: gen. of the place traversed is common with verbs of motion in Homer; here, by extension, of the eye's movement across the plain. δι- eases the use of the gen.

547[873] ἤματι κείνωι: Homeric clausula.

548[874] Imitation-cum-variation of *Il.* 12.23 καὶ ἡμιθέων γένος ἀνδρῶν. The Argonauts belonged to the Heroic Age, ἀνδρῶν ἡρώων θεῖον γένος, οἳ καλέονται | ἡμίθεοι (Hes. *WD* 159–60). **ἄριστοι**: sc. ὄντες. Cf. *Il*. 6.209 γένος … οἳ μέγ' ἄριστοι.

549[875] Cf. *Il*. 3.47 πόντον ἐπιπλώσας.

550[876] Πηλιάδες: the nymphs of Mt Pelion in Thessaly, where the timber for the *Argo* was cut (cf. Eur. *Med*. 3–6, Cat. 64.1ff.).

551[877] 'Αθηναίης 'Ιτωνίδος: Athena directed the building of the *Argo* at Pagasae in Thessaly. Iton, where she had a temple, was nearby.

552[878] ἐπικραδάοντας 'wielding'. κραδάω = κραδαίνω, 'brandish'.

553–4[879–80] ὅγ' … Χείρων: such separation of the article from its noun, found already in Homer, is much affected in Hellenistic poetry. **ὄρεος**: Chiron lived on Mt Pelion in Thessaly. **ἄγχι θαλάσσης** 'right up to the sea': a Homeric clausula.

554[880] Φιλλυρίδης: the centaur Chiron, tutor of Achilles, was son of the nymph Philyra. Patronymics and metronymics in -ίδης often take a heavy first syllable for metrical convenience, either by lengthening the vowel or by doubling the consonant. **πολιῆι δ' ἐπὶ κύματος ἀγῆι**: lit. 'on the wave's grey breaking-place', i.e. on the beach, greyish-white with foam. The phrase is a recherché variant on the Homeric πολιῆς ἐπὶ θινὶ θαλάσσης: ἀγή (< ἄγνυμι) is a very rare word.

555[881] βαρείηι χειρί: a Homeric phrase. **κελεύων** 'urging them on'. **πολλά** is virtually an adverb.

556[882] 'He propitiously pronounced on (ἐπ-) them a safe return as they set out.' πηρός = 'maimed', so ἄπηρος / -ής = 'unharmed'.

557[883] σὺν καί οἱ = καὶ σύν οἱ. **παράκοιτις**: her name was Nais or Chariclo. **ἐπωλένιον**: Achilles is a babe 'in arms' (ὠλέναι).

558[884] Πηλεΐδην ᾿Αχιλῆα: a Homeric formula. The *Iliad* has as its theme μῆνιν... Πηληϊάδεω ᾿Αχιλῆος (1.1). For the *Argonautica* this is a significant moment: Peleus leaves behind his son and Apollonius leaves behind the conventions of traditional 'heroic' epic. **δειδίσκετο**: in Homer this verb means 'greet' or 'pledge'; here, uniquely, Ap. uses it as a synonym of δείκνυμι (to which it is not in fact related).

XVI

After a lengthy stay with the women of Lemnos, who had murdered their husbands, the Argonauts are finally persuaded to leave the island by Heracles, who despises time spent on unheroic amatory pursuits. Having passed through the Hellespont they reach the land of the Doliones, and are hospitably received by King Cyzicus; but on leaving they are blown back to land and in the darkness kill their former host in a confused mêlée. Departing after the funeral they compete to see who can row the longest; Heracles easily wins, but breaks his oar.

Heracles is not suited to this new type of epic. He is a hero of the old school – strong, direct, self-reliant. He refused the Argonauts' offer of leadership; he kept sullenly by the ships while his companions engaged in heterosexual diversions on Lemnos; and in the present passage his exaggeratedly heroic prowess finally reduces him to astonished impotence. He is not at home in this company; and it comes as no surprise to find him written out of the poem in the next scene, where he ranges the Mysian countryside distractedly in search of his beloved Hylas, whom the nymphs have stolen away. The Argonauts put to sea without him (see *835* n.), and the sea-god Glaucus prophesies that he must instead perform the Twelve Labours. In Libya towards the end of the poem he is glimpsed dimly on the horizon as he makes off with the Hesperides' golden apples, which he has removed by brute force after killing their guardian serpent. His action there contrasts with Jason and Medea's removal of the Golden Fleece from its tree after Medea had charmed its guardian snake to sleep. Heracles is thus a foil to contrast with the new, subtler, more 'romantic' ethos of Apollonian epic.

1153[885] ἔρις 'spirit of rivalry' to see who would stop rowing last.

1154[886] ἀμφί: adv., 'all round'.

1155[887] ἐστόρεσεν ... κατὰ δ᾿ εὔνασε: both bed-metaphors:

στόρνυμι of making a bed smooth, κατευνάζω of putting to sleep, i.e. making calm.

1156[888] γαληναίηι πίσυνοι: i.e. confident that the calm would last – wrongly, as it turned out (1159). ἐπιπρό 'onward': common in Ap. but not found in earlier poetry.

1157–8[889–90] οὐ . . . οὐδέ: the reinforced double negative is of a type standard in Greek of all periods: οὐ qualifies κίχον and οὐδέ ('not even') Ποσ. ἵπποι. διέξ suggests that the ship cut through (δι-) the waves at such speed that she kept leaping out (-έξ) of them.

1158[890] Ποσειδάωνος . . . ἵπποι: for Poseidon's horses and their breathtaking speed over the sea cf. *Il.* 13.23–31. κίχον: aor. of κιχάνω, 'overtake'.

1159[891] ἔμπης 'nevertheless' (in spite of the γαληναίη in which they had been πίσυνοι). ἐγρομένοιο σάλου: gen. abs. Another sleep-metaphor.

1160[892] νέον: freshly each day. ἐκ 'from the direction of'. ὑπὸ δείελον 'as evening approaches'. δείελον = 'afternoon' in Homer, 'evening' often in later writers. ἠερέθονται 'rise up' (form of the root ἀειρ-).

1161[893] μετελώφεον: the imperf. implies that they kept stopping, i.e. each man (but not all at once) kept resting.

1161–3[893–5] ὁ . . . Ἡρακλέης: *879–80* n.

1162[894] πασσυδίηι μογέοντας: they kept rowing with all possible speed (πᾶν + root σεύομαι), but wearily. κάρτεϊ χειρῶν: a Homeric clausula.

1163[895] The power of his rowing shook the ship's timbers. Cf. *Hom. Hymn to Apollo* 403 τίνασσε δὲ νήια δοῦρα.

1164–6[896–8] They are sailing just out from (1166 τυτθὸν ὑπέκ) the coast of Phrygia along the SE shore of the Propontis, into which flows the river Rhyndacus, dividing Phrygia from Mysia.

1165[897] μέγα τ' ἠρίον: <*Il.* 23.126. Αἰγαίωνος: a hundred-handed giant mentioned in the *Iliad* (1.396–406) and elsewhere.

1166[898] παρεμέτρεον 'passed by'. Homer has μετρέω = 'traverse': cf. Lat. *iter metiri*. εἰσορόωντες 'keeping in sight' the river and barrow.

1167[899] Lit. 'levering up furrows from the turbulent swell', i.e. making furrows with his hugely deep oar-strokes. τέτρηχα is irregular perf. of ταράσσω, but Hellenistic poets probably thought it cognate with τρηχύς.

1168[900] ἄξεν: aor. of ἄγνυμι. τρύφος: acc. neut., 'fragment' (from θρύπτω, 'smash in pieces') – a Homeric *hapax* (*Od.* 4.508).

1169[901] ἄμφω: this word, like δύο, is sometimes indeclinable. πέσε δόχμιος: 'he fell over sideways'.

1170[902] παλιρροθίοισι 'on the backwash'.

1171[903] παπταίνων 'looking around'. The word is often used of persons in an agitated mental state. Heracles looks round for the oar without which he feels uncomfortable. ἀήθεσον: imperf. of ἀηθέσσω, a Homeric *hapax* (*Il.* 10.493) = 'be unaccustomed'. ἠρεμέουσαι: ἠρεμαῖος and its cognates are Attic words (= ἥσυχος) not found in earlier epic poetry.

XVII

After numerous adventures the Argonauts at last arrive in Colchis. At the start of Bk 1 the poet had invoked Apollo; but as Bk 3 begins he calls on Erato, Muse of love-poetry, for inspiration. The new invocation heralds a new, romantic element within the epic, foreshadowed already by Jason's attractions for the Lemnian queen in Bk 1. Bk 3 opens with a witty scene on Olympus, in which Hera and Athena persuade Aphrodite to let Eros shoot Medea, daughter of the Colchian king Aeetes, with one of his arrows, so that she will fall in love with Jason and use her magic powers to help him gain the Fleece. When Jason courteously presents his case, the king refuses to hand over the Fleece unless Jason can emulate him in performing a frightful task – he must yoke and plough with fire-breathing bulls, sow dragon's teeth and reap the crop of armed men which springs from them. In despair, Jason accepts the challenge.

Thanks to Eros' dart Medea has already fallen in love with Jason and has responded favourably to an appeal to help him. Bk 3 is largely concerned with her mental turmoil, torn as she is between love for Jason and loyalty to her father. In a series of monologues, of which 771–801 is the third and longest, she strives in vain against her divinely inspired obsession. Brooding, atmospheric description and vivid simile (744–70) lead into her anguished and vacillatory speech, which culminates in a short-lived resolution for suicide. At last, however, the inevitable decision is made, and she waits impatiently for daybreak (802–24). Later, at a private rendezvous, she will hand over drugs to make Jason invulnerable, and he will promise to take her home as his wife. The book closes with his successful accomplishment of the task.

For most readers Apollonius' 'psychologizing' treatment of Medea is the high point of the epic. Virgil's portrait of Dido and Ovid's wavering heroines in the *Metamorphoses* owe much to Apollonius. Apollonius in turn owes much to the impassioned Medea of Euripides: compare, for example, 771–801 with *Medea* 1019–80, where she agonizes over the murder of her children. Allusions of this type are important in reminding us of the later history of Medea and Jason. In the *Argonautica* itself Medea is presented in ambivalent terms. In Bk 3 Apollonius plays down her darker aspects, concentrating mostly on the young girl's conflicting emotions; but to some degree in Bk 3, and increasingly in Bk 4, we realize that as descendant of Helios and priestess of Hecate she has great power – for evil as well as for good.

These lines make an interesting contrast with Theocritus' second *Idyll* (*574–738*): in both passages a young sorceress, alone in the silence of the night, tries vainly to come to terms with the irresistible power of Eros. **744ff.[904ff.]** These lines are underpinned by echoes of *Il.* 10.1–16 (the Greeks have been routed, and Agamemnon is sleepless with worry) ἄλλοι μέν... | εὗδον παννύχιοι μαλακῶι δεδμημένοι ὕπνωι· | ἀλλ' οὐκ Ἀτρεΐδην Ἀγαμέμνονα ποιμένα λαῶν | ὕπνος ἔχε γλυκερὸς πολλὰ φρεσὶν ὁρμαίνοντα. | ὡς δ' ὅτ' ἂν ἀσπράπτηι πόσις Ἥρης ἠυκόμοιο | ... | ὡς πυκίν' ἐν στήθεσσιν ἀναστενάχιζ' Ἀγαμέμνων | νειόθεν ἐκ κραδίης, τρομέοντο δέ οἱ φρένες ἐντός... In addition to the basic similarity of situation ('everyone except X was asleep') there are specific verbal echoes: 2 ἀλλ' οὐκ ~ 751 ἀλλὰ μάλ' οὐ, 5 ἀστράπτηι ~ 756 ἐνιπάλλεται αἴγλη, 9 πυκίν' ~ 755 πυκνά, 9 ἐν στήθεσσιν ~ 755 στηθέων and 760 στήθεσσι, 10 νειόθεν ἐκ κραδίης ~ 755 κραδίη, 10 τρομέοντο ~ 760 ἐλελίζετο, 10 ἐντός ~ 755 ἔντοσθεν. The reader must recognize this allusion and appreciate the fact that Ap. has transferred the words from a martial to an erotic context (see p. 8): it is with this sort of Homeric reference that the *Argonautica* points its originality. Here the basic Homeric structure is filled out with unusual detail. As night approaches the sailors remain vigilant; traveller and doorkeeper think of rest; and a bereaved mother (a dissonant element of foreboding) is wrapped in the sleep of exhaustion. Silence reigns throughout the city, but Medea is in inward turmoil. This passage was the source for *Aeneid* 4.522ff. (*nox erat...*).

745[905] Ἑλίκην: another name for Ἄρκτος, the Great Bear (*314* n.) or Wain, used for night-time navigation because in antiquity it revolved (ἑλίσσειν) round the pole and never set.

746[906] ἔδρακον: aor. (of δέρκομαι): 'had turned their eyes towards . . .'. **τις ὁδίτης** 'many a traveller'. For this use of τις see LSJ s.v. A.II.1–2.

747–8[907–8] τινα παίδων | μητέρα τεθνεώτων 'a mother of dead children'. Who she is, and why her children have died, is not elaborated. Exhausted with grief, she has fallen into a deep slumber (**ἀδινὸν . . . κῶμ'**). In a previous scene (616ff.) Medea was overcome by ἀδινὸς ὕπνος, only to be shaken by terrible dreams. (Some critics see this mother of dead children as an allusion to the fears of Medea's sister Chalciope, whose sons have incurred the king's wrath by helping the Argonauts. Others point out that ultimately Medea herself will be the mother of dead children.)

749[909] θρόος 'hubbub', a Homeric *hapax* (*Il.* 4.437) but common thereafter.

750[910] ἠχήεις: ἠχώ means simply 'noise' as well as 'echo'. **μελαινομένην:** *pres.* part., 'growing dark' (similarly imperf. ἄγεν, 744).

751–2[911–12] Adapted from *Od.* 15.7–8 Τηλέμαχον δ' οὐχ ὕπνος ἔχε γλυκύς, ἀλλ' ἐνὶ θυμῷι | νύκτα δι' ἀμβροσίην μελεδήματα πατρὸς ἔγειρεν.

752[912] Αἰσονίδαο: Jason, son of Aeson.

753[913] δειδυῖαν: one would expect from the Homeric perf. part. δειδιώς / -ότος a fem. δειδιυῖα. Ap.'s form is presumably a contraction of this. **οἷσιν** 'by which'. **ἔμελλε:** sc. Jason.

754[914] ἀεικελίηι 'unseemly' (< ἀ + εἰκός), i.e. not a worthy end for such a hero. **νειὸν "Αρηος** 'fallow land of Ares' – the ground in which King Aeetes was accustomed to sow the dragon's teeth and reap his crop of armed men.

755–60[915–20] Fränkel wished to transpose these lines after 765, arguing that (1) Medea's pity (761) should arise from the idea of Jason's impending doom (753–4), not from her own confused thoughts (755–60); (2) that 752–4 + 761–5 is a neatly framed unit; (3) that the simile illustrates Medea's unsettled mind, and ought to be juxtaposed with lines 766–9, which describe her confused state. (See *A.J.Ph.* 71 (1950) 126–7.) The suggestion is attractive; but it might be replied that (1) the simile illustrates not the indecisiveness of 766–9 but Medea's μελεδήματα (752), which prevent her from sleeping (751–4); and (2) that it is hardly surprising to find abrupt transitions in a passage which describes extreme mental turmoil.

755[915] πυκνὰ . . . ἔθυιεν: lit. 'seethed thick and fast', i.e. was in furious turmoil.

756–9[916–19] A famous simile (> Virg. *Aen.* 8.20–5): Medea's heart wavered like a sunbeam reflected indoors from water swirling in a basin or pail. The main point, ἔνθα καὶ ἔνθα, is picked up again in Medea's words at 771, νῦν ἔνθα κακῶν ἢ ἔνθα γένωμαι ..; There is some evidence to suggest that the image may be borrowed from a Stoic philosophical source: see Hunter ad loc.

756[916] ὥς τίς τε: the so-called 'epic' τε (LSJ s.v. B, *862*), introducing a generalization. Untranslatable. **ἐνιπάλλεται:** πάλλομαι is often used of a racing heart.

757[917] τό: relative. **νέον:** adv., 'freshly'.

758[918] γαυλῶι 'pail', a Homeric *hapax* (*Od.* 9.223).

759[919] στροφάλιγγι: the swirling of newly poured water.

761–5[921–5] This surprisingly technical description of Medea's headache owes much to contemporary researches on sensation and perception by the physicians Herophilus and Erasistratus. The **ἀραιὰς | ἶνας** are the body's fine nerves; **ἰνίον** = the bottom-most part of the skull. See F. Solmsen, *M.H.* 18 (1961) 195–7.

762[922] τεῖρ': sc. αὐτήν. **σμύχουσα:** the 'smouldering' fire of love. **χροός:** χρώς = 'flesh' as well as 'skin'.

763[923] ὑπὸ . . . ἄχρις 'right up under'; ἄχρις adv.

764–5[924–5] ὁππότ' . . . | . . . ἐνισκίμψωσιν 'whenever they hurl...'. In epic, relative and temporal clauses sometimes take the subj. without ἄν / κε when the reference is to a general condition: Goodwin, *GMT* §538.

765[925] ἀκάματοι . . . ἔρωτες: perhaps 'feelings of desire, which never slacken off' rather than 'the Erotes, untiring in their attentions': the personalized pl., though commonly used of Aphrodite's attendants in the Hellenistic period, would be rather odd in a book which has Eros himself as a major character. (The distinction between Ἔρωτες and ἔρωτες is, however, a modern typographical one, and does not correspond to separately definable ancient concepts.)

766–7[926–7] ἄλλοτε goes with φῆ, **οἱ** (= Jason) with δωσέμεν (fut. inf.). Enclitic pronouns tend to be attracted towards the beginning of a sentence, even if their verb is some distance away: cf. *22* n.

766[926] θελκτήρια φάρμακα ταύρων: the gen. is dependent on the adj.: 'drugs to charm the bulls'. Medea has promised to provide these charms the next day (736–8).

767[927] οὔ τι 'not at all' (sc. δωσέμεν). **καὶ αὐτή:** as well as Jason, whom without her help the bulls will kill.

768[928] αὐτίκα 'presently' (a third option): cf. *1209–10* n. **θανέειν:** Homer has several 2nd aor. infinitives in -έειν. Their origin is in doubt.

769[929] αὔτως 'just as she was'. **εὔκηλος** 'doing nothing', lit. 'at one's ease' (cf. *431*). **ὀτλησέμεν:** ὀτλεῖν, 'bear' (cognate with τλάω, etc.), is not found in extant pre-Hellenistic poetry.

770[930] δοάσσατο 'was in two minds' (from δοιάζω, cognate with δοιός, 'double'): cf. 819. In Homer δοάσσατο (apparently from a different root) means 'seemed'.

771–801[931–61] At lines 766–9 Medea has mentioned three options: (1) giving the φάρμακα to Jason; (2) not giving them, but committing suicide; (3) doing nothing. In this soliloquy she first thinks about (3) (778–9), then seems to be considering (1) (779–82); then (3) again (783–5). This leads to a new possibility, giving the φάρμακα *and* committing suicide (785–90); but this is rejected as likely to bring disgrace (791–8). At last she turns without conviction (ἂν ... εἴη, 798) to (2) (798–801); but the sequel shows that she in fact chooses (1), which has never been fully discussed.

771[931] Indirect question, dependent on πάντηι ... ἀμήχανος, which effectively = οὐκ οἶδα. ἔνθα ... ἢ ἔνθα + gen. = 'in this state of ... or that?'.

772[932] ἀλκή + gen. = 'defence against'.

773[933] ἔμπεδον 'continually' (lit. 'in the ground', i.e. steadfastly). ὡς: exclamatory.

774[934] 'Αρτέμιδος ... βελέεσσι: in Homer sudden death in women is attributed to the shafts of Artemis: cf. e.g. *Od.* 11.172. (Medea is instead a victim of the shaft of Eros.) πάρος 'earlier', defined by the following clause.

776[936] Χαλκιόπης υἷας: Medea's nephews, sons of Phrixus and her sister Chalciope. On the death of their father, who had been originally carried to Colchis on the back of the Golden Ram, they set sail for Orchomenus in Boeotia to claim his property. But Medea is wrong in thinking that they 'reached the Achaean land': they had in fact met the Argonauts (in Bk 2) on the Isle of Ares in the Black Sea, and had sailed back with them to help win the Fleece. (Fränkel's conjecture νῆα κομίσσαι in 775 avoids this difficulty of Medea's mistake ('before the Achaean ship brought Chalciope's sons'); but κεῖθεν in 777 can hardly refer to anywhere but Greece.) τις is to be understood with θεός.

777[937] πολυκλαύτους . . . ἀνίας 'woes causing much weeping' – in appos. to τούς.

779[939] λελάθοιμι: redupl. aor. opt. of λανθάνω, 'escape the notice of. . .'.

780[940] μησαμένη . . . μῆτις: an allusion to the etymology of her name: Μήδεια = 'plotter', 'contriver'.

781[941] ἐπίκλοπος . . . ἀρωγῆς 'serving to conceal my help'.

782[942] προσπτύξομαι 'address him in a friendly manner', lit. 'embrace him' (sc. with words). Medea is thinking about the meeting already arranged with Jason (737–9).

783–4[943–4] δύσμορος refers to herself. Even though Jason should die (κατ. περ ἔμπης, gen. abs.) she cannot expect her troubles to cease.

785[945] ἀπαμείρεται: in Eng. it is natural to say 'I shall grieve when he *is* deprived of life'; but in Gk the fut. is much commoner, the pres. rare. αἰδώς: her reputation for decency and maidenly modesty in the eyes of others.

786[946] ἀγλαΐη: the trappings of royalty. σαωθείς: aor. pass. part. of σαόω (=σώιζω). ἵνα 'wherever' (sc. ἂν ἦι νέεσθαι).

788[948] ἐξανύσειεν: aor. opt., attracted into the mood of τεθναίην. One would expect a fut. indic.

789[949] λαιμὸν ἀναρτήσασα μελάθρωι 'hanging my neck from, lit. to, the roof-beam', i.e. fastening a rope *to* the beam and hanging herself *from* it. Hanging is the traditional method of suicide for women in Gk literature (e.g. Antigone, Jocasta, Phaedra).

790[950] πασσαμένη: epic aor. mid. part. of πατέομαι, 'eat', 'swallow' (the σ is doubled for metrical convenience). Ap. alludes to the Homeric ὀδυνήφατα φάρμακα πάσσων (*Il.* 5.401, etc.); but he has changed the drugs from 'pain-stilling' to 'destructive', and the verb from πάσσων ('sprinkling') to the similar sounding πασσαμένη. ῥαιστήρια . . . θυμοῦ = θυμοφθόρα (807): ῥαίω = 'shatter'.

791–7[951–7] Echoes of the Nausicaa-episode in *Od.* 6 are an important aspect of Ap.'s presentation of Medea. These lines are an allusion to Nausicaa's speech at 276–88, in which she imagines how the Phaeacians will slander her if they see her in the company of Odysseus.

791–2[951–2] μοι ἐπιλλίξουσιν . . . κερτομίας 'people will leer insults at me', i.e. talk about me with leering expressions of condemnation. ἐπιλλίζω seems to mean 'stare' or 'wink' (cf. *Od.* 18.11).

792[952] τηλοῦ 'far and wide'.

793–4[953–4] An allusion to Helen's words at *Il.* 3.411–12 Τρωιαὶ δέ μ' ὀπίσσω|πᾶσαι μωμήσονται ('will criticize'). Medea, like Helen, fears a reputation for shamelessness. **κεν … μωμήσονται:** in epic poetry κε / ἄν + fut. ind. is almost equivalent to the potential opt. (Goodwin, *GMT* § 196): cf. *366* n.

793[953] διὰ στόματος 'on their lips'.

798[958] ἦ τ' 'indeed'. ἦ is often strengthened by the addition of one or two particles: see LSJ s.v.

800[960] ἀνωίστωι here might mean either 'mysterious' (no one would know why she hanged herself) or 'unforeseen' (no one expected it): cf. *1017, 1119, 1342*.

801[961] οὐκ ὀνομαστά 'not to be mentioned', i.e. ill-omened, unmentionable.

802[962] φωριαμόν 'box' (in Homer = 'chest'). **μετεκίαθεν** 'went to fetch' (epic aor. form).

802–3[962–3] An allusion to *Od.* 4.230 (Helen's φάρμακα) πολλὰ μὲν ἐσθλὰ μεμιγμένα, πολλὰ δὲ λυγρά.

805[965] ἀσταγές 'not in drops' (στάζω = 'drip') – understatement for 'in streams'.

806[966] ὀλοφυρομένης: gen. abs. **ἵετο:** the mid. of ἵημι = 'hasten', 'be eager to…'.

807[967] τόφρα: for final conj. ὄφρα, 'in order that'. Hellenistic poets similarly use adverbial τόφρα for ὄφρα ('as long as') and τόθι for ὅθι. **πάσαιτο:** aor. opt. of πατέομαι: see 790 n.

809[969] ἐξελέειν: sc. φάρμακα.

811[971] ἔσχετο: aor. mid. of ἔχω used passively by extension from cases such as *Il.* 17.695–6 δὴν δέ μιν ἀμφασίη ἐπέων λάβε … | … θαλερὴ δέ οἱ ἔσχετο φωνή, where ἔσχετο is in fact middle ('his voice halted').

812[972] μεληδόνες 'cares' in the sense of 'pleasant concerns', 'interests'. **(ἀμφὶ …) ἰνδάλλοντο** 'flashed before her mind'.

814[974] ὁμηλικίης: her friends of the same age. **οἷά τε κούρη** 'as one would expect a girl to do'. For this idiom see LSJ s.v. οἷος v.2, Dawe on Soph. *O.T.* 763–4, *1053* n.

816[976] Lit. 'if she truly handled each thing in her mind', i.e. if she weighed her advantages with care.

817[977] τήν: sc. φωριαμόν (fem.). **σφετέρων:** originally σφέτερος was the 3rd pers. pl. possessive adj., 'their' (<σφεῖς); but its extension to the meaning 'own' in all persons began early in Greek (e.g. Hes. *WD* 2). Cf. *1070, 1329*.

818[978] Ἥρης ἐννεσίηισι 'at the prompting of Hera', who finally resolves her doubts. At the beginning of Bk 3 Hera determines to help Jason in return for a kindness he once did her when she was disguised as an old woman. **βουλάς**: internal acc.

819[979] ἄλληι: adv. **δοιάζεσκεν**: 770 n. **ἐέλδετο** rounds off this section of the narrative with an echo of 747, where the traveller and gatekeeper 'look forward to' sleep. The whole night has passed in agonizing, and Medea now waits impatiently for the day.

820[980] θελκτήρια 'magical'. Contrast 766.

821[981] συνθεσίηισι: Medea had promised her sister Chalciope that she would help her sons (776 n.) – and by extension the Argonauts – in the face of Aeetes' threats. **ἀντήσειεν ἐς ὠπήν**: a variation on the Homeric ἤντησας ὀπωπῆς (*Od.* 3.97, 17.44). ὠπή is not found before Ap.

822[982] ἀνὰ . . . λύεσκε: a more optimistic gesture than the suicidal opening (ἀνελύετο) of the box at 808.

824[984] Ἠριγενής 'the Early-Born', i.e. Dawn. Homer has Ἠριγένεια. **ἔκαστοι** 'each separate person': cf. LSJ s.v. II.1.

XVIII

The Argonauts encounter Talos, the bronze guardian of Crete, who is vulnerable only in the ankle. Medea afflicts him with the evil eye, so that he strikes his ankle against a rock and bleeds to death.

In Book 4 Medea charms the serpent-guardian of the Golden Fleece, and the Argonauts set off for home with their prize. Apsyrtus, brother of Medea and leader of the pursuing Colchians, is treacherously murdered by Jason. A circuitous return journey via the Danube, the Adriatic, the Po and the Rhône leads them finally to round the toe of Italy and make for mainland Greece; but they are blown off course to Libya, where they are forced to carry the *Argo* across the desert. Throughout these wanderings characters and episodes from the *Odyssey* are presented in a novel way – the Argonauts encounter Circe, Scylla and Charybdis, the Sirens, and Alcinous and Arete, rulers of Phaeacia. Talos might be seen as Apollonius' equivalent of the Homeric Cyclops, who pelts the departing Odysseus' ship with rocks at *Od.* 9.480–6, 537–42.

No other literary treatment of the story survives. It appears that in some versions Medea overcame Talos by her drugs or by treachery (Apollod. 1.9.26); but vase-paintings show the Dioscuri playing a prominent part in removing the vital nail which held in his blood (for references see M. Robertson, *J.H.S.* 97 (1977) 158–60). It seems quite possible that Apollonius himself invented the evil eye story to further his own narrative purposes. This is the last, and in many ways the most impressive, occasion on which Medea comes to the aid of the frightened and dispirited 'heroes'. Her destruction of Talos concludes, too, a series of brain-vs-brawn confrontations in the *Argonautica*; and it shows Medea at the height of her powers overcoming her victim not by treachery or drugs, but by pure, concentrated evil (κακὸν νόον, 1669). The poem, and the Argonauts' journey, will soon come to a successful conclusion; but our last glimpse of Medea shows her physically and mentally isolated and superior, imperious, malignant, irresistibly powerful. She and Jason did not live happily ever after.

1629–30[985–6] ἀστήρ | αὔλιος 'the homing-star'. This is a good example of Ap.'s allusion to Homeric philological problems. At *Il.* 11.62–3 Hector is compared to a star: ἥμος δ' ἐκ νεφέων ἀναφαίνεται οὔλιος ('baneful') ἀστὴρ | παμφαίνων, τοτὲ δ' αὖτις ἔδυ νέφεα σκιόεντα, | ὣς Ἕκτωρ ... Some versions, however, had the variant αὔλιος ἀστήρ, i.e. Hesperus, the evening star, at whose appearance men and animals retire to rest in their dwellings (αὐλαί). In Homer the word occurs in the fifth foot. Ap. places it prominently in the first foot, and adds an explanatory 'gloss' – the star is αὔλιος because it 'brings relief to wretched ploughmen', i.e. signals their return home. Nor is this mere pedantry: the 'gloss' is particularly apt, since 'ploughing the sea' is a common metaphor for rowing. The ploughmen can rest; but the heroes' work is only just begun (1633–5). Cf. *906–7*.

1631[987] λιπόντος: intrans., 'having died down'.

1632–3[988–9] κλίναντες | ἱστόν: ancient ships' masts were lowered when not in use.

1634[990] Cf. *Od.* 7.288 εὗδον (n.b.) παννύχιος καὶ ἐπ' ἠῶ καὶ μέσον ἦμαρ. ἐπ' ἤματι δ' αὖτις ἰοῦσαν 'coming in turn after the day'.

1635[991] ὑπέδεκτο δ' ἀπόπροθι: probably intrans., 'appeared next in the distance' (LSJ s.v. ὑποδέχομαι IV.2). In Homer ὑποδέχομαι often = 'greet', 'welcome', and αὐτούς might be understood here; but Carpathus, a small island between Crete and Rhodes, is rocky and inhospitable.

1637[993] Κρήτην: acc. of motion after περαιώσεσθαι, 'cross over to ...'. **ὑπερέπλετο**: the verb is not found elsewhere, and its meaning here is uncertain: either 'was bigger than the others ⟨to the sailors' view⟩' or (less likely, unless the past tense is generic) = ὑπέρκειται, 'is the outermost ⟨in the view of a mainland Greek⟩' (cf. *Od.* 13.257 τηλοῦ ὑπὲρ πόντου).

1638[994] σκοπέλοιο 'promontory', literally 'lookout point' (< σκο-πέω) – an appropriate word for Talos as watcher over the island (1643).

1639–40[995–6] Talos 'prevented them from fastening their cables to the land as they arrived at the shelter of the harbour of Dicte', lit. 'the Dictaean shelter of a harbour'. Mt Dicte was apparently situated on the eastern extremity of Crete.

1641–2[997–8] At *WD* 106–201 Hesiod lists the five ages of man, each inferior to the last: Gold, Silver, Bronze, Heroic and Iron (the present). Ap. describes Talos as a relic (λοιπὸν ἐόντα) in the age of heroes (μετ' ἀνδράσιν ἡμιθέοισιν) of the bronze 'stock' (ῥίζης) – an appropriate word, since men of the bronze race were born from ash-trees (ἐκ μελιᾶν, *WD* 145 > μελιηγενέων). Hesiod's metallic classification is of course metaphorical; but Talos is literally bronze.

1643[999] Εὐρώπηι: cf. *1202–10*.

1644[1000] τρίς: he 'roamed a triple course round Crete on bronze feet'. We know from Apollodorus (1.9.26) that Talos roamed round Crete three times a day – why does not Ap. say so? Fränkel's conjecture, τρὶς περὶ (adv.) χαλκείοις ποσὶν ἤματι δινεύοντα, is attractive – Κρήτην may have arisen from a scribe's marginal explanation of νήσου in 1643.

1645[1001] Another allusion to Homeric criticism (cf. 1629–30 n.). *Il.* 23.454–5 describe a horse ὃς τὸ μὲν ἄλλο τόσον ('so far') φοῖνιξ ἦν, ἐν δὲ μετώπωι | λευκὸν σῆμα τέτυκτο περίτροχον ἠΰτε μήνη; but some texts replaced the archaic adverb τόσον with δέμας, a variant to which Ap. refers here.

1647[1003] σῦριγξ αἱματόεσσα 'a blood-filled vein'. σῦριγξ perhaps originally meant 'shepherd's pipe'; but its semantic range increased in a way similar to that of Eng. 'pipe'.

1647–8[1003–4] Fränkel's conjecture ἄμφ' ἄρα, though by no means certain, gives good sense: 'around it (the σῦριγξ) a thin membrane held the division of life and death'. The MSS read αὐτὰρ ὁ τήνγε | λεπτὸς ὑμὴν κτλ., which might just conceivably mean, 'and its thin membrane enclosed it, the division . . .'; but the expression is very awkward, and ὁ is in any case unwelcome.

1648[1004] ζωῆς ἔχε πείρατα καὶ θανάτοιο: these words seem to be an allusion to *Il.* 6.143 ὥς κεν... ὀλέθρου πείραθ' ἵκηαι, where LSJ translate 'doom'. The basic meaning, however, is 'division', 'boundary', 'limit': the ὀλέθρου πείρατα are what a man crosses when his state changes from living to dead. Similarly here the thin membrane's breaking or not breaking means to Talos the difference between life and death.

1650[1006] ἀναχρούεσκον: the verb is rare in poetry, and is not found in Homer. In the middle voice it is a semi-technical term for 'backing water' (Thuc. 7.38, etc.); here 'pushed off' from shore, or perhaps 'rowed backwards away from the land'.

1651–2[1007–8] Two spondaic fifth feet signal their weariness.

1651[1007] ἠέρθησαν: aor. pass. of ἀείρω, = 'get under way': LSJ s.v. 1.5.

1654[1010] μούνη: the emphatic position of this word suggests that the meaning is 'by myself' rather than 'only I 〈, not you〉'.

1655–6[1011–12] Talos, like Achilles, is vulnerable only in the heel: Ap. echoes *Il.* 20.101–2 (Aeneas boasts that he might defeat Achilles) οὐ κε μάλα ῥέα | νικήσει', οὐδ' εἰ παγχάλκεος εὔχεται εἶναι. (The *Iliad* makes no mention of Achilles' heel.)

1656[1012] ὁππότε μή: 'provided that... not', a parallel extension of meaning to ὅτε μή = 'if not': cf. e.g. *Il.* 14.247–8 οὐκ ἂν ... ἱκοίμην | ...ὅτε μὴ αὐτός γε κελεύοι, *Od.* 16.196–8, 23.184–6. **ἐπ' ἀκάματος πέλοι αἰών:** ἐπ'... πέλοι = ἐπείη: cf. Pind. *Pyth.* 8.97 λαμπρὸν φέγγος ἔπεστιν ἀνδρῶν (= ἀνδράσι) καὶ μείλιχος αἰών. **ἀκάματος** is difficult. The meaning may be 'continuing tirelessly for ever' (cf. Eur. fr. 594.1 ἀκάμας χρόνος); or perhaps there is a reference to the gods' life νόσφιν ἄτερ τε πόνων καὶ ὀιζύος (Hes. *WD* 113). In either case the basic meaning is 'I will overcome him unless he is immortal'.

1657[1013] θελήμονες: 'calmly' (= ἥσυχοι): cf. West on Hes. *WD* 118. **ἐρωῆς** 'range' (cf. *Il.* 15.358) rather than 'force'.

1658[1014] εἴξειε δαμῆναι: for εἴκω + inf. used of yielding up an object for a certain purpose cf. *Od.* 5.332 Ζεφύρωι εἴξασκε διώκειν (sc. νῆα).

1659[1015] ὑπὲκ βελέων ἐρύσαντες: < *Il.* 18.232.

1660[1016] ἐπ' ἐρετμοῖσιν: they held the ship still 'on the oars'. **δεδοκημένοι:** irreg. perf. part. of δέχομαι, 'await' (= δεδεγμένοι).

1661[1017] μῆτιν: a very common word in the *Arg.*, cognate of course with Μήδεια (< μήδομαι, 'plot', 'devise'); cf. *940* n. **ἀνωίστως:**

probably with ῥέξει rather than δεδοκημένοι: 'they waited to see what plan she would mysteriously put into action'. Cf. *960* n.

1661–72[1017–28] Medea prepares to fix Talos with the evil eye (κακὸν νόον, 1679), usually termed βασκανία in Greek (cf. *1* n.). In real life any inexplicable trouble, especially lingering disease, is attributed to its malign influence. Medea, a sorceress of supernatural power, can produce an instantaneous effect by concentrated malignity. She shields her eyes (1661–2) to avoid harming the Argonauts, invokes the destructive Keres (1665–7), meets Talos' gaze with her own and affects him with hallucinations (δείκηλα, 1672). Rays emanating from the eye can be the channel of hatred as well as of love (cf. *1129* n.). For a discussion of how βασκανία operates see Plut. *Quaest. Conu.* 5.7.

1663[1019] ἐπ' ἰκριόφιν: the old instrumental -φι(ν) is sometimes used instead of a gen. ending in Homer. ἴκρια (n. pl.) is the half-deck at a ship's stern.

1663–64[1019–20] Jason leads her between the rows of benches – perhaps because the ship is rolling, perhaps because she is in a trance.

1665[1021] 'With spells (ἀοιδῇσιν = ἐπαοιδῇσιν) she propitiated and won over the Keres.' The MSS read δέ for τε, making two clauses: 'she concentrated her mind with spells (a very rare use of μειλίσσομαι) and won over the Keres'. Some MSS have μέλπε for θέλγε; but 'celebrate' seems less apt than 'beguile', 'win over'. μέλπε perhaps by assimilation to μειλ- of the preceding word. **Κῆρας**: spirits of doom and death, daughters of Night: cf. Hes. *Theog.* 213–17.

1666[1022] κύνας: often of divine agents or ministers, 'faithful servants' of the gods.

1667[1023] ἐπὶ ... ἄγονται: continues the metaphor of κύνες – ἐπάγειν is used of 'setting on' dogs in the hunt (cf. *350* n.).

1668–9[1024–5] τρίς ... τρίς: the magic number: cf. *616*.

1669[1025] θεμένη 'putting on', 'adopting': cf. *Il.* 9.629 ἄγριον ... θέτο ... θυμόν (cf. 639).

1670[1026] ὄμμασι: at 4.726–9 we are told that descendants of Helios are instantly recognizable by the flashing glance of their eyes. Here Medea puts her ancestral power to devastating use. ἐμέγηρεν = ἐβάσκανε, a unique extension of the normal meaning '(be)grudge' (*332*). ὀπωπάς: Ap. is the first writer to use this word to mean 'eyes'; in Homer it = 'view' or 'power of sight'.

1671[1027] ἐπί οἱ πρῖεν χόλον: 'she gnashed her rage at him'. πρίω = 'saw', then (with ὀδόντας) 'grind'; hence this metaphorical use with an object. ἀίδηλα 'destructive'; or perhaps 'obscure', 'uncertain' (< ἀ- + ἰδεῖν).

1672[1028] δείκηλα 'images', 'hallucinations': a rare word, first attested in Democritus and Herodotus.

1673–7[1029–33] The narrator makes a rare personal appearance, exclaiming in astonishment at the power of magic. The lines complement a similar outburst earlier in the book (4.445–9), where Ap. exclaims against the destructive power of Eros, which led Medea to kill even her own brother.

1673[1029] ἄηται 'is blown this way and that', i.e. 'is stirred': for the metaphor cf. 1682–6.

1675[1031] ἀντιάει: sc. ἡμῶν: 'death comes to us not only from diseases and wounds, but...'. χαλέπτοι: potential opt.; governed by εἰ (1674).

1676[1032] echoes Medea's words at 1658.

1677[1033] βρίμηι 'might' – attested only once in earlier poetry (*Hom. Hymn* 28.10). ἄν = ἀνά (*303* n.). Tmesis.

1678[1034] ἐρυκέμεν: final ('consecutive') infin.: 'heaving up stones *to prevent* them from reaching...': cf. *1586*.

1679[1035] στόνυχι: στόνυξ is a sharp point. In surviving pre-Hellenistic literature only at Eur. *Cycl.* 401. χρίμψε 'grazed'; Homer uses the compound ἐγχρίμπτω with this meaning.

1680[1036] ἴκελος μολύβωι: metallic simile for a metal man. Ap. is adapting the words of Numenius, a third-cent. didactic poet, who in his Θηριακά mentioned ἰχώρ | ἠερόεις, τοτὲ δ' αὖ μολίβωι ἐναλίγκιον εἶδος (*SH* 591.1–2).

1682–6[1038–42] The falling-tree simile is found already in Homer (*Il.* 4.482–7, 13.389–91 = 16.482–4, all of falling warriors); but the two-stage collapse is Ap.'s innovation. Cf. Virg. *Aen.* 2.626–31.

1685[1041] ῥιπῆισιν 'the blasts'.

1686[1042] πρυμνόθεν 'from the bottom'; first attested in Aeschylus (*Sept.* 71, 1056).

1687[1043] ἀκαμάτοις: the 'tireless' feet which took him around Crete three times every day (1644). Being metal he is never fatigued. ἐπισταδὸν ἠιωρεῖτο: probably 'swayed from one foot to the other', i.e. ἐπισταδόν = 'successively' (as in Homer), not 'upright'.

1688[1044] ἀμενηνός: all his μένος has drained away, and he is 'tireless' no longer.

XIX

Moschus

Epyllion.   The term 'epyllion' is sometimes applied by modern scholars to poems written in epic hexameters but on a small scale, dealing often with epic themes in novel, witty and surprising ways. Few complete examples survive in Greek (Theoc. *Idylls* 13, 22, 24, [Theoc.] 25, *Europa*), though Latin epyllia help to fill out the picture (Cat. 64, *Moretum*, *Ciris*; cf. Orpheus / Aristaeus in Virg. *Geo.* 4.315–558, Baucis and Philemon in Ovid, *Met.* 8.611–724). But so great were the differences in length (c. 75–c. 1500 lines), style, subject-matter and treatment that closer definition is hardly possible. The most famous poem of this type in antiquity was Callimachus' *Hecale* (p. 84).

Moschus and the Europa.   Moschus (fl. c. 150 B.C.) was a grammarian from Syracuse in Sicily. Fragments of his bucolic poems, in the tradition of Theocritus, survive; but the *Europa* is his only extant complete work. It promises (1–15) to be an aetiological poem on the name of Europe; but in fact it consists in an elegant and witty narrative recounting the abduction of Europa by Zeus disguised as a bull. At the beginning of the poem we are told that Europa dreamt that two women, representing Asia and 'the land opposite', fought over her, and that the latter claimed Europa as her prize (1–15). Europa leaps out of bed and reflects on the dream in naive wonderment (16–27). She gathers together her companions and prepares to go to the seashore to pick flowers; her flower-basket's allegorical scenes are described at length (28–62). When Zeus sees Europa picking flowers he is overcome with desire. He changes himself into a beautiful white bull and gains the girls' confidence (63–107). Europa climbs on to his back and is rapidly borne away across the sea. She maintains an elegant pose as she reflects naively on her ravisher's ability to run over the waves (108–52). The rest of the story is dismissed summarily in a short coda (153–66), and the naming of Europe is not even mentioned (if the poem is complete – see 165–6 n.).

Sources.   The Europa-myth was treated by, amongst others, Hesiod, Simonides and Bacchylides; but Moschus seems not to be indebted to

any particular source. The dream and the decoration on the flower-
basket are probably his own invention. In a wider sense, however,
Moschus is highly derivative. His language is very closely Homeric. The
present commentary records some of the many verbatim borrowings;
but syntax, rhythm and vocabulary are all traditional. There are
several borrowings, too, from Apollonius (9, 31, 35, 48, 101 nn.). The
general outlines of the following scenes are derivative: (1) Europa's
dream and her trip to the meadow are inspired by Nausicaa's dream
and her trip to the seashore in *Odyssey* 6, and by Medea's dream and her
ride to meet Jason in *Argonautica* 3: in both cases a nubile young girl
travels, accompanied by her handmaidens, to an erotic encounter. The
reader is constantly aware of the poem's similarities to and differences
from these two stories; and the narrative both challenges recognition of
derivative elements and demands admiration for a fresh treatment of
similar themes. (2) The personification of the two continents in
Europa's dream (8–15) is based on Aesch. *Persae* 181–7, where the
Persian queen Atossa sees Europe and Asia as two women in native
dress. The general import of Europa's dream has something in common
with that of Io in [Aesch.] *Prom.* 645–54, where Io is exhorted to go to
the Λέρνης βαθὺν | λειμῶνα to meet Zeus, who is in love with her. Io is an
ancestress of Europa, and is depicted on the wondrous basket. (3) The
theme of abduction whilst gathering flowers in a meadow is derived
from the *Homeric Hymn to Demeter* 1ff., 406ff., where Persephone is
snatched away by Hades whilst picking flowers with her attendant
Oceanids. (4) Another traditional element is the set-piece ('ecphrastic')
description of Europa's basket (37–62), which in layout appears to be
directly modelled on Theocritus' famous description of a rustic beaker
at *Idyll* 1.27–56. Moschus links the basket both thematically and
genealogically with his heroine (39–42 n.); and this stress on lineage and
pedigree provides an interesting parallel with the self-conscious literary
ancestry of the ecphrasis itself, which is part of a venerable line
stretching back to Homer's Shield of Achilles at *Iliad* 18.478–608.

The Europa and art. Europa's basket is an imaginary work of art, a
wonder to behind (38 θηητόν, μέγα θαῦμα), itself depicting wonderment
amongst the crowds who gaze on the swimming cow (49 θηεῦντο). But
the poem's links with art go deeper than this. A large number of
contemporary paintings and mosaics show various stages of Europa's
'seduction' by the bull: a favourite scene is of the girl sitting sidesaddle

and grasping one horn as she is borne across the sea in an elegant pose (see W. H. Roscher, *Ausführliches Lexikon der gr. u. röm. Mythologie* I (Leipzig, 1884–90) 1409–18). Io and Argus were popular subjects, too. Thus the poem is closely linked with contemporary taste in pictorial representation; and it is interesting that critics have often described its charm as 'rococo'.

The Europa as art. Unlike a picture, the poem has temporal progression: it relates the metamorphosis of Europa from virgin (7 ἔτι παρθένος) to mother (166 μήτηρ), from mortal girl to continental eponym. Four tableaux make up the story: Europa in bed, in the meadow, crossing the sea, canonized as mother. But in addition to this temporal progression the poem is constructed with the same harmony and symmetry which characterize the basket itself, ostensibly a 'real' work of art: (1) The poem is framed by prophecy: Europa's prophetic dream is complemented by Zeus's forecast of her future at the close. (2) Within the prophecy-frame stand two speeches of Europa (21–7, 135–52), enclosing the main part of the narrative. Both consist of questions and exclamations expressive of naive wonderment, and both end with a prayer beginning ἀλλά... (27, 149–52). (3) Within this inner frame are two set-piece descriptions, of the basket (37–62) and of Europa crossing the sea on the Zeus-bull (115–30). The latter is directly inspired by contemporary art; the former purports to reproduce in words a real work of art. (4) In addition to this formal symmetry the lengthy ecphrasis of Europa's basket stands in counterpoint to the main narrative by retailing the parallel story of Io, ancestress of Europa: in both stories love is the motive for a bovine transformation of beloved (Io) or lover (Zeus); Io crosses the sea from Europe to Asia, Europa from Asia (Phoenicia) to Europe; both stories end with a return to human form; and both are implicitly aetiological.

The whole ethos of the poem – small-scale, Homeric in diction, unhomeric in treatment, ecphrastic, pictorial, pseudo-naive – is, so far as we can judge, typical of the Greek epyllion.

Bibl.: Edn: W. Bühler (*Hermes Einzelschrift* 13, 1960). Gen.: R. Schmiel, 'Moschus's Europa', *C.Ph.* 76 (1981) 261–72; K. Gutzwiller, *Studies in the Hellenistic epyllion* (Königstein / Taunus, 1981) 63–73.

>Hor. *Odes* 3.27; Ovid, *Met.* 2.836–3.2, *Fasti* 6.603–20.

1–5[1045–9] Night. A young girl sleeps sweetly. Aphrodite is at work.

ὅτε . . . ὅτε . . . εὖτε elaborate the opening statement, and dreams frame the whole (1 ὄνειρον, 5 ὀνείρων).

1[1045] Εὐρώπηι: the first word provides the poem's title. **ἐπὶ . . . ἧκεν:** tmesis. Cf. *Od.* 2.395 (Athene on the suitors) ἐπὶ γλυκὺν ὕπνον ἔχευε.

2[1046] τρίτατον λάχος: < A.R. 3.1340. The division of night into three parts is Homeric (*Il.* 10.251–3). **ἐγγύθι δ' ἠώς:** < *Il.* 10.251.

3[1047] Cf. *Il.* 10.26 ὕπνος ἐπὶ βλεφάροισιν ἐφίζανε. **γλυκίων μέλιτος:** < *Il.* 18.109.

4[1048] Doubly oxymoronic: sleep both loosens and binds, and his bonds are soft ones. The line is compounded from *Od.* 23.342–3 γλυκὺς ὕπνος | λυσιμελής (cf. *Od.* 20.56–7) + *Od.* 23.16–17 ἐξ ὕπνου . . . | ἡδέος, ὅς μ' ἐπέδησε φίλα βλέφαρ' ἀμφικαλύψας (M. therefore derived ἐπέδησε from πεδάω, not ἐπιδέω) + *Il.* 10.2, etc. μαλακῶι δεδμημένοι ὕπνωι. **πεδάαι . . . κατά** = καταπεδάαι: *317* n. **φάεα** 'eyes', as occasionally in Homer (LSJ 1.3); cf. *223*.

5[1049] ἀτρεκέων . . . ὀνείρων: dreams seen just before daybreak were thought to be true ones. **ποιμαίνεται** 'is roaming afield' – an apt metaphor, considering the importance of cows and bulls in this poem: cf. *82*.

6[1050] ὑπωροφίοισιν ἐνὶ . . . δόμοισι = ἐν ὑπερώιοις, the women's quarters located upstairs, 'under the roof' (ὑπωρόφιος < ὑπό + ὄροφος, with 'metrical lengthening').

7[1051] Φοίνικος θυγάτηρ: Phoenix gave his name to Phoenicia, where the poem is set.

8[1052] ὠίσατ': this augmented form of ὀίομαι is first attested in Hellenistic poetry. Homer has ὀίσατο.

9[1053] ἀντιπέρην: not named, of course – the poem is indirectly an αἴτιον of why Europe is so called. ἀντιπέραν / -ας is elsewhere an adverb, 'opposite'; but here it must be a fem. adj. (= ἀντιπεραίαν) used substantivally. Aesch. has πέρα as a noun at *Ag.* 190 and *Supp.* 262. **οἶα γυναῖκες:** M. has borrowed the expression from Ap. Rh. 4.1189 αἱ δὲ πολυκμήτους ἑανοὺς φέρον, οἶα γυναῖκες, where οἶα has its idiomatic meaning 'as X tend to' (*974* n.); but in adapting the phrase M. has integrated it into the syntax of the sentence so as to mean 'they had an appearance like women' (sc. ἔχουσι). One would have expected οἵην or γυναικῶν.

11[1055] ἐνδαπίηι 'native', cognate with ἔνδον (cf. ἀλλοδαπός < ἄλλος).

12[1056] ἔτικτε: the imperf. of this verb is often found where one would expect the aor.: cf. LSJ s.v. 1.1, *1575*.

13[1057] βιωομένη: formed from βιάω by analogy with e.g. μνωόμενος, which is derived from μνάομαι by (1) contraction (μνᾱόμενος > μνώμενος), (2) 'diectasis', addition of a vowel to restore the original scansion. Cf. epic εἰσορόων.

14[1058] εἴρυεν: imperf. of attempted action ('conative'). οὐκ ἀέκουσαν: predicative. εἶο: with γέρας (15), 'her prize'. The MSS read φάτο μόρσιμον εἶναι, which is a Homeric clausula and may be right; but a word for 'her' needs to be supplied somewhere.

15[1059] Cf. *Il.* 2.787 πὰρ Διὸς αἰγιόχοιο.

16–28[1060–72] She leaps out of bed (16), sits down (18) and finally stands up and goes out (28). It seems unlikely that ἀπὸ ... λεχέων θόρε refers to her sitting up in bed, as Bühler suggests: see Richardson on *Hom. Hymn to Dem.* 285.

16[1060] Cf. *Hom. Hymn to Dem.* 285 κὰδ δ' ἄρ' ἀπ' εὐστρώτων λεχέων θόρον.

17[1061] παλλομένη κραδίην: < *Il.* 22.461. Acc. of respect. τὸ ... ὄνειρον: the def. art. is separated from its noun, and at first sight seems to be a relative referring to the previous sentence. Such separations are frequent in Hellenistic poetry. Cf. *879–80* n. ὡς ὕπαρ: she regarded it as real.

18[1062] ἀκὴν ἔχεν: in Homer ἀκήν is an adverb, and it may be so here (cf. εὖ ἔχειν, etc.); but Hellenistic poets may have considered it a noun (cf. Ap. Rh. 3.521). Cf. on 9 ἀντιπέρην.

20[1064] ἀνενείκατο: unaugmented aor. mid. of ἀναφέρω, a Homeric *hapax*: *Il.* 19.314 μνησάμενος δ' ἀδινῶς ἀνενείκατο ('fetched up his breath deeply') φώνησέν τε. Some ancient scholars wrongly understood an acc. with Homer's verb; and hence Ap.Rh. could write ἀδινὴν ἀνενείκατο φωνήν (3.635), adapted by M. here and at 134.

21[1065] τίς qualifies ἐπουρανίων.

22[1066] ποῖοί: see on 139.

23[1067] ἡδὺ μάλα κνώσσουσαν: < *Od.* 4.809. ἀνεπτοίησαν: πτοέω is very often used of sexual excitement, and ἀν. may well have sexual overtones here (cf. 25 πόθος): the dream was, after all, inspired by Aphrodite.

24[1068] ὑπνώουσα: ὑπνώω is a Homeric by-form of ὑπνόω.

26[1070] Cf. *Il.* 9.480–1 ὁ δέ με πρόφρων ὑπέδεκτο, | καί μ' ἐφίλησ' ὡς εἴ τε πατὴρ ὃν παῖδα φιλήσηι. **σφετέρην:** *977* n.; cf. 163.

26[1070] ὡς 'like' – not in series with exclamatory ὡς...ὡς in 25.

27[1071] εἰς ἀγαθὸν ... ὄνειρον, echoing (though not syntatically parallel to) 1 γλυκὺν...ὄνειρον, rounds off the first section of the poem. **ἀλλά ...** is often used in speeches to introduce a formal prayer-ending: cf. 149, *401* n. Here, however, the meaning might equally well be adversative: 'but, ⟨whatever the dream might betoken,⟩ make it good'. **κρήνειαν:** the MSS read κρίνειαν; but the role of gods is to 'fulfil' dreams (κραίνω), while to 'interpret' them (κρίνω) is that of seers.

28[1072] ὡς εἰποῦσ' ἀνόρουσε: < *Od.* 14.518.

29[1073] All-adj. lines are found in Homer and Hesiod (*Od.* 15.406, *Theog.* 320, 925). Here M. produces a stately crescendo-effect with words of 3, 4, 4 and 5 syllables (cf. *401*). **ἤλικας** and **οἰέτεας** (a Homeric *hapax* – *Il.* 2.765) seem to be synonymous.

30[1074] ἐς χορὸν ἐντύναιτο: < Call. *Hymn to Ap.* 8. ἐντύνω / -ομαι usually = 'get ready'; but since she played with her friends whilst dancing, not whilst preparing to dance, the phrase must mean 'when she entered the dance'.

31[1075] φαιδρύνοιτο χρόα: *305* n. **προχοῆισιν ἀναύρων:** Ap. Rh. 3.67 ἐπὶ προχοῆισιν...'Αναύρου. προχέω = 'pour forth' or 'forward'; hence προχοή = either 'river's outlet' or 'flowing stream' (LSJ is inadequate here), in this line perhaps the former. The -αυρος suffix is found in many nymph- and river-names, and may represent an old word for 'water'. Ap. Rh.'s Ἄναυρος was a particular river in Thessaly, but the word was used by extension (1) for any mountain torrent (2) simply = 'river' (cf. the alleged extension of 'Αχελῶιος to 'water' in general – Hopkinson on Call. *Hymn to Dem.* 13).

32[1076] Young girls who pluck flowers do so at their own risk, as the sequel shows. Europa stands in a long line of literary heroines who are themselves plucked in flower-meadows by gods. Persephone is the best known example (*Hom. Hymn to Dem.* 1–18, 406–33); cf., too, Eur. *Ion* 887–96 (Creusa) and *Helen* 241–51 (Helen).

33[1077] Cf. *Od.* 10.397 ἔφυν τ' ἐν χερσὶν ἕκαστος.

34[1078] δέ: M. imitates the Homeric usage by which a short open vowel can be treated as metrically heavy before λ, e.g. *Il.* 12.459 πέσε δὲ̄ λίθος. Cf. *51* n.

35[1079] τ': 91 n. ὁμιλαδὸν ἠγερέθοντο: <Ap.Rh. 1.655. ἠγερ-έθομαι (cf. 122) is an epic form of ἀγείρομαι, 'assemble'.

36[1080] ῥοδέηι . . . φυῆι: i.e. ῥόδοις ἃ ἔφυεν.

37[1081] Cf. *Od.* 4.125 Φυλὼ δ' ἀργύρεον τάλαρον φέρε.

38[1082] μέγα θαῦμα: a Homeric phrase (*Il.* 13.99, etc.).

39–42[1083–6] The lineage of the basket. (Cf. the impressive pedigree of Agamemnon's sceptre, another work of Hephaestus, at *Il.* 2.102–8.) M.'s account presupposes the following family-tree: Inachus → Io + Zeus → Epaphus (+ Memphis) → Libye + Poseidon → Phoenix + Telephassa → Europa + Zeus (→ Minos, Rhadamanthys, ?Sarpedon). Thus Europa's basket belonged to her grandmother Libye, who was raped by a god and gave her name to Libya; and it depicted the rape by a god of *her* grandmother Io, eponym of Ionia. Europa inherits not only the basket, but also the experiences depicted on it.

39–40[1083–4] ἐς λέχος . . . | ἤιεν: a euphemism.

39[1083] 'Εννοσιγαίου: Poseidon, god of the earthquake.

40[1084] Τηλεφαάσσηι: elsewhere spelled Τηλεφᾶσσα or -φάεσσα ('Far-Shining'); -αάσσηι perhaps by vowel-attraction, on the analogy of forms with so-called 'diectasis' (13 n.).

41[1085] ἥτε οἱ αἵματος ἔσχεν: an odd expression. The Homeric αἵματος εἶναι, etc., is nowhere else found with the dative. If the text is sound, οἱ must = σφετέρου; but Gow's ἥ θ' ἑοῦ is attractive. ἀνύμφωι: but not for long.

43[1087] δαίδαλα πολλά: the phrase is used of Achilles' shield at *Il.* 18.482 and of Jason's cloak, another ecphrastic description, at Ap. Rh. 1.729. τετεύχατο: -ατο is an epic pl. ending.

44–61[1088–1105] Io, daughter of Inachus, great-great-grandmother of Europa, was an Argive priestess of Hera. Zeus desired her and metamorphosed her into a cow to escape his wife's notice. But Hera requested the cow as a gift, and set many-eyed Argus to keep watch over her. Argus was killed by Hermes, and the peacock arose from his blood; in revenge Hera tormented cow-Io with a gadfly, which drove her to Egypt via the Bosporus and the Ionian sea. There Zeus touched her and restored her true form; from the touch she conceived Epaphus (<ἐπαφάω). A version of the story is told by Ovid, *Met.* 1.583–754.

44, 50[1089, 1096] ἐν μὲν ἔην . . . ἐν δ' ἦν: Homer and Ap. Rh. introduce each section of their set-piece descriptions of shield and cloak (43 n.) with such phrases.

44[1089] Cf. *Il.* 18.574 αἱ δὲ βόες (n.b.) χρυσοῖο τετεύχατο κασσιτέρου τε (Achilles' shield). Cf. 54.

46–7[1090–1] The meaning is unclear. Line 46 tells us that she was treading on top of the waves; but νηχομένηι ἰκέλη suggests that she was swimming. Perhaps the artist is imagined as having used his licence to depict the swimming cow as actually out of the waves. The Zeus-bull, however, charges across the sea 'with unwetted hooves' (114).

46[1090] φοιταλέη: the word has overtones of madness and distraction. Io wandered over the Ionian sea, which was named after her.

48–9[1092–3] Io is shown passing through the Bosporus, whose etymology is hinted at in the words ποντοπόρον βοῦν (cf. 49 n.); on both shores (δοιοῦ...αἰγιαλοῖο) stand amazed onlookers. Elsewhere in Greek sing. δοιός = 'double', not 'both'; but in all other respects Hermann's emendation is perfect, restoring both visual and logical sense.

48[1092] ἐπ' ὀφρύσιν αἰγιαλοῖο: <Ap. Rh. 1.178 (where Αἰγ. is a proper name – cf. on 31). 'Brow' is used in Greek for 'bank', 'side' or 'rim'; cf. Lat. *supercilium*.

49[1093] ποντοπόρον βοῦν: a piquant etymological play (48–9 n.) on the Homeric formula ποντοπόρος νηῦς.

50[1094] Ζεὺς Κρονίδης: <*Il.* 16.845. **ἐπαφώμενος**: from ἐπ-ἀφάω. Another etymological allusion – see 44–61 n.

55–61[1099–1105] The shields of Achilles and Heracles have Ocean around their edges (*Il.* 18.607–8, *Scutum* 314–17), and the rustic beaker in Theoc. *Idyll* 1 is bordered with acanthus. Presumably M. intends something similar here; but it is difficult to imagine how the peacock 'covered the rim' (περίσκεπε χείλεα, 61) of this basket. Perhaps we are to think of the bird's tail trailing around the whole circumference; but the position of Argus and Hermes in relation to the other scenes is unclear. See 60 n.

55[1099] ἀμφὶ δέ is the third item in the series ἐν μέν (44), ἐν δ' (50). **δινήεντος**: elsewhere δινήεις = 'eddying'; but here it must = 'rounded'.

56[1100] Ἑρμείης: according to some accounts it was by killing Argus that Hermes earned his epithet Ἀργειφόντης.

57[1101] ἀκοιμήτοισι: Argus was renowned for his unwinking vigilance. Even in death his eyes remain open; they are transferred to the tail of the peacock, sacred bird of Hera.

59[1103] Cf. *Il.* 2.462 ἔνθα καὶ ἔνθα ποτῶνται ἀγαλλόμενα πτερύγεσσι.

60[1104] ἀναπλώσας: <ἀν-ἁπλόω, 'spread out'. **ὠκύαλος νηῦς:** <*Od.* 12.182, 15.473. The 'wings' (i.e. tail?) are spread out to resemble the oars on either side of a ship, a vivid comparison for most birds; but the peacock's tail actually forms one huge mass.

61[1105] ταρσοῖς: originally ταρσός was a flat basket for drying (τέρσομαι) cheeses; but the word came to be applied to a variety of flat, outstretched objects: see LSJ s.v.

62[1106] echoes 37, rounding off the ecphrasis section.

63[1107] αἱ δ' ἐπεὶ οὖν: a common Homeric opening. **λειμῶνας . . . ἀνθεμόεντας:** cf. *Od.* 12.159, *Il.* 2.467.

64[1108] θυμὸν ἕτερπον: <*Od.* 1.107.

66–7[1110–11] ἔραζε . . . θαλέθεσκε: elsewhere ἔραζε is an adverb of motion, 'to the ground'; but here it must = 'on the ground'. χαμᾶζε, too, is found with no idea of motion.

67[1111] πέτηλα: like φύλλα (*518*n.), this word for 'leaves' can occasionally mean 'flowers' (not mentioned in LSJ): cf. Eur. *Ion* 889, *Helen* 244.

68[1112] θυόεσσαν: from θύον, 'incense'; hence 'fragrant' in general. **κρόκου . . . ἔθειραν:** a heightened poetic expression for the whole flower: cf. Virg. *Geo.* 4.137 *comam mollis . . . hyacinthi.*

69[1113] δρέπτον: δρέπτω is a rare by-form of δρέπω.

70[1114] ἀγλαΐην πυρσοῖο ῥόδου: another high poeticism (cf. 68 n.). The rose was queen among flowers, and a symbol of love. Europa stands out amongst (69 μέσσηισιν) her companions like the rose amongst other flowers. In plucking the rose she prefigures her own ravishment. At Eur. *Helen* 244 Helen is snatched while gathering roses.

71[1115] This simile reinforces the erotic overtones of 69–71. It is inspired by *Od.* 6.102–9, where Nausicaa amongst her handmaidens is compared to Artemis with her band of nymphs. The adaptation of Homer's chaste simile to a suggestively erotic one is pointed. **'Αφρο-γένεια:** Aphrodite, born from the foam (ἀφρός) produced when Cronus cast into the sea the genitals of his castrated father Uranus.

72[1116] Cf. Ap. Rh. 3.1133–4 οὐ μὲν δηρὸν ἀπαρνήσεσθαι ἔμελλεν | ῾Ελλάδα ναιετάειν. The line is an echo and variation of 64. **οὐ μέν:** adversative. **θυμὸν ἰαίνειν:** a Homeric clausula.

73[1117] ἄρα conveys the sense 'as we now see in retrospect' – often thus with ἔμελλε = 'was not to…' (cf. Denniston, *GP* 36). **ἄχραντον:** the girdle is 'defiled' by the male hand which removes it.

74[1118] ὡς . . . ὥς 'when . . . then': see *654* n. **ἐόλητο**: a pluperf. pass. form of uncertain derivation. Some connect it with εἰλέω, 'oppress' (cf. LSJ s.v. B); but at Ap. Rh. 3.471 the ancient commentator glosses it ἐτετάρακτο, which seems more suitable in the present context.

75–6[1119–20] Metaphorical ὑποδμηθείς and δαμάσσαι prefigure Zeus's literal conversion to a bull: the bull is to be subdued not by work (83 ὑποδμηθείς) but by love.

75[1119] ἀνωΐστοισιν 'unexpected': *960* n. **θυμόν**: acc. of respect, probably to be taken with both ἐόλητο and ὑποδμηθείς.

76[1120] Aphrodite and Eros are often characterized as the only gods able to overpower Zeus: cf. *Hom. Hymn to Aphr.* 36–40, *1588–9*.

77[1121] δὴ γάρ gives a strong emphasis, stressing the length to which Zeus was prepared to go.

78[1122] Cf. *Il.* 18.567 παρθενικαὶ δὲ καὶ ἠΐθεοι ἀταλὰ φρονέοντες + *Od.* 13.277 οὐδ' ἤθελον ἐξαπατῆσαι. **ἀταλόν**: 'childish' or 'simple' seems to be the most likely translation of this adj. here ('young', 'gay' LSJ). The etymology is uncertain: cf. West on Hes. *Theog.* 989.

79[1123] Three syntactically parallel main clauses, each longer than the last, give the line an animated rhythm, reinforced by alliteration of κρύψε and τρέψε and anaphora of καί. **κρύψε θεόν**: a bold concretization, 'god' for 'godhead': cf. Virg. *Aen.* 2.590–1 *in luce refulsit | alma parens, confessa deam*, Ovid, *Fasti* 5.504 *dissimulantque deos*, Cat. 63.6 *sensit sibi membra sine uiro*. **γίνετο**: for the imperf. for aor. cf. *12* n., *166*.

80–3[1124–7] This was no ordinary bull.

80, 82[1124, 1126] ἔνι, ἔπι: *427–8* n.

81[1125] ὦλκα: a recherché Homeric form of αὔλακα.

83[1127] μάστι: the MSS read ὅστις; but οἷος ὅστις seems intolerable, especially considering the parallelism of 80 and 82. μάστι is by no means certain, and the correption of -ί is rather harsh; but it makes good sense and is palaeographically closer to ὅστις than other suggestions.

84–5[1128–9] For the Homeric source of these lines see *1001* n.

86[1130] ὑπογλαύσσεσκε: 'shone brightly (the original meaning of γλαυκός) from under (ὑπο-) ⟨his μέτωπον⟩'. The verb is found once in Call. (*Hymn to Art.* 54), who may have invented it. **-εσκε**: Homer, too, has a sing. verb with ὄσσε (e.g. *Il.* 12.466), i.e. the neut. dual is treated as n. pl. **ἵμερον ἀστράπτεσκεν**: Zeus is god of the lightning. His eyes flash forth ἵμερος, which in turn kindles ἵμερος in the onlookers (cf. 91). Often in Greek the eyes are described not only as the seat of love, but as the channel of its communication: cf. e.g. Soph. *Ant.* 795–7 ἐναργὴς βλεφάρων ἵμερος εὐλέκτρου νύμφας.

87[1131] ἐπ' ἀλλήλοισι: 'over against each other', i.e. symmetrically. **κέρᾱ:** contracted from κέραα. **ἀνέτελλε καρήνου** 'rose from his head', gen. of separation. ἀνατέλλω is used both for the rising of heavenly bodies and as a technical term for growing horns (e.g. Aristotle, *De Gener. Anim.* 743a12).

88[1132] 'Like crescents of the horned moon with its rim cut in half' (ἀντ. ἡμ. qualitative gen. defining κύκλα), i.e. like two crescent moons, each of which is like a half-rim of the moon.

90–1[1134–5] ἔρως and ἱμερτοῖο point the latent sexuality which characterizes this whole scene.

91[1135] τοῦ τ': the redundant 'epic' τε qualifying the relative – not a conjunction. **ἄμβροτος ὀδμή:** gods are often described as accompanied by a divine fragrance: cf. *Hom. Hymn to Dem.* 277–8, [Aesch.] *Prom.* 115, Eur. *Hipp.* 1391, Virg. *Aen.* 1.403.

94[1138] οἱ: dat. of interest.

95–6[1139–40] This is a wittily novel kind of sexual encounter: the ultra-naive Europa does not understand the meaning of her own reactions to the bull. For the phraseology cf. Call. *142–3*, Ap. Rh. 3.1352–3.

95[1139] ἠρέμα χείρεσιν: as Zeus lovingly touched cow-Io ἠρέμα χερσί (50), so Europa lovingly touches bull-Zeus.

96[1140] ἀπομόργνυτο: mid. for act., not unusual in Hellenistic poetry (cf. *1219, 1591*). **ταῦρον** for μιν, though the object is the same as for the preceding verb. The line is parallel in construction to 94, where κούρην is similarly used. Bühler, however, sees the emphasis on ταῦρον as pointedly indecent.

97[1141] Cf. *Il.* 10.288 αὐτὰρ ὁ μειλίχιον μῦθον φέρε Καδμείοισι. M. surprises with divergence from his source half-way through a word.

98[1142] Μυγδονίου: Mygdonia was part of Phrygia; the Phrygian pipe was known for its low note. One suspects that the recondite adj. was chosen for its alliterative quality (97 μει-, μυ-, 98 Μυγ-, ἠπυ-, etc.). **ἀνηπύοντος:** elsewhere the pres. tense of ἠπύω and compounds has a short ῠ; only here and at 124 ῡ in extant Greek. A similar variation is seen in e.g. λύω.

101[1145] Cf. *Od.* 6.238 (Nausicaa) δή ῥα τότ' ἀμφιπόλοισιν ἐϋπλοκάμοισι μετηύδα: as Bühler notes, M. has changed the common ἐϋπλοκάμοισι to βαθυπλ., attested only once elsewhere (Ap. Rh. 1.742), and μετηύδα similarly to μετέννεπε, another Apollonian *hapax* (3.1168).

104[1148] ὑποστορέσας: suggestive, because commonly used of beds: 'making a couch of his back'. **οἴά τ' ἐνηής**: either οἴά τε = ἅτε, 'because' (sc. ὤν), or οἴα alone = ἅτε (LSJ s.v. οἷος ii.3) and τ' is displaced from its proper position after ἐνηής (i.e. ἐνηής τε πρηΰς τε).

107[1151] αἴσιμος: in Homer 'destined' or 'appropriate'; but here it seems to mean little more than 'friendly', 'well disposed'. **ἀμφιθέει**: literally, 'runs around him', i.e. 'animates him' – a rather forced expression. **μούνης . . . αὐδῆς**: little does she know (cf. 153).

108[1152] ὡς φαμένη: Homeric post-speech formula.

109[1153] ἀνεπήλατο: aor. mid. of ἀναπάλλω (not of ἀνεφάλλομαι).

111[1155] <*Il.* 8.258, etc. τῶι δὲ μεταστρεφθέντι + *Il.* 10.522, etc., φίλον τ' ὀνόμηνεν ἑταῖρον (cf. 28).

112[1156] Cf. *Od.* 16.357 τὴν (sc. νῆα) δ' οὐκ ἐδύναντο κιχῆναι + the use of οὐ(κ) (ἐ)δύνα(ν)το in Iliadic battle-narrative of friends unable to help a comrade in difficulties (*Il.* 15.650–2, etc.).

115[1159] ἐρχομένοιο: gen. abs., with the noun understood.

116–17[1160–1] Cf. *Il.* 13.27–9 (Poseidon's sea-chariot) ἄταλλε δὲ κήτε' ὑπ' αὐτοῦ | πάντοθεν ἐκ κευθμῶν, οὐδ' ἠγνοίησεν ἄνακτα· | γηθοσύνηι δὲ θάλασσα διίστατο.

116[1160] Διὸς προπάροιθε ποδοῖιν: the dual may be a learned joke, since Zeus is temporarily quadruped; but the reference could be to the front pair of legs. Less charitable critics might argue that M.'s eagerness to sound 'Homeric' has led to an elementary oversight. (Hexameter poets occasionally use dual for pl., with nouns as well as verbs (cf. West on Hes. *WD* 186); but this is unlikely to be relevant here.)

117[1161] κυβίστεε: several Homeric verbs in -άω have ε-vowel in the imperf., perhaps because the identity of aor. and fut. forms (-ησα, -ήσω) was extended by analogy to the imperf.

118[1162] αἱ δ': in epic rel. + δέ does not always point to a change of subject.

120[1164] βαρύδουπος: of the sea's roar. **ὑπεὶρ ἁλός**: this seems to make better sense than the reading ὑπεὶρ ἅλα of some MSS – 'above the surface' rather than 'across the sea'; and ἅλα Ἐνν- involves an improbable hiatus.

122[1166] Cf. *Il.* 3.231 ἀμφὶ δέ μιν Κρητῶν ἀγοὶ ἠγερέθονται. See on 35.

123–4[1167–8] Both lines end with rhyming four-syllable words, giving two successive fifth-foot spondees. This is to represent the deep tone and ponderous rhythm of primitive instruments.

123[1167] Τρίτωνες: sea-divinities with human bodies and fish-tails, companions of Poseidon. The shell-trumpet is their characteristic feature. **πόντοιο . . . αὐλητῆρες**: that is, they are the sea's equivalent of terrestrial pipers.

125[1169] ἐφεζομένη: in art she is usually shown sitting side-saddle; a pornographic mosaic shows her astride, naked, kissing the bull.

127[1171] πέπλου: the MSS read κόλπου; but the κόλπος is a loose fold falling from above the girdle – it could hardly be wetted in the waves. It is, however, possible that M. deliberately strained the normal meaning of κόλπος in order to prepare for the metaphor of κολπώθη in 129. **μιν** = πέπλον.

128[1172] ἐφελκόμενον: with μιν. **πολιῆς ἁλός**: a Homeric phrase. **ἄσπετον**: literally 'unspeakable', hence 'unspeakably large' (cf. *Od.* 5.100–1 ὕδωρ | ἄσπετον). Here the adj. lends a high epic tone to the narrative.

129[1173] ὤμοισι: locatival dative (cf. e.g. *Il.* 1.45). The conjecture ἀνέμοισι is attractive; but artistic representations show the πέπλος billowing around Europa's shoulders.

131–3[1175–7] Cf. *Od.* 12.403–4 ἀλλ' ὅτε δὴ τὴν νῆσον ἐλείπομεν, οὐδέ τις ἄλλη | φαίνετο γαιάων, ἀλλ' οὐρανὸς ἠδὲ θάλασσα...

131[1175] γαίης ἄπο πατρίδος: three times in Homer.

132[1176] ὄρος αἰπύ: Homeric clausula.

133[1177] Virgil's *caelum undique et undique pontus* (*Aen.* 3.193; cf. 5.9). **ἀήρ**: in Homer this word seems always to mean 'mist' or 'haze'; but later poets use it for 'air'. **πόντος ἀπείρων**: cf. *Il.* 24.545 Ἑλλήσποντος ἀπείρων, Hes. *Theog.* 678.

134[1178] ἀμφί ἑ παπτήνασα: <*Il.* 4.497 = 15.574. **τόσην ἀνενείκατο φωνήν**: 20 n.

135–52[1179–96] Throughout this speech Europa veers between naive wonderment and half-realization that this must be the work of some god (135, 140, 152).

135[1179] θεόταυρε: 'bull with something divine about you'. **ἔπλεο**: Homer uses the aor. of πέλομαι, lit. 'have become', for 'to be'.

136–7[1180–1] θάλασσα(ν) at the end of successive lines emphasizes her incredulity.

136[1180] εἰλιπόδεσσι: lit. 'of rolling gait', a Homeric adj. for oxen, here used substantivally.

139[1183] ποῖόν σοι ποτὸν ἡδύ;: sc. ἐξ ἁλός. Sometimes ποῖος loses its specific meaning 'what sort of?' and conveys a sense of surprised incredulity: 'What about fresh water 〈which bulls need to drink〉?' These are rhetorical questions, not enquiries after fact. ἡδύ: ~ πικρόν of the salt sea.

140[1184] Cf. *Od.* 16.183 ἦ μάλα τις θεός ἐσσι.

141[1185] τι 'at all'. For adverbial τι cf. *146, 189, 250, 253*.

142[1186] στιχόωσι: Homer has only στιχάομαι; the act. is found first in Hellenistic poetry – perhaps a third-cent. innovation. **χθόνα καὶ κατὰ πόντον:** for the prep. with the second of two nouns cf. *45*, Virg. *Aen.* 6.692 *quas ego te terras et quanta per aequora uectum | accipio!*

144[1188] ὑπὲρ ἠέρος ὑψόσ' ἀερθείς: i.e. up above the lower air (133 n.) and into the higher αἰθήρ. There is word-play here: some ancient etymologists derived ἀήρ from ἀείρω (cf. Plato, *Crat.* 410b). **ὑψόσ' ἀερθείς:** < *Od.* 8.375 = 12.432.

146[1190] ὤμοι ἐγώ: common in Homer. **μέγα δή τι δυσάμμορος:** < Ap. Rh. 1.253. Adverbial μέγα δή τι = 'very greatly' is frequent in Hellenistic poetry: cf. *253*.

147[1191] ἑσπομένη: aor. part. of ἕπομαι, which often means 'accompany' rather than strictly 'follow'.

148[1192] ξείνην: ξε(ι)νος sometimes = 'odd', 'unfamiliar'.

150[1194] ἔλπομαι: here expressing her diffidence: not 'expect', but 'suppose', 'suspect'.

151[1195] τόνδε πλόον is object of κατιθύνοντα; **προκέλευθον** agrees with ὄν.

152[1196] οὐκ ἀθεεί: < *Od.* 18.353. **ὑγρὰ κέλευθα:** Homeric clausula.

153[1197] ἠύκερως = εὐκέραος (cf. 52), with epic lengthening to ἠυ- and contraction of α + ο to ω. The accent is anomalous.

154[1198] Cf. *Od.* 4.825 θάρσει, μηδέ τι πάγχυ μετὰ φρεσὶ δείδιθι λίην, *Il.* 24.171 θάρσει... μηδέ τι τάρβει. **οἶδμα:** originally of a swelling (οἰδέω) sea, but often a synonym for πόντος.

155[1199] ἐγγύθεν: 'on close inspection'.

156[1200] ὅττι θέλοιμι: one would expect a subj. (ὅττι θέλωμι cj. Hermann), since the main verb is in primary sequence; but opt. for subj. + ἄν is occasionally found (K.–G. 1 252–3), and Bühler may be right in suggesting that the Homeric clausula ὅττι θέλοιεν (*Od.* 15.317) has influenced M. here.

157[1201] Cf. *Od.* 5.100 τίς δ' ἂν ἑκὼν τοσσόνδε διαδράμοι ἁλμυρὸν ὕδωρ; **σὸς . . . πόθος** = πόθος σοῦ (< *Od.* 11.202); contrast 25. **ἀνέηκε:** 'let go', hence 'incite', 'urge'.

158[1202] ἐειδόμενον: the form with 'prothetic' ἐ-vowel is a Homeric metrical alternative (∼ 155 εἴδομαι) in the aor. part. **ἤδη** with reference to the near future = 'immediately'.

159[1203] ἥ μ' ἔθρεψε καὶ αὐτόν: most ancient accounts agreed that Zeus was brought up, if not actually born, in Crete, away from the murderous designs of his father Cronus: cf. *274–327*. **νυμφήια:** not a formal marriage, of course; but bull-Zeus's prophetic language raises the encounter from the level of ingeniously contrived casual liaison to that of historically significant event. γάμος, the commoner word for 'marriage', has a very wide range of meanings, from 'rape' to 'holy wedlock'. Contrast 41 ἀνύμφωι.

160[1204] κλυτοὺς . . . υἷας: Minos, Rhadamanthys and Sarpedon, according to Apollod. 3.1.1, Hes. fr. 140. They were kings of Crete, the islands and Lycia respectively.

163[1207] ἀνελάζετο: λάζομαι is the Ionic equivalent of λαμβάνω; ἀνα- = 'back again' (cf. ἀναχωρέω, etc.).

164[1208] A ὕστερον πρότερον (inversion of logical order), since her girdle was loosed in the bedchamber after it had been prepared. **λέχος ἔντυον Ὧραι:** the Horae, goddesses of charm and beauty, are associated with Aphrodite; and γάμου ὥρα is a standard phrase for 'marriageable age', i.e. the right time to be married (cf. *Od.* 15.126). Preparation of the bed was a formal part of the marriage ceremony: cf. *70*.

165–6[1209–10] Several critics have felt that these lines are unsatisfactory. (1) Is the poem incomplete? The conclusion is abrupt; and one might have expected a poem with this theme to have ended with an αἴτιον for the name of Europe. (2) αὐτίκα γίνετο in 166 looks as if it may be cobbled together from γένετ' αὐτίκα in 165: in 165 αὐτίκα has its usual meaning but in 166 it means 'presently'. Is this tolerable? (3) The two clauses of 166 are in the reverse of logical order: she became a mother by bearing Zeus's children. A possible defence: (1) The epyllion specialized in surprise and disproportion. M. omits the aetiological information well known to his audience and concentrates on a single aspect of the story, the abduction of the girl Europa. Certainly 165–6 are in keeping with the summary tone of 162–3, which give the impression of a hasty rush through the remainder of the myth. (2) (a) Immediacy, suddenness and lack of delay are a mark of the divine (cf. *323, 329*, Pind. *Pyth.* 9.66–70), and M. may be attempting somewhat heavy-handedly to stress this aspect. (b) αὐτίκα with the meaning 'presently' (166) is perfectly acceptable *per se*: see LSJ s.v. 1 3. (c) M. may have considered the variation of tense and word-order between γένετ' αὐτίκα and αὐτίκα γίνετο particularly elegant. He is by no means averse to repetition: cf. 1 & 3, 43 & 44, 61 & 62, 136–7. (d) There seems to be a self-conscious word-play in 166 between τέκε and αὐτίκα, reinforcing the swiftness of her becoming a mother. (3) The ὕστερον πρότερον is not much harsher than 164 (see n. ad loc.).

XX–XXI

Bion

Bion of Smyrna (fl. c. 100 B.C.) was the latest in the canon of Greek bucolic poets, Theocritus and Moschus being earlier. The fragments and short poems which survive (*OCT Bucol. Gr.* 159–65) are much concerned with the subject of Eros; and the *Lament for Adonis* (*1227–1324*), Bion's only long extant work, is a tour-de-force of erotic narrative.

XX

This, so far as we can tell, is a complete poem. The setting and Doric dialect are 'bucolic'; but the emphasis lies elsewhere. The poem describes how a young boy tries to catch winged Eros perched in a tree, and how a worldly-wise old man warns him against courting disaster. The poem is clearly allegorical: the boy is not yet ready for love, and Eros keeps away; but soon there will be no escape from his onset (13 φεῦγε, 14 ἔλθῃς of the boy; 15 ὁ νῦν φεύγων, 16 ἐλθών of Eros). The wise old man, possessed of both technical skill (9) and worldly wisdom, stands in a long tradition of ἐρωτοδιδάσκαλοι, the best known of whom are Diotima in Plato's *Symposium* and Philetas in Longus' *Daphnis and Chloe* (2.3–7). His comments indirectly tell us why Eros is always shown with wings: he comes 'out of thin air', sudden, unavoidable, unpredictable.

Fowling. A sticky substance made from mistletoe (ἰξός, Lat. *uiscum*) was smeared on the end of a rod (κάλαμος); the fowler stood under a tree and stealthily extended his rods to the required length by slotting one into the end of the other (5) in the manner of a modern chimney-sweep. A final darting movement ensured that the (small) bird became stuck fast. Another (and, one suspects, more successful) method was to lime short stakes, scatter food, hide in a bush and imitate birdsong – the post-prandial perch was their undoing. See A. J. Butler, *Sport in classic times* (London, 1930) 184–91. In Hellenistic epigrams Eros is himself some-times depicted as a fowler who catches his victims unawares: cf. e.g. Mel. *AP* 12.132a = *HE* 4104–9 (Mel. 21) = *OCT* 4148–53 and *AP* 12.92 = *HE* 4620–7 (Mel. 116) = *OCT* 4664–71. Bion's poem seems to be an ingenious inversion of this idea.

1[1211] ἐν ἄλσεϊ δενδράεντι: < *Od.* 9.200.

2[1212] ὄρνεα: the form ὄρνεον is a Homeric *hapax* (*Il.* 13.64), not uncommon in later writers. ὑπόπτερον: Eros is conventionally depicted as winged, symbolizing perhaps his qualities of suddenness and fickle-ness. He is called ὑπόπτερος at Mel. *AP* 5.178.3 (*HE* 4202; *OCT* 4246) and elsewhere. The MSS read ἀπότροπον, which might just be understood as 'withdrawn apart' (cf. *Od.* 14.372), allegorical of the boy's unreadiness for love (cf. 15 ἀπάλμενος). But then τόν ('the famous …') has no point, and the sense is much inferior. Perhaps τανυσίπτερον ('with his wings outspread') should be read for τὸν ἀπότροπον: the adj. is applied in Homer and Hesiod to birds both large and small (e.g. *Od.* 22.468).

3[1213] ποτὶ κλάδον: acc. because the verb 'implies previous motion' (LSJ s.v. πρός c.i.2).

6[1216] μετάλμενον: < μεθάλλομαι. The lack of aspiration in this participial form (and in aor. ἆλτο) is a quirk of epic dialect. In Homer the prefix μετ- signifies close pursuit, going 'after'; but here it is used of change, 'first one then the other' (cf. μεταμείβω, etc.). ἀμφεδόκευε 'lay in wait for'. ἀμφ- suggests watchfulness all round.

7[1217] χὠ παῖς stresses his childish simplicity: the subject is the same as for the previous sentences. οἱ τέλος οὐδὲν ἀπάντη: we say 'he met with no success', Greek 'no success met with him'. τέλος = 'satisfactory conclusion'. ἀπάντη = Attic ἀπήντει: App. A. 3.

8[1218] ῥίψας: the simple verb can = 'throw *away*' (cf. ῥίψασπις). ποτ': ποτί. ἀροτρέα: ἀροτρεύς for ἀροτήρ is found first in Hellenistic poetry.

9[1219] ἐδιδάξατο: the mid. was properly used for having someone taught; but here it is for metrical convenience. Cf. *1140, 1591*.

10–11[1220–1] πρέσβυς and **παῖδα** at successive line-ends emphasize the contrast between the qualities of youth and age.

11[1221] Cf. *Il.* 17.442 (Zeus) κινήσας δὲ κάρη προτὶ ὃν μυθήσατο θυμόν . . .

12[1222] φείδεο τᾶς θήρας: sc. τοῦδ᾽ ὀρνέου (not from hunting in general).

13[1223] μακράν: fem. as adverb (cf. 6 τᾶι, *1062* n.).

14[1224] εἰσόκε = εἰς ὅ κε, Lat. *donec*. **ἀνέρος ἐς μέτρον ἔλθηις**: cf. *Il.* 11.225 ἥβης . . . ἵκετο μέτρον. ἀνέρος . . . μέτρον is the whole of a man's prime; ἢν . . . ἔλθηις = 'when you embark upon . . .'.

15–16[1225–6] Cf. Sappho's lover: καὶ γὰρ αἰ φεύγει, ταχέως διώξει (fr. 1.21).

16[1226] ἐλθὼν ἐξαπίνας: <*Il.* 15.325. **κεφαλὰν ἔπι**: unpleasant things are often described as landing on one's head: cf. *1341–5* and *Il.* 19.91–4, quoted ad loc. **καθιξεῖ**: Doric fut. of καθίζω (Attic καθιεῖ). Is there a pun on ἰξός ('you can't stick to him, but he will soon clap his ἰξός on you')? The poem begins ἰξευ- and ends -ιξεῖ.

XXI

The cult of Adonis, Mesopotamian in origin, spread to the Greek world in the seventh century B.C. via Syria and Palestine. In the east the god's name was Tammuz; *ādōn*, Phoenician for 'Lord', was only a title. He was said by the Greeks to be the offspring of an incestuous union between Cinyras, a Syrian settler in Cyprus, and his daughter Myrrha, who was metamorphosed into a myrrh-tree (Ovid, *Met.* 10.298–518). Adonis grew to be a beautiful youth and became the lover of Aphrodite; but he soon lost his life hunting, gored in the thigh by a wild boar. Each year in many Greek cities the women commemorated Adonis' death with lamentations. An effigy of the dead youth was placed on a bier and bewailed by the celebrants; incense was burnt; and small pots called 'Gardens of Adonis' were planted with seeds which germinated and quickly died, symbolizing the brevity of Adonis' life. After a day of mourning it appears that both 'gardens' and effigy were thrown into a river or into the sea. Theocritus' 15th *Idyll*, the Ἀδωνιάζουσαι, is a dialogue between two women who go to visit a celebration of the Adonia staged in the royal palace at Alexandria by Arsinoe, wife of Ptolemy

Philadelphus. At lines 100–44 of that poem a female singer addresses Aphrodite and describes the scene: Adonis-gardens in silver baskets, golden flasks of perfume, various foods laid out, an arbour with effigies or pictures of the lovers in each other's arms, Cupids flitting about. This tableau is of course far more magnificent than the average Adonia-presentation; but it gives some impression of the ritual context in which Bion's poem is to be imagined as taking place.

The gory death of Adonis and Aphrodite's lament for him were popular subjects for vase-paintings and frescoes. Bion's poem may well be inspired by such works of art in its vivid visual detail; but it is not descriptive of a simple tableau such as that described in Theocritus *Idyll* 15: there are several changes of scene (Aphrodite's bed, Adonis in the hills, Aphrodite and the dying Adonis, Aphrodite's palace), and the emphasis is on speech and movement. On a formal level the poem owes much to the 'mimetic' hymns of Callimachus (to Apollo, Athena (*132–273*) and Demeter), in which details supplied in passing by an anonymous 'master of ceremonies' allow readers to construct for themselves a dramatic context (see p. 111).

The imaginary context, we gather, is the day of mourning at the Adonia – probably just before Adonis' image is carried to the sea. On that occasion the women uttered a ritual θρῆνος or lament, perhaps in rhythmic prose, perhaps consisting only of ritual cries and simple exclamations. Sappho appears to have written a *Lament for Adonis* in lyric metre (fr. 140); and the lyric θρῆνος for performance at wakes was well established as a literary form by the sixth century. Bion has thus produced another example of Hellenistic generic fusion by combining the metre and dramatic format of the Callimachean hymn with Doric dialect (perhaps suggested by Theocritus *Idyll* 15 or the Callimachean hymns to Athena and Demeter) and with a threnodic subject of a type previously treated in lyric poetry. But this is not the only novelty. Surviving fragments of lyric θρῆνοι (e.g. Pindar frr. 128a–137, Simonides *PMG* 520–31) are stately, gnomic and consolatory. Bion's poem has a far different effect. It is not the poet who speaks, but a female participant in the rites: detached reflection is replaced by mimetic realism. The poem sets out to recreate the strident tones and heightened eroticism of an exotic foreign festival; and this effect is achieved by an adaptation into the hexameter format of characteristics of real funerary laments. (For a similar but more restrained lament cf. *Il.* 24.723–76.)

Hence the extraordinary amount of anaphora, repetition, alliteration and assonance (cf. Meleager's elegiac lament for Heliodora, *1502–11*); hence, too, the predominantly dactylic rhythm with frequent pauses at the bucolic diaeresis, producing an effect of rapid movement and animation. The refrain, which is perhaps borrowed in conception from *Idylls* 1 and 2 (= *574–738*) of Theocritus, represents the repeated interjections of woe characteristic of all Greek laments. It is artfully varied in structure (1–2 n.) and refers now to Adonis (1, 2, 6, 15, 67), now to Aphrodite (28, 37, 63, 86).

These formal devices suggest something of the antiphony and responsion of a real lament. Despite its various changes of scene the narrative as a whole is structured antithetically. Lament lends itself to contrasts: between past and present, praise and reproach, living and dead. Here the narrator focuses alternately on Adonis and Aphrodite – on his senselessness and her sense of loss, on his death and her inability to die, on his peace and her disturbed state. The contrast is between past happiness and present grief. At the same time, however, parallels are drawn between living and dead – his literal wound is her mental wound (16–17), his bodily disfigurement is equalled by hers (19–22), her tears flow like his blood (64–6). The still figure of Adonis is the focal point for a series of ingenious conceits.

Bibl.: Edn: M. Fantuzzi (Liverpool, 1985). Adonis: M. Detienne, *The gardens of Adonis* (Eng. trans. by J. Lloyd, Hassocks, 1977). In art: *Lexicon iconographicum mythologiae classicae* 1 (Zürich/Munich, 1981) 1.222–9, 2.160–70. Lament: M. Alexiou, *The ritual lament in Greek tradition* (Cambridge, 1974). Bion: V. A. Estevez, ''Απώλετο καλὸς 'Αδωνις: a description of Bion's refrain', *Maia* 33 (1981) 35–42.

> Cf. Ovid, *Met.* 10.503–59, 708–39; Shakespeare, *Venus and Adonis*; Shelley, *Adonais* (based on this poem and the anonymous *Lament for Bion* – *OCT Bucol. Gr.* 140–5).

1–2[1227–8] These lines, together with 97–8, define the poem's ritual context. They contain three of the four half-line elements which, in various combinations appropriate to the context, will form the refrain.

2[1228] ἐπαιάζουσιν: ἐπ- implies an antiphonal response.

3–5[1229–30] Aphrodite is urged to rouse herself from sleep and bewail the dead Adonis (knowledge of the myth is taken for granted). These lines look forward to the lengthy description of the goddess's couch, which will serve as Adonis' bier, at 69ff.

4[1230] κυανόστολα: proleptic: 'beat your dark-robed breast' = 'put on dark robes and beat your breast'. For κυάνεος as a funereal colour cf. *859*. **καί:** postponed: *15* n.

8[1234] λευκῶι λευκόν (sc. μηρόν). Interlaced word order represents the penetration of soft white thigh by hard white tusk. This leads into the colour-contrast of dark blood on pale skin, a recurrent theme (9–11, 25–7, 64–6).

9[1235] λεπτὸν ἀποψύχων 'faintly breathing out his life' – his breath is 'thin', 'weak'. Throughout the poem Adonis is described sometimes as dying, sometimes as already dead (e.g. 70 νεκρός). This is because for the Greeks death took place not in an instant but as the result of a protracted struggle by the soul to break free from the body (ψυχορραγεῖν). Cf. 46–50 n.

10[1236] ναρκῆι: usually of physical numbness; here 'grow dim' of eyes glazed in death.

11[1237] τὸ ῥόδον φεύγει: his lips grow pale. The metaphor looks forward to the miraculous birth of roses from his blood at 66. Cf. *158–9*. **τήνωι:** sc. τῶι χείλει.

12[1238] μήποτε . . . ἀποισεῖ: he is unconscious, and cannot therefore bestow on her a kiss to 'take away'. Perhaps a very strong negative is intended here, equivalent to earlier Gk οὐ μήποτε + fut. (Goodwin, *GMT* § 295); more likely, however, μή stands for οὐ, as often in later Gk.

14[1240] ὅ = ὅτι, as often in Homer. Cf. 57. **θνάισκοντα:** cf. 9 n.; but the pres. can mean 'be dead' as well as 'be dying': cf. 58 and Dawe on Soph. *O.T.* 118.

16[1242] ἄγριον: because caused by a 'savage' beast.

18[1244] This line is an echo of Theoc. 1.71 (Daphnis dying) τῆνον μὰν θῶες, τῆνον λύκοι ὠρύσαντο. In our passage ὠρύονται is a conjecture by Hermann for MSS ὠδύραντο; but it cannot be called certain, since some MSS of Theoc. have ὠδύραντο, and Bion may have read it there too. The conjecture is nevertheless preferable: (1) it seems more effective to have dogs and nymphs lamenting together (pres. + pres.) than in sequence (aor. + pres.) (cf. 83–5, however, for the alternation of tense); (2) ὠρύομαι is a much rarer word than ὀδύρομαι, and is the technical term for dogs howling.

19[1245] Νύμφαι . . . Ὀρειάδες: the mountain-nymphs of Cyprus, natural patronesses of the hunt, by whom, according to some accounts, Adonis was reared.

21[1247] νήπλεκτος ἀσάνδαλος 'with unbraided hair and barefoot' – the ritual dishevelment of mourning.

22[1248] ἐρχομέναν 'as she goes along'. κείροντι: a strong word, 'tear at', 'rip', paralleling Adonis' ἄγριον ἕλκος (16) and perhaps also alluding to the self-laceration practised by mourning women. In addition, κείροντι and δρέπονται involve an ironic conceit, since both verbs are often used with plants as their *object*: κείρω = 'mow down', δρέπομαι = 'pluck'. Nature seems hostile to Aphrodite – a reversal of the 'pathetic fallacy' (cf. 31–9 n.).

23[1249] φορεῖται 'is borne along', implying random and distracted motion.

24[1250] πολλὰ καλεῦσα: cf. the Homeric πολλὰ λισσόμενος (*Il.* 21.368, etc.). The MSS read πόσιν καὶ παῖδα καλεῦσα, which would mean that instead of being quoted directly her cries ('"Ασσύριε πόσι" and "παῖ παῖ") are made objects of the participles. But why she should call Adonis 'child' or 'my boy' is not clear. 'Ασσύριον . . . πόσιν: a reference either to the eastern origins of Adonis' cult or, more specifically, to the Syrian ancestry of his father Cinyras (see p. 217).

25–7[1251–3] If the text is sound we must translate 'But on him, about his navel, floated the black blood, and his chest grew crimson from ⟨the wound in⟩ his thighs, and Adonis' breast, formerly snow-white, became dark in colour': Adonis seems to be lying with his thigh higher than his head and chest, so that blood flows from the wound over the upper part of his body. The pose is in itself improbable, and is not shown in any of the surviving pictures. Particular suspicion attaches to ἀιωρεῖτο: how can blood 'float' or 'be suspended' (cf. *1043*)? Homer has ἠρώησε (< ἐρωέω) twice of blood 'rushing' from a wound; but the aor. is unwelcome here. Fantuzzi's conjecture ἠρωεῖτο is therefore attractive, even though the mid. of ἐρωέω is otherwise unattested.

26[1252] ἐκ μηρῶν: this phrase, too, is suspect, involving an awkward ellipse (see translation, 25–7 n.). Rossbach's ἐκ πληγῶν, 'from the wound', makes better sense; but perhaps a dat. adj., parallel syntactically to 'Αδώνιδι in 27, should be restored. ὑπό: probably in tmesis with πορφύροντο, the prep. suggesting gradual encroachment. Some commentators understand στηθέων from the preceding clause.

28[1254] Κυθέρειαν: a title of Aphrodite, who had a temple on the island of Κυθήρα (cf. 35). For the acc. after an exclamation cf. 3*i*, *220* n.

29[1255] σύν: adverbial, 'at the same time'.

30[1256] μέν: the contrast is between ἦν (to be understood with Κύπριδι) and κάτθανε (31).

31–9[1257–65] All nature shares in mourning Adonis' death. This is the so-called 'pathetic fallacy' (cf. 22 n.): natural country sounds (e.g. 31–3 echoing hills, rustling branches, bubbling rivers) are taken to be purposely made in sympathy with a human event.

35[1261] ἐρυθαίνεται: perhaps 'turn brown', i.e. wither (cf. 76), rather than 'turn red' – roses are specified at 66, but not here. **Κυθήρα:** the island, or its nymph, mourning in sympathy with Aphrodite.

36[1262] κναμώς: κνημός = densely wooded lower slope of a mountain. **οἰκτρόν:** adv.

39[1265] αἰνόν: 'terrible' in the sense of 'extreme' (cf. δεινός). **τίς οὐκ ἔκλαυσεν ἂν αἰαῖ** 'who could have failed to cry "Woe" at ...?' If the text is sound, αἰαῖ κλαίειν is to be taken as a verb = αἰάζειν; but Ludwich's ἐν αἴαι ('who in the world did not ...?') may be right.

40–78[1266–1304] The imaginary scene changes. After her distraught wanderings Aphrodite has found Adonis. She utters a long lament, the centrepiece of the poem (42–61). The narrator instructs her to set Adonis on their 'marriage'-bed, which will now become his bier.

40[1266] ἄσχετον 'unstaunchable'.

42[1268] ἀμπετάσασα: aor. part. of ἀμπετάννυμι (epic form of ἀναπετ-): 'with her arms outspread', a characteristic pose of lamenting women.

43[1269] κιχείω: irregularly formed aor. subj. of κιχάνω. The meaning is presumably 'so that I can hold you for the last time', a slight extension of the usual meaning 'meet with', 'reach'.

45[1271] τὸ δ' αὖ πύματον 'once more, for the last time'.

46–50[1272–6] Aphrodite begs Adonis to kiss her with his dying breath – that will be a 'sweet stimulant' (48) which will make her desire him ever afterwards. Some critics see an allusion to the Stoic idea of the soul as a vaporous exhalation (ἀναθυμίασις). But the concept of the liver as seat of passion(s) is normal and not specifically Stoic; and it was a common custom to catch a loved one's last breath as a way of continuing the union after death on a (literally) spiritual plane (see Pease on Virg. *Aen.* 4.684). The passage combines images of sex and death in a suggestively erotic manner.

46[1272] ὅσον ζώει τὸ φίλημα 'as long as the kiss has life', i.e. until you die in the act. Cf. 13.

47–9[1273–5] ἄχρις . . .: words meaning 'until' occasionally have the subj. without ἄν: see Goodwin, *GMT* §620.

48[1274] φίλτρον: some interpret this word in its obscure anatomical sense of 'dimple in the upper lip' (LSJ s.v. II); but the normal meaning of 'love-charm' or 'stimulant to desire' seems suitable here. ἀμέλξω: lit. 'milk' – the suction of a kiss.

50[1276] ὡς 'as if it were'.

50–3[1276–9] A paradoxical conceit: Aphrodite's immortality thwarts her desire to join Adonis. These lines exploit a secondary meaning of φεύγειν and διώκειν, which often signify amorous flight and pursuit (cf. *567*, *1225–6* n.).

53[1279] ἐμμί: this is usually thought to be the Aeolic form of εἰμί, but Hellenistic poets may have found it in Doric works now lost. Cf. on 84.

55[1281] ἐς σὲ καταρρεῖ: lit. 'flows down to you'; the Eng. metaphor is 'falls to you'. The words are borrowed from Theoc. 1.5 (of a prize).

56[1282] πανάποτμος: twice in Homer (*Il.* 24.255, 493), both times of Priam mourning his dead son Hector: the word thus confers status on Adonis' tragic death.

57[1283] ὅ: 14 n. φοβεῦμαι 'hate', i.e. 'flee ⟨in loathing⟩', a meaning not given by LSJ.

58[1284] τριπόθητε: the prefix has intensive force, as in e.g. τρίσμακαρ. πόθος: probably '⟨object of⟩ my desire' rather than 'feelings of desire'; but to decide between these two meanings is perhaps over-pedantic. Cf. Theoc. *715*. ὡς ὄναρ ἔπτα: an adaptation of *Od.* 11.222 ψυχὴ δ᾽ ἠΰτ᾽ ὄνειρος ἀποπταμένη πεπότηται. ἔπτα is an act. aor. form of πέτομαι.

59[1285] κενοί 'unoccupied' – gone is the object of their ministrations. δώματ᾽: Aphrodite's palace.

60[1286] σοὶ δ᾽ ἅμα κεστὸς ὄλωλε 'my love-girdle has perished with you'. The words seem to represent Aphrodite's distraught incoherence: they have no logical connexion with what precedes and follows (despite γάρ). Aphrodite's κεστός was a belt of material with seductive powers. At *Il.* 14.214 she gives it to Hera to aid the Διὸς ἀπάτη. Here the meaning is perhaps that any use she had for the κεστός is now gone together with Adonis, whom she charmed with its help. κυνάγεις: imperf.

61[1287] The text is doubtful. Translate 'Why, being fair, were you so mad ⟨as to⟩ (sc. ὥστε) struggle with the beast?'. Köchly's repeated τί seems desirable and characteristic in this anaphoric style.

64[1290] ἁ Παφία: Aphrodite had a famous temple at Paphos in Cyprus.

65[1291] τά: tears and blood, which became flowers (ἄνθη is predicative). **ποτὶ χθονί**: ποτί because they fell *to* the ground; dat. because they flowered once they were *on* it. Cf. *1585*.

66[1292] ἀνεμώναν: the anemone (lit. 'wind-flower'), which was proverbially short-lived: Ovid, *Met.* 10.738–9 *namque male haerentem et nimia leuitate caducum | excutiunt idem qui praestant nomina uenti.*

69[1295] 'A lonely pile of leaves is not a good bed for Adonis.' **ἐρήμα** because he is still imagined as lying in the hills.

71[1297] καί 'even'. **οἷα** 'as if'; the sing. οἷον is commoner.

72–8[1298–1304] The text of these lines is very uncertain.

72[1298]: see 3–5 n.

72–3[1298–9] '... in which he used to slumber when he toiled with you through the night in sacred sleep.' Neither the construction of τὸν ἱερὸν ὕπνον (cognate acc.?) nor the meaning of ἐμόχθει is clear, and as a sexual euphemism the whole line sounds grotesque. (An intelligible meaning could be gained by reading ... οἷσι κάθευδεν | ὡς ... τὸν ἱερὸν ὕπνον ἴαυεν (cf. *56*, Theoc. 3.49): if κάθευδε fell out after καθεύδων immediately above, ἴαυεν might have been transposed. But ἐμόχθει remains unexplained.)

73[1299] ἱερὸν ὕπνον: i.e. sleep with the divine goddess. (At *1484* the phrase has a different meaning.) ἱερός is a recurrent epithet of Aphrodite in this poem (cf. 22, 29); this makes it unlikely to be relevant here that Archilochus uses the phrase τὸ θεῖον πρᾶγμα as a euphemism for sexual intercourse (*SLG* 478.15).

74[1300] παγχρυσέωι κλιντῆρι: a couch of gold befitting χρυσέη Ἀφροδίτη. But κλιντήρ can also = 'bier'. Another variation of the 'love and death' theme. **πόθες**: aor. imper. of προσίημι (ποτ(ι)-ἕς – cf. *577* ποθίκει), 'put him on your golden couch'. The MSS have πόθει (imper. of ποθέω) or ποθεῖ. **καὶ στυγνόν** 'even though he is a fearful sight', disfigured by his injuries. στυγνός seems occasionally to = 'dishevelled' (not in LSJ; but cf. [Moschus] 3.4); but that meaning is less apt here.

75–8[1301–4] At the Adonis-festival the effigy on its bier was sprinkled with flowers and perfumes. Here the narrator hints at the origin of this custom: all flowers died with Adonis (cf. 35) and Adonis was Aphrodite's μύρον ('sweet favourite'), so that all perfumes ought to be poured on him, too.

75[1301] πάντα σὺν αὐτῶι: it would be better to understand εἴη than ἐστί: 'let everything be with him', i.e. 'let him have everything'; but the ellipse of the opt. is harsh, and the sense is even then not good. The phrase may be corrupt; one would expect a second imperative to parallel ῥαῖνε... ῥαῖνε in 77.

76[1302] ὡς 'when'.

77[1303] Συρίοισιν ἀλείφασι: Syria was famous for its unguents and perfumes; but the adj. is especially apt here because of the Syrian origins of Adonis' family. According to Ovid's account (*Met.* 10.503–14) Adonis was born from the myrrh-tree into which his mother had been metamorphosed, and was anointed with the myrrh which dripped from it, his mother's 'tears'.

79–96[1305–24] Another change of scene. Adonis is lying on Aphrodite's golden couch, now his bier, and is mourned by the Loves and Graces. This was a popular scene in Greek and Roman art.

79[1305] ἀβρός: the word has overtones of luxurious ease as well as of beauty.

81[1307] ἐπ': probably 'in honour of'; but there is evidence (e.g. *Il.* 23. 135–6) that mourners' hair was actually strewn *on* the corpse. (Cf. 81–2 for other articles so strewn.)

82[1308] ἐπὶ ... ἔβαλλεν: tmesis. **πτερόν:** presumably a feather from his wing, though this does not fit well with the other articles of equipment.

84[1310] φορέοισιν: cf. 94 ἀνακλείοισιν. The -οισι 3rd pl. ending is Aeolic (cf. *807*); but it may have occurred instead of the usual -οντι in some Doric writings (e.g. choral lyric with Aeolisms). Cf. 53 n. Participles in -οισα (for -ουσα) are found in both Aeolic and literary Doric: App. C. 9. **μηρία:** here for μηρούς, 'thighs'; usually = 'thighbones'.

85[1311] ὄπιθεν ⟨standing⟩ behind'. **ἀναψύχει** 'tries to revive' him with a cooling draught.

87–90[1313–16] Hymenaeus, god of marriage, had celebrated the lovers' union with torches, garlands and wedding-songs at the bedroom door; but this joyful attitude now changes to one of grief. Cf. *1516–19*.

88[1314] ἐξεκέδασσε 'scattered in shreds': aor. of ἐκκεδάννυμι.

90[1316] ἔτι πλέον ἢ Ὑμέναιον 'even more, i.e. more loudly/frequently, than ⟨he once sang⟩ "Hymen"'.

93[1319] πολὺ πλέον ἢ Παιῶνα 'even more than ⟨they once sang⟩ the paean', a solemn choral performance particularly associated with

Apollo; as Apollo's attendants the Graces might be expected to have sung it at the 'wedding' of Adonis and Aphrodite. The line-end echoes 90. Παιῶνα is Ahrens' conjecture for the MSS τύ, Διώνα (apparently an echo of 651), which is unsatisfactory in sense: why should the Graces out-mourn Aphrodite herself?

94–6[1320–2] The Fates try to call Adonis back from the dead, but he cannot obey because Persephone will not release him (sc. because she is in love with him herself?). There may be a reference to a less well known version of the myth in which Adonis is not killed by a boar but is placed in a chest by Aphrodite and entrusted to Persephone, who refuses to release him; as in the case of Persephone herself, a compromise is reached whereby Adonis will spend half the year above earth and half below.

94[1320] ἀνακλείοισιν: 84 n. κλείω is a lengthened form of κ(α)λέω. ἀνακαλεῖν is the technical term for summoning the dead back to earth.

95[1321] ἐπαείδουσιν 'they conjure him with incantations' (ἐπωιδαί). **οὐκ ἐπακούει:** this verb is often used of 'giving ear to one who prays' (LSJ).

96[1322] οὐ μὰν οὐκ ἐθέλει: οὐ μάν qualifies the negative: 'it is not, indeed, that he does not want to ⟨give ear to them⟩'. **Κώρα:** Doric for Κόρη, Persephone.

97–8[1323–4] In a two-line coda, formally corresponding to 1–2, the narrator signals the end of this year's lament and looks forward to the next Adonia.

97[1323] κομμῶν: the word is derived from κόπτω, i.e. a 'beating of the breast'; but here its transferred meaning of 'dirge' is equally appropriate.

98[1324] εἰς ἔτος ἄλλο: a standard sentiment at the end of hymns, promising renewed celebration at the next festival: cf. Call. *Hymn to Dem.* 123 ἔτος δ' εἰς ἄλλο φυλαξεῖ (sc. ἡμᾶς), 'she will preserve us for another year'. Here, however, εἰς is untranslatable: cf. 616 ἐς τρίς and phrases such as εἰσάπαξ and εἰς αὔριον.

XXII

Rhianus

Rhianus (third cent. B.C.), a Cretan slave turned scholar, produced editions of the *Iliad* and *Odyssey* and probably lived for a time in

Alexandria. His poems included a long Ἡράκλεια, 'ethnographical' epics on the Thessalians, Achaeans and Eleans, and epigrams. His best-known work was the Μεσσηνιακά, which appears to have focused on the heroic (and occasionally romantic) deeds of Aristomenes, who attempted to liberate his country from Spartan domination in the Second Messenian War (c. 650 B.C.). The present lines inveigh gloomily in traditional gnomic language against the folly of mankind – the poor complain but make no effort to better themselves, while the rich and powerful aspire too high and are eventually punished, since Ate pursues them and brings down their arrogant pride. If this is a complete poem it is possible to see indirect criticism of the divine aspirations of Hellenistic monarchs (see p. 4); but if, as seems more likely, it is a fragment of one of the lost epics, ignorance of its context must make us suspend judgement. Rhianus' diction is for the most part Homeric, with some borrowing from Hesiod (ἁμαρτίνοοι, εὐοχθῆισι) and elsewhere.

Bibl.: *CA* pp. 9–10.

1–3[1325–7] The gods' gifts can 'tilt' either way, can be good or bad: Theognis 157–8 Ζεὺς γάρ τοι τὸ τάλαντον ἐπιρρέπει ἄλλοτε ἄλλως, | ἄλλοτε μὲν πλουτεῖν, ἄλλοτε μηδὲν ἔχειν. But men are so 'thoughtless' that none bears his lot wisely (3–16).

1[1325] ἦ ἄρα δή: Homer has ἦ ἄρα and ἦ δή in strong affirmations, but never all three particles together.

2[1326] φέρομεν 'cope with'.

3–8[1327–32] The ἀχρήμων blames the gods, underestimates himself, feels inferior in the presence of the rich, is cast down in helpless despair. (He ought to be trying to make the best of things.)

4[1328] στρωφᾶται 'wanders around ⟨aimlessly⟩' because he has no means of sustenance. Pres. subj. after ὅς κ'.

5[1329] σφετέρην: *977* n.

6[1330] Cf. Theognis 177–8 καὶ γὰρ ἀνὴρ πενίηι δεδμημένος οὔτε τι εἰπεῖν | οὔτ' ἔρξαι δύναται, γλῶσσα δέ οἱ δέδεται, 667–70. **νοέειν** suggests that he cannot even form his thoughts coherently, let alone give them expression.

7[1331] ὅθι τ': cf. *1079*.

8[1332] θυμὸν ἔδουσι: a Homeric metaphor: cf. e.g. *Od.* 10.378–9 τίφθ' οὕτως, Ὀδυσεῦ, κατ' ἄρ' ἕζεαι ἶσος ἀναύδωι | θυμὸν ἔδων;

9–16[1333–40] The rich and powerful man forgets that he is mortal, tries to rival Zeus, acts insolently, aspires to heaven: traditional ὕβρις.

9[1333] εὐοχθῆισι: a Hesiodic word (*WD* 477) of uncertain etymology meaning 'do well'. -ηισι is the Homeric 3rd pers. subj. ending; here -ῆισι <-έηισι.

10[1334] πολυκοιρανίην: once in Homer (*Il.* 2.204), = 'rule by many'; here 'rule over many'.

11[1335] The foot-imagery prepares us for 17–21.

12[1336] 'With insolence and errors of discretion': ὑπεροπλίη is a Homeric *hapax* (*Il.* 1.205); ἁμαρτωλή occurs only at Theognis 327. **ἁμ. νόοιο** picks up ἁμαρτίνοοι (1).

13[1337] ἴσα Διὶ βρομέει: for the expression cf. Call.'s famous βροντᾶν οὐκ ἐμόν, ἀλλὰ Διός (*20*). If a particular reference is intended it is to Salmoneus, legendary king of Elis, who was thundersmitten *dum flammas Iouis et sonitus imitatur Olympi* (Virg. *Aen.* 6.586); Apollod. 1.9.7 calls him ὑβριστής . . . τῶι Διὶ ἐξισοῦσθαι θέλων.

14[1338] μνᾶται δ' εὔπηχυν 'Αθήνην: an act of this type was proverbially hybristic: cf. Alcman, *Partheneion* (*PMG* 1) 16–17 μή τις ἀνθ]ρώπων ἐς ὠρανὸν ποτήσθω | μηδὲ πη]ρήτω γαμῆν τὰν 'Αφροδίταν. Rh. may have chosen Athena here because she is a virgin goddess; but there may be a specific allusion to Cotys, king of Thrace from 382 to 358 B.C., who once set up a marriage-feast for himself and Athena and drunkenly awaited his bride (Theopompus, *FGH* 115 F 31). According to one account Prometheus' punishment was a consequence of his having lusted after Athena (Duris of Samos, *FGH* 76 F 47).

15[1339] ἀτραπιτὸν . . . Οὔλυμπόνδε: again proverbially hybristic (cf. Alcman, 14 n.). Homer alludes to the story of Otus and Ephialtes, who piled up mountains in order to scale heaven and fight with the gods (*Od.* 11.305–20). **τεκμαίρεται** 'plans', 'designs', a slight development of the Homeric meaning 'fix', 'arrange'.

16[1340] μετ' ἀθανάτοισιν ἀρίθμιος: tmesis of the adj.: cf. *Hom. Hymn* 26.6 μεταρίθμιος ἀθανάτοισιν, *693–4* n.

17–21[1341–5] Ate pursues such arrogant men and hovers unperceived and invisible above their heads, standing by old sins as a young woman and by young sins as an old woman, helping Zeus and Dike. She helps them by striking men with a fatal blindness, so that they bring about their own ruin. For the operation of Ate cf. *Il.* 9.505–12 and especially 19.91–4, which Rh. is echoing here: πρέσβα Διὸς θυγάτηρ ῎Ατη, ἣ πάντας ἀᾶται, | οὐλομένη· τῆι μέν θ' ἁπαλοὶ πόδες· οὐ γὰρ ἐπ' οὔδει | πίλναται, ἀλλ' ἄκρ' ἥγε κατ' ἀνδρῶν κράατα βαίνει | βλάπτουσ' ἀνθρώπους. Rh. may be expanding the implications of Homer's πρέσβα and θυγάτηρ in making Ate νεωτέρη to old sins and γρηῦς to young sins, though the significance of the contrast is not quite clear: perhaps he means that she crops up unexpectedly to punish sins committed long ago, and that in the distant future she will punish sins which now seem recent. (It may be in this sense that Dike has τὸ γρήιον ἴχνος in Euphorion, *SH* 415 ii 6.) For the unpredictability of Ate's onset cf. Solon fr. 13.74–6 κέρδεά τοι θνητοῖς ὤπασαν ἀθάνατοι, | ἄτη δ' ἐξ αὐτῶν ἀναφαίνεται, ἣν ὁπότε Ζεὺς | πέμψηι τεισομένην, ἄλλοτε ἄλλος ἔχει, Theognis 203–8.

17[1341] ἁπαλοῖσι: because they never touch the ground: cf. *Il.* 19.92 (17–21 n.). She is thus contrasted with the arrogant men, who forget that they are mortals who tread the earth (10–11). **μετατρωχῶσα** 'runs after', 'pursues'. τρωχάω is an epic form of τρέχω.

18[1342] ἄκρηις: at *Il.* 19.93 (17–21 n.) our MSS of Homer read ἀλλ' ἄρα ἦγε; but clearly Rh. knew of an alternative (and better) reading ἀλλ' ἄκρ' ἦγε (or ἀλλ' ἦγ' ἄκρα) . . . κράατα: see Pfeiffer, *HCS* 1 149. **ἀνώιστος** 'unforeseen': cf. *960* n.

19[1343] γραίηισι: γραῖα, like γέρων, can be used adjectivally: cf. *1444*.

20[1344] ἐφίσταται: this verb is often used for the appearance of visions and dreams.

21[1345] ἐπίηρα φέρουσα = χαριζομένη. In Homer ἦρα is a noun (= χάριν); but some ancient critics read phrases such as ἐπὶ ἦρα φέρων (tmesis) as ἐπίηρα φέρων: in the fifth cent. b.c. a poetic adj. ἐπίηρος, 'pleasing', appears. If our MSS are to be trusted, Rh. had the phrase as two words.

XXIII

Lycophron

Lycophron was born at Chalcis in Euboea, and seems to have lived in Alexandria c. 275–250 b.c. He classified and perhaps edited the comic poets for the recently established Library and produced a large work Περὶ κωμωιδίας, which probably dealt with rare and obscure words found in comedy. Later grammarians counted him a member of the Pleiad, a name given by them to the seven leading luminaries of tragic composition in the third century. Of his 46 or 64 tragedies, and of his satyr-plays, only a few fragments remain (*TGF* 100 F 1–9). He is the first recorded maker of anagrams (Πτολεμαῖος > ἀπὸ μέλιτος, Ἀρσινόη > ἴον Ἥρας – *SH* 531).

Lycophron's only extant work is the *Alexandra*, a 1474-line tour-de-force of riddling obscurity. Written in the strict iambic metre of Hellenistic tragedy (West, *GM* 159), the poem is an extended 'messenger-speech': a guard set to watch over Cassandra (= 'Alexandra', sister of Alexander = Paris) relates to her father, Priam, the prophetess's inspired ravings. It was Cassandra's fate never to be believed. Lycophron provides a new reason for this traditional feature of the myth: she was not only not believed, but not even understood. Grammatically and syntactically her speech is relatively lucid; but her recondite vocabulary and obscurely allusive references make the poem a puzzle soluble only by readers with an extremely wide knowledge of mythology and earlier literature. It has been calculated that 518 of the 3000 different words in the poem are found nowhere else, and that a further 117 occur in the *Alexandra* for the first time. Gods and men are referred to in riddling periphrases, with much use of obscure cult-titles (cf. 352, 356, 359) and oracular animal-imagery (357–9).

Cassandra's prophecies cover the Trojan War and the fall of Troy, the return journeys of the various Greek commanders and their individual fates, and finally cryptic allusions to the rising power of Rome and the unification of Europe and Asia. The *Alexandra* subsumes within the framework of a tragic messenger-speech subject-matter from the *Iliad* and *Odyssey*, epics such as the Νόστοι ('Heroes' Returns'), and many of the myths treated in fifth- and fourth-century tragedy; its general tone, moreover, owes much to the riddling hexameter oracles which circulated in large numbers in the ancient world. The poem thus constitutes another novel combination of form and subject-matter. For most readers it typifies the unacceptable face of 'Callimachean' poetry: recondite, inaccessible, self-indulgently obscurantist. It is tempting to see the whole monstrous enterprise as an elaborate joke.

In this extract Cassandra riddlingly prophesies her own rape by Ajax son of Oileus and the shipwreck of the homeward-bound Greek fleet on the coast of Euboea, an act of retribution by Athena for Ajax' sacrilege. *Bibl.*: Edn: E. Scheer (2 vols., Berlin, 1881–1908), L. Mascialino (Teubner, 1964). Comm.: C. von Holzinger (Leipzig, 1895), G. W.

Mooney (London, 1921). Trans. and notes: A. W. Mair (Loeb, 1921, with Call. and Aratus). Gen.: S. West, 'Lycophron italicised', *J.H.S.* 104 (1984) 127–51.

348–65[1346–63] 'And I, wretched girl, the one who refused marriage, within the masonry of my stony maiden-room without ceiling, hiding my body in the roofless chamber of my dark prison – I who rejected from my virgin bed the eager god Thoraeus, Lord of Ptoön, Ruler of the Seasons, since I had taken eternal virginity ⟨as my lot⟩ to uttermost old age, in emulation of Pallas, Giver of the Spoil, Wardress of the Gates, marriage-hater – then (sc. at the fall of Troy), ⟨like⟩ a dove to the nest of the vulture, shall I in frenzy be dragged with crooked talons, I who often invoked the Maiden, Yoker of Oxen, the Sea-gull, as my helper and defender from marriage. And, turning up her eyes to the ceiling of her wood-carved shrine, she shall be angry with the army, she who fell from heaven and the throne of Zeus ⟨to be⟩ a most precious possession for my ancestor the king.'

348[1346] ἡ γάμους ἀρνουμένη: as priestess of Athena Cassandra had vowed eternal virginity, as she explains at 354–6.

349–51[1347–9] Having frightened the Trojans with her gloomy rantings, Cassandra has been immured by her father in a windowless stone building in the shape of a pyramid or dome (hence 'roofless' 350 and 'dark' 351); the guard/messenger has been set to watch over her.

350[1348] ἀνώροφον στέγην 'roofless chamber': Lyc. is playing on the primary meaning of στέγη, 'roof', to produce an apparent oxymoron. The shape of Cassandra's prison (349–51 n.) means that it both is and is not 'roofed'.

351[1349] ἀλιβδύσασα: a word of uncertain etymology. Ancient grammarians derived it from ἀλί + βδύω (supposedly Aeolic for δύω), i.e. 'plunge into the sea', 'submerge'; Lyc. uses that meaning metaphorically here.

352[1350] Θοραῖον: a Laconian cult-title of Apollo, 'God of Fertility' (θορός = 'semen'). **Πτῷον**: Apollo had a temple on the Ptoan hill in Boeotia. **Ὡρίτην**: because as sun-god he brings in the seasons (ὧραι).

353[1351] δεμνίων: to be taken with both λίπτοντ' and ἐκβαλοῦσα: he was eager *for* her bed, and she rejected him *from* it. It was this rejection which, according to some accounts, led to her prophecies always being disbelieved: cf. Aesch. *Ag.* 1202–12.

356[1354] Λαφρίας 'Giver of Spoil' (λάφυρα), a rare equivalent of the Homeric Ἀγελείη (λεία/λήϊα = 'booty') and Ληῖτις. **Πυλάτιδος**: representations of Athena were often placed over doors and gateways.

357[1355] τόργου: the 'vulture' is Locrian Ajax, son of Oileus, who raped Cassandra in the very temple of Athena.

358[1356] ἅρπαις οἰνάς: a triply tricky expression. One's first instinct is to translate οἰνάς 'vine' and ἅρπαις 'bill-hook'; but φάσσα (357) suggests that οἰνάς may have its other meaning, 'dove', and that ἅρπαις = 'talons'. It seems, however, that οἰνάς means neither 'vine' nor 'dove', but qualifies φάσσα as a fem. adj. meaning 'affected with οἶνος', i.e. frenzied, prophetically inspired.

359[1357] Βούδειαν: a Thessalian title of Athena: she first taught men to use the plough by fastening (δέω) oxen (βοῦς) to it. **Αἴθυιαν**: 'Sea-gull', a Megarian title for Athena as sea-goddess.

361-4[1359-62] When Troy falls Cassandra will no longer be in her dark prison, but in the temple of Athena. Athena's statue, the Palladium, which fell from heaven when the city was founded, will avert its eyes from the terrible sight of the priestess's rape. For a vase-painting which may show Athena's averted gaze see J. Davreux, *La Légende de la prophétesse Cassandre* (Liège, 1942) 158-9 no. 91, fig. 55.

361[1359] δουρατογλύφου: lit. 'beam-carved' (δόρυ, γλύφω).

364[1362] πάππωι: Ilus, who founded Ilium = Troy. **χρῆμα τιμαλφέστατον**: because the city was destined not to fall as long as the Palladium remained within the walls. Its theft by Odysseus and Diomedes was narrated in the *Little Iliad*, a lost epic poem; cf. *166-73* n.

365-72[1363-70] 'And because of the sin of one man all Hellas shall mourn the empty tombs of ten thousand children – ⟨tombs⟩ not in receptacles of bones but perched on the rocks(?), nor hiding in urns the ritually disposed last ashes from the fire, as is the due of the dead, but ⟨instead Hellas shall mourn⟩ a piteous name and inscriptions on empty cairns, bathed with the hot tears of parents and of children and the mourning of wives.' The bodies of the shipwrecked Greeks will not be recovered, so that they will neither be laid to rest in sarcophagi (ὀστοθήκαις) – as would happen if they died at home – nor be cremated and sent home as ashes in urns – as is the custom for men who die abroad: their relations will have only cenotaphs over which to mourn. Such, at least, ought to be the meaning; cf. 367 n.

365[1363] ἑνὸς δὲ λώβης ἀντί: Virgil echoes this passage or its source at *Aen.* 1.39-41 *Pallasne exurere classem | Argiuum atque ipsos potuit summergere ponto | unius ob noxam et furias Aiacis Oilei?*

367[1365] χοιράδων 'the hog's-back rocks' of Cape Caphereus, on to which the fleet was lured by Nauplius, whose son Palamedes had been treacherously killed at Troy by his Greek allies. But the 'ten thousand children', not the 'empty tombs', ought to be described as 'perched on the rocks'. The line seems to be corrupt, and no convincing emendation has yet been proposed.

368[1366] τέφρην: one would expect τέφραν, but Lyc. uses some Ionic forms (e.g. 370 οὔνομ').

369[1367] ἢ θέμις φθιτῶν = the Homeric ὃ γὰρ γέρας ἐστὶ θανόντων (*Il.* 23.9). ἢ θέμις ἐστί *uel sim.*, with or without a qualifying gen., is a common expression.

XXIV

Herondas

Herondas flourished c. 280–265 B.C.; it is not known where he was born or where he lived. Even the form of his name is not certain, some sources having Herodas. He sprang to fame in 1891, when a papyrus was published containing eight of his μιμίαμβοι and fragments of two more. They are dramatic scenes from low life: a procuress and her 'victim', the impudent lawcourt speech of a pimp, a schoolboy's flogging, women discussing art in a temple, a mistress' revenge on her unfaithful slave-lover, women discussing dildoes, their visit to a shady cobbler, a dream of the poet *qua* humble cottager. Herondas was at first hailed as an ultra-realist; but it has since been shown that his work fits in well with the literary approach of his contemporaries Callimachus and Theocritus. His invention of the μιμίαμβος is another example of that fusion of genres typical of the new poetics: (1) The low subject-matter and character-types are based on those of the mime, a form of dramatic popular entertainment dealing with (often sordid) scenes from daily life. Only in the works of Sophron of Syracuse (mid fifth cent.) had the mime achieved real literary status. Sophron wrote in his native Doric dialect in a kind of rhythmical prose, and he was much read in the third century (Theocritus *Idylls* 2 (*574–738*) and 15 adapt themes from Sophron into Doric hexameters: see p. 155, 217–18). (2) Language, metre and Ionic dialect are borrowed from Hipponax, a sixth-century Ephesian writer of bitter lampoons. He, too, was popular in the third century, inspiring most notably Callimachus' *Iambi* (frr. 191–225; cf. p. 83–4). He used the so-called 'limping iambic' (σκάζων, χωλίαμβος), an iambic line with long penultimate syllable, to produce a dragging effect of 'deliberate metrical ribaldry' (West, *GM* 41). The μιμίαμβοι are thus far from 'realistic' in that they employ metrical, linguistic and dialectal forms unused for several centuries.

If they were performed at all, the μιμίαμβοι were probably recited by a single talented declaimer rather than produced with a full 'cast'. They share with New Comedy an interest in character-drawing (ἠθοποιία) and the depiction of types. Womankind emerges from the pages of Herondas with little credit. The focus of interest in this first poem is not the faithful ἑταίρα (?: cf. 89 n.) Metriche but the old bawd Gyllis, who attempts to persuade her to take a new lover in the absence of her 'steady' partner Mandris. Both characters speak in clichés and pro-verbial language. By wedding precious and recherché form with platitudinously garrulous content Herondas has produced a strange mixture of pseudo-realism and extreme artifice.

Dialect. The most notable features of E. Ionic literary dialect in this poem are η for ᾱ, κ for π in κου, κοτέ, κόσος etc., and lack of rough breathing ('psilosis'); εο usually contracts to ευ (Attic ου).

Text. In places the papyrus is damaged or illegible. The text printed here is supplemented to show what seems to be the most likely meaning. Many of these supplements are extremely doubtful.

Bibl.: Edn: W. Headlam & A. D. Knox (Cambridge, 1922); I. C. Cunningham (Oxford, 1971). Gen.: Fraser II 876–8; G. Mastromarco, *The public of Herondas* (Eng. transl. by M. Nardella, Amsterdam, 1984); W. G. Arnott, 'Herodas and the kitchen sink', *G. & R.* n.s. 18 (1971) 121–32. Metre: West, *GM* 160–1.

> For the procuress figure cf. Ovid, *Amores* 1.8.

Title. The papyrus gives the title as Προκυκλί[ς] ἢ Μαστροπός. The latter word is a common term for 'pimp' or 'procuress' (cognate with μαστεύω, 'search out'); it may have been added by an ancient editor to explain προκυκλίς, a word of obscure etymology, which is found only here in extant literature.

1–2[1371–2] Hearing a violent knocking, Metriche assumes that some boorish rustic has arrived 'from the country'. There are several problems: (1) μή τις '⟨see⟩ if anyone . . .' is not a certain restoration, so that (2) παρ' ἡμέων is difficult in both sense and construction. 'Someone of ours', i.e. 'someone in our service' is possible (cf. Men. *Dysc.* 375 τὴν παρ' ἐμοῦ = 'mine'); the conjecture παρ' ἡμέας is much easier ('to our house'). Alternatively, -έων might suggest that a pres. part. should be restored. (3) In the papyrus ἀγροικίης is corrected from ἀποικίης, which some see as a reference to Mandris' absence in Egypt; but it is unlikely that a Greek would call Egypt simply 'the colony', even if it was at the forefront of his mind.

3[1373] τίς τὴν θύρην;: sc. ἀράσσει. **ἐγῶδε** = ἐγὼ ἥδε, 'me!'.

4[1374] ἦν: interj., = Lat. *en.*

5[1375] εἰς: Ionic for εἷ; found in Homer. **Φιλαινίδος:** a notorious fourth-cent. ἑταίρα called Philaenis wrote *On sexual positions.* The name of her daughter betrays Gyllis' dubious character.

6[1376] ἔνδον: with ἄγγειλον. εἴσω would be more normal, unless the implication is 'step in and shout your message' rather than 'go to your mistress and tell her...'.

7[1377] κάλει 'call her'. It is not at all clear who speaks this word. The text printed here assumes that it is an imperative spoken by Gyllis. Other editors attribute it to Threissa, who is immediately interrupted by Metriche (Θρ. καλεῖ – Μ. τίς ἐστιν;); others again attribute it to Metriche (κάλει . τίς ἐστιν; – 'call in ⟨whoever it is⟩. Who is it?'). **ἀμμίη:** child's word for nurse. Perhaps we are to assume that Gyllis brought up Metriche as well as Myrtale and Sime (89). Nurses often cause trouble where ἔρως is concerned: cf. Eur. *Hippol.*, etc.

8[1378] στρέψον τι: a phrase of uncertain meaning; probably 'withdraw a little', the trans. use (LSJ s.v. στρέφω D). **μοῖρ':** ironically high-flown.

9[1379] Γυλλίς: nom. for voc. (contrast 18, etc.) for metrical convenience. τί σὺ θεὸς πρὸς ἀνθρώπους; 'why the divine visitation?' (sc. ἥκεις) – further irony.

10[1380] κου = Lat. *fere*, 'about'.

11[1381] οὐδ' ὄναρ 'not even in a dream', a colloquial expression, = 'not at all'.

13[1383] μακρήν: adv.: *1223* n. λαύρηις 'alleys'.

14[1384] ἄχρις ἰγνύων προσέστηκεν 'approaches up to the knees', i.e. 'stands knee-deep'. ἰγνύς / ἰγνύη is properly the hollow at the back of the knee.

15[1385] δραίνω μυῖ' ὅσον: lit. 'I have strength as much as a fly'.

15–16[1385–6] τὸ . . . παρέστηκε: portentous moralizing. Gyllis refers repeatedly to old age and the brevity of life (19, 32, 37–8, 42–7, 63) in order to reinforce her *carpe diem* proposal.

16[1386] σκιή: the shadow of death.

17[1387] σίγη: imperative (Attic σίγα). **μὴ τοῦ χρόνου καταψεύδεο** 'don't slander your age', i.e. don't falsely accuse your years of diminishing your abilities. For this use of χρόνος for 'age' see LSJ s.v. II.

18[1388] εἰς: 5 n. **ἄγχειν** 'squeeze', a technical term in wrestling also used of violent lovemaking. Gyllis is not 'past it' sexually, but will have 'others yet' (**καὶ ἑτέρους**).

19[1389] σίλλαινε 'have your joke' (σίλλος = 'lampoon') implies 'my days for love are gone'. **ταῦτα** probably refers to ἄγχειν and lovemaking in general, not to σίλλαινε: joking is not a natural characteristic of young women, but lovemaking is – or so Gyllis wishes to argue.

20[1390] πρόσεστιν 'belongs to', i.e. 'is characteristic behaviour of', a common use. **ἀλλ' οὐ τοῦτο μή σε θερμήνηι**: the speaker and the meaning of these words, and the force of οὐ...μή, are uncertain. οὐ μή + aor. subj. usually indicates strong denial. Evidence for the same construction indicating strong prohibition is not watertight (see Goodwin, *GMT* §§ 301, 364), but that may be the sense here. If Gyllis speaks, the meaning might be '⟨young women are made for love⟩ but don't let that put ideas into your head (lit. 'put you on heat'). *But* ⟨despite that warning⟩ what a long time you've been suffering chastity...'. If Metriche speaks she might mean 'but don't let this (the fact that young women are made for love) put ideas into your head' (sc. about finding a lover for me). Some critics, taking ταῦτα in 19 to refer to σίλλαινε, take Metriche to mean 'but don't let this (sc. my jesting) make you angry'. Of these possibilities the first seems most likely.

21–48[1391–1418] Gyllis 'softens up' Metriche by casting doubt on Mandris' fidelity. Egypt is a place of unrivalled attractions. Life is uncertain; all one's eggs should not be in the same basket.

21[1391] χηραίνεις = χηρεύεις, 'you are separated ⟨from Mandris⟩'. The verb is not found elsewhere.

22[1392] τρύχουσα 'wearing out' the bed during restless, lonely nights.

24[1394] οὐδὲ γράμμα 'not even a single letter ⟨of the alphabet⟩'.

25[1395] πέπωκεν ἐκ καινῆς 'he has drunk from a new ⟨cup⟩', i.e. he has found a new mistress: an appropriate image from the lips of a bibulous old woman (cf. 67–82 n.).

26[1396] κεῖ = ἐκεῖ: cf. (ἐ)κεῖνος. **τῆς θεοῦ**: Aphrodite, goddess of pleasure.

27[1397] ὄσσ' ἔστι κου καὶ γίνετ(αι) 'whatever exists and is produced', an all-inclusive phrase.

28–32[1398–1402] Egyptian allurements tumble from the lips of garrulous Gyllis in amusing disorder – eulogy of the Ptolemies from an unlikely source.

28[1398] δύναμις: Egypt is the centre of power. εὐδίη 'peace', lit. 'fair weather'.

29[1399] θέαι 'shows', 'spectacles'. See p. 4. νεηνίσκοι: potential friends (or boyfriends) for Mandris.

30[1400] θεῶν ἀδελφῶν τέμενος: Ptolemy Philadelphus and his sister-wife Arsinoe were deified (while still living) in 272/1 B.C. χρηστός: sc. ἐστι.

31[1401] Μουσῆιον: see p. 4.

32–3[1402–3] οὐ negates κεκαύχηται: women 'as many as heaven does not boast it bears stars', i.e. more in number than heaven has stars.

32[1402] τὴν Ἀιδεω Κούρην: Kore = Persephone, wife of Hades.

34[1404] τὴν δ' ὄψιν 'in appearance', acc. of respect, as καλλονήν in 35.

35[1405] κριθῆναι: infin. of purpose.

35–6[1405–6] λάθοιμ' αὐτὰς | γρύξασα: Gyllis superstitiously hopes that she has escaped the notice of the goddesses – they might be angry at her comparison.

36–7[1406–7] κοίην ... ψυχὴν | ἔχουσα 'what's got into you...?', 'why this attitude of...?'.

37[1407] θάλπεις τὸν δίφρον 'warm your chair' like a lethargic stay-at-home.

37–8[1407–8] κατ' οὖν λήσεις | γηράσα = λήσεις οὖν καταγηράσα 'you'll be old before you know it'. οὖν in tmesis with compound verbs, conveying liveliness and immediacy, is a feature of Ionic; here, if the supplement is right, a verb is interposed between the prep. and its participle.

38[1408] σεῦ τώριον τέφρη κάψει 'ash will devour, lit. gulp down, your youthful bloom (τὸ ὥριον)'. Her beauty is bright fire hidden under gradually encroaching ash.

39[1409] ἄλληι: adv., 'elsewhere'.

40[1410] κιλαρὴ κατάστηθι 'and make yourself well disposed'.

41–2[1411–12] Ships generally had two anchors to prevent drifting.

42[1412] κεῖνος ἦν ἔλθηι 'if He should come', meaning Death.

43[1413] οὐ μηδὲ εἶς: οὐ μή makes this a strong negative, 'absolutely no one': cf. 20 n. Hiatus is allowed between οὐδέ /μηδέ and εἶς: cf. 45, 48, 73.

44[1414] δεινά: adv.

45[1415] καταιγίσας 'arriving with a rush'. καταιγίς = 'hurricane'. ἔπνευσε: gnomic aor.

47[1417] μήτις: when a negative reply is sought the question is introduced by μή ('there isn't anyone near, is there?').

48–66[1418–36] The proposition: Gryllus, a wealthy and wholesome international athlete, has fallen in love with M.; she should make him her second anchor. Gyllis attempts to make Gryllus an attractive prospect by emphasizing that despite his physical prowess he is gentle and modest. In describing him she uses terms more appropriate to a girl: he is given a double metronymic (50); he 'would not move a straw' (54), a phrase elsewhere used of demure maidenly behaviour (Arist. *Lys.* 474; cf. Herondas 3.66–7); he is 'an untouched seal as regards Aphrodite' (55), an image far more appropriate to female than to male virginity; and he cries piteously like a girl in love (59–60). This flattering picture, which is intended to inspire Metriche with pity for the wretched virgin, is undercut by Gryllus' name. Γρύλλος means 'Grunter'; and Γρύλλοι was the name given to ludicrous-looking dancers with disproportionate limbs depicted on vases and wall-paintings: cf. Pliny, *Hist. Nat.* 35.114. Cf. 5 n.

49[1419] χρεῖζουσ' = Attic χρήιζουσα (cf. 1 Θρέισσα = Θρῆισσα). The order is ἅ σοι ἀπαγγεῖλαι χρεῖζουσ' ὧδ' ἔβην.

50[1420] 'Gryllus son of Mataline daughter of Pataecion' (both women's names).

51[1421] νικέων 'the winner of...'. ἐν Πυθοῖ: Pytho is a poetic synonym for Delphi, where the Pythian games were held. Cf. 862.

52[1422] ἐν Κορίνθωι: the Isthmian games. τοὺς ἴουλον ἀνθεῦντας 'those in bloom as to their down', i.e. adolescents blooming with downy cheeks. Understand καθεῖλε from 53.

53[1423] Πίσηι: synonym of Olympia. καθεῖλε 'overcame', lit. 'brought down'.

54[1424] τὸ καλόν 'nicely'. οὐδὲ κάρφος . . . κινέων 'he wouldn't move a straw', roughly equivalent to our 'he wouldn't hurt a fly'. Strong but gentle.

55[1425] ἄθικτος ἐς Κυθηρίην σφρηγίς: athletes in training abstained from sexual activity; but Gyllis is no doubt exaggerating.

56[1426] ἰδών σε: 46, 638 nn. καθόδωι τῆς Μίσης 'at the ⟨festival of the⟩ Descent of Mise'. Mis(m)e is an obscure figure, originally perhaps daughter of Isis. καθόδωι suggests that she descended to the underworld like Persephone (ἡ Κάθοδος = second day of the Thesmophoria).

57[1427] ἔρωτι: perhaps to be taken with both verbs: love made his inwards seethe and goads him on.

58[1428] μευ οὔτε: scanned as two syllables: cf. 69 ἐγὼ ἐξ, 80 τοῦ ἀκρήτου.

59[1429] μευ καταχλαίει 'he weeps all over me' (=κλαίει κατ' ἐμοῦ).

60[1430] ταταλίζει: τατί is a term of endearment; so the meaning must be 'wheedle', 'coax': he wants Gyllis to approach Metriche on his behalf.

61[1431] ὦ τέκνον μοι: the phrase is used several times in Eur. (e.g. *Orestes* 124) in solemn addresses. Gyllis hopes to lend dignity to her dubious proposal. μοι: the so-called 'possessive' dat. (K.–G. 1 423), which is in fact a relic of an old gen. form μοι.

62[1432] δὸς τῆι θεῶι: she should 'offer up' her error to Aphrodite, who will be pleased with it (imagery of a votive offering).

62–3[1432–3] κατάρτησον | σαυτήν: very obscure. καταρτάω τι ἔκ τινος = 'hang up X on Y'; so perhaps 'hang yourself on pleasure', i.e. dedicate yourself to it, continuing the imagery of 61–2.

63[1433] προσβλέψαν: catching sight of you, i.e. reaching you, before you know it. The participle is attracted into the tense of the main verb, with which it coincides in time. This attraction is regular with λανθάνω: see Goodwin, *GMT* § 144.

64[1434] πρήξεις 'will gain'.

65[1435] δοθήσεταί τι: Gryllus gratified will be generous. σκέψαι: 2nd pers. imper. mid. of σκέπτομαι.

66[1436] πείσθητί μευ: πείθομαι is sometimes found with gen. instead of dat., perhaps by analogy with ἀκούω, etc.

67–82[1437–52] Metriche rejects Gyllis' improper suggestions with gentle indignation and tries to divert her with the offer of a drink. Old bawds were notoriously bibulous: in *Amores* 1.8 Ovid calls his *lena* Διψάς, 'Thirsty'.

67[1437] τὰ λευκὰ τῶν τριχῶν 'the whiteness of your hair'.

68[1438] κατάπλωσιν: she swears by (her confidence in) his return.

71[1441] 'I would have made her lame to match her lame songs', χωλ(ά) obj. of ἀείδειν, χωλήν obj. of ἐξεπαίδευσα. There is a sly reference to the poem's choliambic metre – cf. Call. fr. 203.13–14, 65–6 τὰ μέτρα . . . | τὰ χωλὰ τίκτειν.

74–5[1444–5] There are two possible meanings, depending on whether the stress is placed on πρέπει or on νέηις: either 'you should talk to young women in terms befitting your (venerable) age', i.e. 'you should know better at your age', or 'make your old wives' propositions to *younger* women' (sc. I'm old enough not to be taken in – contrast 19). ὄν = ὅν (sc. μῦθον); γρήιη for γραῖα (=γραῦς) is found only here. For the adjectival use cf. *1343* n.

76[1446] τὴν Πυθέω 'daughter of Pythes'. The patronymic lends dignity to Metriche's repudiation of the proposal. (It may not be coincidental that Pythes was the father of the poet Hipponax, whose metre and dialect Her. imitates.)

78–9[1448–9] Either (1) a formula of transition, 'Gyllis doesn't need words such as these' (sc. 'let's change the subject' or 'the words she *does* need are an invitation to drink') or (2) a formula of dismissal, 'Gyllis doesn't need talking to like that', i.e. she knows the facts well already. φασί: this, too, is ambiguous: it may refer either to the proverbial nature of the whole expression ('as the saying goes') or to the fact that G. is a well known bibber ('they tell me . . .').

79[1449] τὴν μελαινίδ᾿ ἔκτριψον 'rub clean the cup'. The μελαινίς was a black shell. Cups were often named after objects whose shape they resembled.

80[1450] ἐκτημόρους τρεῖς 'three sixth-parts', i.e. half a χοῦς, the size of which varied from area to area.

81[1451] ἐπιστάξασα: lit. 'add by dripping': she should 'go easy' on the water – Gyllis likes a strong tipple. καλῶς: probably = 'no, thanks' – only a token refusal. See Gow on Theoc. 15.3.

82–5[1452–5] Text, meaning and speaker-attributions in these lines are extremely uncertain.

82[1452] δεῖξον: 'show it ⟨to me⟩' makes poor sense, and δέξον (<δέχομαι) would be little better. Perhaps Her. is using δεῖξον in the sense of Homeric δεικνύμενος, etc. (<δεικανάομαι), 'toast'; but since the end of the line is lost nothing can be said with confidence. παραλλάσσειν 'to change your course', i.e. to persuade you to veer from the straight and narrow.

83[1453] τῶν ἱρῶν: cf. 61–2. Metriche ought not to neglect Aphrodite's holy rites in stubborn chastity.

84[1454] ὧν οὕνεκέν μοι – : she tries to revive the subject of Gryllus, but Metriche cuts her short. ὤνα' οὐδ' ὅσσον 'you have profited not a bit', i.e. you've got nowhere. ὤναο = ὤνησας, aor. of ὀνίνημι. οὐδ' ὅσον is a standard phrase: see Gow on [Theoc.] 9.20.

85[1455] ὥς σοι εὖ γένοιτο 'cheers!', raising the cup. ὥς = οὕτως. μᾶ: an exclamation of admiration, indignation, etc. used only by women. Its original meaning seems to have been 'mother'.

88[1458] εὐτύχει: a standard formula for 'farewell'.

88–9[1458–9] ἀσφαλίζευ . . . | σαυτήν 'take care of yourself'. σώζου is commoner.

89[1459] Μυρτάλη τε καὶ Σίμη: ἑταῖραι over whom Gyllis has greater control. She hopes that they will stay young = attractive = profitable. The fact that Metriche is classed with them suggests that she, too, is a ἑταίρα, not a married woman. The names of these two are appropriate to their profession: myrtle was associated with things venerean; snub-nosedness betokened a wanton temperament (σιμός a common epithet of goats).

90[1460] ἔστ(ε) 'as long as'.

XXV

Machon

Machon (fl. c. 270–250 B.C.), comic poet and scholar, was born in Corinth or Sicyon but lived most of his life in Alexandria. Of his highly acclaimed comedies only two short fragments survive (19–20 Gow), but we have considerable remains of his Χρεῖαι or *Useful Anecdotes*. The χρεία-genre had existed at least since the fourth century, and may have been intended originally for pedagogical purposes. In Machon's case the title is a joke: *his* anecdotes are far from improving. They record, in chatty language and comic iambic metre, the scabrous, salacious and amusing *bons mots* of famous courtesans, parasites and musicians of the fifth and fourth centuries. In the following anecdote Philoxenus, writer of dithyrambs (*PMG* 814–35, ?836) and notorious epicure, resigns himself to a suitable death in language befitting his profession (14–17, 19–21).

Bibl.: Edn: A. S. F. Gow, *Machon* (Cambridge, 1965). Gen.: Fraser I 621–3, II 878–80.

1[1461] ὑπερβολῆι 'exceedingly', qualifying ὀψοφάγον (3). Emphatic position to stress the overall extravagance of his character. **Φιλόξενον**: Philoxenus of Cythera (435–380 B.C.). He lived for a time in Syracuse at the court of Dionysius I. Whilst imprisoned in the stone-quarries on a charge of treason he composed his famous dithyramb Κύκλωψ ἢ Γαλάτεια, which inspired Theocritus *Idylls* 6 and 11 (see pp. 148–9).

3[1463] εἶτα 'and so', denoting vague consequence and implying a chatty raconteur (cf. 7). **πηχῶν δυεῖν**: about three feet long. Gen. of quality. The form δυεῖν coexisted with δυοῖν in Attic after the fourth century.

6[1466] ὑπό: for this use of ὑπό + gen. for the onset of illness, etc., see LSJ s.v. A.II.3 and cf. *612*.

7–9[1467–9] ἰατροῦ τινος . . . ὃς εἶπεν: such transitions from gen. abs. to nom. are not rare in Greek, even without the intervening relative. Goodwin, *GMT* §850, says their purpose is 'to make the participial clause more prominent'; but here perhaps the effect is one of chatty inconsequence.

8–9[1468–9] φαύλως πάνυ | φερόμενον 'in a very bad way'.

10[1470] διατίθου: often of 'putting one's affairs in order'.

11[1471] ὥρας ἑβδόμης: the gen. implies 'in the course of...'. The seventh hour of the day, day of the month and month of the year were considered critical for illness.

13[1473] δεδιώικηται 'is set in order'. The form with both reduplication and augment (cf. reg. δεδιήιτηκα from διαιτέω, and aorists such as ἠνεσχόμην and ἠνώχλησα) is rarer than simple διώικηται.

14–17[1474–7] He speaks of his poems as grown children honoured with wreaths of victory, and consecrates them to the Muses and to the trusteeship of Aphrodite, goddess of charm and grace, and Dionysus, patron of dithyrambic competitions.

14[1474] σὺν θεοῖς 'by the gods' grace'. **καταλιμπάνω**: *459* n.

16[1476] συντρόφοις: he was a genius from the cradle.

17[1477] There is no verb to govern ἐπιτρόπους. Meineke assumed words were missing after Μούσαις; the text printed here follows Gow in making Philoxenus break off in his haste to proceed to more important matters.

19–21[1479–81] Timotheus of Miletus (450–360 B.C.), lyric poet

(*PMG* 777–804) and contemporary of Philoxenus. Nothing of relevance is known of his *Niobe*. Lines 20–1 are probably a parody of a passage in Timotheus or Philoxenus: **μοῖρα νύχιος** and **κλύειν** are high poeticisms.

21–2[1481–2] 'You can't take it with you' is a piece of proverbial wisdom (cf. *1737–8*); but the octopus will be safely stashed away inside Philoxenus.

22[1482] ἀποτρέχειν: he has to hurry because the ferry (πορθμίδ') is about to depart (20 χωρεῖν) – εἴ τις ἔτι πλεῖ, σπευδέτω is Charon's cry at Arist. *Frogs* 197. This ἵνα-clause is displaced so that the 'punch-line' can come at the end.

23[1483] ἀπόδοτε: addressed to his servants.

XXVI

Epigrams

From the time of the introduction of writing in Greece until the end of the Byzantine era the epigram, especially in the form of epitaphs and celebratory inscriptions, never lost its popularity. Its aim – to give fresh expression within a small space to the all-too-familiar themes of public beneficence and private grief – made it a form of obvious appeal to Hellenistic poets, who may have been the first to compose non-functional, literary epigrams. (Poems of this type attributed to Anacreon, Simonides and Plato are probably by later hands – see *FGE* pp. 119–27.) Epitaphs and dedications, both real and fictitious, were produced in large numbers, and the genre was expanded to include subjects familiar from early lyric poetry and drinking-songs – love, sex, humour, the symposium. (Short elegiac poems in the Theognidean corpus had treated similar themes.) Imitation and variation were of the essence: poets attempted to describe similar objects or bemoan similar deaths in novel and interesting ways (cf. *1558–61, 1562–9*). That striving for 'point' so noticeable in the poems of Martial and in e.g. the post-Lear limerick is not often to be found in Hellenistic epigrams. Some poets, especially Callimachus, experimented with unusual metres; but the vast majority of poems were written in elegiacs or iambic trimeters. Most epigrams are written in epic/Ionic dialect, some in Doric, and some apparently in a mixture of both.

A collection of epigrams by 40 Hellenistic and supposedly pre-Hellenistic poets was made by Meleager (q.v. below) in about 100 B.C.; it was entitled Στέφανος, or *Garland*. This, together with several anthologies of poems from the Roman imperial period, provided material for a huge collection by Constantinus Cephalas in the early tenth century. Cephalas' work in turn formed the basis for the *Greek Anthology* or *Anthologia Palatina* (*AP*), compiled later in the same century, which disposes its 3700 poems according to theme (epitaphs, dedications, erotic and satirical pieces, etc.). In the selection given here, which follows a similar arrangement, ten named poets are represented:

Alcaeus of Messene (fl. c. 210–190 B.C.), author of a number of vitriolic attacks on Philip V of Macedon and of various more conventional pieces.

Antipater of Sidon (fl. mid-second cent.) was famed as an extemporizer of verses (Cic. *De oratore* 3.194). He specialized in elaborately rhetorical epitaphs and dedicatory poems.

Anyte of Tegea (first half of third cent.). Her interest in animals and the countryside, and the fact that she lived in Arcadia and wrote in Doric, have led some to believe that she is linked with the origins of bucolic poetry. Almost all of her poems are quatrains.

Asclepiades of Samos (born 340–320 B.C. – contemporary with Philetas, older than Callimachus), also called Sicelidas, praised by Theocritus (*Id.* 7.39–41) but included among the Telchines by the ancient commentator on Callimachus' *Reply* (see *9–12* n.). He was of great importance in the development of the literary epigram; his innovations possibly included the 'snatch-of-conversation' poem and epitaphs on earlier poets. Most of his poems deal with heterosexual love, and it seems likely that he originated subjects which later became clichés of erotic poetry. Like Anyte, he favoured the quatrain. His poems, together with those of Hedylus and Posidippus, may have been published in a collection called the Σωρός ('Heap'). He wrote hexameter and lyric poems, now lost: the Asclepiad metres were named after him (see p. 173).

Callimachus (see p. 83–4): 63 epigrams by Callimachus survive. They formed only a small part of his total oeuvre; but they show him to be the foremost exponent of the genre in antiquity. Here, too, his striving for variety is apparent: the poems are highly original, often personal, strikingly phrased, experimental in both metre and subject-matter.

Heraclitus of Halicarnassus (?older contemporary of Callimachus). See on *1496–1501*. *1488–95* is his sole surviving poem.

Leonidas of Tarentum (early / middle third cent.), most influential and most imitated of Hellenistic epigrammatists. His poems reflect contemporary artistic and poetic interest in the depiction of lower-class life (cf. Theocritus' pastorals, Callimachus' *Hecale,* Herondas, etc.). He wrote numerous epitaphs for humble craftsmen and fishermen, and dedication-poems for the tools of their trades. This semi-technical subject-matter means that his work is full of neologisms and recondite vocabulary. A high proportion of spondees results in a slow, dragging effect peculiar to Leonidas' verse.

Meleager of Gadara (fl. 110–90 B.C.) was born of Syrian parents and spent his youth in Tyre (*1570*); in old age he became a citizen of Cos. He prefaced his *Garland* with a long poem comparing each contributor to a different flower; and in amongst the selection he scattered epigrams of his own, variations on themes treated by these earlier writers. His elegant and mannered poems display an exceptionally wide range of style and treatment: see *HE* II pp. 591–3, where Gow / Page characterize him as 'concise, lucid and picturesque'. His love-poems, with their ingenious imagery, were particularly influential in later times. He wrote Menippean satires in a mixture of prose and verse, now lost (*1573* n.).

Philodemus of Gadara (c. 110–c. 40 B.C.), Epicurean philosopher and many-faceted scholar, flourished in Rome under the patronage of L. Calpurnius Piso and influenced many contemporary Roman writers. His prose works were unknown until excavations of Piso's villa at Herculaneum unearthed several long fragments. As an epigrammatist he is clearly in the tradition of his fellow-countryman Meleager, specializing in original and stylish variations on erotic themes.

Posidippus of Pella in Macedonia (fl. 280–270 B.C.) probably lived for part of his life in Alexandria. He may have published a collection of poems jointly with Asclepiades and Hedylus. (see p. 244).

Bibl.: All epigrams in the present selection are to be found in *HE, GP* or *FGE,* and in D. L. Page's Oxford Text *Epigrammata Graeca* (1975; abbreviated to *OCT*); see app. crit. for references. There is a Loeb text of the whole *Greek Anthology* by W. R. Paton (5 vols, 1916–18). Gen.: Fraser I 553–617, II 791–869; G. Giangrande, 'Sympotic literature and epigram', *Entretiens Hardt* 14 (1967) 93–174; D. H. Garrison, *Mild frenzy: a reading of the Hellenistic love epigram = Hermes Einzelschriften* 41

(1978); S. L. Tarán, *The art of variation in the Hellenistic epigram* (Leiden, 1979).

1

An epitaph for Saon, son of Dicon, from Acanthus (probably the place of that name in Chalcidice). Whether or not he was a real person is unknown. His name, father and place of origin are listed without elaboration, and the closing sentence is phrased with equal spareness. These two simple sets of words serve to highlight by contrast the central metaphor, which ties the lines together. Saon 'sleeps a holy sleep', holy because 'the righteous dead' (G.–P.) are holy. Sleep and rest are death-clichés in Greek as in English ('Here lies . . .', 'R.I.P.'); but Call.'s words here are far from banal. (1) The metaphor is a Homeric allusion: *Il.* 11.241–2 (Iphidamas brutally killed by Agamemnon) ὣς ὁ μὲν αὖθι πεσὼν κοιμήσατο χάλκεον ὕπνον | οἰκτρός. Call. changes death's aspect by substituting ἱερόν for the unyielding χάλκεον; and in doing so he changes the order of verb and noun-phrase. (2) The second sentence is tellingly ambiguous. Most editors choose to print a colon after κοιμᾶται, making the second sentence an explanation of the choice of words in the first: 'Do not use the word "die" in connection with good men', because (e.g.) it is too final, too harsh. This meaning is suggested, too, by the juxtaposition of κοιμᾶται and θνήισκειν, which conveys the emphasis 'sleeps ⟨yes, *sleeps*⟩, not "is dead" . . .'. But the words θνήισκειν μὴ λέγε τοὺς ἀγαθούς literally mean 'Do not say that good men die' – the implication being that they in some sense survive (e.g. through their good works and in the memories of men). This is the meaning if a full stop is placed after κοιμᾶται. A dash preserves the ambiguity. (In Call.'s time there were no such subtleties of punctuation to hinder the range of meaning.) The poem is thus simultaneously praise (he was good) and consolation (he is not altogether 'dead').

2

An epitaph, possibly fictitious, for a 12-year-old boy: another brilliant distich. Nicoteles was everything to his father, and it is fitting that δωδεκέτη . . . Νικοτέλην, words in agreement and of identical rhythm, should enclose the whole poem. The boy's age is mentioned first, sounding the note of pathos: δωδεκέτη in this position serves a semi-predicative function, the sense being 'Twelve years old was his (τόν) son when...'. In the middle stands the father's name, ending the first line as that of his son ends the second. Juxtaposition of παῖδα and πατήρ points the unnaturalness of father burying son. ἀπέθηκε suggests deposition of a precious object (ἀποθήκη = place for storage); but this most precious of all possessions can never be retrieved. In laying down his son Philippus has laid aside his expectations of contented old age: the son is dead, but the father lives on – in hopelessness. The poem is heavily alliterative, especially in π/φ and δ/τ.

3

On Aretemias of Cnidus, who died in giving birth to twins, only one of whom survived. The poem purports to be an epitaph; but in fact the epitaph is quoted in lines 5–8, and the poem as a whole is a carefully contrived dramatic scene. Greek tombs were often placed at the roadside, and often in epitaphs the reader is addressed as 'passer-by' or 'stranger' (thus ξεῖν' in 5). This poem takes that convention outside the epitaph itself: an ill-defined and undefinable speaker addresses a traveller and, apparently out of curiosity at the sight of a newly dug grave, urges that they should read the inscription. The poem thus consists of a pair of speeches, the second quoted by the speaker of the first – curiosity aroused and satisfied.

The tone of the four-line epitaph spoken by Aretemias ('Virtuous'), wife of Euphron ('Kindly'), conveys the gentle personality of the (probably fictitious) dead woman and serves to counteract the effect of the desolate scene sketched in lines 1–2. Briefly she lists her name, place of birth and husband. She 'came to his bed', a common expression for marriage; but the marriage-bed soon became bed of pain (ὠδίνων), childbed, deathbed. It is not her nature to complain: ὠδίνων οὐκ ἄμορος is a brave understatement. She bore twins, and one died with her; but the final couplet glides over the negative fact of these deaths and looks to the future: one child may be dead, but the other survives and will care for her husband, its father, when he is old. She in turn keeps one child as a reminder of him: 'a novel turn', as G.–P. remark, since 'memories are usually left by the survivors to the dead'.

1[1488] ἀρτίσκαπτος 'newly dug'. μετώπωι 'face'. Wilting garlands, laid against the tombstone, move in the wind.

2[1489] φύλλων: ancient funerary garlands consisted of leaves, not flowers.

3[1490] διακρίναντες: an unusual use of the verb, perhaps combining the meanings 'make out', 'decipher' and 'investigate', 'examine'. For this use of the aor. participle expressing time coincident with that of the main verb see Goodwin, *GMT* § 150 and cf. *1433* n.

3–4[1490–1] 'The construction is ἴδωμεν τίνος ὀστέα φατὶ ὁ πέτρος περιστέλλειν' (G.–P.).

4[1491] λευρά 'smooth', presumably of bones stripped of flesh by cremation. **περιστέλλειν**: the rarer meaning 'protect' is more suitable for a tombstone than the more usual 'enclose'. **τίνος** is unusually delayed, perhaps to emphasize that it is the *identity* of the dead person which is important. Cf. *1614*.

7[1494] δισσά: sc. τέκνα.

4

A brief elegy on the death of Heraclitus of Halicarnassus, author of the preceding epigram, about whom nothing of substance is known. The tone shifts from melancholy to optimism. Lines 1–3 evoke the shock of bad news: 'someone mentioned' Heraclitus' death, perhaps casually in conversation. As soon as Callimachus heard the news, he wept and remembered: the simple connective δέ's and the juxtaposed verbs in line 2 reproduce the quick sequence of emotions from hearing to sorrow to remembrance. What he fondly remembered is 'how many times we both set the sun in talk': their words continued into the night. After this brief recollection of former happiness the poet moves back to his sense of loss. ἀμφότεροι at the end of line 2 is the link between the sorrowing με at the end of 1 and σύ in the same metrical position in 3. ἀλλὰ σὺ μέν που, four small words preceded by a strong pause, give a diminuendo effect which reinforces the uncertainty (που) about Heraclitus' death: how and when he died are unknown. Line 4 gives a reason for the poet's ignorance: Heraclitus was his ξένος in far-away Halicarnassus. 'Four times long ago' Heraclitus became dust and ashes; but his 'nightingales' live on. It is possible that a collection of Heraclitus' poems was entitled

'Αηδόνες. Even if this is not so, and the word is only a picturesque synonym for ἐλεγεῖα, the point is the same: Hades will not lay his plunderer's hand on them, and they will remain as Heraclitus' μνῆμα for future generations. Thus the sadly retrospective ἐμνήσθην of line 2 is counteracted by the last phrase of the poem, the more optimistic future οὐκ ἐπὶ χεῖρα βαλεῖ (and τεαὶ...ἀηδόνες complements τεὸν μόρον). Nightingales are particularly apposite here: (1) They sing after dark and thus, metaphorically, after death – a parallel to Callimachus' and Heraclitus' conversations long into the night. (2) There may be an allusion to the supposed derivation of ἀηδών from ἀεί + ᾄδω (cf. *Et. Gud.* p. 29 de Stephani). (3) The nightingale's song was proverbially a lamentation (ἐλεγεῖον): Heraclitus' ἀηδόνες can be imagined as bewailing their own poet's death.

1–2[1496–7] ἐς δέ με δάκρυ | ἤγαγεν probably = 'brought me to tears', ἐς qualifying δάκρυ, not the interposed με. It seems just possible, however, that ἔς με could = ἐμοί (cf. Call. *Hymn to Dem.* 17 ἃ δάκρυον ἄγαγε Δηοῖ); and the idea of a messenger bringing tears might be thought superior.

3[1498] ἠέλιον . . . κατεδύσαμεν: a transitive version of the Homeric ἠέλιος κατέδυ, 'the sun set'. **λέσχηι:** a Homeric *hapax* (*Od.* 18.329), = 'lounging-place'. Here, however, the later meaning 'conversation' is more suitable.

4[1499] τετράπαλαι: a colloquial formation, perhaps to lend a conversational tone. **σποδιή:** another Homeric *hapax* (*Od.* 5.488).

5[1500] ἀηδόνες: cf. *13–16*n.

6[1501] ἀρπακτής: a variation (if MSS -ής is right) of the Homeric *hapax* ἀρπακτήρ (*Il.* 24.262).

Classical scholars have approved this poem as a heartfelt expression of grief miraculously untainted by Callimachus' usual learned predilections. It is therefore important to note that even so 'sincere' a poem as this depends for full appreciation on a knowledge of etymology and of the Homeric lexicon. To a learned Hellenistic reader the poem's appeal lay not in its 'emotional' strength alone, but in the combination of that aspect with the telling use of etymology and Homeric words and phrases to produce a complex and sophisticated whole: *ars latet arte sua.*

Bibl.: J. G. MacQueen, 'Death and immortality: a study of the Heraclitus epigram of Callimachus', *Ramus* 11 (1982) 48–56.

5

An elegy on the death of Heliodora. The poem is a tour-de-force of repetition and responsion, characteristics of the Greek ritual lament (δάκρυα 1 & 3, -δώρα 1 ∼ δωροῦμαι 3, δάκρυα δυσδάκρυτα 3, μνᾶμα... μνᾶμα 4, πόθων 4 ∼ ποθεινόν 7, φιλο- 4 ∼ φίλαν 5, οἰκτρά... οἰκτρά 5, αἰάζω 6 ∼ αἰαῖ 7, Ἀχέρ-... χάριν 6, ἅρπασεν 7 & 8, παν-... παν- 9; cf. p. 218–19), and of elegant variation (νέρθε 1 / εἰς Ἀΐδαν 2 / ἐν φθιμένοις 5 / εἰς Ἀχέροντα 6; στοργᾶς 2 / πόθων & φιλοφροσύνας 4; λείψανον 2 / μνᾶμα 4 / χάριν 6; θάλος 7 / ἄνθος 8). Each of the first three pentameters begins with a spondaic first-person verb; lines 2 and 6 have in addition a strong pause after this first word, followed by parallel appositional phrases. In lines 1–2 there may be a play on Heliodora's name, which means 'gift of the sun': now she is in the darkness of Hades, where Meleager will send his own gifts of tears. His feelings towards her are described in terms of affection (στοργᾶς, 2) and kindliness (φιλοφροσύνας, 4) as well as desire (πόθων, 4); and ποθεινόν in line 7 means 'missed' as well as 'beloved'. λείψανον (2) and μνᾶμα (4), 'relic' and 'memorial', are here unusually applied to the survivor rather than the deceased (cf. on *1488–95*). After the heightened emotion of 1–6 the final couplet (which G.–P. call 'dull') is a gentle prayer, a novel variation on the theme 'May earth not lie heavy on your bones'. G.–P. feel that 'the note of true sorrow is not sounded' in this poem. Quite what the role of 'true sorrow' might be in so self-conscious a genre as the Greek epigram is not an easy question to answer.

1–2[1502–3] καὶ **νέρθε** goes with σοι, **διὰ χθονός** with δωροῦμαι.

1[1502] Ἡλιοδώρα: one of several perhaps fictitious female addressees of Mel.'s poems.

3[1504] δάκρυα δυσδάκρυτα 'tears wept in wretchedness'.

5[1506] οἰκτρά: n. pl. as adv.

7[1508] ἐμοί: probably with ποθεινόν ('missed by me') rather than with ποῦ. **θάλος**: epic word for a youthful, thriving person (< θάλλω); cf. *57* ἀμφιθαλεῖ. **ἅρπασεν** "Αιδας: cf. *1501*.

8[1509] ἔφυρε: aor. of φύρω, 'defile'. **κόνις**: perhaps an allusion to the ashes of cremation.

9[1510] ἀλλά: this word often introduces prayers (cf. *401*, *1193*); but here it could be adversative, implying 'but ⟨despite the fact that her flower is defiled⟩ ...'.

10[1511] ἐναγκάλισαι: aor. imper. of ἐναγκαλίζομαι, 'take in one's arms'.

Bibl.: S. G. P. Small, 'The composition of "Anth. Pal.," vɪɪ, 476', *A.J.Ph.* 72 (1951) 47–56.

6

On a girl who died on her wedding night. At least two *Garland* poets, Erinna and Antipater, had composed (pseudo-) epitaphs on this theme. Like theirs, Meleager's version plays upon the similarity between the trappings of marriage and of death: lights, noise and a bed. Neither husband nor cause of death is mentioned. The poem is symmetrically constructed in four end-stopped couplets, the sense running on at the end of each hexameter: (1) The theme stated: not marriage but death. (2) Marriage: joyful sounds at evening. (3) Death: mournful sounds at dawn. (4) Death and marriage: the same torches served for both.

1[1512] ἐπινυμφίδιον 'on her wedding day' she received not γάμον (her first sexual experience) but death. Cf. Soph. *Ant.* 810–16.

2[1513] παρθενίας ἄμματα: i.e. the knots fastening the girdle which symbolized her virginity: cf. *1208*.

3[1514] νύμφας ἐπὶ διχλίσιν: the double doors of the bedchamber (= θαλάμων θύραι, 4). ἄχευν: Doric for ἦχουν.

4[1515] θαλάμων ἐπλαταγεῦντο θύραι: a bride was consigned to her bedroom to the accompaniment of an ἐπιθαλάμιον, a song sung to the pipes by a chorus of girls (cf. Theoc. *Id.* 18). ἐπλαταγεῦντο probably refers to their beating the doors in a token ritual attempt to 'rescue' their companion.

5[1516] ἀῶιοι: *64* n. In the morning the same chorus returned to sing the διεγερτικόν or 'waking-up song'; but Clearista would never wake again. ἀνέκραγον: sc. οἱ λωτοί. ἐκ: with σιγαθείς (tmesis); aor. of sudden action.

6[1517] γοερὸν φθέγμα μεθαρμόσατο 'the Marriage-God changed his sorrowful voice', i.e. changed it so that it became sorrowful. μεθαρμόζω is usually constructed with εἰς or πρός, but occasionally it is found with a simple acc. and a 'proleptic' adjective.

7[1518] ἐδαιδούχουν 'cast light' (LSJ do not recognize this meaning of the verb).

8[1519] νέρθεν: not used of motion towards: so 'they showed her the way in the world below' (not 'the way to Hades'). Torches were left in Greek tombs to light the corpse's way. Clearista's death followed so swiftly on her marriage that the same torches served for both ceremonies.

7

On Teleutagoras, a merchant lost at sea; ostensibly perhaps an inscription for his cenotaph (7–8). The poem evokes pathos for a domestic tragedy – a young man lying drowned on a lonely beach, his father left weeping at an empty tomb (cf. *1363–70*). The names of father and son occur in the first and last lines. Every pentameter has the maximum number of long syllables, and three of the four hexameters begin with a spondee; this gives a lugubrious effect. Line 1 is heavily alliterative (σσ, τ). καταπρηνόω (3), ἰχθυβόρος (5) and λαρίς (5; usual form λάρος) seem to be coinages of Leonidas.

1[1520] ἠχήεσσα θάλασσα: < *Il.* 1.157. **τόν**: sc. υἱόν.

3[1522] ἄγρια: n. pl. as adv.: cf. *1533*. **χειμήνασα**: this might be transitive, with Τελ. as obj.; but it seems more likely that ἄγρια χειμήνασα is a self-contained phrase. **καταπρηνώσαο** 'made him capsize' (πρηνής = 'headlong').

4[1523] λάβρον κῦμ': < *Il.* 15.624–5 (κῦμα... λάβρον). **ἐπιχευαμένη**: mid. for act. in this verb is found in Homer, e.g. *Il.* 8.158–9.

5[1524] χὠ μέν που: cf. *1498* n. **καύηξιν . . . λαρίδεσσι**: sea-birds.

6[1525] τεθρήνητ': the gulls have sung his dirge. For the unusual elision of -αι cf. *496*.

7–8[1526–7] κεκλαυμένον . . . δακρύει: the cenotaph was wept over when it was erected (perf. part.); now it inspires tears in Timares whenever he gazes at it.

8

A dead shepherd prays that those who survive him will pay rustic honours to his tomb, and promises that their kindness will be requited. The poem is a short pastoral elegy, ostensibly for inscription on the grave.

1[1528] οἰοπολεῖτε 'haunt in solitude' (G.–P.), from οἰός + πολέω.

There is a pointed assonance with ὄις (2); and in fact some ancient authorities thought that the adj. οἰοπόλος meant 'a place where sheep wander' (Schol. *Il.* 13.473).

2[1529] εὐείρους 'fleecy' (εἶρος = 'wool'). **ἐμβοτέοντες** 'pasturing'.

3[1530] προσηνῆ 'comforting' (sc. ἐμοί) (G.–P.).

4[1531] χθονίης εἵνεκα Φερσεφόνης: Persephone, stolen away from the upper world by Hades, might be expected to sympathize with the herdsman's request.

5[1532] βληχήσαιντ': aor. opt. of βληχάομαι, 'bleat'.

6[1533] πρηέα 'softly' (with συρίζοι). πρηΰς is an epic equivalent of πρᾶος.

7[1534] λειμώνιον ἄνθος ἀμέρξας: cf. *1076*.

9[1536] εὐάρνοιο 'well lambed', i.e. having plenty of milk for this rustic libation.

11–12[1538–9] θανόντων . . . ἀμοιβαῖαι . . . χάριτες: 'favours done by the dead in return ⟨for those granted them by the living⟩'. **ἐν φθιμένοις** is, strictly speaking, redundant, since οἱ φθίμενοι = οἱ θανόντες.

9

On a cock killed by a predator. Anyte may well have been the originator of the animal-'epitaph'; poems by several imitators are preserved in the *Anthology*. There is no evidence of genuine inscriptions for the graves of animals until at least a century later; perhaps, therefore, this is a case of literature influencing life. The tone of the present poem, with its highfalutin vocabulary and domestic subject-matter, is difficult to assess. One expects a 'sincere' expression of sorrow, but the lines might equally well be an exercise in ironic deflation: the cock, rather pompously described, prided himself on rising early, but an unseen 'destroyer' caught him napping and fixed its claw in the songster's gullet.

1[1540] πυκιναῖς πτερύγεσσιν: variation on a Homeric phrase (πτερὰ πυκνά *Il.* 11.454, πυκινὰ πτερά *Od.* 5.53). **ἐρέσσων:** birds in flight are often described as 'rowing' with their wings, the resemblance being to the two banks of oars beating in unison on either side of a ship; but the use of the word here, of a cock shaking himself down in the morning, is perhaps tongue-in-cheek.

2[1541] ἐξ εὐνᾶς: probably with (με) ὄρσεις, not with ἐγρόμενος.

3[1542] ὑπνώοντα: ὑπνώω is an exclusively epic form of ὑπνόω. σίνις: a very rare word meaning 'ravager' (< σίνομαι), 'predator'. Some sort of cat, perhaps. λαθρηδόν = λάθραι; not found elsewhere.

4[1543] ἔκτεινεν: 1st aor. of κτείνω. ῥίμφα 'swiftly', another high poeticism. καθείς: aor. part. of καθίημι, 'put down into' – i.e. fixing its claw in the gullet.

10

What's in a name? This poem describes and solves the rebus ΦΦ supposedly inscribed on a gravestone: the dead woman's name was Φειδίς (φεῖ + δίς), literally 'frugal' (< φείδομαι) – the economy of lettering is thus particularly appropriate. ΦΦ might be called a 'Callimachean' γράμμα (2): it is the product of hard work (9 καμών; cf. 3), 'sparing' with words (cf. *1644–5*) and accessible only to the 'intelligent' reader (10 ξυνετοῖς) who is on 'the right path' (6; cf. *25–8* and Pind. *Ol.* 2.83–9, p. 88–9). The pattern-poems (*822–33*) and Lycophron's *Alexandra* (*1346–70*) show a similar fascination with τὸ γριφῶδες.

1[1544] ὅτου χάριν 'for what reason' (ὅτου = οὗτινος: LSJ s.v. ὅστις).

2[1545] γράμμα 'as its inscription'; in apposition to δισσάκι φεῖ.

3[1546] κεχολαμμένον: perf. part. pass. of κολάπτω, 'cut', 'engrave'.

4[1547] τᾶι: with κευθομέναι. Χιλιάς: φ as numeral = 500, so ΦΦ = 1000. This first attempt at a solution is conceptually the opposite of the 'frugal' truth (cf. *6* for Call.'s dislike of χιλιάδες). Needless to say, Χιλιάς was not a real Greek name.

5[1548] τοῦτο = the name Χιλιάς. κορυφούμενον 'summed up', lit. 'brought to a peak'. The usual verb is κεφαλαιόω, lit. 'bring to a head'.

6[1549] τὸ μέν: the conjecture just made.

7[1550] ἔπλετο: *1179* n. Φειδίς: this and Φειδώ are real Greek names.

8[1551] Οἰδίπος: this form of the nom. is not found elsewhere, though the gen. Οἰδίπου occurs in tragedy. Cf. epic τρίπος for τρίπους. ἐφρασάμαν 'I have perceived it', i.e. seen through it, solved it.

9[1552] αἰνετός: sc. ἐστί. οὐκ = ὁ ἐκ. δισσοῖο: 'double' both because it consists of two letters and because it is simultaneously φέγγος and ἔρεβος. τύποιο 'incised letter' (G.–P.).

11

Fictitious epitaph for Archeanassa, a courtesan from Colophon (she was reputedly Plato's mistress). This is the earliest surviving poem with the theme 'desirable even in old age', a popular idea in later amatory epigrams. If Archeanassa was so attractive at the time of her death, what must have been the experience of her early lovers?

1[1554] ἔχω: the grave speaks.

2[1555] ἐπὶ ῥυτίδων . . . ἔζετ(ο): a witty adaptation of the commonplace of love 'sitting' (e.g.) in the eyes.

4[1557] πρωτόβολοι 'you who were first struck', sc. with love for her. πυρκαϊῆς 'conflagration', an imaginative intensification of the 'ἔρως-as-fire' motif (for which see e.g. *574–738 passim*).

Bibl.: see *FGE* pp. 167–9.

12

The *Anthology* contains a large number of poems on poets, many of them fictitious epitaphs. This and the next celebrate the fourth-century Telian poetess Erinna, who died at the age of 19. She was best known for her *Distaff* ('Ηλακάτη, *SH* 401; cf. p. 173–4), a short, polished poem of some 300 hexameters lamenting the death of her newly married friend Baucis.

This poem is an ingenious conceit based on two familiar themes: (1) the poet as bee gathering sweet honey (Pind. *Pyth.* 10.54, Bacch. 10.10, etc.); (2) the young girl abducted while gathering flowers (see p. 201 on Moschus' *Europa*): Erinna, like Persephone, was stolen away by Hades as she gathered 'flowers', i.e. as she composed her poetic bouquets. The closing words are a quotation from an epitaph by Erinna for Baucis (*AP* 7.712; *HE* 1789–96 (=Erinna 2); *OCT* 643–50): the same early death befell her as the friend whom she mourned.

1[1558] νεάοιδον: perhaps 'recently become a singer' rather than 'singing youthfully' (LSJ). ἐν ὑμνοπόλοισι 'amongst poets': ὑμνοπόλος is sometimes used with no strictly hymnic overtones. The -πολ- element is cognate with πολεῖν ('range about'), a particularly appropriate image for the flitting bee.

3–4[1560–1] "Αιδας . . . 'Αἴδα: Hades' name frames the couplet, with a variation of prosody.

4[1561] βάσκανος 'grudging' – envying men her presence he took her for himself. **ἔσσ'**: ἐσσί, epic form of εἶ.

13

Antipater's epigram on Erinna, like the riddle-poem *1544-53*, emphasizes the λεπτότης of its subject in imagery reminiscent of Callimachus' *Reply*: Erinna is brief and swan-like in expression and justly famous, while a huge mass of later poems, croaking like jackdaws (cf. Pind. *Ol.* 2.83-9, p. 88-9), have already fallen into oblivion. The epigram is spoken by these inferior productions, which address the reader as ξεῖνε (6) in the manner of a grave-inscription; but the demonstrative τοῦτο in line 2 suggests that the poem is to be imagined at the head of a copy of the *Distaff*.

1[1562] παυροεπής 'of few verses' (G.–P.).

2[1563] ἔπος 'poem', probably nom.: it 'has its share of the Muses'.

3[1564] μνήμης: perhaps an allusion to the fact that the Muses are daughters of Memory (Hes. *Theog.* 53-5). **ἤμβροτεν:** epic aor. form of ἁμαρτάνω, 'miss'. There may be a pun on ἄμβροτος, 'immortal'.

4[1565] νυκτὸς . . . πτέρυγι: Night is often represented as winged: cf. Virg. *Aen.* 8.369 *nox ruit et fuscis tellurem amplectitur alis.* **κωλύεται:** apparently 'is constrained' or 'confined' (G.–P.).

5-6[1566-7] ἀναρίθμητοι . . . μυριάδες: perhaps 'countless tens of thousands of verses', contrasting with παυροεπής (1): cf. Call.'s πολλαῖς . . . χιλιάσιν (*4*).

5[1566] νεαρῶν: though recently produced they have been quickly forgotten. **σωρηδόν** 'in heaps', piled up in neglect.

7[1568] κύκνου . . . μικρὸς θρόος: poets are often compared to swans. Cf. Lucr. 4.181-2 *paruus ut est cycni melior canor, ille gruum quam | clamor in aetheriis dispersus nubibus austri,* which may be a direct borrowing from this epigram.

8[1569] εἰαριναῖς: jackdaws croak in the spring nesting-season; but in view of *aetheriis* in Lucr., Stadtmüller's αἰθερίαις is very attractive.

14

One of three autobiographical poems by Meleager in the form of epitaphs – more elaborate variations on a theme already used by Callimachus and Leonidas. After outlining his life and career the poet claims that his Syrian background should not cause surprise, since we are all 'citizens of the world' and have a common origin (5–6). The last two couplets are reminiscent of Callimachus' *Reply* (*1–40*), in which the poet says that although he is old (*6, 37–8*) he wants to sing only like the delicate cicada (*29 ff.*). Here Meleager characterizes himself as an old man who is still a charming 'chatterer', i.e. singer (λαλεῖν can be used of the cicada); and he adapts the traditional χαῖρε-formula to wish the reader / passer-by a similarly 'garrulous' old age.

1[1570] τεκνοῖ: the pres. is common with verbs of giving birth, indicating the state resulting from past action.

2[1571] 'Ατθίς: Gadara, remotely situated in the province of Syria ('Ασσυρίοις = Συρίοις), had a flourishing literary community, and is hence proudly called 'Attic'. **Γάδαρα**: neut. pl. in appos. to 'Ατθὶς πάτρα ναιομένα ἐν 'Ασσυρίοις.

3[1572] ὁ σὺν Μούσαις 'companion of the Muses' (cf. Theoc. *Id.* 7.12).

4[1573] 'I who first (i.e. as my first literary production?) ran along with the elegances of Menippus.' Menippus, a third-cent. Gadarene, wrote elegant satires in a mixture of prose and verse. There is a pun on the title of Mel.'s compositions, which were called Χάριτες.

5[1574] μίαν . . . πατρίδα κόσμον: the idea of the κοσμοπολίτης is at least as old as Euripides (fr. 777): see Pease on Cic. *De nat. deorum* 1.121.

6[1575] ἔτικτε: for the imperf. cf. *1056* n. **Χάος**: *828* n.

7[1576] Two translations are possible: (1) 'As an old man I wrote these words on my (wax) tablets before ⟨I went to⟩ my tomb'; (2) 'As an old man I inscribed these words on the (funerary) tablets in front of my grave'. The second of these seems the more reasonable thing to say.

8[1577] 'For old age ⟨is⟩ a near neighbour to death.' Most editors read gen. γήρως, translating 'for a neighbour of old age ⟨is⟩ close to Hades'; but that seems even weaker.

9[1578] λαλιόν: Mel. appears to have coined this word, which he uses twice elsewhere, instead of the usual λάλος (cf. 10). **πάρος**: the sense is, 'having first greeted me . . . may you, too, . . .'.

Bibl: J. J. Pollitt, *Art in the Hellenistic Age* (Cambridge, 1986) 13 (on 'cosmopolitanism').

15

Lovemaking provides a relief like the satisfaction of summer thirst or sailors' joy that the frustrations of winter inactivity are past. The poem is constructed as an ascending tricolon, three clauses each longer than the last, pointed by anaphora (ἡδύ ... ἡδύ ... ἥδιον), and it is cast in the form of a 'priamel', 'a series of detached statements which through contrast or comparison lead up to the idea with which the speaker is primarily concerned' (Fraenkel on Aesch. *Ag.* 899–902 (q.v.), a passage which Asclepiades echoes here).

1–2[1580–1] ἡδύ ... ἡδύ: in the first sentence ἡδύ qualifies ποτόν; in the second it is predicative, i.e. ναύταις ἡδύ ⟨ἐστιν⟩ ἰδεῖν ...

1[1580] θέρους 'in summer', gen. of undefined time. **χιών** 'ice-cold water'. Cf. *1717* n.

2[1581] ἐκ χειμῶνος 'after winter'. **εἰαρινὸν Στέφανον**: the Crown or Corona Borealis, which begins to rise in the evening in early March, a signal that it is again safe to sail.

3[1582] τοὺς φιλέοντας: Greek uses the masc. for male + female as well as male + male.

4[1583] χλαῖνα: Greeks commonly used their cloaks as blankets. **αἰνῆται**: lovemaking is the homage due to Aphrodite.

16

Let Zeus do his worst; no bad weather will prevent the poet from leading a κῶμος to the door of his beloved. Asclepiades is the earliest known composer of 'mimetic' epigrams set at various stages of the κῶμος: see Tarán 53–114. In this poem the humour lies partly in Zeus's dual role as lover and weather-god. Inflated language and hyperbole add to the humour, and a literary allusion in lines 1–2 makes the love-poet a new Prometheus, echoing the defiance of [Aesch.] *Prom.* 1043–53.

1[1584] χαλαζοβόλει 'shower hail' – not found elsewhere. **αἶθε κεραυνούς** 'set burning your thunderbolts'. The MSS reading αἶθε, κεραύνου (i.e. two imperatives) is unsatisfactory. The tautology is not a serious problem; but both these verbs ought to be transitive, and it is awkward to understand με. Moreover, αἶθε κεραυνούς gives the line a more resounding close.

2[1585] ἐν χθονὶ σεῖε: *627* n.; or perhaps ἐν ... σεῖε in tmesis.

3[1586] ἀφῆις ζῆν 'let me off so that I live' – infin. of result (Goodwin, *GMT* § 775).

4[1587] χείρονα: neut. acc. pl.

5–6[1588–9] A reference to the story of Danaë, who was visited by Zeus in a shower of gold after her father had confined her in a bronze chamber.

6[1589] διά: implying perhaps that golden brightness pervaded the whole room.

17

A remark made by the poet to his neighbour at a symposium: he has seen a young guest sighing and has recognized from his own experience the signs of love. The epigram is based on a poem by Asclepiades (*AP* 12.135; *HE* 894–7 (=Ascl. 18); *OCT* 1049–52), in which a similar event is described in the past tense. The final couplet creates an impression of lively colloquial speech by use of vivid imagery and proverbial expression.

1[1590] ἕλκος: a wound made by love's arrow. **ἐλάνθανεν:** the imperf. implies that he had successfully been concealing his feelings until now. **ὡς:** exclamatory.

2[1591] πνεῦμα: a sigh. Probably acc., with ἀνηγάγετο mid. for act.

3[1592] τὸ τρίτον: commentators see a reference to the libations poured at the beginning of symposia to Zeus Olympius, the Heroes and Zeus Soter (cf. *274* n.), neat wine being drunk with each. In that case it is unclear, perhaps irrelevant, why the ξεῖνος should sigh at this particular moment. But the poem of Ascl. is more explicit: αἱ πολλαὶ προπόσεις, too many toasts, had made Nicagoras drunk and maudlin. Here, then, τὸ τρίτον may refer not to these preliminary libations but simply to his third cup of wine.

3–4[1592–3] He was garlanded with roses, which dropped their petals and fell to the ground. 'The falling garland is a sign of the lover' (G.–P.), reflecting his drooping spirits.

4[1593] ἐγένοντο χαμαί: having fallen they were all on the ground.

5[1594] ὤπτηται 'he is roasted' (perf. pass. of ὀπτάω) – picturesque variation (found first in Soph. fr. 474; cf. *1609*) on the love-as-heat image. **μέγα δή τι:** *1190* n., *253*. **οὐκ ἀπὸ ῥυσμοῦ:** a phrase of uncertain meaning. ῥυθμός (Ionic ῥυσμός) means 'rhythm', 'measure', 'proportion'; perhaps translate 'not at random' or, as G.–P. suggest, 'not out of step', i.e. reasonably.

6[1595] φωρὸς δ' ἴχνια φὼρ ἔμαθον: cf. Eng. 'set a thief to catch a thief'. The image of ἴχνια, 'traces', 'tracks', is perhaps suggested by the rose-petals lying as evidence on the ground.

18

Callignotus swore that Ionis would always be first in his affections; but now he is in love with a boy, and Ionis is out of the reckoning. This is a poem of amused detachment: two commonplace proverbial references (4, 6) are used to comment ironically on this all too familiar situation, and μήτε φίλον . . . μήτε φίλην (2) is mockingly echoed by οὐ λόγος οὐδ' ἀριθμός at the close.

3[1598] λέγουσιν: that lovers' oaths are not binding and go unpunished if broken is a commonplace as old as Hesiod (fr. 124).

3–4[1599–1600] τοὺς ἐν ἔρωτι | ὅρκους: oaths ⟨sworn when one is⟩ in love.

4[1600] μή: verbs of swearing are amongst those which have μή rather than οὐ + inf. in indirect speech: see Goodwin, *GMT* § 685.

6[1602] ὡς Μεγαρέων: the Megarians once asked the Delphic oracle τίνες κρείττονες τυγχάνοιεν (cf. κρέσσονα, 2); but the reply listed many other towns and ended ὑμεῖς δ', ὦ Μεγαρεῖς, οὔτε τρίτοι οὔτε τέταρτοι οὔτε δυωδέκατοι οὔτ' ἐν λόγωι οὔτ' ἐν ἀριθμῶι ('out of account and out of reckoning') – Schol. Theoc. 14.48–9.
> Cat. 70.

19

The poet's soul is fevered; but that is no more than he deserves, since he nurtured and encouraged Eros without foreseeing the inevitable result. For the common Hellenistic conceit of Eros as a baby or young boy cf. *822–33, 1211–26, 1610–19*. Lines 3–6 allude to the proverbial theme of the 'viper in one's bosom', the ungrateful offspring or fosterling which at last grows too strong for its parents (cf. Aesch. *Ag.* 717–35, *Cho.* 928). The mannered ingenuity of the last line is typical of Meleager.

1[1602] δ': this word is sometimes found 'in passionate or lively exclamations, where no connection appears to be required' (Denniston, *GP* 172).

1–2[1602–3] ἄρτι . . . ἄρτι 'at one time . . . at another. . .'.

2[1603] ἀναψύχεις: the usual meaning is 'revive' (trans.); but here

Mel. plays on the similarity of sound with ψυχρός (cf. 6): the soul revives when no longer αἰθομένη, i.e. when it is ψυχρά. (The Stoics actually derived ψυχή from ψυχρός, believing that the soul was acquired at the moment of birth when the child was 'tempered', i.e. made cool, by the air (Chrysippus, *SVF* II 804–8); but such theories are probably not relevant here).

3[1604] τί κλαίεις;: an echo of Thetis' words to Achilles, τέκνον, τί κλαίεις; (*Il.* 1.362). **ἄτεγκτον** 'unsoftened' (< τέγγω), i.e. hard-hearted.

4[1605] σοί: emphatic: 'against *you*'.

5[1606] καλῶν: ironical: 'all too good'.

6[1607] πῦρ . . . χιόνα: love blows hot and cold, like fever.

8[1609] ὀπτῶι καιομένη μέλιτι: cf. *1594* n.: love is sweet yet painful, γλυκύπικρον (Sappho fr. 130.2).

20

This poem is inspired by Moschus *Idyll* 1, in which Aphrodite proclaims Eros as a runaway slave and gives a long, semi-allegorical description of his appearance. The language is based on that of the town-crier – in both poems Eros is a 'wanted man', and he may even now be lying in wait for innocent members of the public. Each poem plays on Eros' paradoxical status as both elemental force and captivating child. But whereas Moschus ends abruptly with a warning that Eros is dangerous and should not be approached, Meleager adds a novel twist: there he is, after all, hiding in Zenophila's eyes, i.e. her eyes dart arrows of desire (hence τοξότα in 10: see *1129* n.).

1[1610] ἄρτι . . . ἄρτι: intensificatory repetition: 'this very moment'.

2[1611] ὤιχετ' ἀποπτάμενος: < *Il.* 2.71.

3[1612] γλυκύδακρυς: a variation on the idea of ἔρως as bitter and / yet sweet (cf. *1609*). **ἀθαμβής**: lit. 'unastonishable', i.e. unabashed, froward.

4[1613] σιμὰ γελῶν 'laughing pertly'. For the overtones of σιμός see *1459* n.

5[1614] πατρὸς . . . τίνος: sc. ἐστί. 'Wanted' notices or proclamations (some of which survive on papyrus) gave a brief physical description of the runaway and details such as parentage and country of origin. **οὐκέτ' ἔχω φράζειν** 'I cannot go on to say' (G.–P.): cf. *775*. A teasing reference to the much debated question of Eros' parentage.

5–6[1614–15] Many allegorical genealogies existed for Eros; but Mel.'s point is that he is equally abhorred by the whole world (which he pervades as generative principle).

8[1617] ἄλλα 'for other people', sc. now that his attention is elsewhere. λίνα 'nets' for souls. The soul is traditionally winged and is sometimes depicted in art as a butterfly, the Gk for which is ψυχή.

9[1618] κεῖνος 'there he is!' περὶ φωλεόν 'lurking about his lair', picking up the imagery of τὸν ἄγριον in 1.

10[1619] τοξότα Ζην–: there is Homeric precedent for a short final syllable failing to be lengthened by the double consonant ζ beginning a proper name (e.g. *Il.* 2.634 οἵ τε Ζάκυνθον ἔχον): see G.–P. ad loc. for further details.

21

This famous epigram is attributed by ancient sources to Plato, who is said to have composed it for a boy astronomy pupil called Ἀστήρ (Aristippus ap. Diog. Laer. 3.29). Both ascription and anecdote are almost certainly false (see *FGE* pp. 125–7 and *FGE* 584–5 nn.), and there is no need to assume play on a proper name. The poem combines three common ideas: (1) the metaphor of ἀστήρ for a person to be gazed at or admired (cf. *48* n., *155–6* n.); (2) the notion of heavenly bodies 'looking down' on human affairs (cf. *1622–7*); (3) the 'would-that-I-could-become...' motif (cf. e.g. Ovid, *Amores* 2.15 on his mistress' ring). *Bibl.*: W. Ludwig, 'Plato's love epigrams', *G.R.B.S.* 4 (1963) 77–80.

22

An address to the moon, inviting her to look down on the poet and his mistress as they make love; she will be a sympathetic observer, having herself been in love with Endymion. Three adjectives in asyndeton provide a stately opening reminiscent of hymnic invocations (cf. *370*, *401*). G.–P. note the poem's 'sensuous tone and exquisite phrasing'.

1[1622] δίκερως: of the two 'horns' of the crescent moon. Cf. *1132* n., Hor. *Carmen saec.* 35–6 *bicornis ... luna*. φιλοπάννυχε 'you who love all-night revels'. The παννυχίς was an all-night festival, over which Selene might be thought to preside. Such festivals often provided opportunity for seduction.

2[1623] εὐτρήτων: lit. 'well pierced' (<τετραίνω), i.e. latticed.
βαλλομένη: Greek, like English, has the metaphor of light being 'cast'.

3[1624] αὔγαζε: both 'illumine' (of the moon) and 'gaze upon' (of the moon-goddess). **χρυσέην**: 'as if Callistion were a second χρυσέη Ἀφροδίτη' (G.–P.).

4[1625] κατοπτεύειν: the verb suggests close observation or keeping watch. **οὐ φθόνος**: the phrase οὐ φθόνος + inf. is used when a speaker does not begrudge a favour.

5[1626] ὀλβίζεις 'you consider us fortunate'. **ἡμέας** = ἐμέ; rather awkward in this context.

6[1627] Ἐνδυμίων: whilst Endymion slept in a cave on Mt Latmus in Caria he was espied by the moon, who fell in love with him. According to one version of the myth she bore him 50 daughters (Paus. 5.1.4); another version tells how she sent him to sleep for ever so that she could kiss him without his knowledge (Cic. *Tusc.* 1.92).

23

The poet asks a mosquito to hum a summons in the ear of the absent Zenophila. If the insect is successful he will adorn it with a club and lionskin, fitting reward for the completion of a Herculean task. This poem is the second of a pair by Meleager dealing with mosquitoes. In the first he rebukes them for troubling his mistress; here one of their number is enrolled on the poet's own side and ironically promoted to the status of 'divine messenger' (ταχὺς ἄγγελος of a bird-omen at e.g. *Il.* 24.292, *Od.* 15.526). The minute insect, which is humorously taken to be suitable as poet's messenger because its monotonous hum is supposedly a sign of musicianship (4 φιλόμουσε), is urged to deliver its message ἥσυχα (5) – as if it could do anything else. The final couplet paints a fantastic and ludicrous picture.

1[1628] πταίης: aor. opt. of πέτομαι – a polite request.

1–2[1628–9] οὔασι δ' ἄκροις . . . ψαύσας: ψαύω occasionally takes the dat. rather than the usual genitive. ἄκροις suggests not the tips of her ears, but 'just touching her ears'. Cf. Aesch. *Ag.* 891–2.

2[1629] The assonance is remarkable.

3[1630] λήθαργε 'forgetful of', + gen.

5[1632] καὶ σύγκοιτον 'the man sleeping with her, too'.

6[1633] ζηλοτύπους ὀδύνας 'pains caused by jealousy' (<ζῆλος + τύπτω) – her partner will be jealous if he hears the message.

24

An address to the musical cicada, exhorting it to strike up a fresh song
and lull the poet to sleep at noon. The epigram is largely descriptive,
with the love-theme introduced only at the end in an ὄφρα-clause (cf.
1698–9); if the cicada's song is sufficiently diverting the poet will be able
to escape temporarily from the pangs of ἔρως. G.–P. note the elaborate
variation of vocabulary used to describe the cicada's musicianship.

1[1636] δροσεραῖς σταγόνεσσι μεθυσθείς 'drunk on dewdrops' (supposedly the cicada's only sustenance: cf. 29–36 n.) – a witty paradox.

2[1637] ἀγρονόμαν . . . μοῦσαν 'a country-haunting song'.

3[1638] ἄκρα . . . πετάλοις: probably 'aloft on the leaves' rather
than 'just on the surface of the leaves' (cf. 1628) or 'on the leaf-edges'.
ἄκρα n. pl. adv. **πριονώδεσι κώλοις** 'with your saw-like legs' – an error,
since cicadas, unlike grasshoppers, 'stridulate by vibrating a membrane
in the thorax' (G.–P.).

4[1639] αἰθίοπι . . . χρωτί 'with tawny skin', a very loosely constructed dative. The adj. Αἰθίοψ elsewhere = 'Ethiopian'; here, uniquely,
Mel. has used it for αἴθων or αἶθοψ.

5[1640] ἀλλά: 401 n.

5–6[1640–1] τι νέον . . . παίγνιον 'some fresh ditty'.

6[1641] ἀντωιδὸν Πανί 'in response to, i.e. accompanying, Pan'
rather than 'in competition with' him. At mid-day gods are abroad:
201–15 n.

7[1642] ὄφρα . . . ὕπνον ἀγρεύσω 'so that I may snatch some sleep'.
ἀγρεύσω is probably aor. subj., though occasionally in Homer ὄφρα is
found with fut. ind.

Bibl.: D. F. Dorsey, 'The cicada's song in Anth. Palatina 7.196', *C.R.* n.s.
20 (1970) 137–9.

25

Offering of a rough oak club to Heracles by Archinus, a Cretan:
Callimachus gives a novel turn to the standard dedicatory distich. The
object itself speaks, as often in dedicatory poems; but even a distich is too
much for this laconic hero: he cuts short the club's reverential address
and brusquely elicits all the information he needs in less than a single
pentameter.

1[1644] τίν: Doric for σοί. **λεοντάγχ(α):** voc. of λεοντάγχης, 'strangler of the ⟨Nemean⟩ lion'. On this labour of Heracles see p. 85. **ὦνα** = ὦ ἄνα: cf. *306* n. **συοκτόνε**: 'slayer of the ⟨Erymanthian⟩ boar', which Heracles perhaps killed after he had displayed it alive to his taskmaster Eurystheus. **φήγινον ὄζον**: lit. 'oak-branch', i.e. a branch roughly fashioned into a club like that carried by Heracles himself (cf. *1635*).

26

On a nautilus-shell found near Iulis on Ceos and dedicated by Selenaea, daughter of Cleinias of Smyrna, in the temple of Aphrodite-Arsinoe at Zephyrium, a promontory west of Alexandria. Before her death in 270 B.C. Arsinoe (p. 4) was already identifed with Aphrodite; the seaside temple at Zephyrium, founded during her lifetime (Fraser I 239–40), was later to be famous for the dedication of the Lock of Berenice (Call. fr. 110, Cat. 66: see p. 85). The poem has other strong links with Arsinoe. Ceos, where the shell was found, was part of the Ptolemaic empire, and the harbour which served Iulis had recently been renamed Arsinoe (Fraser I 587–8, II 835). Smyrna, on the coast of Asia Minor, had been re-founded on a new site by Arsinoe's first husband Lysimachus, king of Thrace. Thus both dedicatee and dedicated object can claim a particular right to the goddess's favour. Moreover Aphrodite, born from the foam, was associated with shells in literature and art, and was often depicted standing on one as she rose from the waves ('Αφροδίτη ἀναδυομένη – cf. Botticelli's *Birth of Venus*).

The last epigram dealt in the smallest possible space with a large, heavy piece of wood. This long and highly elaborate poem, the first ten lines of which form a single sentence, has as its subject a small, delicate and elegant nautilus-shell. (The nautilus is a small squid-like creature; the female is protected by a paper-thin shell. Aristotle, in a passage which may have been one of Call.'s sources here (*De Nat. Anim.* 622b5–18), describes the nautilus' 'sail' (4 n.) as λεπτόν.) The contrast between these two epigrams tells us much about Callimachus' poetic art; and the present poem illustrates perfectly 'his ability to transform the material of his studies in other fields . . . into poetry' (Fraser I 588): details of natural history and etymological references are an integral part of the epigram's sophisticated brilliance.

1[1646] **παλαίτερον** 'formerly', irreg. comparative of παλαιός. The nautilus was once a (living) shellfish and is now an ἄνθεμα.

2[1647] πρῶτον: since this is her first offering, we deduce that Selenaea is a young girl. Her motives are not specified.

3[1648] ναυτίλος: attracted into the nom. because it is subject of the following verb. ἀῆται: nom. pl. of ἀήτης, as at *606*: sc. ἦσαν.

4[1649] Two of the nautilus' tentacles are larger than the other six. These were mistakenly believed to be used as halyards (πρότονοι) to support a membranous 'sail' (Aristotle above). In fact the nautilus is jet-propelled. οἰκείων 'my own', i.e. part of the nautilus' body.

5–6[1650–1] The nautilus was thought to move in calm weather by rowing with its tentacles – hence 'see how my name ('sailor') befits my action'.

5[1650] Γαληναίη = Γαλήνη, mentioned as a sea-nymph at Hes. *Theog.* 244 and occasionally found personified elsewhere. λιπαρή 'of the *oily smoothness* of a calm sea' (LSJ). οὖλος 'vigorously': cf. *325* n.

7[1652] ἔστ(ε) 'until at last'. παρά: when παρά + acc. expresses position 'with ref. to past motion' (LSJ c.i.2) the translation 'on' is often more appropriate than 'beside'. γένωμαι: ὄφρα quite often takes the subj. rather than the opt. after past tenses.

8[1653] περίσκεπτον παίγνιον 'admired toy', though παίγνιον also suggests 'dainty object'. Aphrodite is a playful goddess.

9–10[1654–5] The halcyon, a mythical bird, is said to have laid its eggs in the nautilus' shell. Quite how this could happen is not clear. Neither Aristotle nor any other source mentions this procedure: the halcyon is generally said to have built a nest during the Halcyon Days at mid-winter, when the sea remained calm. ἀλκυών was derived by some ancient etymologists from ἁλὶ κυεῖν, 'conceive in the sea'.

9[1654] μηδέ = ὄφρα δὲ μή.

10[1655] νοτερῆς 'sea-wetted' (lit. 'damp').

11–12[1656–7] οἶδε γὰρ ἐσθλὰ | ῥέζειν: she knows how to behave well towards others, and herself deserves to be well treated by the goddess.

12[1657] Σμύρνης . . . Αἰολίδος: the ancient city of Smyrna was inhabited by Aeolians until 688 B.C.; but as applied to the new town the adj. is historically evocative rather than literally accurate.

27

A mock dedicatory epigram. Eudemus offers up his salt-tub to the Cabiri in thanks for his escape from 'storms' of debt: by eating nothing but salt with his bread he lived frugally enough to be able to pay off what he owed. The salt-tub which rescued him is pictured as a ship, 'aboard which' (ἐφ' ἧς, 1) he escaped the threatening χειμῶνας (2 – a common metaphor for troubles); he was thus saved ἐξ ἁλός (4) – not only 'from the sea', but also 'by means of ⟨eating only⟩ salt'.

1[1658] ἁλίην: a tub for storing salt. **ἐπέσθων** 'eating in addition' (sc. to his bread).

3[1660] θεοῖς Σαμοθρᾶιξι: the Cabiri, protectors of seafarers. Their cult was based in Samothrace. **ὅτι:** the 'redundant' use, introducing direct speech (Goodwin, *GMT* § 711): the actual words of his dedicatory inscription were Εὔδημος τήνδε ὧδε θέτο, κτλ. **τήνδε:** sc. ἁλίην. **κατ' εὐχήν** 'in accordance with his vow', i.e. he had vowed to make the dedication if he escaped his debts.

4[1661] ὦ λαοί: the words 'call the attention of the public to the dedication' (G.–P.) – a sort of town-crier's formula. **ἐξ:** instrumental (LSJ III.6) as well as local, saved '*by* salt' and '*from* the sea'.

28

Another parodic 'dedication', based on a similar epigram by Asclepiades (*AP* 5.203; *HE* 832–7 (= Ascl. 6); *OCT* 987–92). Sporting equipment was often set up in temples in thanks for victory. Mention of a whip and reins in Homeric language in line 1 of this poem leads us to expect the commemoration of a win in the horse-race; but in fact the dedicatee is a prostitute who has 'ridden' her client to satisfaction more quickly than a rival could 'ride' hers. The poem is a clever elaboration of the *double entendre* in κέλης, which besides meaning 'horse for riding' can also refer to the sexual position in which the woman sits astride the supine man. Line 4 is 'a brilliant but blasphemous parody' (Fraser II 813) of Callimachus' *Bath of Pallas* 2 (*133*) τᾶν ἵππων ἄρτι φρυασσομενᾶν | τᾶν ἱερᾶν ἐσάκουσα – words describing the sacred mares of the chaste goddess Athena are adapted to refer metaphorically to the 'whinnying' men whom these prostitutes have 'ridden'.

1[1662] μάστιγα καὶ ἡνία σιγαλόεντα: a Homeric run of words (e.g. *Il.* 5.226). These items are probably intended as a symbol of her 'riding'-victory, not as actually used during the 'race'.

2[1663] Πλαγγών 'Dolly' – the name of a famous fourth-cent. prostitute. **εὐίππων . . . ἐπὶ προθύρων:** the dedication is imagined as made at the entrance to a temple of Aphrodite (Κύπρι, 5). The adj.

εὐίππων leads in to the κέλης-joke; but its literal meaning in this context is not clear.

3[1664] Φιλαινίδα: another notorious character: see *1375* n. **πολύ-χαρμον:** χάρμη = 'joy of battle' (LSJ): Philaenis has enjoyed many such contests.

4[1665] πώλων: a *double entendre*, since πῶλος is a common poetic word for a young person (cf. Anacreon's 'Thracian filly', *PMG* 417.1); here apparently of the 'colts' just ridden. **ἄρτι** 'just now': she rushed out and made the dedication as soon as she won.

5[1666] σὺ δέ: *1602* n.

5–6[1666–7] πόροις νημερτέα . . . δόξαν 'give her sure fame', i.e. ensure that she remains famous.

6[1667] ἀείμνηστον τήνδε τιθεῖσα χάριν 'by making this gift (the dedication) never-forgotten'.

29

The poet orders mice to leave his hut – he has not enough to feed them. Leonidas here affects to be living like one of the characters from his poems: he says he is a poor rustic living on a frugal (λιτός) diet of bread and salt (cf. *1658–61*). For the rustic hut cf. e.g. Call.'s *Hecale* (p. 84) and the *Moretum*: for the mice Call. *SH* 254–65 (*Aetia* Bk 3), in which the peasant Molorchus is so tormented by his 'tiresome neighbours' that he invents the mousetrap (see p. 85). The themes of frugal eating and the simple life are often implicitly or explicitly linked with Hellenistic poetic theory: Callimachus is advised by Apollo to keep his Muse thin and pictures himself as a cicada living only on dewdrops (*23–4, 34*). The *locus classicus* for style as mirror of the man is Seneca's 114th *Letter*. The equation underlies many literary anecdotes, e.g. Philetas' lead boots (p. 9).

1[1668] σκότιοι 'living in the dark' or perhaps 'furtive' (G.–P.).

2[1669] μῦς: acc. pl. **σιπύη** 'grain-bin'. **οἶδε** 'has the power to' (LSJ s.v. εἴδω B.2): cf. *368* ἐπίσταται, Fr. *savoir*.

3[1670] δύο κρίμνα 'two lumps of coarse meal' – the entire contents of his σιπύη.

4[1671] 'I am content with this life ⟨inherited⟩ from my fathers.' **ᾐνέσαμεν:** vivid aor. for pres., an Attic idiom with this verb: LSJ s.v. I.5.

5[1672] φιλόλιχνε: λείχω can be used of dainty sampling of food as well as of actual licking.

6[1673] σκυβάλου 'scraps'.

8[1675] πλειοτέρην . . . ἀρμαλιήν 'fuller rations'. πλειότερος is a Homeric comparative form of πλέως.

30

On the famous allegorical statue Καιρός ('Opportunity') by Lysippus of Sicyon, a fourth-century B.C. sculptor. The poem is a dialogue in which Καιρός explains to an interlocutor the meaning of his unusual features (winged feet, razor in right hand, large forelock, head bald behind). Like *1544–53*, in which the passer-by finds the solution himself, this epigram is a piece of interpretation, a commentary.

Copies of the original statue survive only in relief. Some show Καιρός holding a pair of scales as well as a razor.

1[1676] τίς πόθεν;: a Homeric phrase: 'who ⟨and⟩ from whence?'.

3[1678] ἐπ' ἄκρα 'on tiptoe'.

3–4[1678–9] ταρσοὺς| . . . διφυεῖς 'double wings', i.e. two wings on each foot. Cf. *1105*.

4[1679] ἵπταμ(αι): a post-classical equivalent of πέτομαι. **ὑπηνέμιος:** probably '⟨swift⟩ as the wind' rather than 'wind-borne'.

6[1681] 'I am sharper than any ⟨sharp⟩ edge' (Paton) (?). This is presumably a reference to the proverbial phrase 'on a razor's edge' (ἐπὶ ξυροῦ ἀκμῆς), used of crucial moments. Perhaps the meaning is that The Fleeting Moment is briefer in duration than any razor's edge is narrow in space.

7[1682] κατ' ὄψιν 'over your face'. **ὑπαντιάσαντι λαβέσθαι** 'for the person who meets me to grasp hold of': a reference to the proverb 'Grasp Time by the forelock'.

8[1683] εἰς τί . . .; 'for what purpose?'.

9–10[1684–5] 'No one will any longer (ἔθ') ⟨be able to⟩ seize me from behind once I am past, ⟨even if⟩ he wants to' – τόν looks forward to με; ἔθ' is presumably to be taken with δράξεται, if the MS reading is correct. οὔτις ἐφημερίων, 'no mortal', would be easier.

11[1686] τοὔνεχ' 'for what reason?'. **εἵνεκεν ὑμέων** 'for your (i.e. mankind's) sake'.

12[1687] διδασκαλίην 'to be a lesson to you'.

Bibl.: Καιρός in art: A. B. Cook, *Zeus* II 2 (Cambridge, 1925) 859–68, C. Picard, *Manuel d'archéologie grecque* IV 2 (1963) 553–65, A. Stewart, *A.J.A* 82 (1979) 163–71, J. J. Pollitt, *Art in the Hellenistic age* (Cambridge, 1986) 53–4.

31

Another dialogue, this time a brief conversation between a prospective client and an accommodating prostitute. The appeal of this witty 'mime' lies partly in its 'realism', the apparently effortless assimilation of everyday colloquial language into the elegiac verse-form (cf. Theoc. *Idd.* 14.1ff., 15.1ff.).

1–2[1688–9] μήπω | τοῦτο φιλοσπούδει 'Don't be in a hurry as regards that'. The verb is a conjectural emendation and does not occur elsewhere; but in sense it is plainly preferable to the MS reading φιλόσπουδος, which could only be taken as an abrupt exclamation.

2[1689] μή τιν' ἔχεις; 'Are you engaged?'. μή hopes for a negative answer: *1417* n.

3[1690] αἰεὶ τὸν φιλέοντα = τὸν αἰεὶ φ., 'Whoever happens to fancy me'.

5[1692] ξένον 'unusual'.

7[1694] ποῦ γίνηι; πέμψω 'Where are you? (i.e. where will you be?). I'll send for you'. καταμάνθανε 'You can find out'. The meaning is unclear; perhaps she is imagined as pointing to her house.

8[1695] πρόαγε 'Lead on'.

32

An inscription for a spring, inviting passers-by to drink in the shade; a much imitated poem. G.–P. believe that ἅπας (1) and πόνοις θέρεος (3) imply an address to a group of harvest labourers on a particular farm; but it seems possible that ἅπας could imply any passer-by and that πόνοις θέρεος might be more general, 'toil in the heat'. For the relaxed description cf. *1636–43*, which ends similarly with an ὄφρα-clause.

2[1697] ὡραίου 'lovely'(?). With inanimate objects this meaning recurs only in late Greek (though it is common enough of persons 'in their prime' in Plato and Xen.); but the more usual meaning 'seasonal', 'timely' makes poor sense here.

3[1698] φίλα γυῖα: a Homeric phrase (φίλα = 'one's own'). Here the meaning is 'body', not 'limbs'.

4[1699] τυπτόμενα: cf. *Il.* 11.305–6 νέφεα Ζέφυρος... | ...λαίλαπι τύπτων; but the verb seems strangely forceful in this context.

33

Philodemus prays for a safe voyage as he sets sail for the Piraeus. The poem consists of a single sentence – four lines of elegant invocation and two lines of prayer.

1[1700] ᾿Ινοῦς ὦ Μελιχέρτα: driven mad by Hera, Ino, daughter of Cadmus, killed her son Melicertes and leapt with his body into the sea. As sea-goddess she was called Leucothea; both she and Melicertes, also called Palaemon, helped sailors in distress (Ovid, *Met.* 4.519–42, Apollod. 3.4.3).

3[1702] κύματα: he asks the κύματα to carry him διὰ πλατὺ κῦμα (5) – possible, perhaps, but rather awkward. Schmidt's cj. κυανοχαῖτα ('dark-haired', a Homeric epithet of Poseidon) is attractive.

4[1703] Θρήϊξ: Zephyrus blows from the west, not from the Thracian north. Perhaps he is called Θρήϊξ here because Aeolus, who controlled all the winds, was thought by some to have lived in Thrace. G.–P. think there may be a reminiscence of *Il.* 9.5 Βορέης καὶ Ζέφυρος, τώ τε Θρήικηθεν ἄητον.

6[1705] γλυκερήν: the harbour will be a sweet sight to him after the long voyage.

XXVII

Drinking-song

A fragment of a scolion or drinking-song. The stanzas are linked by their *carpe diem* theme, and were probably intended to be sung by individual guests at symposia. The initial letters of each stanza are in alphabetical order, perhaps as an aid to memory. The subject-matter has less in common with other surviving scolia (*PMG* 884–916, *SH* 521–6) than with certain poems in the Theognidean collection (cf. especially Thgn. 1039–70b) and with sympotic epigrams. Certain features of language show that the diction is influenced by popular speech (4, 6, 8, 18, 24, 26, 29 nn.). The papyrus on which the lines are preserved is Egyptian and dates from the first century A.D.; the poem itself may well be post-Hellenistic.

Metre. The so-called στίχος μύουρος or 'mouse-tailed' hexameter, with a short penultimate syllable: see West, *GM* 173–4. The standard example cited by metricians is *Il.* 12.203 . . . αἰόλον ὄφιν (which should probably be written ὄφϝιν). We know of very few poems composed in this metre, and none from the Classical period. The present lines show a strong preference for the masculine caesura (‑³‑ | | ∪∪, not ‑³‑∪ | | ∪). The final syllable is long except in line 23, and the accent on the final word is almost always paroxytone, representing a falling pitch on the last syllable. Neither of these characteristics necessarily suggests a late date: see W. S. Allen, *Accent and rhythm* (Cambridge, 1973) 265–8.

3[1707] διαφρονεῖν 'quarrel'. δια- in compounds sometimes = 'at variance': cf. *Il.* 1.6 διαστήτην ἐρίσαντε, and διαφέρω, διαφωνέω, etc.

4[1708] πονέσεις: this form of the fut. is found first in Aristotle (-ήσω in Classical Gk).

5[1709] αὔλει μοι: an order addressed to the piper. Perhaps each guest uttered these words before singing his stanza to the pipe accompaniment. (Cf. Theognis 1055–6 ἀλλὰ λόγον μὲν τοῦτον ἐάσομεν, αὐτὰρ ἐμοὶ σὺ | αὔλει, καὶ Μουσῶν μνησόμεθ' ἀμφότεροι.) Alternatively, αὔλει μοι might represent a refrain which was written out in full only after the first stanza, which is lost.

6[1710] ἴδες = εἶδες. ει and ι were already being confused in pronunciation in the late fourth cent. B.C.: see W. S. Allen, *Vox Graeca* (3rd edn, Cambridge, 1987) 70. **διόλου** 'they are the same for ever' (as opposed to ephemeral man).

7[1711] ἀπέχει: sc. ἡμέρας. **τὰ τεταγμένα** cognate acc., 'in due order'.

8[1712] κοπία 'toil', a popular usage found in literature only in Biblical Greek. The usual meaning is 'be tired'.

11[1715] αὐτορύτους 'flowing of their own accord': Pind. *Pyth.* 12.17. **ἤθελον** 'I should like', desiderative imperf., rare without ἄν: cf. Goodwin, *GMT* § 425 (ἐβουλόμην).

13[1717] χιονέων '⟨cool as⟩ snow'. Snow, expensive out of season, was used to cool drinks at symposia: see Gow on Machon 270; cf. *1580.*

14[1718] κατά: distributive (LSJ ii.1): 'at each spring'.

16–17[1720–1] Λύδιος . . . Φρύγιος: the pipes were, according to some accounts, invented in Lydia or Phrygia. Cf. *1142*.

16[1720] Λύδια παίγματα: the Lydian ἁρμονίαι, dismissed by Plato in the *Republic* (398e) as μαλακαί, συμποτικαί and χαλαραί ('effeminate').

18[1722] ὅτᾱν: a false quantity, perhaps by analogy with ἐᾱν.

21–2[1725–6] There are no limits (μέτρα) to acquisitiveness: cf. Solon fr. 13.71 πλούτου δ' οὐδὲν τέρμα πεφασμένον ἀνδράσι κεῖται. **μέτρα πενίας** is added for the sake of antithesis; perhaps the implication is that no one ever realizes that he has escaped poverty.

21[1725] ἄν . . . ἀνεύρατο: an unusual form of tmesis. The prefix ἀν(ά) stands for the verb, which appears in the next clause: easier is Pind. *Nem.* 9.8 ἀνὰ μὲν . . . φόρμιγγ', ἀνὰ δ' αὐλὸν ὄρσομεν, where there is tmesis in both parts.

24[1728] ὁ τάλας 'wretch that he is'. βασανίζεται 'is tormented'. This metaphorical use is not found in Classical literature, but is common in the κοινή.

26[1730] ποθ' ἵδης: rough breathing by analogy with ὁρᾶν. Misplaced analogical aspiration of this type is a feature of the κοινή, e.g. καθ' ἔτος by analogy with καθ' ἡμέραν: see J. H. Moulton, *A grammar of New Testament Greek* II (Edinburgh, 1928) 98–9. It is impossible to say whether the error here belongs to the scribe or to the poet. **μνήματα κωφά** 'silent tombs'. κωφός suggests mute, deaf, senseless. **παράγηις** 'pass by'. παράγειν is not used transitively with this meaning in Classical Greek.

27[1731] κοινὸν ἔσοπτρον ὁρᾶις: the common fate of mankind stares you in the face. οὕτως προσεδόκα: the dead man when he was alive looked at corpses and tombs and expected to die just as you do.

28[1732] τὸ ζῆν: obj. of δανίσας.

28–9[1732–3] Cf. Lucr. 3.971 *uitaque mancipio nulli datur* ('life is granted freehold to no one').

29[1733] ἀποδιδοῖς: διδοῖς (Attic δίδως), originally an Ionic form, is found in Homer, but also in Biblical Greek.

31[1735] Overweening arrogance: cf. *1336–40*. The word-order suggests the nuance 'A king was Xerxes, the one who claimed to share everything with Zeus'.

32[1736] δυσὶ πηδαλίοις: a ship was steered by two long oars, one at either side of the stern. The rhetorical exaggeration of Xerxes' ignominious escape is a commonplace: see Mayor on Juv. 10.185. **Λήμνιον ὕδωρ**: the sea south of the Hellespont, which Xerxes had arrogantly bridged. (Λήμνιον κακόν was proverbial for any terrible misfortune; for the origin of the expression see Herod. 6.138, Garvie on Aesch. *Cho.* 631–8.)

33[1737] Κινύρας: king of Cyprus, favourite son of Apollo. He unwittingly committed incest with his daughter Myrrha (see p. 217) and killed himself in shame.

34[1738] ὀβολοῦ: placed in a corpse's mouth as fare for Charon, ferryman of the dead.

Bibl.: Edn: *CA* pp. 199–200; D. L. Page, *Greek literary papyri* (Loeb, 1941) 508–12; D. Young, *Theognis* (Teubner, 1961) 119–21. Gen.: T. F. Higham in *Greek poetry and life: essays presented to Gilbert Murray*... (Oxford, 1936) 299–324.

APPENDIX
DORIC DIALECT[1]

The literary Doric of Hellenistic writers, though more pronounced in some poems than in others, is an artificial amalgam of basically epic language and Doric characteristics borrowed from earlier poetry; it represents neither in broadness nor in consistency the speech of any Doric area. Epic or Attic forms are often juxtaposed with Doric forms within the same poem (e.g. κε and κα, 2nd decl. gen. sing. in -οιο and -ω, *636* ἐοῖσα ∼ *648* εὖσα). Manuscripts are unreliable in preserving Doric forms, because their scribes often unconsciously substituted the κοινή forms with which they were familiar; but it is not safe to restore Doric everywhere, since poets seem to have allowed considerations of sound and other criteria to override dialectal consistency. In many cases where manuscripts disagree a modern editor is reduced almost to random choice.

Here are listed the commoner features of the Doric texts in this volume, viz. Callimachus *Hymn* 5 (*132–273*), Theocritus *Idylls* 2 (*574–738*), 10 (*739–796*) and 11 (*493–573*), Bion *Lament for Adonis* (*1227–1324*) and fr. 13 (*1211–26*), Simias *Wings* (*822–33*), and some epigrams. References are not exhaustive. Particularly unusual forms are discussed in the commentary.

[1] A full account of Doric can be found in C. D. Buck, *The Greek dialects* (2nd edn, Chicago, 1955). For a useful discussion of Theocritus' dialect see Dover xxvii–xlv.

A. Vowels

(1) Original Indo-European ᾱ is retained where Attic changes to η: ἁ μάτηρ, etc.

(2) ω for Attic ου in some words: *636* μῶνος; *1233* ὦρος = epic οὖρος, Attic ὅρος; *524* ὥς = οὖς; *577* ὦ = οὖ. Cf. D.2.

(3) Contraction. ε + ο and ε + ου > ευ (Attic ου): *228* βαλεῦ, *581* βασεῦμαι, *1281* ἐμεῦ. α + ε > η (Attic ᾱ): *727* ἐφοίτη, *606* σιγῆι (Attic σιγᾶι).

B. Consonants

(1) σδ for ζ, except initially: *501* γενειάσδων. (Only in Theoc., and even there not consistently.)

(2) ν for λ before τ and θ: *139* ἦνθε (Attic ἦλθε).

C. Verbs

(1) 1st pers. pl. indic. act. in -μες: *578* τεθνάκαμες (Attic τεθνήκαμεν).

(2) 3rd pers. sing. indic. act. of -μι verbs in -τι: *540* προῖητι (=προῖησι), *1491* φατί (= φησί).

(3) 3rd pers. pl. indic. act. in -ντι: *618* φαντί (=φασί), *585* τρομέοντι (=τρομέουσι).

(4) Contracted futures in -έω / -έομαι: *534* ἑξεῖς from ἑξέεις (Attic ἕξεις), *254* γνωσεῖται from γνωσέεται (Attic γνώσεται).

(5) Verbs in -ζω have fut. and aor. in -ξ-: *761* ἐργαξῆι (Attic ἐργάσηι), *756* χροΐξεῖται (Attic χρώισεται).

(6) Perf. act. sing. has pres. endings: *739* πεπόνθεις (=πέπονθας), *493* πεφύκει (=πέφυκε).

(7) Contracted verbs. -άω verbs in Attic seem sometimes to be -έω in Doric: *561* ὀρεῦσα (Attic ὀρῶσα from ὀράουσα).

(8) Infinitives in -εν: *530* συρίσδεν.

(9) Participles. Fem. pres. and aor. act. participles in -οισα / -αισα: *588* ἔρδοισα, *631* τρίψαισα.

(10) The verb 'to be'.
   3rd pers. sing. pres. ἐντί (*1223*).
   1st pers. pl. pres. εἰμές (*578*).
   3rd pers. pl. pres. ἐντί (*543*).
   3rd pers. sing. imperf. ἦς (*650*).
   infin. ἦμεν (*542*).
   fem. part. εὖσα (*648*) and ἔσσα (*200*).

D. *Nouns and adjectives*

(1) First decl. gen. sing. of nouns in -ης in -ᾱ (Attic -ου): *642* Θευμαρίδα.

Fem. acc. pl. in -ᾰς (Attic -ᾱς): *732* Μοίρᾰς, *776* καλᾰς. (Only in broader dialect.)

Fem. gen. pl. in -ᾶν, contracted from -άων (Attic -ῶν): *235* Μοιρᾶν.

(2) Second decl. gen. sing. in -ω (Attic -ου): *259* βιότω.

Acc. pl. in -ως (Attic -ους): *144* ἀλαβάστρως.

E. *Pronouns*

(1) 1st pers. sing. gen. (ἐ)μεῦ (*560, 628*); dat. ἐμῖν (*494, 536*).

(2) 2nd pers. sing. nom. τύ (*703*), acc. τέ or τυ (*753, 764, 520*) or τίν (*531, 547, 560*); gen. τεῦ (*251*) or τεῦς (*544, 547*) or τεοῦς (*517*); dat. τίν (*521*).

(3) 1st pers. pl. acc. ἀμέ (*534*); dat. ἀμῖν (*499*).

F. *Doric words*

Different forms of individual words include:

αἰ for εἰ (*542, 548*).

κᾱ for κε, ὅκκᾱ for ὅταν (*514*).

Μοῖσα for Μοῦσα: cf. C.9.

ὅκα for ὅτε (*198, 232*), ποκά for ποτέ (*188, 554*).

ὄρνιχας (from ὄρνιξ) for ὄρνιθας (from ὄρνις) (*254*).

ὀστία for ὀστέα (*594*).

πρᾶτος for πρῶτος (*236, 591*).

τῆνος for (ἐ)κεῖνος (*590*), τηνεί for ἐκεῖ (*670*).

INDEXES

Non-italic numbers refer to pages, italic numbers to individual notes in the Commentary.

I SUBJECTS

Acaeus, *124–8*
Acanthus, 246
accentuation, 173, *801*, *1197*
accusative: exclamatory, *220*, *1254*; of extent, *28*; in apposition to sentence, *860*; internal, *212*, *285–6*, *325*
Achilles, 183, *884*, *1011–12*, 201, *1099–1105*, *1604*
Acmon, *822*
Acontius and Cydippe, 102–10
acrostic, 137, 143–4, 271
adjectives: comparative, *167*, *345*, *438*, *468–9*; concessive, *853*; 'double superlative', *478*; masc. with fem. noun, *469*; nom. in -ιν, *36*; predicative, *163*, *1580–1*; proleptic, *1230*, *1517*; temporal, *64*, 577; 'transferred epithet', *624*
Adonis, 217–26
Adrasteia, *320*
Adriatic, 194
Aeetes, 187, *914*, *981*
Aegaeon, *897*
Aeolus, *1703*
Aeson, *912*
Aesop, *29–36*
Aeschylus, 8, 89–90, *340*, *362–3*, *483*, *1042*, 201, *1053*, *1135*, *1351*, 258 (bis), 260, *1736*
aetiology, 8, 85, 102, *58–63*, 58, *136–43*, 143, 176, 178, *842–3*, 182, 200, *1090*, *1209–10*
Agamede, *589*
Agias and Dercylus, 112, *187*
Aidos, *429–30*
Ajax, son of Oileus, 230, *1355*
Alcaeus of Lesbos, 146, 172–3
Alcaeus of Messene, 244, 254

Alcinous, 194
Alcman, *362–3*, *1338*
Alexander, 2, 4
Alexandria, 2–6, 146, 181, 217, 227, 229, 241, 245, 265
allegory, 215, 269–70
alliteration, *1142*, 247
Amalthea, *322*
Amyclae, *78*, *773*
Amymone, *178–9*
anacoluthon, *62*
Anacreon, 243
anagram, 230
Anaurus, *1075*
anchor, *1411–12*, *1418–36*
Ananke, *824*
anaphora, *132–63*, *201–15*, *279–80*, *364–9*, *376–400*, 219, *1287*
Anaxo, *638*
anemone, *1292*
Antagoras of Rhodes, *278*
Antigone, *949*
Antigonids, 2, 136
Antimachus, 8, 87, *1*, *9–12*, 142
Antioch, 2
Antipater of Sidon, 244, 256
Antiphanes, 7, *173*
Anyte, 244, 253–4, 270–1
aorist: gnomic, *38*, *709*, *1415*; 'instantaneous', *702*, *1671*; for state resulting from past action, *30*; with πολλάκις, *196*
Aphrastus, *124–8*
Aphrodite, 111, *144—63*, *154*, *159*, *507*, *703*, *800*, 187, *1045–9*, *1067*, *1115*, *1120*, *1208*, 217–26, *1396*, *1453*, *1474–7*, *1583*, 261, 265, *1653*
Apidanians, *287*, *314*
Apis, *287*